# PT

## A COHERENT PLAN FOR A STRESS-FREE, HEALTHY AND PROSPEROUS LIFE WITHOUT GOVERNMENT INTERFERENCE, TAXES OR COERCION

### SEVENTH EDITION

### 1996

by

# Dr WG Hill

SCOPE
INTERNATIONAL
LIMITED

PT – The Perpetual Traveler
© Dr WG Hill 1996

Scope International ltd
Forestside House
Rowlands Castle
Hants PO9 6EE
England
UK

7th Edition 1996

British Library Cataloguing in Publication Data

A catalogue record for this book is available from the British Library

ISBN 0 906619 24 6

Typeset by Scope International Ltd
Printed by Hartnolls, Bodmin, Cornwall, England, UK

# CONTENTS

## PART 1 – IT IS YOUR MONEY

## PART 2 – USING MAIL DROPS FOR FUN AND PROFIT

## PART 3 – BETTER LIVING THRU' TECHNOLOGY

## PART 4 – MOVING ABOUT: THE A+A EXPANDED

## PART 5 – THE PT TOOLBOX

perjured, purchased testimony of her own accountant. He testified that she directed him to wrongly categorize personal expenses as business expenses. Appeal documents clearly indicated he lied (according to the *Wall Street Journal)* at government urging. In one of the most memorable moments of her show trial, a maid observed that Leona had once said "Only little people pay taxes." A strange statement in view of the fact that Leona paid more income taxes than 99.99 per cent of the USA population. This testimony was part of a hatchet job by the Federal Prosecutor, Giuliani, a ruthlessly ambitious politician, who turned public opinion against her. At the age of over 70 she received a jail sentence she began serving in 1992. Her husband, Harry, who was in his eighties had a stroke after he was indicted, and never recovered. In prosecuting them, the IRS violated its own long-standing rule of thumb that "tax fraud" consisted of failing to pay an amount of more than one-third of the gross amounts due. In the Helmsley case, the amount of tax not paid was approximately two per cent of the tax actually paid. The amount involved, while over one million dollars, was such a tiny percentage of the Helmsley's net worth, that it could have made no difference to a childless, very old couple whose entire multi-billion dollar fortune was already left to charity.

**Mike Millkin:** Brilliant young financier associated with Drexel Burnham and Company. He "invented" junk bond financing. Convicted of such exotic crimes as "Stock parking" and other offenses (crimes only in the USA), he was subjected to public defamation, fines and forfeitures that will wipe out his personal billion dollar not worth. He was also given a jail sentence of ten years that is more than most rapists and murderers will serve. Millkin and Helmsley are examples of the new government thinking (and seeming public opinion) that **anyone who is rich or successful is a criminal** and should be prosecuted.

**Reverend S.Moon:**Founder of a religious sect. At a time when he had signature power over approximately one billion dollars and could have legally used those funds at his discretion, he was indicted and convicted of illegally diverting under $2,000 of church funds to a personal account. The lesson here is that the leader of any popular but **minority** sect or religious group stands a very good chance of being framed on some technicality.

**Patty Hearst:** Kidnapped daughter of a famous publisher who was obviously brainwashed and forced to participate in bank robberies with the gang (Symbionese Liberation Front)that had kidnapped her. She was convicted of crimes she would never have been involved in if not under the influence of her captors. But the federal prosecutor was able to get a conviction – as federal prosecutors do in 95 per cent of all cases they undertake. It didn't hurt to have a dad with a chain of newspapers. After several years of favorable publicity in Pop's papers, she received a pardon from Jimmy Carter.

**Alphonse Capone:** Notorious founder of The Crime Syndicate dealing from Chicago in prohibition era booze. Why should we include this infamous character on our list of those deserving sympathy? Only because it was for poor Al that the Government developed a new theory: it was OK to deny selected personages their constitutional rights and to develop special new standards and laws just for them. It was decided that if a person was as bad as Al reputedly was, a prosecutor could take extraordinary (and otherwise illegal)) steps to put them in jail and keep them there forever. This Al Capone precedent has evolved to the point that today, a prosecutor can, at his discretion, put away any man woman or child he chooses as his target. A main criteria for prosecution these days is the potential political benefit (i.e. publicity) to the prosecutor! Thus we see why high profile individuals (guilty or not) get more attention than they deserve.

The PT book series is dedicated to those unfortunates (like the above) who lost their money and their freedom. They were physically, mentally and financially abused and injured by a government which, in many cases, should have awarded them medals instead.

We hope that PT Theory and Practice will be used as tools for those readers who still have any money or freedom worth preserving. Intelligent and productive individuals of the world are the new victims of an unprecedented wave of government abuse and persecution. High-profile individuals in particular must be extremely wary. Any individual talented or lucky enough to have become independently wealthy or notable in their particular field of endeavor must take steps to preserve their asses and their assets. This involves internationalizing oneself as more fully explained here in this book and in *PT 1*. Strange as it may seem, the USA has a written policy that tells agents and prosecutors to seek out, investigate and destroy high profile successful people. This is in direct violation of the Constitution's Equal Protection Clause which forbids the persecution of any particular class or type of person. Unfortunately, to their discredit, the Courts of the USA, and more particularly the USA Supreme Court has decided to ignore the constitution and proceed illegally. In this practice of persecuting high profile or wealthy people, the USA joins most of the countries of the Western World where it is no longer safe to be outstanding or wealthy.

*PT 1* shows the Basic Path. How to make yourself invisible to all "Authorities." *PT 2* (and hopefully others to follow) offers more practical suggestions and explores some resources available for the truly worthwhile people of the Earth (producers, not takers). If you want to know how to live free in an unfree world, read on. And remember: The PT research team includes you! Do not hoard your PT ideas, case histories and discoveries for yourself. Submit them to the author or publisher for inclusion in revised editions or new volumes. If your material is used, you will be presented with a free copy of the deluxe leather-bound edition using your contribution (or perhaps another book that you want!).

Bon Voyage on your Perpetual Travels!

## W.G. Hill

Note: The Name W.G. Hill is a Pen Name assigned to and 100 per cent owned by Scope International Ltd. The designation PT may be freely used by any person or author desiring to do so, but we ask that a copy of any articles or books written be lodged with us for research purposes. Readers from all countries are urged to send us material suitable for the next edition of *PT 2* and the Hall of Frame.

# HOW GOVERNMENT STEALS FROM YOU (& HOW TO KEEP YOUR ASSETS & YOUR FREEDOM)

The growth of government budgets, leads directly to a decline in your freedom – UNLESS YOU TAKE EVASIVE ACTION.

The growth of government as measured by us is simply how much more government spends now than it did in prior years. The *tax and spend* growth rates of most Western governments during the past 60 years have been phenomenal. From a base of nearly zero, close to two-thirds of all wealth generated in the Western Democracies is now spent by politicians, not by the people who create or earn wealth. But worse than this bad news is that the percentage of wealth being confiscated is still growing. Government spending grows faster than national income, personal income, per capita income, adjusted after inflation income or as a percentage of gross national product. In grossly overtaxed Europe, it seems clear that the new bureaucracy of the EU will add another layer of parasitic bureau-rats with new taxes to support them. If "someone" takes more and more of your earnings and assets, that "someone" is obviously eroding your freedom. In most industrialized countries, the typical citizen can no longer choose how to spend, invest or bequeath most of his own money. If such choices are made for you by someone else, you are obviously, less free. The PT can achieve a much higher degree of physical and economic freedom than the average man or woman. In this chapter we get a quick overview of what is at stake.

A government can spend only by taxing its subjects. Yet some types of taxes are hidden from the people who must pay the bills.

Taxation takes three main forms:

1) **Income taxes and hidden taxes like sales taxes, import duties or VAT** which raise prices. Sales taxes are generally believed to have a greater impact upon the poor since they (wage-earners and State-supported individuals) tend to spend a greater amount of their earnings on consumer items. In France, much more money is raised from sales-type taxes than from the income tax. Why? Probably because the wealthy French, who are supposed to be hardest hit by income taxes, have evaporated and now live abroad.

2) **Borrowing** which is a deferred tax. The class of persons who will have to pay it being at first, unclear. In an expanding economy with moderate inflation, an increase in national debt can be a healthy thing if the debt is used to pay for infrastructure (like highways and communications systems) that facilitate commerce and generate funds to retire the debt. In an ideal world, users of improved facilities would pay for them. But, more typically, funds raised by government borrowing are squandered. They end up being exported. The poor may buy imported consumer goods. The wealthier recipients of government largesse invest abroad. The country is thereby impoverished, and living standards drop. Who must pay the debt? No one and everyone! With a debt that becomes too large to service with taxes, the country cannot simply roll over the debt and issue more paper to pay off maturing bonds and the interest on them.

The government has a hard choice: it can end the game with a default (as many Latin American countries do, from time to time) or more likely, it will issue ever-more worthless currency (see below) to pay the debts. Russia has taken this rampant inflation route. **The burden of the borrowing and the default falls on those who have not had the financial ability or good sense to ship their assets abroad.** [Note: How much money has been sent abroad to offshore money and tax havens? Recent figures unearthed by us indicate that more American dollars (presumably owned by Americans), have been deposited abroad in secret accounts in the past 30 years than *the total now on deposit in all banks in the United States*. This amazing situation of more than half the national wealth having being exported has been the response of the smart money to the growth of a rapacious government. The situation in the USA is not unique. Many Europeans have done the same thing. With a new repressive tax regime in Spain, private Spanish wealth is now seeking haven abroad. The French bourgeoisie, ever distrustful of government, bury their money in gold coins and bars, or keep it "offshore." Most liquid wealth in most industrial countries is now beyond the reach of the tax-collectors, regulators and planners. Financially at least, everyone of substantial wealth is already a PT.

The most common form of taxation in the past has been

3) **Printing unbacked currency** which by law, must be accepted in payment of all debts, public and private. This running of the printing presses, by causing inflation, erodes the value of creditor's holdings (thereby reducing or eliminating government debt) and raising general price levels. This is a tax on those with assets in the form of cash, bonds, secured or unsecured debts due from others, in the form of bank savings deposits or the equivalent. Inflation shifts wealth from the creditor class (who are owed money) to the debtor class (borrowers) for a time, but eventually erodes all wealth and endangers stability. In times of inflation, no one can make long term plans or invest in plant or equipment. Even a farmer can't safely raise a crop of cattle or pigs. The creation of real wealth (growth) always declines when there is double digit inflation (over 10 per cent).

What can you as an individual do, to protect yourself? Strangely enough, governments who squeeze their own citizens, offer incentives to foreigners to use them as a tax haven. Ireland, with one of the most repressive tax systems on Earth welcomes visiting Americans with signs at Shannon Airport inviting the deposit of funds in special inflation-protected, tax-free, high-interest, secret accounts. For high-rollers there is an entire section newly-built at Dublin Docks devoted to the management of money of foreigners who seek to avoid their home-country's taxes. The only people who can't use these schemes and facilities are the Irish themselves. But then Great Britain provides similar services to the Irish (and anyone else) at the Channel Islands and the Isle of Man. Even the worst, repressive Communist regimes had special banks offering such services for foreigners. Their successors have kept these banks functioning as a profit center as almost every other State-owned facility disintegrates. It is a strange paradox that almost every country offers facilities to assist tax evaders of every nationality but its own! This reminds us of the statistic in a Hite (sex) report that almost every husband has had affairs with several marrried women, but believes his own wife to be faithful. The conclusion: either some married women are having all the fun, or some husbands are living in a dream world. With governments trying to seduce foreign tax evaders, and at the same time trying to convince the remaining few loyal and patriotic taxpayers that they shouldn't go "offshore," we wonder who is fooling whom.

Moral of the story? Get your assets out of your home jurisdiction. Have the paperwork ready to export your corpus if and when it becomes necessary. In short, be Prepared Thoroughly. Be a PT.

# 4000 YEARS OF TAXES

*A history of the world, submitted by loyal reader, PT, George Rip Van Vanden Heuvel. We don't know if this is his pen name or not! As you can guess, this is a tongue in cheek article. We have edited it down somewhat from the original 60,000 pages. Mr. Rip Van Vanden Heuvel gets a free book of his choice. Editor's Note: If you can contribute a chapter of good information, general interest or humor to our PT series, you too will get our thanks, your name and address in print, or not, the adulation of our thousands of readers, and a free book, not to mention "literary immortality!"*

In the beginning, there were high taxes. There were those in the 100 per cent bracket (slaves) and those who worked for the tax collectors. The tax collectors at that time were all the nobles and their bosses were the kings.

Then came Alexander the Great. At the head of the great Army of Macedon, he announced across-the-board tax cuts for everybody that gave up to him without a fight. No more sales taxes, preference taxes, property taxes, value-added taxes, user fees, or revenue enhancements. "Pay me and my army 10 per cent, keep the rest, and I will destroy all the tax collectors". His army marched, sacking and burning the IRS Service Centers in Persia, Asia Minor, Egypt and the rest of the known world. Cities built monuments to him BEFORE his army even got there. Everywhere mankind frantically pleaded, "Please, conquer us, too".

The known world under "Low Tax Alex", as he was known at the time, enjoyed explosive economic growth. Production soared. People had time to think and write and create. Great cultural advances were made. Then Alexander died, and some other Greeks took over after him.

During the next few hundred years, successor rulers raised taxes. As a result, their empire collapsed. The Romans took over, promising lower taxes to those who surrendered without a fight. Everybody joined. Except for a few socialists in Israel whom they crucified. The Romans decreed the known world would be taxed AT A VERY LOW RATE, and the folks back home in Italy would pay no taxes at all. The Roman Empire advanced everywhere, bringing prosperity, law and culture. Rome itself became the most swinging fun city the world ever knew (or has ever known). They invented bondage and domination and other sports I read about in Sex Havens for Tax Fiends, I mean Tax Havens for Sex Fiends, a best seller by the famous Roman author, Lascivious. Everyone in Rome had lots of orgies, slaves and swell houses. Porny pictures were painted on walls as murals. You can still see a lot of them in Pompeii. They even set up offshore tax havens in Delos and a few other places. [I shudda been born 2000 years ago.]

A few centuries later, the new generations of Roman rulers shut down the offshore centers, raised taxes and this wonderful empire collapsed. Europe was taken over by a new gang of tax collectors. They were called vandals. The believed in a 100 per cent tax followed by death for the taxpayers. This didn't do much for the tax base. Despite tax-relief crusades by Attila the Hun and Ghengis Khan, an era of high taxes collected by feudal lords and the Churches in Europe prevailed for centuries. It was called The Dark Ages. Reason? Nobody could afford to turn on the lights.

But during this period, the Arabs took over all of Europe except for parts of France and Germany and under their benevolent despotism and low taxes, people enjoyed great prosperity. Actually, the majority of Christians enjoyed being ruled by the Arabs who were more efficient than the feudal lords. They believed in free enterprise, freedom of expression and thought, tolerance and low taxes. They didn't even make you join their church, I mean Mosque. Arab taxes had 20 per cent as the upper limit.

Then a few isolated trading communities not yet conquered by the Arabs – like Venice in Italy – cut their tax rates. Trade and commerce exploded. Low taxes brought wealth and joy everywhere.

The Arabs were tossed out on a promise of lower taxes. In order to deliver their promises, the new Spanish kings sent out Columbus. America was discovered. One hundred per cent taxes were imposed on the native indians whose gold supported the Europeans. They paid 100 per cent and were worked to death as slaves. Where there was no gold, the local European colonists had to work too hard. An American tax revolt threw out the British. It took 125 years to get taxes back to where the British had them, but the Democrat Party was formed and IT raised taxes. Everybody who loved freedom headed west for the Frontier. By 1914 the frontier was closed and, as there was nowhere else to hide, Congress passed the American Income Tax. Everybody, including Ernest Hemingway and Gertrude Stein, left for Paris. But then the French put up taxes to pay for the Maginot line, a group of dancers at the Follies Bergere and other frivolous projects.

Tax rates shot up throughout the world. Everybody was feeling mean, so we had World War I.

After the war, a reparations tax of 100 per cent was imposed on Germany. They could not possibly pay, so German industrial and mining areas were seized by the French. This was not enough for the greedy French who actually expected to be paid for the war damage. So the lifetime savings of all Germans were confiscated through an inflation tax. It was still not enough. Taxes went up all over. The world depression came. Germans owed several times what their properties were worth. Foreclosures were rampant, unemployment was total, and anarchy threatened. The Communists were the largest party in urban areas and hope for the future was gone.

Germany cried for "a man on a white horse". In rode Hitler.

Hitler wanted to be the world's ONLY tax collector. He (like many conquerors before him) liked a 100 per cent rate and anyone who wasn't German he wanted either dead or in slavery. Some people didn't agree. They went to the gas chambers and paid 100 per cent tax on the way. To avoid this fate, the rest of the world decided to oppose Hitler and we had World War II.

After the war, defeated Germany and Japan were force-fed the American tax code with the high 1945 tax rates. For ten years, the defeated nations got nowhere. They produced only junk, poverty and unhappiness.

Then Germany said "We'll keep your lousy tax code, but give us one little loophole: all overtime pay would be tax free." Japan did something similar by making all investment profits, dividends and interest earned on savings tax free. This encouraged wealth-building. Suddenly, with the possibility of getting rich legally open to them, the essentially lazy Germans and the copycat robot Japanese became innovative and hard-working again. Their economies soared.

Meanwhile in the Red World, China was having famines, year after year. The tax rate on communes was cut by the Commies (who got something right for a change!) from 100 per cent to nothing. Agricultural production exploded. Soon China was EXPORTING food. Famines were gone for good. Then they started economic free zones where all the Chinese who live there became millionaires while those under traditional communism still stagnate.

In America, when the Kennedy tax cuts went into effect, the economy, and tax revenues, grew so fast that America had its only balanced budget since World War II. This was the Latter Curve at work showing that as tax rates go down, tax collections go up.

Then Johnson, Nixon, Ford and finally Carter enacted a series of "fiscally responsible" tax reforms (= increases). The American economy turned to mush. Ronald Reagan came in with a "simple solution". He cut taxes. Latter's curse was at work again. The American economy expanded. New jobs were created faster than anywhere on Earth. The only problem was that the Democrats in Congress kept spending money (welfare) on marijuana-smoking degenerates faster than it could be collected. Now the UK suffers from EC imposed socialism.

Great Britain went nearly extinct with tax rates up to 98 per cent. Margaret Thatcher came, immediately slashed tax rates, and rid the country of socialism. Every day in England until Thatcher left, the future looked brighter than it did before.

Except for the worst countries of the third world, tax rates were, for a while, dropping around the earth. Communist countries, with nothing to lose but their chains, are cutting taxes and worshipping at the altar of capitalism. But their mentality is so warped by Communism that it will be many years before they get it together.

The only place in the world where tax increases are FAVORED is in the United States Democrat-controlled Congress. Congressmen may be very sincere and they mean well.

But there was another leader in the Americas who had good intentions. This king's name was lost to antiquity when he told his people, in a famous speech, "Our latest tax hike is to balance the budget and reassure the credit markets". His people turned and ran into the jungles. On that sad day, the ancient and irreplaceable Mayan civilization came to an end.

USA president George Bush said "Read my lips . . . no new taxes". He said that just to get elected. But his bureaucrats believe in persecuting the rich, famous or productive people of America. Confiscation and forfeitures (100 per cent taxes) and jail await anyone who dares to succeed financially, or speak the truth. Bush is no student of history – he just doesn't see what's going on. 100 per cent taxes and death or loss of freedom for the most productive elements of society have never worked. These days, Americans are fleeing the country and renouncing "the most expensive passport in the world," more than ever before. Just like the Mayans did.

PT has become an underground best seller among the oppressed rich yearning to be free. All the worthwhile people read it. Then they see the light, take their chips and leave. I hope the last person to leave the USA will turn off any remaining lights.

The irreplaceable American entrepreneurial civilization of yesteryear has evaporated. The US economy is going downhill like a toboggan. More of the same and it will all come to an end with a whimper as it did in Russia. All productive and worthwhile people buy the large red book *(PT 1)*, and disappear into the jungle, just like W.G. Hill did. And me too.

See you in Monaco, Campione, Andorra, Singapore, or Swaziland.

# HOW TO STAY FREE

This book is dedicated to showing you how to stay FREE. Free, in every sense of the word – by using your cunning and your knowledge of the present, the past and of what makes the world tick, instead of merely running, as it were. Although you may also have to do a bit of that, depending on your own circumstances.

Free – from what? From problems, frustrations, fears, harassment, extortion, lawsuits and the implications and ramifications of all of these. While you may consider yourself a "free man" (or woman), chances are that you are not. The bad news is that even if you are currently living a fairly normal and happy life, events may conspire to turn against you. Others may steal your money, your freedom – and, ultimately take your life. Most people are sitting ducks – unless they take precautions before such events come to pass. The good news is that there are plenty of things that you may do to thwart dangers likely to pop up. Just a modicum of effort and expense can give you the sort of insurance you can't get from an insurance company.

Do you believe that "an ounce of preparation is worth about a ton of cure"? If so, this book is for you. If you are content to just "let things happen" then put this book back on the shelf.

This book exists to give you the low-down, no-nonsense, straight facts: how to set up those seemingly elusive safeguards that may shield you in times of trouble. If you put the information in this book to practical use you will find that you, too, can keep your money, your freedom and your life.

# PART ONE

# IT IS
# YOUR MONEY

# Chapter 1

# BEWARE: DANGER AHEAD

Planet Earth is not a safe place to be. So far, however, it is the only planet offering homes and gardens. That being so, it will serve you well to do whatever you can to make your life as long, safe and pleasant as possible.

If you want to keep your money, your life and your freedom, the first thing you must do is to to seek **maximum privacy**.

By using *perfectly legal* techniques you will be able to keep your money, your life and your freedom.

In today's world, it is absolutely essential to know what "tricks of the trade" you may use to *get away with just about anything* – even if that is 'merely' keeping your life and avoiding getting robbed blind by criminals in or out of government.

Did you know that using your own, personal and thoroughly valid credit card may be a one-way ticket to either divorce court or prison?

Did you know that even using *cash* for *legal purchases* may get you thrown in jail?

Did you know that for less than the cost of a few bus tickets per month, you will be able to immediately "disappear" forever and never be found, should the need one day arise?

When you have read this report, you will know how to disappear.

You will also know how to find out if your spouse, your business partners or your employees are cheating on you or stealing from you. How to substantially reduce, or even eliminate, your taxes. And how to protect yourself from robbers, kidnappers and extortionists.

If you are an honest person, this is The Bad News: there are a lot of mean, vicious criminals both on the streets and in government – and your luck may very well be about to run out! Now, here's The Good News: you can beat most cheats, crooks and criminals by using the methods described in this volume.

## THE MOST DANGEROUS PLACE ON EARTH IS WHEREVER YOU ARE

Let us briefly assess the potential dangers that you may have to deal with.

First of all there are, of course, those posed by Mother Nature. Earthquakes, floods, hurricanes, typhoons, droughts, diseases, swarms of locusts and so on. Not a lot you can do about those except trying to avoid getting caught in the middle of one. Umbrellas, mosquito nets, vaccinations and the proper use of prophylactics aside, we can think of only two trouble-shooting hints to let on about how to beat the dangers of natural disasters and inconveniences. If finding yourself uncomfortably close to the epicenter of an earthquake, go stand in a doorway. According to scientists this offers the best protection against falling debris and has been shown to be the least unsafe place to be when the local Richter-scale goes berserk. The other tip is not to invest your life's savings in real estate that may be wiped out if the tree-huggers and nature-lovers turn out to be right and the much-talked-about "greenhouse effect" actually sets in: even a modest rise in sea levels will wipe out investments in low-lying real estate. Someone once said that you should "buy land, 'cause they're not making any more of it". Sounds about right. But if you do, as a general rule, make sure that the land you buy is on sufficiently high ground to remain land and not suddenly turn into a lake.

# DEADLIER THAN THE FEMALE: GOVERNMENT

The number one threat to your life and your livelihood is not a natural disaster. It is your fellow man, which means anyone who is in a position to hurt you or your interests, directly or indirectly – intentionally or not. Depending on circumstances and the way you generally tend to lead your life, it takes just one malevolent, stupid or merely ignorant person to turn your life upside down, cause you considerable grief – or wipe you out altogether.

These days, many malevolent, stupid or merely ignorant people are found in government. They can be the most dangerous. Some are misguided by socialist ideology. **All** of them have power. They make their own rules. More peoples' lives have been wrecked by governments than by all other disasters put together. Today, the bureaucrat is deadly. Avoid whenever possible.

This report will teach you how to insulate yourself. It will show you how to prevent disasters from happening. Dangers lurk everywhere. You **will** have to re-evaluate some "truths" to adjust to the New World Order. An example:

You have to travel from, say, New York to London or vice-versa. You cannot drive a car across the Atlantic and swimming is not a practical option either. In other words, you decide (by default, really) to fly over. So far, so good. In order to get on the plane you need to purchase an air ticket. With me so far? Now see if you can find "the hidden danger" in the preceding sequence of events. Give up? The answer is: the way in which you choose to pay for that airline ticket may, under the present circumstances, land you in considerable trouble if you do it the wrong way. You basically have three options: pay in cash, by check or by credit card. Each of these could create problems. If you pay by check or credit card a lasting record is created that will allow anyone with access to the proper files to determine that you went abroad and deduce some sinister purpose for your travels. For instance, that you went on an innocent holiday, on an innocent business trip or on a highly suspect visit to a country well known for its banking secrecy laws (in the event that the one doing the checking is employed by the IRS). In other words, you may have good reason to avoid leaving any evidence of the trip behind for posterity. The seeming solution would be to pay for the ticket in cash. Cash is fairly untraceable, right? But that is exactly the catch: precisely because cash is just about the only way in which you may purchase anything without leaving a trace behind, it is generally assumed by authorities to be the monetary conduit of choice for criminals in general . . . and drug dealers and elusive money launderers, in particular. In other words, making large purchases and paying cash may make you a potential suspect in the eyes of those engaged in the much-touted "war on drugs".

Sounds too far-fetched? This, exactly, was what happened to "Joe". He bought a one-way, first class airline ticket from Honolulu, Hawaii to Miami, Florida. He paid the fare in cash. Not in counterfeit notes, mind you, but in good and (relatively) solid greenbacks, issued by the US Treasury. This aroused the suspicion of the airline ticketing clerk who duly informed her supervisor – who then, in his turn, informed the local police. On his arrival in Florida, Joe was picked out from the other passengers and his luggage was searched. It turned out to contain not only the standard items of clothing and toiletries but $6,000 in cash he intended to use as spending money. The cash was confiscated until he could prove a legal and tax-paid "source of funds". Bear in mind that this was on a *domestic* flight and *not* an international trip.

Paying for all purchases in cash is not necessarily the safest. It may be – but as with everything else, it depends on the circumstances.

"Joe" was now labelled in government files as a money laundering criminal in the eyes of the law. You may argue that he *ought* to be arrested and thrown in jail. That the ticketing clerk merely did her civic duty by being alert to an irregular situation and informing her supervisor about this suspicious character. Where's the harm in that? Give that lady a medal!

Alas, that is not the point.

This search could have happened to anybody, whether involved in drugs or not.

It could have happened to you, me and any other good, upright citizen with no ties to the criminal underworld whatsoever, who paid cash for a long-distance airline ticket. There might be any number of reasons why you did not use a check (the airline might not accept it before allowing several days or weeks for it to clear) or a credit card (perhaps you got mugged the day before and had not yet received replacements for your stolen credit cards, forcing you to fall back on cash). Take a minute to ponder that one. If you pay cash for anything in many countries you may more or less automatically fall under suspicion of being a criminal.

This, in turn, might lead to just a waste of time. You could get strip-searched (which means discomfort). It may even mean a permanent record being created in government files to the effect that you had once been apprehended and checked out as a potential drug-runner. If then, years down the line, you were to be justly or unjustly accused of a crime, the old "drug suspicion" case would surely be drawn out of the files and presented in court, perhaps resulting in you being convicted of and incarcerated for something you did not, in fact, do. Merely because of the doubt about prior arrests that this past "incident" would create in the minds of any jurors and/or judges.

## HOW AN HONEST BANKER HAD TO FLEE TO STAY HONEST

You may also be targeted if you are trying to avoid aiding and abetting criminals: this happened to "Raj", a medium-level bank officer working in a Pakistani branch of the later so ill-fated BCCI bank. Raj saw that inadvertently he had been caught up in a criminal operation. He tried quietly to sell his house and unload his local investments in order to flee the country before push came to shove. Unfortunately for him, this came to the attention of his BCCI employers who decided that it would be easier to dissuade the man from talking (by threats and intimidation) if he stayed in Pakistan – and very hard if he fled the country. To warn him off, they first conspired to have his brother killed, cut a hand off the corpse and had it delivered to Raj's home. The poor fellow is now in hiding somewhere in America – not only from his former employers but also from the authorities, afraid what may befall him if he is forced to testify.

You may not work at the BCCI or any other criminal outfit but then you could stumble into a situation where you are the only person who can testify against someone your government very badly wants to nail. Even with witness protection programs in place, you may not be willing to co-operate and see your life changed beyond recognition just so that a prosecutor may rejoice in seeing someone else – even a gangster – go to jail for ridding society of yet another piece of scum. And don't even think of trying to play "hostile witness" or you may still get landed in jail for "contempt of court". People who testify in many criminal cases are under extreme government pressure to deliver testimony desired by the prosecutor. If they don't help convict, they may be the next target.

Which brings us back to the original point. The number one threat we all have to deal with in this life is **other people.** It is, quite simply, the basic premise which you have to keep in mind at all times. If there were no other people on this planet but you, this would not be so. However, such a hypothetical situation would also imply that there would be no one you could pay to bring you food, for instance, so you would have to hunt or gather for yourself. There would be no hospitals or surgeons to save your life if you happened to develop appendicitis. Simply keeping a low profile and becoming a PT keeps you from making enemies and insulates you from bureaucrats.

## LEND A HELPING HAND TO YOUR BEST FRIEND, YOURSELF

You (and everybody else) are essentially *alone* in life. Whatever else happens it is up to you, and no one else, to make sure that your remaining lifetime is spent as pleasurably, comfortably and safely as possible. You may try to abregate this personal responsibility, if you will, but the results are sure to follow: whatever you neglect doing in terms of enhancing your own safety and security, nobody else will automatically do for you.

Is this a trifle disconcerting? It should not be. As opposed to an animal, man possesses a conceptual consciousness of himself and the world around him. A cow does not rationalize that it has to eat grass in order to stay alive and make a nicer, fatter piece of beef when it is time for a one-way trip to the slaughterhouse. A man, however, has the ability to know that if he does not wake up in the morning and go to work, he will be laid off. If he gets laid off, paychecks will stop coming. If that happens, he will have two options: either to find some other way of getting money for food and rent or start living rough once the dole checks run out.

But man's conception of life and the world around him is not an instinct, it is purely volitional. If he chooses to exaggerate his perception of the dangers around him, man is free to turn into a raving psychotic. The reverse is also true: we may choose to ignore or deny the existence of the world's opportunities and dangers, and become, in effect, not a Homo Sapiens but rather a Homo Ostrichus – mentally sticking our heads in the sand, pretending to ourselves that there is no danger and nothing to fear.

Take a brief look at your daily newspaper, then ask yourself if you really wish to play make-believe and imagine that no one can hurt you.

In this life, you have two choices: one, to take charge of the task of ensuring you have prepared yourself very, very thoroughly for whatever potential dangers lie in whatever remaining lifetime you have ahead of you; or, number two, to lethargically muck around with your life and get a surprise whenever someone decides to exert a malevolent influence. Remember, the first option entails some effort, thinking and acquiring of knowledge on your part. The latter means you can go on without a care or a thought for tomorrow – until the day comes when a lawsuit, divorce, dispute with City Hall or other problem makes a wreck of your life. Even the Boy Scouts have the same motto as a PT. They say "Be Prepared" – we say PT means "Prepare Thoroughly".

# RATS, RATS & MORE RATS

Big Brother is expanding to the EC. Back on his home turf, the USA, all businesses and professionals have been informants or "rats" for years. In Britain, a rat is a "Super grass." The rule is squeal or get squashed. What to tell about? All large or "unusual" cash transactions or "suspect travel plans" must be reported on special forms. These reports trigger a special multi-bureau team of criminal investigators to check up on things. Often this takes the form of arresting and giving the third degree to the person denounced. Don't inform and you may be accused of "aiding and abetting." It's not the Nazi, Communist or Fascist scheme it appears to be. No, it's all just part of the ever-expanding drug war, they say. Of course Hitler and Stalin had only the *good of society* at heart when they set up similar informers' networks. At first bankers and stockbrokers were the only American civilians dragged into the Bureau-Rat Auxiliary. Those who didn't report cash transactions made to entrap them by "G-Men" or government agents, like First Boston Corporation, suffered heavy penalties. Corporate officers got jail sentences. This brought the industry into servile compliance. Then accountants, lawyers, car dealers, travel agents, airlines, retailers and almost every other business handling cash were forcibly enlisted as unwilling, unpaid informers. Today, in the USA, the fee you pay a lawyer must pass the smell test. If your money (cash or otherwise) is not Lily White, it may be confiscated from the lawyer who then will **not represent you, despite having been paid.** A strange situation indeed – where legally speaking, an American is *presumed innocent until convicted.* It seems those who use cash in the USA today are presumed guilty of drug trafficking until they prove otherwise. In the United States, citizens may be searched "on suspicion," and all unusual amounts of cash on your person can now be confiscated. Even buying an airline ticket with US $100 bill could result in you being reported, detained, and your money confiscated until you prove it was not illegally earned and that it was going to be reported for income tax purposes. Students of logic know that proving a negative is difficult, if not impossible.

The USA government wants other countries to adopt its theories and methods. Canada, Australia and Britain seem to be falling in line. There are only a few European countries where petty cash transactions are not assumed to be a badge of criminality. This is where cash transactions are not generally reported: Germany, Luxembourg and Switzerland. But even in these countries, large cash transactions by *new customers* may result in a police interview.

**Rodent Control Tip:** One PT reports that after attempting to pay for an air ticket with a US $100 bill, and then being detained "on suspicion" and missing his flight, he sued the airline for the maximum amount ($1,000) in small claims court. The airline didn't defend, presumably because costs of sending in a lawyer would have cost them more than the maximum award. Our PT collected $1,000 for unwarranted harassment and damages. The judge felt that persons paying for a domestic flight in cash certainly had that right. Consider suing each time your life is interfered with. On second thoughts, it's probably better to keep a low profile and follow the basic PT formula for self-preservation: *know the local game and never call attention to yourself by doing anything considered unusual.* In other words to keep your ass and your assets, *When In Rome, Do As The Romans Do.*

US banks abroad were inducted into the informants network years ago. But as of 1993, British banks, travel agents and airlines have agreed to report all suspicious transactions, such as big cash bankrolls or unusual travel plans to police. We don't like the arbitrariness of the current war on drugs which is more of a war upon privacy, with no apparent deterrent effect on drugs. The Final Word? PTs can retain their assets, their privacy and their freedom by simply knowing how to keep a low profile and staying out of trouble. Hoist your five flags and sail free.

# Chapter 2

# SHRUGGING IT OFF

How come that we need to "do something to preserve our freedom"? It was Oscar Wilde who said that "most men live in a state of quiet desperation". A few years later, Wilde himself was sent to prison for committing the crime of being a homosexual. Even today, several States in the supposedly "free" United States have laws on the books making unmarried sex a criminal offense. These same States make it a felony to perform "an unnatural act" with your own wife, and such unnatural acts include your wife giving you a little kiss anywhere below the belt or vice versa.

The very real and present danger of being harassed or even indicted and incarcerated for committing any number of victimless crimes should, in itself, be enough for any intelligent individual to take proper precautions. Such an individual – **you** – should seek to limit to the fullest possible extent the risk of being made a martyr by a world in which politicians, the media and a sheep-being-led-to-the-slaughter public are constantly ranting and raving about how "something ought to be done" about whatever. Or whomever. Unfortunately, "whomever" it is that "something just ought to be done about" may very well turn out to be *you* one day – if it is not already.

Should "something be done" about tax-evaders? Even if, like Leona Helmsley you fork out over $50 million per year of your money to a state or government, you may still find yourself officially designated as a "tax-evader" – a target, to be hunted down and thrown in jail.

Should "something be done" about men who refuse to pay alimony to a greedy ex-spouse? You may one day count yourself among the great number of men sought by the authorities for not paying up to an ex-wife who betrayed you.

Should "something be done about drug-dealing vermin"? You may one day find your phone tapped or yourself arrested and all your assets seized on an unfounded suspicion that you are such a person. Even if you are subsequently cleared you should expect no apologies for the "inconvenience" nor any remuneration for the financial losses you "just happened" to suffer in the process.

After all, whatever happened – or happens – to you at the hands of the authorities is "all for the good of the country". And "countries" (meaning, in effect, states and authorities) are not usually given to apologies or to paying damages to innocent people who inadvertently get caught up in their wars. Which, incidentally, is especially true as far as the "war on drugs" goes.

## THE MYTH OF LAW-ABIDING JOE PUBLIC

If you are an upright citizen, pay your taxes and do not engage in drug-dealing nor obtain a financially crippling divorce (perhaps because you have been wise enough to stay single) then, surely, any such situation would not befall you. And even if, for some odd reason, you suddenly were to find yourself under suspicion for some crime which you did not commit, then that would merely be a tiny misunderstanding to be speedily cleared up, right?

Wrong. No matter how strait-laced and impeccably law-abiding you are, you may at a moment's notice find yourself being referred to not as "Mr Joseph Public" but, rather, as "the Defendant". Remember how the politicians and the media literally make their living from screaming to the public that "something ought to be done" about this or that. More and more "things" (which means people) are created about whom something should be "done". You eventually find that you are one of the victims of government.

An example: "Something ought to be done about those heinous environmental polluters". Unless you have been spending the past ten years backpacking in Nepal, you will know that newspapers in just about every country regularly feature stories about how "evil, privately-owned Big Businesses" are polluting the environment and how those same evil businessmen must be forced to pay for the environmental clean-up thus necessitated.

How can this affect you? Here's an example: until the late Sixties, government environmental agencies in most countries actively urged companies to dispose of chemical waste by sealing it in containers and burying it. Yes, that's right – bury containers full of that toxic chemical stuff. Unfortunately, it turned out that this advice was not a smart move. Steel drums rust and let chemicals leak into the ground, polluting the water supplies. Massive scandals have erupted involving companies which were following government guidelines in the past. Now they find themselves in the position of being sued for huge damages when that government advice of 20 years earlier turned out to be unwise. But that is not all. Courts in the United States have ruled that it is in the "public interest" that "the polluters be made to pay". It is the new order of things not only to sue companies that have polluted in the past – but also their "collaborators". This means if a company buried toxic waste somewhere 20 or 30 years ago, it may be sued today – even if it was following official guidelines in the past. If the company is bankrupted, the legal way is now wide open to sue instead those companies and individuals who "collaborated" with the now-bankrupt polluter. It is possible to sue a trucking company which 30 years ago undertook a contract to haul chemical waste to the dumpsite. If you just happened to buy that trucking company many years after that contract was completed then you may still be sued for damages. And if that trucking company that you bought just happens to be a privately- owned business and not incorporated anywhere, that means that you – personally – may be liable for the damages stemming from another company that followed bad government advice a generation ago! Lloyd's and other insurers are also being stuck with clean-up costs that should be spread over the entire populace.

## WHY ANYONE WITH ANY MONEY WILL BECOME A TARGET

Courts increasingly operate on the "deep pocket" theory. If someone can point to a damage or a grievance suffered, someone else may be made to pay for it. If that "someone" is either no longer in existence (because of death or bankruptcy) then anyone with just the tiniest connection to the (real or imagined) "culprit" may be sued. In the USA these days, it is not inconceivable that a man may sue a feminist author for the "emotional damages" he suffered when his wife divorced him after reading a "how-and-why-you-should-get-a-divorce-from-your-chauvinist-husband" book.

If someone sues it means that you will either have to defend yourself – incurring huge legal costs – or be found guilty by default. Even if you are cleared (or found unculpable), after years of litigation you may have had to divest yourself of all your assets in order to pay your lawyers' fees. As a rule of thumb, anyone may sue anybody for anything, anywhere. Governments do it every day to quell dissidents, corporations do it for money and individuals and business competitors do it to harass each other. It's one giant merry-go-round in which the only assured, long-term winner is "the house" – the lawyers. It is in their economic interest to see that anyone with visible assets becomes a victim of the Deep-Pocket theory.

As the world becomes more and more integrated, national borders are of decreasing importance and protection. A court in the United States recently threatened to levy big fines on the US subsidiary of a Swiss bank unless the Panamanian branch of that bank agreed to disclose the identities of its American customers. Needless to say, the court did not give a hoot about the lack of formal connection between the US and the Panamanian branches of a foreign owned bank – nor about the fact that, if abiding by the court order, the Panamanian branch would be breaking the banking secrecy laws in Panama – leading to the potential prosecution of managers of the Panamanian branch for complying with the ruling of a United States court.

## THE CASE OF DAVID SIMPSON

Dave Simpson operated a trading company out of Torrance, California, brokering contracts between Taiwanese electronics manufacturers and American importers. He did that so well that he earned a significant amount of money in a few, short years. Not trusting US banks, he put most of his hard-earned fortune in a bank based in the Cayman Islands. He did not try to conceal this fact to the IRS, disclosing the existence of his foreign bank account on his 1040 tax-form. By being a law-abiding citizen he ought to have protected himself, right? Wrong. A couple of years into the relationship with his Cayman Island bankers, his bank became involved in a drug-money laundering scandal. All assets deposited in the USA by this bank were frozen by the US Government, pending outcome of an investigation if where the money had originated i.e. which accounts contained "dope money".

The investigation dragged on for four years with a final outcome not expected for another five or six years. Result: when his company needed cash, Simpson was unable to access his personal assets in order to save the company, not to mention paying his mortgage. His business went bust and the bank foreclosed on his house, evicting him onto the streets. He is theoretically a millionaire, yet he cannot gain access to his savings because the United States government has decided that it has a very serious beef with some Colombian drug lords *who just happened to use the same bankers*. Tough luck – for Simpson.

Similar fates befell Iranian citizens in the aftermath of the fall of the late Shah when the US government ordered all "Iranian-owned" private assets frozen in retaliation when a mob of Iranian students seized the US embassy in Teheran and held American citizens as hostages for 444 days.

Similarly, expatriate Kuwaiti citizens found their private bank accounts in most countries blocked until further notice when Iraq invaded Kuwait in an attempt to take over the country and its assets, both domestic and foreign-held. During World War II, the USA seized all French, Swiss and British private accounts.

In all instances, private individuals were unjustly penalized by having their bank accounts frozen and their credit cards cancelled. Kuwaitis recently wound up depending on handouts from Kuwaiti embassies to tide them over. A "regrettable" result of a Big Brother state striking back at its enemies, real or perceived. But also something that those affected could have done much to prevent had they taken future dangers and upheavals into account instead of relying on the status quo to remain unchanged. The worst part is that United States federal agents never had a near-good case for freezing "Kuwaiti assets" across the board to prevent Saddam Hussein and his henchmen from looting and pillaging private Kuwaiti bank accounts abroad. Most of the American Kuwaiti accounts seized were owned by Kuwaitis living in New York or London.

## WE'D LIKE YOU TO MEET A VERY SPECIAL LADY . . .

If you find yourself in need of a deeper explanation of why things work the way they do, one is readily available. It is also, unfortunately, one of which few people have ever heard: the case of Ayn Rand.

A Russian expat who fled to the United States from Soviet Russia in the 1920s, Ayn Rand went on to become one of the leading – and some would say the number one – authors of the century . . . based, not only on the public acclaim of the novels and philosophical volumes she produced but, especially on the basis of her no-nonsense message: life belongs exclusively to the individual who shall, in turn, be absolutely free to do with it whatever he pleases – as long as the rights of others are not transgressed.

In 1957, Rand published her stunning and immensely significant novel *Atlas Shrugged* (out of print in Britain, it is still available from Signet Books, New York). And whereas the socialist George Orwell secured a more lasting, mainstream place in history for himself with the publication of *1984*, *Atlas Shrugged* explains exactly how things work in the real world and what may happen if too many people forget the facts – the basics. The terrifying bit is that much of what Rand predicted might happen to western civilizationhas come true.

Set in the United States of America (without mentioning any specific year), the backdrop for the novel is industry and the people who make it work. The heroes, according to Rand, are not unionized workers who alternate between whining for shorter hours and demanding more pay for less work, but rather a few, rare capitalists, without whose constant quest for efficiency and profit the engine ot the world would stop.

In *Atlas Shrugged* a number of senseless laws are introduced by government. All are, officially, passed ''for the common good'' and ''the public welfare''. Competition is restricted by law, lest old and inefficient companies with bloated payrolls lose ground to new, ambitious upstarts. Plans are introduced to ''spread profits around'', lest a few attain ''excessive'' riches. An industrialist, Hank Rearden, invents a revolutionary metal, Rearden Metal. Suspicious, at first, over this new product, it soon dawns on the world that the invention holds supreme advantages over steel and will recolutionize just about every sector of industry. To make sure that Rearden Steel does not discriminate against those customers who initially refused to buy his product, laws are passed that require Rearden Steel Mills to put a quota-system into operation so that allcomers will get his state-guaranteed ''right'' to buy his ''fair share'' of the output. Even so, Rearden profits mightily due to his years of research and hard work. Soon rival mills, unable to compete against him with their old-fashioned steel, are driven to the brink of bankruptcy. Making no excuses for his success, Rearden is in due course blackmailed by the government into giving up his patent rights so that ''all may share'' in the benefits of his invention. The following excerpt from the book is a verbal exchange between Rearden and Ferris, the emissary of Big Brother, visiting the mills to announce the blackmail.

*Ferris: ''You honest men are such a headache. But we knew you'd slip up sooner or later – and this is just what we wanted.''*

*Rearden: ''You seem to be pleased about it.''*

*Ferris: ''Don't I have good reason to be?''*

*Rearden: ''But, after all, I did break one of your laws.''*

*Ferris: ''Well, what do you think they're there for?''*

*Dr. Ferris did not notice the sudden look on Rearden's face, the look of a man hit by the first vision of that which he had sought to see. Dr Ferris was past the stage of seeing; he was intent upon delivering the last blows to an animal caught in a trap.*

*''Did you really think that we want those laws to be observed?'' said Dr Ferris. ''We want them broken. You'd better get it straight that it's not a bunch of boy scouts you're up against . . . We're after power and we mean it. You fellows were pikers, but we know the real trick, and you'd better get wise to it. There's no way to rule innocent men. The only power any government has is the power to crack down on criminals. Well, when there aren't enough criminals, one makes them. One declares so many things to be a crime that it becomes impossible for men to live without breaking laws. Who wants a nation of law-abiding citizens? What's there in that for anyone? But just pass the kind of laws that can neither be observed nor enforced nor objectively interpreted – and you create a nation of law-breakers – and then*

*you cash in on guilt. Now that's the system, Mr Rearden, that's the game, and once you understand it, you'll be much easier to deal with.''*

Translate this to modern-day politics. The "war on drugs" is, in fact, nothing but an elaborate scam to make it "legal" for the state to invade the privacy of you, me and everybody else, and to create a situation where prosecutors can select and convict almost anyone of a "drug-related" crime.

## WHY DOES MILTON FRIEDMAN WANT LEGAL DRUGS? HERE'S WHY:

The ordinary folk who support the "war on drugs" certainly do not realize they are being conned. It is also doubtful that more than a handful of politicians admit even to themselves that this is the real *raison d'etre* of the many laws on laundering of money is to require full disclosure from everyone of the exact sources of their funds.

Did you really think that the American President cares much about a non-voting "crack mamma" in Harlem? He knows, however, that people can be worked up enough to be furious about the "drug threat to our children". The fact remains, however, that some people will take drugs of their own free will. The demand for drugs is created by people who want them, serious and proven side-effects notwithstanding – or those who crave it to seek some sort of solace for a mind battered by the psychological problems.

But drug use cannot be wiped out for the very simple reason that, like prostitution, it has been around from the beginning and will be around long after we are all dead.

Some people use drugs to seek a brief refuge from a reality that is, rightly or wrongly, perceived by them as cruel and unbearable. Others use drugs to seek relief from boredom. And so on. But did you realize that narcotic drugs only came to be outlawed at the start of this century? Sigmund Freud habitually used cocaine but as far as his contemporaries were concerned, that was his own, personal business, not something that society ought to interfere with through laws or regulations.

Before 1913, using drugs was considered a vice. Today, it is a crime only because certain politicians found that stirring up anti-drug hysteria was good for a few votes. But since drug use was *outlawed* drug use has *increased* many times over.

In the US (and possibly other countries) the "drug war" merely is the government's excuse to pry into the privacy of anyone and everyone, and to pass legislation to permit them even more intrusion. The government's ultimate objective is the control of all aspects of every business and individual, and violating their privacy (not just in financial, but in all matters) is a necessary preliminary step. Together with this, the government wishes to control all property, and they are closer to this than most people realize.

Constitutional rights do not apply to most individuals in the US for reasons too complex to cover here. When persons claim "First Amendment Rights" of freedom of expression, "Second Amendment Rights" to bear arms, and so forth, the courts rule against them, and people blame the rotten system. It is rotten, but as the Bill of Rights under the US Constitution do not apply to most people, the government is perfectly within their power to deny the rights the people thought they had. We remind PTs that the drug war is a cover up for governments' intrusion into everybody's affairs, and an excuse that uninitiated people accept. Any transgression on the part of the government, no matter how grievous, can be hidden under the umbrella of the "drug war".

# Chapter 3

# TO PT OR NOT TO PT

There is, to our knowledge, no real life Atlantis where men and women may live freely without an omnipresent state hovering over the waters to interfere with the individual's every action at the behest of a "democratic majority" made up of losers, suckers and fools.

To wit, there are certain countries and jurisdictions that do not have much in the way of laws and taxes. Normally referred to as "tax havens", there are a handful of true ones left: Bermuda, Monaco, Andorra and a couple of the British Channel Islands. These are places where income taxes do not exist, with strict bank secrecy laws in place to protect residents (and sometimes non-residents) against the local government – which tends to be inclined to leave people alone anyway, and against foreign governments – which do not.

The main problem with these agreeable countries is that not only are they scarce in number, but also pretty small in terms of territory. To protect the native population from being totally overrun by tax-wary foreigners, residence and land-owning permits are not only hard to come by but may also be quite expensive (Scope International's guides to no-tax or low-tax jurisdictions such as Andorra, Gibraltar, Campione d'Italia and a particular Channel Island show you little-known shortcuts and reveal the secrets in detail. They are available from Scope, order form at the back of this book).

In addition, not everyone is willing to relocate his physical self to another country "merely" to escape taxation.

Short of merely moving to a tax-haven there is another, more advanced option: to become a "PT". Prior Tax-Payer or Perpetual Tourist.

To facilitate the continued freedom from taxation in the event of future changes in rules, laws and regulations a PT may have procured a second nationality. In the event that his home country decides to do what the United States is already doing and starts taxing its citizens on a worldwide basis, regardless of place of residence, a PT thus has the option of divesting himself of his original citizenship without becoming stateless. He already has a "spare" or "back-up" nationality, complete with passport and other identity papers for use in such a situation.

Initially published in 1988, the original *PT* (now in its fourth revised edition) sets forth not only a lot of very concrete reasons for having extra passports and citizenships but also a view of what life can be like if you are a tax-free, perpetual traveller. It is, to date, the only book of its kind, presenting an integrated, coherent plan for a stress-free life.

If you have not already read *PT 1* we highly recommend that you do so. Just as *Atlas Shrugged* is essential reading. You will quickly grasp *why* and *how* politicians have been able to get away with imposing an ever-increasing number of counter-productive and ultimately anti-human laws, so *PT 1* is a *must-read* if you want the low-down on what the individual – **you** – may do in general terms to make sure that you do not become a victim of "them". The PT-concept, or "way of life", is founded on the premise that if you stop closing your eyes to realities and instead recognize the unfortunate fact that the world looks and works the way it does (and why!), you may then go on to implement a set of general safeguards that will shield you from the most detrimental of real-life dangers – instead of standing idly by, waiting. Registered buyers of the original *PT* report can order the new and expanded third edition of *PT* for half price from Scope International Ltd.

More than 25 years ago, there was formulated a theory of three "flags", since expanded to five, that are at the core of the PT concept. In general terms, they are:

Flag number 1: BUSINESS BASE.
Make your money in a jurisdiction different from your personal, fiscal domicile.

Flag number 2: CITIZENSHIP.
Make certain that you have at least one citizenship (and passport) from a country unconcerned about its non-resident citizens and what they do outside its borders. This is *in addition* to a passport from your home country.

Flag number 3: DOMICILE.
Be legally resident and domiciled in a stable, secure tax-haven.

Flag number 4: ASSET REPOSITORY.
Stash your assets abroad somewhere different from 1, 2, 3 from whence they may be safely and anonymously managed by proxy. It should be a place without currency controls.

Flag number 5: PLAYGROUNDS.
Where you actually and physically spend your time.

The PT-concept is based on the idea that if you adopt all of these flags and structure your life around, them you will attain a higher degree of safety and security, both personal and businesswise. Even if you have been sensibly paranoid about lawsuits, government and police harassment for years, you will learn much in the way of new techniques, things to do – and especially **not do**. Even if you have already read it, pick it from the shelf again and go through it once more. You may have been become too much of a "Master of the Universe" in your own eyes and started slipping since. Re-reading will keep you on your toes. This report *PT 2,* is meant to add new information and readers' suggestions to your repertoire.

# INTERNATIONAL INVESTING

International investing isn't new, of course. Europeans have been doing it for decades. American Depository Receipts (ADRs), which represent whole or partial shares of foreign companies, have been listed and traded in New York since the 1920s. Wealthy Chinese and Russians were forced into it.

"What is new is the escalated scale of the global equities business," says Paul Melton, publisher of the Amsterdam-based *Outside Analyst* an international investing publication.

In 1961, only 150 ADRs were available to American investors. Today, over 600 ADRs exist for stocks of companies in 16 nations. That list includes the likes of Britain's Imperial Chemical, Hanson PLC and Glaxo Holdings, Denmark's Novo Industri, Japan's Sony Corp, Canon Inc., and Hitachi Ltd, etc. In Europe, some international securities are part of every portfolio. Bearer shares are the favorite way to hold stock discreetly.

Overseas holdings by US portfolio managers exploded from around $3 billion in 1980 to something over $4 billion today. In 1980, US investors traded about $17 billion worth of international shares. By 1992, the figure had zoomed to over six times that.

Why should anyone, American or otherwise, be interested in investing abroad? One, because domestic markets around the world steadily progress toward a giant global exchange, and two, you can make more money. Foreigners also jump into America's markets. Ever more Americans pour cash into distant lands. Moreover, foreign markets offer additional opportunities to diversify for safety in well managed portfolios.

Stock markets generally, do not rise or fall together. Why be in the American market if it stagnates while share prices in far lands skyrocket? Wise investors ask themselves that question as they look overseas. They note the nations with promising markets. Then they invest at least some of their funds there.

Not long ago, Paul Melton of *Outside Analyst* provided interesting data about international investing in an article carried by *Personal Finance.*

He said: "During this decade, the average US stock, ignoring dividends, gained 177 per cent, while dollar returns in Singapore/Malaysia, Australia, Canada, Belgium, Holland, Hong Kong, France, Norway and Britain ranged from a low 180 per cent in Britain up to 299 per cent among these nine countries. As for the world's three stock market leaders, Italy and Sweden each had dollar returns above 500 per cent in the decade. Meanwhile, Japan led the pack with a breathtaking dollar return of 1,001 per cent."

Do you need more evidence? In 1988, for instance, the Dow Jones Industrial Average, bell-weather barometer for US investors, climbed 11.8 per cent. A Morgan Stanley Capital International index for world stock exchanges registered a 24.1 per cent increase in the same period when measured in local currencies, and a 21.2 per cent climb in US dollars.

Had you invested your money in the indices of any or all of 15 foreign countries at the start of 1988, you would have beaten the Dow by a wide margin. The Belgium market, for instance, soared by 67.2 per cent in franc terms, and by 48.5 per cent when measured in dollars.

The EAFA (Europe, Australia, Far East Index) showed a 32 per cent gain in local currencies and a 26.7 per cent jump in US dollar terms. Study such data and you must ask yourself how you can afford to ignore overseas markets. Of course in 1991 and 1992, with a rising dollar, it took exceptionally good judgement to make money in dollar terms, but diversification and international nimbleness is the name of the game today.

With adequate information, even small investors can go global, either through ADRs obtainable from a broker, through Yankee bonds bought at the same place or through mutual funds. Yankee bond issues are denominated in foreign currencies (yen, pounds sterling, Swiss franc or whatever), and registered with the SEC in the United States.

The ease of international investing may surprise you if you have overlooked this money-making avenue. ADRs are listed on US exchanges. Some foreign companies list stocks directly on exchanges, Britain's Hanson and Imperial Chemical are two examples. Or consider the Netherland's Royal Dutch Shell. Publications provide quotations of prices. Dividends arrive without trouble (though you may pay foreign taxes, which may be deducted as credits in US returns). You can unload shares of these giant public companies quickly.

Scores of funds offer opportunities for investing in international equities or bonds, or in a foreign currency. Funds sell directly through American offices or through brokers. Offshore banks, for fees of about 0.25 per cent a year, will be only too happy to take your money and invest as per your instructions. You can invest in currencies, commodities, metals, bonds, stocks or mutual funds.

The list includes Fidelity Global Bond, Merrill Lynch Pacific, the Templeton Income, the Putnam Global Government Income, the First Australia, the First Australia Prime Bond Fund and many more.

Single country or area funds proliferate. Among them are: the France, the Germany, the Korea, the Italy, the Scandinavia, the Taiwan and the Scudder New Asia Fund.

Remember, though, that when you invest in a foreign land you become subject to the vagaries of the dollar. When the dollar's value increases against the currency of the host country, your investments in the foreign land decline in dollar terms. Should your stocks also suffer decline at the same time, your investment gives you a double downside hit.

When the dollar slumps, the values of your foreign holdings climb. Sometimes the monetary situation operates in your favor, sometimes not. Should your stocks rise in value in the host country, you will enjoy a double profit. Dividends, if any, are a third bonus.

In 1987, with a weak dollar, international bond funds averaged a total return of 20.8 per cent. In 1988, as the dollar strengthened, yields fell to around 2 per cent. So if you ponder an investment abroad, first check the status of the dollar from your informational sources. Changes in currency valuation may be more important than the actual investment. Once in a foreign investment, you must follow the gyrations of the dollar, selling as soon as you sense a strong strength trend in the US currency. The general historical trend points to a declining pound and dollar. the Deutschmark and Swiss Franc are appreciating.

In addition to newsletters previously mentioned here, consider *World Market Perspective, The International Advisor, Fuller Money* and *Swingtrend.*

Dennis Hardaker, *Advisor* editor, says: "Our publication selects, analyzes and recommends the most promising world stocks and monitors the world's stock markets, offering readers the chance to profit from them." *The International Advisor* is located at WMP Publishing Co., Suite 103, Lee Road, Winter Park, FL 32789, USA.

*World Market Perspective* is also published by WMP Publishing, at the same address. Its analysis aims more at the foreign economic situation than does its sister letter. Jerry Schomp, editor, says: "We only study global markets for specific and general economic trends, and analyze them so that our subscribers can use the information to make better investment decisions."

General investing letters, such as Standard & Poor's *The Outlook*, Doug Casey's *Investing in Crisis, The Wellington Letter* or *Personal Finance*, periodically report worldwide investing opportunities.

In November 1988, *Personal Finance*, phone 800-777-6214 in USA, did a report on the Over-the-Counter Z-Seven, a closed end fund. Z-7 invests in both American and foreign stocks. Gains averaged 31 per cent a year. The same article named three dozen foreign companies which they predicted would show average earnings of 30 per cent a year over the next five years.

Companies included: Western Mining and Alcoa in Australia, Algoma Steel, Ipsco Inc and LSI in Canada; Atlas Fertiliser in the Philippines; Hermes in Switzerland; Davy Corp, Caparo Industries and Renold in the United Kingdom; and Mannesman in West Germany. The results were mixed.

In the two years following the recommendation, Z-7 for instance was flat and made nothing in dollar terms. But in 1991 it picked up and made about two per cent per month. There are no sure things, but in general, foreign stock funds have given investors more upside action than most American funds.

The *New York Times* business section covers major foreign business and financial developments as well as American news. Meanwhile, its worldwide political coverage ranks among the best. That is important.

International investors must pay close attention to world political events. When Iran wars with Iraq, or Iraq invades Kuwait, the world oil market shakes, with consequent reaction in petroleum shares. The development of a full Common Market in Europe from the end of 1992 may force drastic changes in operations of American multinational corporations. That fact will affect their stock prices. South Africa's racial problems can affect its stocks, producing bargains for investors unconcerned about speculative risks and political considerations. When US sanctions were lifted in July 1991, most South African stocks doubled in one day. Bond discounts disappeared. Investors who were positioned to take advantage of the long-anticipated news made another killing!

*The Wall Street Journal* offers several daily pages of non-USA financial news. In one analysis, the Journal's Abreast of the Market column said: "Ideally, investors look for a 'triple whammy' when moving cash abroad. In stocks, that means a dividend payment, rising stock prices and currency profits. In bonds, the potential triple advantage adds up to yield, capital gains and rising currency." The

*Financial Times* of London is sold all over Europe and Asia and gives *The Wall Street Journal* stiff competition.

*Barron's* has its International Trader column plus a page on prices on overseas markets. *Investor's Daily* reports pertinent data. The *Economist*, a London-based weekly magazine, has American and French editions which offer a wide variety of international articles. Virtually every business magazine periodically examines foreign markets. The Associated Press, working with Dow Jones, has developed a cadre of business-orientated reporters abroad. Its dispatches appear in newspapers around the world. Most major financial magazines have English versions.

Asset International Inc., 18 Desbrosses St., New York, NY 10013, USA, recently published *The International Investor's Guide*. Its 450 pages contain a wealth of data, including investor's contacts at more than 1,000 foreign companies. The work isn't cheap at $245 a copy. It could be worth it for serious investors.

No US law prohibits citizens from maintaining a foreign bank account. Of course USA investors must declare any interest income on tax returns.

# Chapter 4

# MAKING THE RIGHT MOVES: REAL FREEDOM IS SPELLED PT

*"Idiots and amateurs talk about 'strategies'.*
*Generals discuss logistics"*
*- Norman Schwarzkopf*

PTs do *not* follow "advice" offered by the mass media – at least not as far as choosing where to live goes.

For the past few years, the popular press has published the "results" of annual "scientific findings" on where to go for the "highest quality of life".

Invariably, the "top scorers" on quality of life test are either Finland or Denmark, with Sweden occasionally thrown in for good measure. We know all of these countries well. You won't find a greater collection of aggressive, perpetually depressed clapped out alcoholics anywhere. So, running the risk of killing off yet another popular delusion, world press "reports" notwithstanding, Scandinavia is great for a visit but for its wealthy and productive citizens who are the most over-regulated and over-taxed people on earth, it stinks. We can even call on witnesses to support this. Not so long ago, we met a middle-aged, somewhat rotund Swedish businessman in the new British Airways business class lounge in Heathrow's terminal three. We talked a bit and asked if he was heading back to Stockholm. The fellow choked violently on his orange juice. Then he spat out that he'd rather die a slow death by munching on glass shards than ever again "setting foot in that evil little altruist-infested, communist Gulag concentration camp." According to him, the only reason the Scandinavian countries don't need walls, barbed wire, minefields and guards with orders to shoot to kill to prevent people from fleeing is an intensive brainwashing of the population that starts in kindergarten. Wow. We knew things were bad up there, but not *that* bad. Other expatriates term Scandinavia one big open prison! They opted out while they still could. Many of them are today's PTs, long off their governments' computers.

Is it advisable to become at PT? It sounds expensive and cumbersome, doesn't it? Moving to another country, then keeping your money and businesses in a third country, officially residing in a fourth country, using identity papers issued in a fifth. Is all that really necessary, just to protect your freedom? Surely, there must be easier ways?

Perhaps there are, if you find them, please let me know.

Consider the national politics of the world's only remaining superpower, the United States of America. Here, the federal government and individual states are spending literally billions of dollars every year to wage a "war on drugs". It is widely accepted by a vast majority of the country's inhabitants as the "right" thing to do. Sit back for a second and consider these two facts: first, that enforcing a strict ban on drugs has created an urban war zone where teenagers do not think twice about gunning down each other (not to mention innocent bystanders) in the street with UZI submachineguns to protect their "exclusive territories" for the sale of drugs – their "turfs". And, second, that this "war" is crippling people's minds to a pitiful degree. In recent polls (as quoted by *Playboy* magazine) close to 70 per cent of the American population expresses a willingness to give up their civil rights if that is what is "needed" to "fight drugs". Given how hard the present set of "civil rights" enjoyed by every American has been fought for, does it make sense to compromise the right of everyone – the right to a fair trial, the right to privacy, the right not to have one's home invaded by gun-wielding law enforcement officers without search warrants on the flimsiest of suspicions – merely to prevent a tiny minority from using dope? Consider also that the very reasons cited for the "war on drugs" – the gangland shootings, the gunfights in the streets, the muggings and robberies galore – arise from two unchangeable factors: there is a lot of money to be made from drugs as long as it is illegal; and it is precisely the prohibition of drugs which creates junkies who are unable to finance their addictions without turning to violent crime.

In the last US presidential election, the alleged "people's candidate" Ross Perot told the American public that if he were in charge he would ask Congress to make an official declaration of war on drug dealers and users alike. Adding, in off-hand manner, that "it would not be pretty". No, it certainly would not – even as it is, it isn't! But when a presidential candidate proposes to "cordon off poor neighborhoods and send in SWAT teams to conduct house-to-house searches for drugs", that raises some very ominous parallels with Nazi Germany.

If you are American, this is the kind of society – and the kind of politicians – that claim you as state property to be forced into service as a tax-payer, to finance one of the many monstrous stupidities initiated by governments.

But if you are not American, do not rejoice too loudly. Other countries have a habit of following America's example sooner or later. Already, authorities (and bank officers) worldwide will sit up straight in their chairs if someone implies that *you* are or even just *may be* involved in illicit drug deals or money laundering. Those same conscientious people who would otherwise show anyone the door who asked snooping questions about your affairs may sell you out in a second if they can be made to believe merely that you are *under investigation* for drug crimes. In several cases the US Federal Government sought to obtain information from foreign sources citing income tax investigations. When stonewalled by banks and local officials citing strict banking secrecy laws, US prosecutors have formally charged people with drug offences only to obtain either tax information or extraditions. You may rest very assured that this is absolutely **not**, as Dr. Ferris put it, "*the time for noble gestures*". Governments in general and the US government in particular are "at war" all right – but with their own citizens. This alone makes the thought even more compelling that perhaps you ought to just "drop out", become a non-person to local authorities by pretending that you are merely "**passing through**" and, as such, of no real interest to anyone but the local tourist-trap operators.

## SHOULD YOU BECOME A PT?

It may be too big a step (both emotionally and financially) for you to resign as an involuntary, conscripted taxpayer by moving to another country. After all, less than 0.2 per cent of the world's entire population lives outside its country of birth – and this figure includes refugees, embassy staffers and foreign-aid workers. Only a miniscule minority of all expatriates have relocated with the sole intent of getting out from under Big Brother's thumb to live anonymous (i.e. safer) lives as permanent tourists. This is, however, no reason why you should not do so.

Ponder the statistics: less than five per cent of all Americans ever obtain a passport! Americans can visit Canada and Mexico without one, but most Americans rarely venture outside their own state. For most Americans just going to Washington, DC is like going to a foreign country. Sad. These are people who will never acquire a sense of the world as being an overflowing treasure-trove of opportunity and new discoveries. They are content to stay at home, watch the tube and – if so inclined – keep up with the Joneses next door. Not much of a life, but you will get little out of life unless you are prepared to put some effort into it.

For most people, "Japan" is just a word with no special meaning besides "Toyota" – they would never dream of going there. Compare the attitude of Sir Edmund Hillary who, when asked why on earth he travelled halfway around the globe to climb Mount Everest answered: "Because it was there".

Perhaps you should think more like Hillary when it comes to guarding your interests and freedom; using whatever tools are available to you – **because they are there.** After all, even if you are too timid to venture outside the country where you live – or to travel to a different continent and climb a big chunk of granite, just for the heck of it – there is every reason why you should, at the very least, make use of tools such as mail drops, offshore corporations, secret bank accounts and advanced means of communication. Couple this with sophisticated ways of using car license plates, travel documents and identity papers. Then you will be supremely equipped to not only retain – or regain – your freedom but also to increase your sense of personal security and safety AND multiplying your income by several times. Plus lifting yourself high above the fray of doubts, fears, insecurities, worries and occasional panics that permeate the lives chosen – by default – by most people. If you use these tools you will find that, bit by bit, you will tend to stop using phrases like "I can't", "it's impossible", "there is no way" and that most dreadfully apathic and damnable of utterances: "you can't escape death and taxes". Knowledge, both theoretical and practical, makes problems disappear and obstacles crumble. Keep in mind that you will be able to solve just about any problem before you, given sufficient knowledge, time and resources. Or, to quote Henry Ford: "If you think you can, or if you think you can't, then you are right."

In your own quest for freedom and privacy – both personal, financial and otherwise – you will find that it pays tremendous dividends to go further in your endeavours, and put more effort into them, than may at first seem strictly necessary. In the words of the late, great advertising executive, Bill Bernbach: "If you reach for the stars you might not quite get one – but you won't come up with a handful of mud, either". Which means, in regard to the aspect of keeping your money and your freedom, that you should not be timid. Rather, think of yourself as what you really are, a soldier caught in enemy territory – or, if this image is more to your fancy, as a master criminal preparing to perpetrate the crime of the century and getting away with it. It should be pointed out that the latter may serve to induce you to plan more carefully than the former. There is nothing "criminal", "illicit" or even "immoral" about trying to protect your freedom. It is your perfect moral right to do so even if society may have passed a number of laws making it "illegal" or merely "severely frowned upon". Especially when engaged in a highly useful, moral and ultimately profitable (in every way) business it pays handsomely to adopt the attitude of spies or succesful criminals to avoid detection, capture or merely avoiding getting in the spotlight.

In the classic movie *Wall Street*, stockbroker Bud Fox obtains insider information from unlocked file cabinets in deserted offices and from following a corporate raider around to establish what sort of takeovers he is contemplating. This is done in order to beat the raider to it (by buying up stocks in a company before he announces his takeover attempt). Now, reverse the setting and do what you must to make sure that no one can obtain confidential information by looking through *your* "file-cabinets" (i.e. your credit card statements or phone records) by following *you* around.

Remember, yet again, that if you not only are consistently aware of *why* you are doing what you do but also remind yourself *why your actions are **necessary*** to protect your own interests, then the quest will seem far less cumbersome and may, in due course, come to be perceived by you as a little game where your cunning serves to keep you out of reach of looters and moochers.

## THE ETERNAL PARADOX

Although much of *PT1* and *PT2* rants and raves about how bad politicians and bureaucrats are, the truth of the matter is that as individuals, these chaps are people very much like us. Most are not left wing idiots or even fundamentalist religious fanatics. Probably, we would even agree on most moral issues and a lot of other ideas.

Sure, I'm a Libertarian, and some of us express rather extreme positions, but most of these are just to get noticed. Just like the PT books, we want to raise the consciousness of people. There **are other ways** of doing things that should at least be given a try. If they work, good. If not, *back to the drawing board.* The entire worldwide privatization movement of the last decade was an idea that came out of the Libertarian Think Tank. Libertarians pointed out that while State-owned utilities and major industries looked like a winner of an idea at the turn of the century, 100 years of experience proved that independently owned, loosely regulated businesses normally did a far better job at lower cost to the consumers. The idea was to give consumers a choice, not just one option: a state owned monopoly that didn't deliver the goods.

Diversity, private ownership and choice are the general tenets of a market-driven system. From it flows, among many ideas, the concept that perhaps education would be improved if you gave vouchers to parents and let them spend them on the type of institutions, private or not, that provide the kind of education wanted for their kids.

None of us wants old people or young mothers starving on the streets, nor dope addicts shooting heroin in hallways and burglarizing our homes to support their habits. Everybody likes well designed cities with open spaces, no pollution, and even a few attractive public buildings and parks. Even Libertarians are willing to pay some taxes and support a limited police force and volunteer military establishment to suppress violence and fraud. No one seems to want what we have: an ever-growing government with more and more people on the public tit. So why is it so hard to make a change, to get away from a bloated bureaucracy and over-regulated world?

Let's look at a few homely little examples.

Years ago in a certain US city there was a tragedy. Several children burned to death in the home of a babysitter who (although she should have been watching the children) neglected her charges. There was a fire and they burned to death. The newspapers and others clamored for a law. Laws were passed. Licenses were needed to offer childcare. Special training and examinations were needed to get the license. A sprinkler system was required. If anything went wrong at other preschools after that, new laws were passed. A kid fell down some stairs. Thereafter babysitters had to do their thing only on ground floors with no steps in their homes. The amount and type of food, toys, activities were all regulated down to the most minute detail. Charges were regulated and limited, and fines imposed if there were any deviations. Eventually there were no childcare facilities in the city. They had been regulated out of existence. Because there was a "need", daycare centers costing much more than private facilities were established as tax-supported facilities. Mothers who took their children there had many complaints – but there were no alternatives. Taxpayers grumbled a little, but the facilities only added half a percentage point to their property tax. Who could be against children? Everyone accepts the status quo.

What's the point?

The point is that government, as usual, went too far.

Trying to solve a problem, the city in question made it impossible for a mother to entrust her children to an individual of her own choosing. The city, responding to thousands of pressures like this, went from a budget of under $1 million twenty years ago, to **$600 million** today. It went from being a minor tax collector to the point where 5 per cent is added on to the price of every hotel and motel room in the city, and 25 per cent is tacked on to every parking bill, not to mention several hundred other new taxes on everything except breathing. The city now has its own income tax on wage earners within the city – to be able to provide "needed services." Those taxes just sneak up on you – and all for very good purposes!

The same thing is true at the federal level. Urgent needs will **always** expand **to soak** up available funds.

Once a government program is in place, there are employees and beneficiaries with a vested interest in the continuance and expansion of any program. They lobby and use public relations to show what a good job they are doing, and how the needs are even greater than their funds and personnel can cope with. Just as in business, expansion and growth is life: if appropriations and staff are cut, it means less power, influence and perks. The continuance and expansion of their program and their appropriations are exceedingly important to those with a financial interest. For legislators, each program, each agency means only a few pennies a year to each taxpayer. There is no person or agency specifically appointed to terminate programs that have outlived their usefulness. Nor is there anyone sufficiently interested in investigating and eliminating 50 out of 100 workers doing something they (the government employees) think is exceedingly worthwhile.

When border controls were to be eliminated in Europe, the border guards went on strike. They sought to justify their continuance by reviewing all the arrests made, the contraband seized, the fines and taxes collected and all the other "good work" they had done over the years. No one was around to show that they had cost the economy of Europe untold billions due to delays and local inspections. The bureaucrats had a lot at stake (their jobs and livelihoods), while the general public had a more vague interest. Usually there is no highly motivated group close to the power who could move in to say "These guys are nothing but an economic impediment, an institution less than worthless." This time, opposing the organizations of customs service employees and border guards, powerful economic interests were around to lobby for greater freedom in the movement of people, services and goods. But most agencies handle some obscure task that goes on and on. Low profile sometimes means survival for bureaucrats too! It is worse in international agencies than in government. At least governments sometimes are obliged to look for ways to cut expenditures. In the international agencies, like the UN, groups of highly paid civil servants are often ex-politicians who got a lifetime no-work job as a reward for faithful service in their home country. We know dozens of individuals drawing down six figure, tax-free salaries who do little more than liaise with colleagues from other agencies and occasionally commission expensive reports from "expert" friends that no one ever reads. Who will ever seek to eliminate this waste? Probably no one.

There are millions of employees in politics, public service and in the international agencies who could be eliminated with beneficial effects for all. Sure, there would be short term discomfort (unemployment) for these employees themselves. But most would find their way into productive enterprises sooner or later. If not, it would still be cheaper to eliminate the job and pension them off. Perhaps up to 98 per cent of all public agencies could be dissolved or eliminated without any ill effects. Post offices and telephone companies have been privatized with great results. Politically appointed and questionably motivated judges could largely be replaced by far cheaper and more efficient private arbitrators. This is not the place to go over all the possibilities for cutting government down to size, but there are many, as we all know.

The eternal paradox is that even under the political regimes of conservatives like Thatcher and Reagan, government budgets and staffing levels continued to grow. Under their less committed successors, they will grow even more. Bureaucrats who benefit from the status quo don't like to give up their positions of power, prestige, pensions and pay. An institution can do a rotten job, and be corrupt from top to bottom, yet politicians and people are often conned that there is no failure, as with the American Drug Enforcement Administration; or that the reason for the failure is underfunding and understaffing. So the government agency or bureau gets more money, becomes more corrupt and an even bigger failure. The only government solution is to throw more money at it, not to think rationally about other approaches.

If you were elected to public office without any particular training in the Libertarian way of solving problems by *leaving them alone,* you might very well have the belief that almost all problems can best be solved by government intervention, government regulation, and government takeovers of industries that are not performing as well as they might be. If, after government intervention things got worse instead of better, you probably would believe in good faith that the solution was *more regulation,* more tax money, or *more* diversion of control from the private to the public sector.

Millions and millions of dollars are appropriated to provide assistance to the refugees as they arrive. Who could refuse to vote them a paltry few million? Normally, they are not given work permits.

But when the ancestors of the Americans arrived at Plymouth Rock to face a cold and hostile environment, was there a social worker there to greet them? When Columbus landed, did the Arawaks appropriate 10 tons of wampum and put him on welfare until he could get "adjusted"? When the millions and millions of poor Germans, Jews, Irish, and Polish arrived from 1895 to 1910, there was *no* welfare. There were *no* social services. *None was expected.* But people got along. **They worked!** They showed some of the pioneer spirit that made this country great. They prospered!

That doesn't happen as much any more.

America began to follow postwar England down the tubes with lower productivity, lower standards of living, and a generally slower pace and less demanding life. There's no secret why. If you give people money not to work, they *won't* work. If you reduce incentives to produce wealth, people will lay back and let someone else do it.

Much of what happens in America can be predicted from what happened in England a few years earlier. Since World War II, the English Socialist "do-gooders" had political control. They believed in meeting "social gods" and "human needs." As a result, there was overregulation of business, excessive welfare programs, socialization of medicine and industry, accomplished at the cost of massive inflation and the lowering of productivity. Once-mighty England foundered economically, landing in the position of a second-rate power.

What's the answer. The obvious and mostly ignored answer for the world is to institutionalize the automatic termination of laws, programs and agencies. They call this a sunset clause. These are as rare in government as clean pigs in mud. Maybe anything that involves public expenditure needs to be voted on and after a death by sunset clause, the next vote needs approval by something more than a simple majority for the expenditures to be continued.

Every civil service position and perhaps most political jobs should be automatically vacated and left vacant for a substantial period every few years. If the world continues to turn, perhaps the job should be eliminated.

The above probably never will happen. Thus to escape from a system that nobody wants, an eternal paradox, there is another answer: we become PTs.

**Chapter 5**

# HOW TO KEEP YOUR OWN MONEY YOUR OWN BUSINESS IN THE NINETIES AND BEYOND

*"First, ya get da money.*
*Then, when ya got da money, ya get da power.*
*And den, when ya got da power, ya get da woman."*
*– Al Pacino in the movie "Scarface".*

Power and the opposite sex aside, it is a fact that your continued existence anywhere in this world is dependent on you having the dough. But if you don't – it is bad news. Without money, you cannot rent a comfortable home nor eat what you want.

Whether you like it or not, it is that simple. The French branch of British-owned fast food chain Burger King launched a campaign called *Politique Social* – Social Politics. In this case, it consisted of selling two cheeseburgers for 10 French Francs, more or less £1 Sterling. But even then, without even that little cash to spare, well . . . I suppose you could apply for welfare assistance.

So what does money have to do with your privacy? Keeping your own money your own business (and nobody else's) is getting increasingly difficult.

Again, the subject of money ties nicely into the subject "your freedom". With sufficient cash and a few other essentials at hand, you may stay free and alive – at least as long as your money (and health) lasts. But if you do something stupid, you will give the rest of the world (which has no vested interest in your particular livelihood) the chance to locate your funds and confiscate them, leaving you destitute. And a good deal closer to starvation and death. In other words: no matter how much money you have, it is folly not to make painstakingly sure that people who wish you ill (or may do so in the future) have an absolute minimum chance of parting you from the very thing – money – that ensures your continued breathing. Not only should you therefore follow the 11th commandment (GTM – Get The Money) but also and perhaps even more seriously the 12th: Keep The Money And Make Sure It Stays That Way.

Unfortunately, a lot of people tend to remember the former and forget the latter, ultimately finding themselves in that most extremely uncomfortable of situations – having caused their own ruin by default. If there was ever a more senseless form of self destruction than that of spending (or moving about) your money in a way that is fit to enable others to rob you of it, we have yet to hear of it.

Whatever else happens one thing is certain: you will need to use money to pay for your physical upkeep – and for the gadgets and services that will come in handy when trying to keep your freedom. That is precisely the crux of the issue. You may have to do a bit of thinking when making various payments lest you accidentally give away either your intentions or your whereabouts. The same, by the way, goes for communications which are covered in a later chapter.

First of all, let us establish the various tools that fall under the category of "money". Basically, there are three: **cash**, **checks** and **credit cards**.

It may seem trivial to go into such exhaustive detail on a subject as mundane as "money". After all, spending it is not all that difficult – right? Getting it is more important? No – not if you want to keep your freedom and your privacy intact and unembattled. If that is your aim then you really have to start thinking consciously about spending. That being so, it may also induce you to spend less which is a nice detail. You build equity faster when you start making a habit of stopping to think for a minute before making a purchase:"How should I pay for this and, after all, do I really *need* this stuff?".

To whet your appetite on the subject of just why money, in all its forms, is so important to use or spend, or move about the *right* way, let us exemplify by way of referring to the 1989 movie *Midnight Run*. A bounty hunter, played by Robert de Niro, manages to apprehend a fugitive embezzler who has jumped bail – having done so by outwitting a rival bounty hunter. To catch up with de Niro's character, the rival bounty-man (on regaining consciousness) calls up the credit card company and, pretending to be de Niro, claims that his credit cards have been lost or stolen. In other words, he effectively renders the cards useless. De Niro later learns he is broke when trying to purchase Greyhound bus tickets to take himself and his prisoner back to the LA county jail. Thus, a simple phone call may be used to put just about anyone (including yourself . . .) in dire straits.

This DOES happen in real life, to real people, several times a week. The scaring fact is that you could become the next victim. In the three following chapters, we will look at CASH, at CHECKS and at CREDIT CARDS one by one. We will examine how to get maximum financial privacy from each of these three monetary tools. But first, a word on investments.

# INVESTMENTS

A typical fund/investment manager at a bank puts together a model portfolio where he has say, 20 per cent in dollars, 30 per cent in Yen, etc. Then the dollars are divided up into demand deposits, bonds and stock and the same with other basic currency groups. The main object of the investment manager is to do what everybody else does. By following the crowd he can't be criticized if something goes wrong. HIS JOB AS HE SEES IT IS NOT TO GO OUT ON A LIMB AND MAKE SOME CONTRARIAN INVESTMENT. The second goal is to generate as many commissions for his employer as he can without being accused of churning by a client.

Where does the "smart money" go? It does not go to the typical fund or investment manager at a bank unless pure low interest preservation is wanted.

Our own personal feelings are that there are far too many variables to be able to go where the mythical "smart money" is. The fact is we personally know all kinds of people whom one would think were "smart money" and they make all kinds of horrible mistakes on their personal investments. They make their money on sure things like underwriting and company takeovers, or whatever their business is. I doubt if there is or ever has been anyone in the world who made a really sizeable fortune on just TRADING. Unless of course he had a pipeline to insider information – which it is illegal to trade upon.

Sure, there are lucky people who keep throwing sevens on the corner outs at the crap table. But they are rare and they never make as much as the guy who owns the casino.

We have yet to meet the reader who made serious money by picking out consistently winning stocks or currencies. Playing the markets is nothing more than a crap shoot. Of course, with AAA investments or conservative stock portfolios you can usually "preserve" your capital – which is about all we expect to do. Passive investments (stocks, bonds, currencies) are what you have to have after all you don't want the hassles of an active business anymore!

But you can't expect to make the same return as you got by buying some land with 5 per cent down and putting a spec house on it with borrowed money. When a friend of ours did that, he could make $25,000 on an investment of zero (or less than zero if he borrowed enough). With State laws like those of California insulating you from personal liability on real estate loans, it can even be done completely without risk. But there are always hassles and the need to put time into "deals". Once you have had enough of deals, it is an unrealistic expectation that you can make a consistent 50 per cent a year on your money. NOBODY DOES. The historic real return on capital over inflation is more like 2-3 per cent per year.

Sometimes you can see something obvious like we saw the decline of the Tokyo stock market coming for 3 years before it happened. But timing to take advantage of the obvious is impossible to get right consistently. If we had followed our instincts and sold short Nippon Telephone when it was issued at a p/e ratio of 300, we would have lost our shirts. Because it went up! We would have had to cover our short sales. When our predictions finally came true, we wouldn't have made enough just to cover our loss of interest. In the stock market, if you want a profit, the answer is to take a course in the Graham & Dodd Fundamentals. Then wait patiently for a buying opportunity (crash) and buy and hold a stock until the market value catches up with the true value – even if it takes ten years.

Our sure bet is some choice real estate in places like East Berlin, Germany, Prague, Budapest. Prices are now 20 per cent of nearby countries and you can get a good return on rents. The risk isn't great and you can probably get mortgages to cover most of the risk. Why don't we do it? Frankly we don't want the hassle of dealing with tenants who don't pay, frozen pipes, insurance claims, etc. we have enough money to meet our simple needs for such things as travelling anywhere we want to go, getting massaged regularly, eating anywhere and living in a pretty nice place. So why should we get into doing administration work on projects to make more money? And above all, with real estate, you spend half your time screwing around with bureaucrats. Its a living, but if you can get along without becoming part of the system, who needs the aggro?

[Publisher's Note: If you don't have quite enough assets to produce the income you need – or if you like to do interesting work just to avoid boredom, we suggest getting a portable trade or occupation – like being an international consultant. The subject of our next book could be how to make a good living without having to cope with any government officials. What do you think about **Portable Trades & Professions** as a title? If you submit a chapter on your PT job, for instance – how to earn enough to live comfortably with no license required, no taxes to pay, no regulations and no border limitations, you will get a free copy of the Special Report of your choice. Naturally, this happens only if we use your material. With so many PT Readers to draw from, we figure on getting enough contributions from readers to put together an interesting book on this subject.]

# DANGERS OF INVESTING IN THE USA (FOR FOREIGNERS)

For the PT, any bank deposits or brokerage transactions (stocks and bond holdings) if made at all, should be made via banks in neutral countries. By investing under the umbrella of a powerful organization with leverage, you protect your privacy better and reduce the risks of personal involvement in a fight that could have disastrous consequences. In other words, we say that no USA property, stocks or bank accounts should ever be held in your own private name. Not under any circumstances! There are many reasons for this. The horror story at the end of this section is probably not the worst case, but it is the most scary of many similar tales we have heard and documented. But this is why you should be wary of USA investments:

**The USA regularly seizes or freezes foreign (as well as domestically) owned assets** for a host of arbitrary reasons:

Although such incidents are occasionally reported in the press, the extent of USA contempt for the sanctity of private property is not generally known nor understood. It is a surprise to this writer that any person should, under the present circumstances, ever invest a penny in the USA. For instance, during every conflict or diplomatic crisis, one of the first things the USA does is to order the seizure of private assets. We are talking about privately owned American assets held in the names of citizens of countries involved in disputes with the USA. Technically, these assets may eventually be recovered after the conflicts are resolved. But making a recovery often involves years of litigation, personal exposure, personal appearances in court, vast expenses, and often bureaucratic denials that the seizure ever took place or that the assets ever existed.

Assets seized in 1941 were still being held by the Alien Property Office thirty years after World War Two ended. Some privately owned assets taken from (presumably anti-Communist) Cuban based capitalists in retaliation for Castro's seizures have never been returned. Another danger, totally unrecognized by foreigners, are the "Unclaimed Property & Escheat Laws." Under these rules, mere *inactivity* for a period sometimes as short as *two years* results in property being taken over by the state and no longer earning interest! Administrative hearings, proofs submitted by a lawyer and formal hearings are needed to reclaim the funds. Fees of a third to half of the amounts involved are common. Many foreigners have deposited a nest egg in an American bank only to find that their money was taken and used to fund an obscure "do-good" project.

If you wish to trade in securities, or make a deposit in an American financial institution, you may do so through (and in the name of) most European or Asian banks. An "offshore financial center" bank or nominee is the fiduciary of choice for these transactions. The services of such an intermediate are not free, but the one-quarter of 1 per cent per year. Suppose you ill-advisedly held an account at an American brokerage in your own name. Unwittingly depositing more than $200 in cash to such an account (even at a foreign branch office) could result in the entire account being seized by US authorities for "money laundering.". It is then not possible to do any trading for many years while your account is frozen and your case wends its way through administrative and judicial proceedings and appeals. You may be kept in positions you happened to be in at the time of the freeze. Or, if your assets are sold, your account is converted into non-interest bearing cash dollar deposit with the Treasurer of the USA. This cashing-in process happens when the government elects a forced liquidation of your assets. There is no recourse for your attorney's fees, lost interest or investment losses; even if you do recover the funds. Remember, this all happens regularly when a foreign based investor with a USA account violates any one of a myriad of highly technical rules. Even with an American lawyer on retainer, it is possible to get into serious trouble. In fact, much trouble is caused by bad advice from lawyers! In some cases, unless your USA asset is in the multi-million dollar range, the inflation adjusted value of frozen assets will not even begin to cover the attorney's fees expended in the recovery.

**Consider the absurdity of many seizures of private property.** Scenario: The Mexican or French government confiscates certain American owned assets. The American government retaliates by seizing all private assets of French or Mexican nationals in the USA. Such a scenario is common and ordinary. It matters not at all that the citizen who owns the seized property or bank accounts may be personally opposed to the regime the USA is having problems with. A few years ago private Iranian owned assets in the USA were ordered seized when a group of Iranian militants seized the USA Embassy staff as hostages. The militants were leftists and Moslem fundamentalist followers of the Ayatollah. The punished Iranians with the USA investments were generally supporters of America's pal, the ousted Shah.

Kuwaiti private assets were seized in the States and in England during the Gulf War. These were the people the USA was pledged to help! After Cory Aquino was placed in power by the American maneuvering, many Filipinos with USA investments found their property seized by American Treasury Agents. Reason? Alleged connections with the Marcos regime. As Marcos was for a while, the darling and staunch ally of Washington, what Filipino could predict that anyone who profited from a government contract would be considered a criminal in the USA.

Seizures and confiscations in the USA each year now run into billions of dollars! Almost any pretext will do to activate a new bureaucracy existing only to grab "enemy" assets. In other sections of this book we discuss how domestic (American) businessmen are also subject to arbitrary seizures, but in this section, we are only concerned with foreigners who are all classed by many government officials as 'the enemy."

Only the enemy is not usually the enemy – it is more often an innocent and powerless victim. We recall reading the autobiography of German-Jewish teenager who was shipped to boarding school in England during the Hitler era. In England he was not permitted to finish the schooling that had been prepaid for him, but was interned as an *enemy alien* for the duration of the war. As we have noted elsewhere, the number one enemy of human beings is not disease, but rather governments. It is they who cause more misery, suffering and premature deaths than any other factor. Some governments are worse than others, but the USA is rapidly taking the lead in institutionalized, legalized crime against humanity. This occurs because of the criminalization of many activities formerly considered the normal exercise of freedom. American jails overflow with individuals who under any civilized international norms could not be considered criminals. But here, for the moment, we are more concerned with the civil aspects – the possibility that you will lose only your assets if they are held in your own name in the USA. As you will see from our examples, there is unfortunately, few areas of activity that don't involve the possibility of being jailed. Criminal law penalties have recently been injected into many activities previously considered purely civil matters. The difference between civil penalties and criminal penalties is great. If you lose a civil case, you pay damages. Where government is involved, civil damages usually involve back taxes and relatively reasonable fines. Where criminal charges are made, you may lose your freedom and all your assets may be confiscated. As criminal cases are easier to win and offer more "fun" for prosecutors, few civil cases remain purely civil these days.

To enforce new laws on insider trading, drug dealing, and money laundering, many substantial investor accounts are seized every day. The only requirement seems to be that there be "unusual activities." These "unusual activities" are of course, classed as crimes. As a result, every foreign owned account is at risk. Stockbrokers and bankers are required to report (upon pain of criminal penalties for themselves) any "unusual activity" to the USA Treasury on special forms. Upon receipt of such reports, accounts are often frozen.

What is "unusual?" No one knows. Depositing cash (even if only the price of a good lunch) is one "unusual" factor, often leading to vast problems. But almost anything could be considered unusual. *"Unusual" exists, like beauty, in the eyes of the beholder!* As a result, seizures in the USA tend to be quite arbitrary. Unless a celebrity is involved, the vast majority of individual cases are not reported in the press. But hundreds occur every day. Like cancer, such problems do not always hit the other guy.

## THE TWO MILLION DOLLAR CONFISCATION

One of our own clients, last year, merely wanted to close out his account at the USA's largest stock broker. The reason for the requested closure and requested transfer of funds to an account abroad was that he was unhappy being in dollar assets. He also had made a minor complaint to the Zürich office branch manager about the poor servicing of some orders for his account. Over two million dollars in assets were in his own name with this broker. When the money never arrived at his Cayman account, the client inquired and was told that the USA Treasury had seized the money (without any notice or court hearings) due to his "unusual activity."

The only thing unusual was that he wanted to cash in his chips. This fact was reported to the Treasury. The client was informed by a computer-generated government form letter that he could recover it only by bringing a lawsuit, and appearing personally in the USA courts. His claim for recovery had to be within a rather short, prescribed period. As he was an Italian and these assets were a big secret from his own government and from his spouse as well, he could not risk the exposure. He kissed his assets goodbye. "It is not a pleasant experience to have two million dollars confiscated!" he wrote us.

## LIFE SAVINGS SEIZED; WIDOW FRAMED & JAILED; FORCED TO SIGN OVER ASSETS

In another case, a non-US woman from Santo Domingo who had never lived in the USA except for short vacation trips owned a Florida condominium, plus bank accounts and securities on deposit in the USA.

The value was "only" half a million dollars, but this was the widow's entire life-savings. Because another person (a complete stranger!) with her relatively common surname was involved in a tax dispute with the USA, all of her personal assets were seized (once again without notice or court hearing) to satisfy a USA claim against this *stranger*. Upon receiving the standard form letter, she protested the seizure by her own letter to the Treasury, but was told once again by form letter, that she had only a very short time to hire a lawyer in the USA. Preliminary inquiries indicated she'd then have to appear personally at a trial in a US District Court in Miami, Florida to prove beyond a shadow of doubt that she had no connection with the accused offender.

It is always difficult or impossible to prove a negative, but the widow Garcia decided she had no alternative but to go to Florida, hire an American lawyer and try to recover her money and apartment. When she explained her need for a visa (to make her claim) for travel to the USA, permission to visit the USA for this purpose was *denied*. This happened at the USA Consulate in her own country where she had applied for the usual six months visa.

The horror story got worse from that point onwards. She entered the USA illegally via Puerto Rico where she made the standard arrangements favored by Dominicans, by acquiring local (Puerto Rican) driver's license as her USA identification. She then flew to Miami and spent her last assets on a retainer for an expensive Florida lawyer. He did nothing. Without money to make her condo and mortgage payments, her property went into foreclosure and was irrevocably lost. After three months of running up hotel bills and waiting for the attorney to file a legal action within the required period, she complained. Within days (suspecting that her own lawyer had turned her in), she was arrested and quickly sentenced to a year and a day in prison for carrying **fraudulently obtained identification** papers and **illegal entry** into the USA. The date for filing a claim now having passed, her assets were irrevocably lost.

Does it get still worse? You bet! While in jail, just before her release date, she was further charged with being part of a drug importing conspiracy with the stranger (call him "Garcia") she had never met nor heard of. She was told that her 'drug tainted Garcia assets' were gone forever. Unless she waived all further claims against the USA, she was told by the Department of Justice prosecutor that she would be given a forty year sentence for drug trafficking. Now without any funds at all, she was advised by her free public defender lawyer to plead guilty to drug trafficking. Mrs. Garcia initially refused, but the deal eventually made was this., If she would make a plea bargain for a ten year suspended sentence, at the end of her year in prison, she could accept deportation to her home country. Anxious to get back home, and with a best-case scenario of being held in a very unpleasant county jail for several months while her trial was pending, she decided to go for the "deal" and get sent back home at USA government expense. The downside was a drug conviction, but she felt that this would not be a problem back in the Dominican Republic. Her plan was to try and live a quiet life with her daughter who was willing to take her in.

Ultimately, she was deported to her home country as agreed in the plea bargain. Upon arrival, she didn't expect what happened next. Instead of being allowed to stay at the home of her daughter as planned, as a convicted and admitted drug-dealer, she was promptly jailed upon arrival back in the Dominican Republic. There was no need for a trial there because under treaty arrangements, deported and convicted drug dealers serve their USA imposed sentences in the Dominican Republic. So much for trusting the USA Department of Justice and her lawyer who failed to mention this little detail. She spent the following two years in a very unpleasant jail in her own country. There she remains with eight years to go. The Santo Domingo government receives grant money from the USA to keep her and several hundred others like her incarcerated. In a letter to me, the widow Garcia stated that "I never had the slightest involvement in drug dealing, nor any remote interest in illegal drugs of any kind. There was no evidence of any kind, nor any testimony against me. I never had a trial for anything except the illegal entry charge. I wouldn't have made any illegal entry if they hadn't confiscated my money and given me only a few months to make a claim in person. The only connection I needed to get into all this trouble is that I have the same name, Garcia, as a shadowy figure who may or not be involved in this drug business.

Nobody seems to know anything about him except that he had the same last name. The government tried to make him out to be my husband or son, but I have no son, and my husband died twenty years ago – long before the drug thing ever became a big deal. As to the other Garcia: his money was also confiscated, but he never made any claim. This name is the most common name in any Spanish speaking country. I am sure that everyone involved in my case knows that there is no connection between me and this other Garcia, but it doesn't matter to them. It is not like in the movies where a prosecutor admits a mistake to free an innocent person. The contrary is true. The more wrong they are, the more vigorously they defend the position that the accused was "properly sentenced after being found guilty as charged."

The widow continued: "This whole story is like a bad dream, but I assure you it is real. I have written letters to Amnesty International and have tried everything to clear myself, and get free but the answer is always, 'You probably wouldn't have pleaded guilty if you hadn't been involved in something illegal.' I suppose because I am not being tortured and am not a political figure, no one except my family knows or cares about me. Truth is, had I not pleaded guilty, the USA could and would have framed me for some new crime anyway. They can always get other inmates to lie about something in return for money or more likely, a sentence reduction. To accuse the USA government of such tactics may sound far-fetched to someone who has never been in their meat grinder, but I assure you that justice in the USA courts or prison system is not something one can count on. There is a bureaucratic need to convict people and to keep them incarcerated for long periods. Innocence or guilt doesn't seem to matter much.

In my USA Federal prison, I saw examples and heard too many stories of bogus secondary charges being brought at the expiration of the first prison term. I had a real fear of spending my entire life in a foreign jail. Nobody really cares about you and my relatives had a very tough time getting dispensation for a three day visa to visit me (in prison, during my trial) from Santo Domingo. The expense of such trips is something they can't really afford. I figured I would be in a better situation **in** my home country where people knew I was not a criminal. I just wanted to go home and live a quiet life. But this was not to be.

The USA has so much money to fight their drug war, they convict many innocent people like me who then become statistics representing their 'success' in interdicting this traffic. Then with their wealth and immense influence abroad, they can continue to make life miserable for people like me. I feel that USA pressure alone is keeping me in jail here. My money was legally earned and saved as a result of my deceased husband's auto-parts business. The original investments in the USA were made by him because we wanted a safe place to keep our savings due to dangers from an often arbitrary government here at home in Santo Domingo. We were also informed in writing by the local US Embassy that we would always be given a visa to spend up to six months a year in our vacation home in Florida. Had I suspected that what happened to me was a possibility, I wouldn't have touched any investment in the USA with a barge pole. Now all my retirement savings money is lost and I am still in jail with little hope of getting out before I die. I am not saying that everyone in jail is an innocent angel, but I have met quite a few people in the States who like me, do not belong in jails. To be in this situation is not a pleasant ending for a 59-year-old widow and grandmother. I might have killed myself, but regular family visits and my Christian faith and prayer has sustained me."

**Xenophobic Big Brother** It is well known that most countries, while welcoming foreign investors, do not want foreigners to stay around too long nor to own local property. The USA was always different, passing out unlimited visit visas and encouraging foreign investors to buy land, farms, real estate and local businesses. Legal protections against seizures and confiscations were given foreigners on the same basis as if they were locals. Special laws like the Edge Act in banking, even gave foreigners an edge, as it were. Foreigners got bank secrecy denied to locals, and there was for many years no reporting on foreign accounts nor withholding of taxes on interest due foreigners. The drug war and other modern concerns, gave the government excuses to withdraw all former asset protection from both locals and foreigners. *New treaties mandate that the USA reports interest paid to foreigners to their own governments.* Assets of local citizens or foreigners can be frozen, sold or seized quite easily.

To confiscate USA property, some snot-nosed teenager from an obscure agency merely has to scribble that he *suspects* a boat, plane or car; a house or bank account is "possibly involved in" environmental offenses, organized crime, tax fraud, insider trading, drug dealing, money laundering, or a long list of offenses. The property is then taken out of the control of the owner. The burden then shifts to the owner to prove he is clean as the driven snow. The record of recoveries in such cases is dismal, from the point of view of the foreign investor. Often, a civil court appearance by an accused, is used as an opportunity to gather evidence or file criminal charges. As a result, the USA is now a treacherous place to do business, to invest, or even to visit as a tourist. Xenophobia is such that the ownership of local property or businesses is made untenable by the selective enforcement of measures against foreigners. Japan bashing is the current fad. Japanese and Asian investors face many restrictions in the form of laws enforced against them, but not others. Local politicians score points by railing against foreigners. In most cases, such problems are not simply bribe demands as they are in say, third world countries. They are institutionalized Xenophobia that can only be cured by the foreigner being "punished." Attempts to buy off the tormentors in the USA may only cause more problems.

We know from personal experience that crime and corruption exist everywhere. In places like Mexico, Brazil and the Philippines one faces a real danger of armed robbery and even greater danger of false accusations by bribe-seeking corrupt police or customs officials. However, up until recently, the only major governments that were essentially legalized thug rule were the Communists. There, restrictions on freedom of personal travel and economic activities were enforced for their own sake. With the disintegration of the Communists, the last remaining superpower has in many ways, become the successor in terms of making life miserable for its people without any discernible or logical reason. Far too many activities are banned, and far too many people are jailed just for the sake of expanding bureaucratic power. Indeed, the closest thing to the fictional Big Brother government portrayed in the excellent fiction of George Orwell *1984,* is now that of the United States.

# USA REPLACES SOVIET UNION AS THE WORLD'S OUTLAW

No question, the USA today is **not a safe place to invest in – nor even to visit.** Beside the danger posed by the government, recent statistics reveal that the chances of being assaulted in a big city are roughly the same as a front line soldier being shot in World War II. In New York City, Washington DC, and Los Angeles, armed robbery is so common that a well dressed tourist walking alone has a better than even chance of being assaulted and seriously injured. Violent crime is more than 20 times as common in Big City America than it is in Europe. Strange when we also learn that 20 times more people (on a per capita basis) are in American jails than are in European jails. Perhaps the wrong people are being incarcerated in America.

We are not saying that if you visit the USA you'll be assaulted either by drug crazed hold-up or by drug-crazed government officials. But a small percentage of foreign investors will share the fate of the two individuals in the above horror stories. If your accounts are not confiscated however, the odds are probably better than 50-50 that there will be some fairly serious tax or regulatory problems with *any* substantial investments held in your own name. For instance, in the event of death, a large tax (55 per cent in recent years) is due, even from foreigners who may never have set foot in the country. The legal and other costs of "administering an estate" or simply getting it paid over to the rightful owner will be about another 10 per cent – if everything goes smoothly. This legalized theft from the unwary has been the law of the land for years.

Your heirs or joint holder of a bank account or securities portfolio may thus get an unpleasant surprise, ending up with 35 per cent on the dollar when they try to close out an account or sell your real estate. The inheritance/estate tax problem at least, is overcome by simply keeping assets in a company name, or as suggested at the outset, dealing through a foreign bank so that your name, ownership (and the fact of your death), never appears on a USA computer.

Now that constitutional protections against arbitrary seizures or confiscations without notices or hearings have been removed by court decisions, the USA is certainly as treacherous a place as any third world dictatorship. It may be more treacherous than most. Why? Because in the third world (and much of the First and Second World as well) most problems can be settled with an appropriate gift or tribute paid to the proper official. While corruption is not desirable, it is in many ways preferable to be able to make a pay-off; a quick financial settlement. Lawyers in such places know there are standard charges for such things. Then you can get on with life and business.

In the United States, once caught in the grind wheels of bureaucracy, one can face endless hassles and often end up in jail. The system, like that of the former Communist Bureaucracy often seems capricious in choosing it's victims. But there is a pattern. It is this pattern we are now warning you about. In the USA, prosecutors admit the fact that they often choose their defendants on the basis of nationality, notoriety, wealth or social standing. These factors are more decisive, it appears, than whether the defendant did anything to hurt anyone. In many cases, the criteria for what is known as "selective prosecution" is simply *how easy it will be to grab assets or get a criminal conviction* from an already prejudiced (against foreigners) jury.

How much publicity or career advancement opportunity will making a seizure or winning a conviction in a given case provide? Guilt or innocence is often not even a factor to be considered. As such, a wealthy foreigner with investments in the USA is a wonderful target not only for the criminals on the street, but also for the criminals in the government suites. Sometimes, because of personal concerns the foreigner will not "cause trouble" by reclaiming assets taken from him. And if he is foolish enough to come into the states to protect his financial interests, he can become a scapegoat, prosecuted and convicted, thus becoming another statistic to show how effective the government is in bringing outsiders to their knees. Most Americans – the silent majority – have a strong prejudice against foreigners with strange names, strange accents and non-white skin colors. Even Blacks and Hispanics who have become part of the bureaucracy often share these prejudices. They consider themselves white and Anglo and are called by their more ethnic brothers "Oreos". An "Oreo" is a type of mass produced cookie that is "Black or brown on the outside, and white on the inside." Thus it is not unusual for a prosecutor (a member of a minority group himself) to pander to the most base racial and anti foreigner prejudices that are to be found within the hearts and minds of the typical juror. These jurors, like judges, seem to relish the power to take away the money or freedom of a person "different" from themselves. In their normal lives they may not really be the middle class, white, patriotic, flag waving, ecology-saviors that they perceive themselves to be. But they will vote that way against you. Foreigners in the USA, beware. You are the most likely candidate for asset stripping.

# Chapter 6

# PAY ZERO TAXES, LEGALLY!

Be a PhT! Here's the "silver bullet" formula to become a Prior Taxpayer.

$$(A + A)^{00} = PT$$

or

If : Ass plus assets

are scattered to Infinity

THEN you = a Prior Taxpayer

Once outside your home country as a non-resident and without visible assets, you pay no more taxes.

Considerable thought to "doing it right" must go into the implementation. Go over this chapter leisurely and in detail. The "banking passport" indicates one way in which an "alternate identity" may be established to collect fees, royalties, etc. The purpose of a banking passport is to make "your" assets disappear into the accounts of your alter egos (you under different names and citizenships). We have explored the Netherlands Antilles and do not find the solution of setting up a company there or anywhere else for that matter as effective as a "silver bullet". New laws in the USA have made the diversion of earned income to tax haven holding companies not something that can be done legally. But a second passport with alternate identity might be something to explore! It may not be strictly legal, but it's more private and less expensive.

Lawyers and accountants want to keep you around forever paying their annual retainers. I try to get people off on their own, conducting their business affairs in COMPLETE PRIVACY. That is why I do not usually recommend setting up trusts, foundations, holding companies and any such structures requiring

A)    Involvement of others who really shouldn't know your business

B)    Unnecessary overhead, legal registration and annual tax charges.

Offshore corporations and such are mostly worthwhile only where an active business is involved and there is no better way to get a regular cash flow of royalties, commissions or interest out of a given country without paying withholding taxes. We regard setting up such legal entities only as a last resort! The exception to this is when you work with someone who lets YOU run the show, who DOES NOT want to get any signing powers or a say in your business and who shares our view that the more you can do yourself, the better. Most offshore advisers will milk you every year with hefty annual fees and charges.

Usually, offshore centers are rich in crooked "corporation mills" that churn out steep bills but do not care about you or your business. We would be happy to advise you and help you to achieve limited liability and anonymity through cheap and serious company formation agents offshore. For many clients, this has been one way of achieving confidentiality and tax-freedom. Ask Scope for details.

Many Americans do not realize that there is nothing illegal about transferring all their shares of stock, cash or other assets to a custodian bank based abroad. Even real estate may be transferred to a foreign based corporation. British based corporations cost only a nominal sum to establish and run. It used to be the rule that if they did no business in the UK, they were tax-exempt in Britain. The USA and other OECD countries pressured Britain into lifting this rule in 1988. Now, all UK companies have to file and pay British taxes regardless of where their source of income may be. Neighboring Ireland, however, was swift to take advantage of the new British rules. When Britain closed down tax-exempt companies, the Republic of Ireland passed legislation allowing for tax free Irish non-resident companies. If no directors live in Ireland and all source of income comes from outside Ireland, then the Irish company does not pay any tax at all! The USA has many reporting requirements for its citizens who own shares of foreign corporations or bank accounts, but you can kiss all the forms and filing requirements goodbye forever if you become a PT.

There are no restrictions on the free flow of capital in and out of the USA, at the present time. This freedom to transfer assets abroad exists in most of Europe, Japan and the "free world". Reporting requirements are a different matter. For instance: if you cross the USA borders in either direction with cash (not recommended), amounts of *around $5,000* are supposed to be reported.If you are searched by customs officials and are carrying undeclared cash, it may be confiscated. But if you carry cash or checks abroad, as to tax-paid, legally earned money, you can take $100 billion – as long as you report it (or attempt to report it) at the time you cross the border. Many clients tell us that USA customs officials at many border points do not have the proper report forms. They tell the traveller who asks for them to "forget about it". Thus, as is typical with governments, Big Brother's iron fist is often rendered impotent by bureaucratic bungling at the front line. Big Brother is not invincible or all-seeing. Like me, bureaucrats are buried under an avalanche of information and forms. They are brought together only if you do something "high-profile" to trigger a look at your affairs.

## HIDING YOUR MONEY

Financial consultants' most commonly asked questions relate to offshore banking. The answers to these questions together with hands-on help in accomplishing the objectives would normally involve at least several private consulting sessions and cost a client several thousand dollars. Although there are often "free seminars" purporting to explain such things, most of the time these seminars are merely clever ploys to get you to purchase something (like annuities or an asset protection plan) that if fully informed, you wouldn't touch with a ten foot pole. If there was any doubt about your getting your money's worth from *PT 2,* consider this chapter payday. Let's explore the questions.

## A. HOW DOES ONE ESTABLISH A SECRET, JUDGMENT PROOF NEST EGG ACCOUNT THAT IS SAFE FROM CONFISCATION?

The first thing to realize about a "secret account" sometimes referred to by the euphemism "offshore account" is that in order to be kept secret from your potential enemies (creditors and tax collectors) it must be kept secret from *everyone!* Generally speaking, a stranger you meet at a bar or ball game isn't the person who turns you in to a tax collector or otherwise blows the whistle on you. Besides Big Brother, your potential enemies include your spouse, lover(s), your business associates or partners, your own kids. These days, you must add to the list of potential informants against you, your accountant(s) or lawyer(s). Your accountant, lawyer, stockbroker or local banker in many jurisdictions, particularly the USA, is personally liable for criminal prosecution if he has knowledge of any concealment of assets, tax frauds, or other peccadilloes; if your own hired hands don't turn you in they may be breaking the law!!! New regulations make these professionals in your home country little more than government agents. They are like Deputy Sheriffs. *If you don't want sheriff Big Brother to know exactly what you are doing then for heaven's sake, don't tell the Deputy Sheriff!* These "professionals" are not on your side. Because of laws that will take away their licenses, livelihood and possibly their freedom, they have been co-opted. They are now in the enemy camp. As such, accountants and lawyers are the last persons you should trust with sensitive information or from whom you seek advice on "offshore matters." Bottom line? You must now establish your secret offshore accounts or secret asset stashes without telling anyone in your home country, and especially without telling anyone in the above categories.

The second thing to realize is that in most countries of the first world, where the vast majority of our readers are located, every citizen is forced to have and use a fiscal identification number. Not using this number or giving a false number is usually an offense in itself. Countries not having such a system are contemplating it. Only recently have Spain and Australia adopted the policy of requiring a fiscal ID number for everyone. In Spain, even tourists who want a telephone, electric service or a local bank account must obtain a fiscal number. In the USA, it's now a major "felony" crime to use the wrong number by mistake (accidentally on purpose), transpose figures or otherwise attempt to defeat the system! In case you had any doubt, there is no such thing as financial privacy in most of our own countries any more. The unique number assigned to you alone enables the government or a creditor to identify and seize any asset in the jurisdiction belonging to you, even if it is deposited in a variant of your name.

For an example of how insidious these seizure powers are, consider this: many years ago, on his child's first birthday one of our American clients opened a bank account at his own bank for his one year old son. The son's name was different from his own, although the surname was of course the same. As the baby had no "social security number" yet, the father gave his own number to meet the bank's requirements. Twenty-eight years later, the son's account had grown to a very substantial sum, all of which had been earned and saved by the son, not the father!

The father became involved in a civil tax dispute. As a result, the US Internal Revenue **without any notice or trial seized every penny in the son's account.** There was no court order, and no notice to his son. His checks just started bouncing. His bank said: "Under the law we must turn over all your money to any IRS agent who presents us with an order. The IRS agent can write it out on the spot without consulting anyone else." The son spent a fortune in legal fees to get his money back, but even after many years of litigating and unquestionable proof that all but $10 was strictly his own money, he was unable to make a recovery. Needless to say, this resulted in a family estrangement! Thus it is obvious that if you want any protection at all against arbitrary seizure, any "secret" account must be in a foreign country where you neither live, do business, have a home, nor have any other connection, property or business interests, aside from the account itself. This assures that the government in the country where your bank account or other assets are deposited has no tax or other claims against you.

Your address, as known to the foreign bank should not be your home address, but rather a mail drop in a third country.

This third country (where you have your mail-drop) is preferably a banking and tax haven unlikely ever to have any information-exchanging treaty or mutual assistance on collections treaty with the country where you bank or where you live. There is always the possibility that a foreign country with no prior tradition of co-operating with the enemy will adopt a new policy. If you have the insulation of three countries you are safer! A) Passport country B) Mail-drop country of presumed residence C) Banking country. All these plus a new name give plenty of insulation!

What happened to Ferdinand Marcos ex-dictator of the Philippines? The US government invited him to take sanctuary and retire in the USA. When he arrived, US customs seized his typed out lists of foreign investments and bank accounts, many of which were held in Switzerland. Then, at the request of the Philippine government, Switzerland froze his accounts, some of which were immediately transferred to the personal accounts of lawyers for the corrupt New Philippines Good Government Association. Note: All recoveries by this organization have already disappeared into private pockets!

Marcos then died. Mrs. Marcos sought to protect her remaining Swiss funds (held in the names of foundations) with a court action. She got Swiss courts to rule that her accounts could not be taken from her without a criminal conviction in her own country for having stolen the money. The criminal cases are pending. Had Marcos not had a typed, uncoded list of his accounts on his person when he crossed a border, his money held in other names and foundations would be safe for his family today. He made the mistake of trusting the US government to honor its promises to him. You should know better. Never trust any government!

Your new account must not be established with funds transferred directly from any bank or source in your home country that is traceable to you. In other words, if you want something to be a secret, don't leave a paper trail. Above all, your new account, if it is to be secret, should be known only to yourself and your new banker. **You must not ever keep paperwork, statements, nor even the name and address or telephone number of your secret offshore bank written down or on your person.** How do you remember it? The information must be in a code that is not obvious and easily broken. Mirror writing (gnitirw rorriM) or writing backwards is so obvious even a child could decode it. Information should definitely not be kept in a safety deposit box in your home country. Such boxes can be easily opened by a creditor or tax collector without your authorization. A box in a foreign country, especially if it is kept in a different (banking passport) name is secure, if you don't identify it for your potential enemies.

Your new account itself, for extra safety, should not be in your own name. Your new bankers should not know your real country of origin (birth), citizenship, residence, nor anything about you to enable them to link you with your true identity and citizenship. One possibility for buffering or insulation, explained in detail in the Hill series of books, is to use a "banking passport" or other alternate identity documents in order to be able to establish and access funds in a totally unrelated name. Another possibility (less good if the new entity is linked to you), is to use a corporation, trust, holding company or foundation to screen your identity. Perhaps the most secure is a combination of both. If a bank account is held in the name of the XYZ Foundation, and the signer is a Swiss lawyer, and on his books the "true owner or party at interest" is registered as Joe Doaks (not you), you have created a three tier impenetrable situation for creditors or tax collectors. Needless to say, all is lost if you open your big mouth and tell a potential informant (like your business partner, wife, or best friend) about your clever method of concealing your assets.

## HOW DOES ONE SAFELY STORE BANK STATEMENTS OR FINANCIAL RECORDS AND OTHERWISE KEEP TRACK OF SUCH THINGS TO KEEP THEM SECRET FROM PEOPLE – LIKE BUSINESS PARTNERS OR SPOUSES?

If we were to suggest a common code or encryption system in this book that you could use to encrypt information about your account, you could be sure the enemy would use it to decode your secrets. Accordingly, we will simply suggest that you write to Eden Press or Scope International and ask them to provide you with code books or books about coding and decoding. If you are a computer freak, there are a wide variety of encryption systems for hiding information you don't want displayed in front of prying eyes. On computers, confidential files can be protected with secret passwords and such. These are secure from all but dedicated computer hackers or a government agency willing to devote very substantial resources to the de-encryption. Eden Press markets a very sophisticated encryption system that can be used to store information on disks in such a way that supposedly not even the CIA can break the codes.

**Nothing beats what we call a "Personal Code".** As long as it is not obvious, a personal code is not easy to break. Here is an example of an obvious code that once served as grounds for a divorce. A prominent businessman must have thought he was pretty clever, but the "code" as you will see, was broken by a judge and jury, who had it explained to them by the wife's lawyer that Mr. X had a secretary named Mrs. VaVoom and another lady friend named Lola.

Here are a few sample entries from Mr. X's appointment book and desk diary:

Dec 31. Dinner with the Smiths. * with Lola in cloak room, then at midnight ** with Joan [Mr. X's wife].

Jan 4. Lunch at Ritz Hotel with Mrs. Va Voom *. Spent afternoon with her and had another *.

Jan 6. Morning * with Joan. At office, VaVoom insisted upon **. Exhausted. Intended to have a quiet afternoon nap, but Lola insisted I drop over for a *. Came home early and Joan also wanted a *. I could do it barely.Do you need three guesses to figure out what activity was represented by "*"? Mr. X tried to say it was a game of racquet ball. Would you believe that? The court gave Joan a divorce for her husband's adultery, or should we say, to many * with Mrs VaVroom.

Moral, your code should be simple enough so you can remember it, but not so simple minded that everyone else can figure it out too!

**For some things just a code word is enough. Bank could be "piggie" or whatever word comes to your mind first, but for more complex matters – particularly if you want no other person to be able to decode things, you need a more sophisticated system.**

One of the best simple codes I know of and one that is virtually impossible to break is the **"book code."** Even if the enemy knows you are using the book code, it is still almost impossible to figure it out. First you select a common book in your library like *Shakespeare's Plays, The Bible,* or maybe even *PT*. Then you devise a personal system that will lead you to words and numbers to help you remember whatever about your accounts is necessary to remember. For instance: 102-13-04 might mean, Page 102, Line 13 from the top, Word 4 from the left. How to access the words in the book is your choice of course and by simply using reverse numbers, it could also mean Page 201, Line 31 from the bottom, and Word 4 from the right. The best thing about a book code is that it is completely personal. Without figuring out that you are using the book code and without knowing which book it relates to, absolutely no outsider can begin to decipher it. The enemy must know and find the book you use (and the proper edition!). Then he must figure out the personal code you use to lead you to the right word or letter. Breaking the book code is quite difficult, if not impossible.

But codes do not have to be in the form of cryptic symbols or numbers or even code words. Sometimes it is good to make a code look like a laundry or shopping list! For instance if "Lettuce" means "Money" to you and if, when you think of "Bobbies" this means "London" and you know you have an account at Lloyds Bank, London, the following memo could be discovered by an enemy and wouldn't, standing alone in your appointment book, mean anything:

**"Pick up 1K of lettuce at Bobby's on next trip".**

Needless to say, if the entire name of your bank was listed in an international bank directory in your personal library, you would not have to use the book code letter by letter. If you have a published commercial directory of banks, you might make underlinings, crosses, checks or a variety of other marks in different colors in front of dozens of bank listings. But only you will know that (for instance) a green dot means that's the spot where your "mother-lode" is on deposit. If you were worried you'd forget the name and address of your bank, the only thing to worry about with this method is that your book will get lost, destroyed or lent out and never be returned. You can have a back up by having a few photocopied pages from the directory kept somewhere else with similar markings.

You might even write in your appointment book or your address book, something like "Joe KL Wong, Painter (224) 0454-3721". That could be a personal code meaning to you that your account number at the bank of Hong Kong, Kuala Lumpur Branch, is 224-454-3721!

The more personal your code is, the more impossible it becomes to break.

Generally, if you just want to keep track of your balances, you can do that with symbols that mean nothing to anyone else: For instance, regardless of where it is kept, H4.5 means nothing to anyone else. But it could mean to you that you have £4,500 at the Bank of Hong Kong, or £450,000 in the Hibernian Bank of Dublin, or £4.5 Million "Hidden" in the "House". With a modern computer, the additional possibilities for playing at codes are endless. On my own computer, random symbols can have a meaning changed or revealed at the push of a button:

To illustrate: I can type my message in the normal, everyday, common typeface known as Courier. Then to encode, before printing I switch typefaces over to "Zapf Dingbats".

Here is the incomprehensible sentence you will then see on the screen or in print:

❁❁✙❀❂❑ ✳❱❁❁❖❏❑❖❃ ☆ ●❏✧❁ ❙❏◆ ❱❁❖❁ ❂❂● ❍❙ ❁❁❏❑❖✂⦾⧀

If I wanted to make it easier for the enemy I could press "Greek Symbols"

What does it mean?

I now just order my computer to print it in Courier:

``Dear Sweetheart, I love you with all my heart!''

Hard as it might be for you to figure out what the symbols or Greek letters mean, an experienced code-breaker could translate it in thirty seconds. How? Read up on code-breaking in some of the Sherlock Holmes stories by Arthur Conan Doyle. Accordingly, this is just an example of an easy-to-break code, not a suggestion for your use in high priority sensitive matters:

More Good Codes? As I said before, the more personal a code is, the less likely it is that anyone else can figure out what it means.


# B. WHAT ARE THE BEST COUNTRIES TO STASH ASSETS IN?

While there is no perfect place, the better countries are easy to choose: they must have bank secrecy, no withholding taxes for foreigners, or if there is a withholding tax, it must be easily avoided as it is in Austria or Switzerland by means of a "fiduciary account." A fiduciary account is simply an account established for you at another bank by your own bank, and kept in the bank's name. Also important is political stability, an unblemished history of honest dealings with foreign investors, and a long tradition of no government confiscation of private assets. There must be no information exchange treaties or other arrangements with your home country and none on the horizon. Obviously the bankers of your banking country should be fluent in your language. Fortunately, English is the universal language of international banking, business and the airways as well. So unless you bank strictly locally, any major international or offshore bank will have officers that you can communicate with in English.

Outside of Europe, it is probably best to deal only with a branch of a major bank whose home base is **not** your home country. Your offshore bank preferably has no branches in your home country that could be pressured to force them to reveal your account details or worse yet, freeze your account. Thus if an Englishman was going to have an account in the Caribbean, first choice might well be a Swiss, Danish or Dutch bank – never a British nor (for safety's sake) a one-horse local outfit. The account for a Brit for instance should be in the Antilles (Dutch) not Cayman (British). If I were an American I'd stay far away from any *de facto* American colony like Puerto Rico or Canada. Or from any American bank like Citibank, Bank of America, etc. Come to think of it, even if I were not an American, I'd stay far away from American banks no matter where located. They are all quite shaky. The Federal Deposit Insurance Corporation is insolvent and American banks (and stockbrokers) are generally subject to the whims of the current political administration back home. The largest banks in the country, Continental Illinois and Bank of America, went through the equivalent of insolvency in recent years. The same instability would be true of all but the biggest Japanese banks.

Never deposit two cents in a third world bank like Banamex (Mexico) or BCCI (Pakistan) nor any Arab bank. The Muslim idea of banking is so foreign to the English speaker that there is no common ground. Receiving interest from a bank (or paying interest under some interpretations of Islamic Law) is an offense that gets your hands amputated or in some countries you might be shot. I am not joking. This is the law in Iran! I would not deposit my money in any offshore branch of a bank with such rules in the home country! As to general morality and honesty, some Mexican bankers I have known make Jesse James and John Dillinger look like honest men (in comparison to them). And while I'm throwing stones, the Mexican Government has a long tradition of luring in foreign investment and then confiscating it. That leaves the major European banks as just about the only serious choices for stashing serious money.

The best countries are Great Britain's offshore islands, plus Luxembourg, Switzerland, and Austria. Austrian banks and Savings Institutions will even open a totally anonymous passbook account where the bank itself doesn't know the customer's name or address. To save a trip to Austria, you can buy a bearer passbook account from Scope International (the publisher of this book) for $400. This amount includes $10 deposit already made for you in an established account. Anyone can make deposits to your Austrian bearer account (if they know the number) by wire transfer, cash deposit in person, mailed in checks, or any other normal way. But *the passbook must be presented to make withdrawals*. If you lose the book – too bad. It is like losing cash.

There are ways to get a duplicate passbook if you have a photocopy of the lost or destroyed one, but it will be a long and frustrating process. This type of account may be useful where you want a potential enemy or adversary to deposit funds for you, but you want to be sure that even with a lawsuit, it would be impossible for him to get any useful information about the account activities. The way to use the account is to have the deposit made there, and then have a hired hand personally withdraw the funds in cash. You wait outside the bank, take the money and deposit the cash somewhere else. Your bank will not be able to identify who got the money or where it went. A neat way to break the paper trail!

Banks of ex-communist countries are now courting this offshore private investor business, and there are plenty of banks pumping for "High Net Worth Private Clients" in places like Hong Kong, Panama, Cost Rica, Malta, Uruguay and Gibraltar. My thought is, the vast majority of people and politicians in these places are socialist oriented. They are Leftists (as they are in Mexico and most of South America). When times get tough, the local politicians think first of defaulting on their international obligations and second, of confiscating the local assets of foreign depositors and investors. For them, foreign investors are a golden goose to be roasted at the first sign of tough going. Never mind losing the golden eggs! Politicians don't think of long term effects. In most countries, confiscation of private property is considered by the leftist majority a moral and proper thing to do. I would give all such thieves a pass! Exception? Major international banks' branches in Gibraltar and Panama are probably OK for short term (up to a year) funds – just keep an eye out for any handwriting on the wall or bad odors emanating from politicians before an election. Move your money at the first whiff of trouble. Stay on top of things by subscribing to one or more newsletters which keep a sharp eye on such matters.

## C. WHERE DOES ONE GET THE BEST INTEREST RATES (AND ASSET MANAGEMENT)?

In recent years, interest rates in most countries have gyrated from double or even triple digits to low single digits. The "true rate of return" is generally considered to be the interest paid less the (anticipated) local inflation rate, less withholding taxes. Thus when the rate of interest in the USA is below 12 per cent, with 6 per cent inflation and a 6 per cent effective tax the American gets a negative return. In 1992/93, some first class German banks paid 10 per cent per annum interest with no withholding tax and historically low inflation. This is an all time high for Germany where the inflation rate has, since World War Two, been under 3 per cent per annum in most years, and there is no withholding on interest paid to foreigners. In the United States during the same period, where inflation has averaged around 10 per cent, interest rates hit below 4 per cent, an all-time low. Thus the important thing to remember is read the financial papers. Keep up with the news. Place your funds in bonds or for nice long periods like a year or more when you are convinced that interest rates are peaking out. If you buy medium to long term bonds, when interest rates go down again, you can sell the bonds at a big capital gain. Some investment newsletters have a pretty good record at recommending when to get in and out of bonds. The only trouble is that for the unsophisticated investor, there are so many recommendations and so many tantalizing investment opportunities discussed, that one seeking only a high interest return is likely to get confused. But better to be exposed to opportunities than to be ignorant of them!

One reason that people are afraid of making a deposit or buying a bond in a foreign currency is the "currency risk." This means that if you put $100,000 into a British institution in pounds, for a year, and if at the end of a year the pound had gone down from a value of $2 per £1 to $1 per £1, you have lost 50 per cent on your money on the currency – *if you go back into dollars.* The fact that you made 15 per cent interest (reduced to 7.5 per cent by the currency decline) in the pound doesn't soften the pain either. But the currency risk factor is also an opportunity to benefit from potential weakness in your own currency. If the dollar goes from a value of £1 = $1 to a value of £1 = $2, during the same year, you have made 100 per cent on top of your 15 per cent interest. The interest in turn has turned into 30 per cent interest because of the upward valuation of the Pound. The smart investor diversifies in currencies as well as in the type of investment.

If you are looking for a country with a relatively stable currency and a relatively high interest rate, banks in the United Kingdom have, until recently, paid an interest rate of between ten and fifteen per cent per annum for the past 25 years. If you keep your money in pounds, the funds are going to be on deposit in a British bank – even if your actual account is with a non-British fiduciary. Thus, remember, you can have an account in sterling with a bank in Vienna, Hong Kong, or anywhere else. Likewise, you could have a dollar account with most international banks of the world. But remember, in the unlikely event that all the major banks of America fail, you will lose your money even though it is with Swiss Bank Corporation. Why? Because an American fiduciary account held in the name of a Swiss bank is not protected against the failure of the American bank(s) where the ultimate asset is held. Note also, that you get a slightly higher interest if you make the deposit direct. The nature of a fiduciary account is to deduct a small slice (usually one-quarter of 1 per cent of your principal) as the service charge for giving you anonymity.

But getting back to the pound as a recommended currency for deposit. During the last couple of decades the pound had had a trading range of between $1.25 and $1.90 for most of that time. At the extremes, the pound has gone as high as $2.50 and as low as $1.05 – for brief periods. There has been very little change in the pound in recent years against European currencies as the pound was, until the fall of 1992, in an internationally sanctioned currency stabilization arrangement known as "The Snake". For purposes of an over-simplified explanation, the Snake doesn't permit more fluctuations than about 12 per cent versus other EU currencies. [Note: To our perfectionists, I know this isn't exactly right, but for now, and for this section, it is a good simple explanation!] Interest rates in the UK are currently low, but history shows they will rise again shortly. The major British building societies (Savings and Loans) all pay 2-3 per cent per year more than the banks. The difference between a bank and a building society is simply that the main business of a bank is supposed to be commercial loans. The main business of a building society is supposed to be lending on long term mortgages. As a result, the building societies pay the highest interest on funds that are tied up for a year or more. In short, they offer less liquidity. Many of these building societies plus all big British banks have "offshore" branches where you can have accounts that draw interest without any tax with-holding or reporting. The Isle of Man, Guernsey, Gibraltar, Jersey and Cayman Islands are probably all equally good as places to keep your money in a major British bank or Building Society. Another thing to consider is that there are less misunderstandings when your banker is a native English speaker. Here are a few suggestions:

**Great Britain – Building Societies:**
Advantages: Government Insurance. Stability. Automatic roll-over of funds. Checking privileges can be arranged. Disadvantage: Illiquidity; Usually some period of notice required to close an account or to withdraw major amounts of money.

Chelsea Building Society Premier Account (over £10,000), tel London 81 959 0427, or Cheltenham & Gloucester GL53 1BR, Great Britain. They, like most building societies, require **no banker's reference to open an account,** will accept any amount in any currency (by check or any other form or bank transfer), and as of early 1993 they paid 6 per cent when most British banks are paying under 4 per cent. For best privacy and interest free of tax deductions, best to insist that any building society account be opened at their offshore branch – preferably at the Jersey or Guernsey, Channel Islands branches.

Other Savings & Loan (Building Society) companies with "Offshore" branches include:

Alliance & Leicester, PO Box 226, Douglas, Isle of Man, G.B. Very big company.

The Woolwich, PO Box 341, St. Peter Port, Guernsey. Fax: (44-81) 715-722 Britain's second largest Building Society. Halifax is first.

Yorkshire Building Society, PO Box 304, St. Peter Port Guernsey. Highest interest rate from a major player.

Cheltenham and Gloucester, C & G Channel Islands Ltd., 2/3 Rue dePre, St Peter Port, Guernsey, fax 44 81 715 496.

As long as the pounds are acquired below $1.50, we feel there is not much currency risk.

# D. HOW DOES ONE ASSURE THAT FUNDS DEPOSITED WITH A BANK ARE SAFE AGAINST THEFT BY THE BANKERS THEMSELVES? OR BANK FAILURE? OR GOVERNMENT SEIZURE?

First, let's deal with the myths: "Deal with an old established bank." This advice had lead many people down the garden path. Often an old established bank is acquired by a hotshot or a downright crook. Or the government takes over and ruins a spotless bank as they did with the near legendary Rothschild Bank in France. Too often an old established bank is taken over by a gang of thieves. It expands, brings in new depositors, and the next thing you know the whole operation (plus your money) goes down the pan. Accordingly, mere oldness is not the only thing to be considered. For banking you must consider (in my opinion) all of these factors:

1) Size of bank: It is less likely that a multi-million dollar bank (one of the major players in any country) will fail than that a small peanut will go under. Big banks like the late, lamented Bank of Credit & Commerce International do sometimes fail, but in the case of this particular bank, it would never have met my other tests: BCCI was established by nationals of a Muslim country (Pakistan) without serious banking traditions that Westerners can relate to. It was backed financially by some newly rich Arab sultans who know nothing about banking, and it was incorporated in a country (Luxembourg) with lax controls over bank holding companies. Further, long before the failure of BCCI, there were substantial warnings in the form of criminal indictments and so on. BCCI was known in the trade as the Bank of Criminals and Con-men. The handwriting was on the wall long before the ultimate failure occurred. Any sensible PT would have bailed out before he lost his money.

Even if a big bank's entire trust department gets taken over by a crook and funds get diverted (as happened with a Swiss Bank's Chiasso Office in the 1970s) it is likely that the big bank's home office will make good any losses. This is necessary to protect its reputation. It is unheard of for a major bank, established in a civilized, conservative country that recognizes and protects private property, established and run by career bankers of good reputation, to be entirely corrupt. But of course anything can happen!

2) Government Regulations and Insurance Schemes: In the USA and other countries, accounts at some banks and Savings and Loan Associations are insured by the government – but only up to certain limits. It is important to determine these limits and never to have more on deposit than the amount insured. Remember too that a predominantly leftist government can always change the rules in mid-stream. In the USA it was customary for wealthy individuals to place funds with brokers for allocation to many banks and Savings & Loan Associations so that the amount in each account was fully covered by the national insurance scheme. Then, when banks and S&Ls started dying like flies, the regulatory

agencies said that this practice was an abuse and only one account was insured for one individual. The ultimate result after some wrangling was favorable to the depositors – but the important thing to remember is that government promises and guarantees are one of the last things to be relied upon in life! Still, they are something to be considered. The Isle of Man, for instance, has a scheme to insure bank accounts. Wherever there is government insurance there is also likely to be some governmental regulation and controls to keep the banks clean and conservative.

3) Always look at *Local Traditions and Customs*: In Switzerland, **it is a crime to be an officer of a bank that fails** with losses to customers. As a result, a Swiss owned major bank in Switzerland is very unlikely to fail. Why "Swiss owned?" Because a foreigner who establishes a Swiss bank is more likely to live abroad or to take a powder in the event of problems. A Swiss generally feels that his home country is the only place in the world worth living. Where banking regulations are substantial and local custom makes absconding or mismanaging customer funds a serious offense, the customer is surely safer from fraud. It is not possible for anyone to go bankrupt in Switzerland. One pays one's bills or goes to jail. Banks in German speaking countries (Germany, Austria, Switzerland) have a long government tradition of dealing honestly with depositors. Of course the Nazis made a big exception for non-Aryans and confiscated the property (and the lives!) of some thirty million individuals just because they were Protestants, Jews, Slavs, Gypsies or a larger number of other categories. But today that is generally regarded as an aberration that won't happen again. [My comment: keep an eye open for handwriting on the wall in any country. When the graffiti indicates that you may become an enemy of the next batch of politicians to take power, have your second passport and your cash already moved!] Today, in spite of the "aberration" of the Nazi era, a major bank in any of these German speaking countries is among the better choices. Austria even has provision for a "Sparbuch" account so secret (later described at length) that not even the bank knows who the owner is!

4) Beware of Dishonest Governments: On the other side of the coin, many countries of the world have a tradition of regularly confiscating privately owned banks, securities holdings, foreign investments and private banking accounts. These I would characterize as essentially or potentially dishonest governments: any government that has ever within recent history (last 100 years) nationalized a bank or private account I'd rate as a potentially dangerous place to leave assets. On my list of potentially treacherous governments today are those of any ex-communist or Leftist country: For instance, Mexico, Costa Rica, Philippines, Ireland, France, Italy, Malta, all of South and Central America except for Chile maybe, all of the Arab and Muslim world, all of Africa, Australia, all of Asia except for maybe Singapore and Thailand. Thailand however has no great tradition of protecting foreigners and so I'd be wary there. Hong Kong's fate under Red Chinese control is too uncertain to risk any serious long term money in. But the giant Hong Kong Bank itself has made provision to be headquartered elsewhere in the event that the Communists start a confiscation binge in violation of their takeover treaty agreement. Does this mean I'd never have any accounts or do any business in any of these potentially dangerous areas? No! For diversification or convenience I might have small or temporary transit accounts in any of these places, or I might have small accounts in their foreign tax-haven branches. The Hong Kong bank is in fact one of my favorites. It is British owned, competently run, and will surely survive into the next couple of centuries. But I would not entrust any serious long term money to 95 per cent of the banks in the world.

5) Privacy: In the USA and Canada there is no privacy. Period! Big Brother can examine and confiscate accounts without any valid reason and without any notice to the owner. In recent history, private US accounts of all Germans, French, Japanese, Iranians, Kuwaitis and others were arbitrarily seized by the USA. These seizures were for political reasons. The possibility that your home country of origin or residence may undertake some unpopular action against (or in regards to) the country where you have your money is reason enough to adopt the protective coloration of a different, preferably neutral country. Another good reason that your banking passport should be from a neutral country. The

residence address as known to your own banker should be in a neutral country like Switzerland or a tax haven like Monaco, Andorra, Bermuda or the Channel Islands.

6) Run like Bambi at the first sign of trouble. When Bambi, the cute Walt Disney deer, smelled an enemy he ran like the wind. The best rule with regard to your money is to keep a large portion liquid. If and when a newspaper refers to your institution as "loss ridden", or "financially troubled", simply transfer your money elsewhere. Forget about loyalty to a bank. In fact, consider changing banks every year or two just on general principles! If negative political changes in your banking country seem to be coming, move out smartly. A PT is aware and agile!

# E. IS THERE ANY WAY TO ESTABLISH AN ACCOUNT WITHOUT LEAVING A PAPER TRAIL LEADING BACK TO YOURSELF?

The only way to eliminate a paper trail is to go in to your new bank personally or through a lawyer and **open your account with untraceable cash or a commodity like gold.** As many banks around the world are required by their governments to restrict or report the amount of cash they accept from **new** accounts, it may be necessary to either open a number of small accounts and later consolidate them, or to take really huge sacks of cash into banks in those remaining few jurisdictions that don't care about conforming to Big Brother's wishes. To avoid putting further pressure on these few remaining countries whose banks will accept any amount you care to deposit in cash, we will not mention them except in private consultations. In Switzerland currently, most banks will accept a maximum of Sw Francs 100,000 from a new customer. This is around $75,000 USA dollars or £45,000 sterling. Accordingly, to open a Swiss account with £1,000,000 in it, it would be necessary to make 25 trips, or to open around 25 different accounts in cash at various branches or other Swiss banks and later combine them into one big account. Once you have a personal relationship with a banker however, he can make special arrangements with you (regarding confidential movements of cash) everywhere in the world – of course not in those countries where Big Brother and the Bureau Rats are in total control. An *established customer* in Switzerland can deal in unlimited amounts of cash if the banker feels his client's source of funds is legal.

Second best for breaking the paper trail is perhaps bearer securities. These are simply shares of companies or bonds that are issued to bearer. The company has no record of who the owner is. They are outlawed in the USA, but available everywhere else. One deposits bearer securities with the new bank and tells the new bank either to hold them, or to sell them and deal with the proceeds as directed. With bearer securities there is a potential trail (very difficult to follow) if you bought the bearer securities in your own name through a stockbroker or bank. Thus it is best to explain to the stockbroker when you buy, that your objective is confidentiality. A good stockbroker will arrange for an anonymous purchase.

A third possibility is to purchase something (an object or commodity) that you know can be shipped abroad and sold. Gold, rare coins, stamps, jewelry, antiques, art works – all these are possibilities. But if you are in a hurry, nothing works as well as cash. But even cash takes up a lot of space in a suitcase if you use sterling (largest bill £50) or dollars (largest bill $100).

## WHICH COUNTRIES HAVE THE LARGEST DENOMINATION (HIGHEST VALUE) BILLS?

Most people believe it is Switzerland. Their thousand franc note is worth around US $750. Canada also has $1,000 notes worth about US $800. But Singapore, with a strong, well accepted currency has $10,000 Singapore dollar notes in common circulation. They are worth closer to $7,000. Using Singapore banknotes, $14 million in USA dollar value can be crammed into an ordinary attache case, and $1 million can be stuffed in a pocket or belly money-belt! If any reader knows of any other high-value banknote, please let us know for future editions. Note: Don't tell us about Italy where everyone pays for dinner with a 100,000 lira note. It sounds like a lot but is worth less than US $100.

## TRANSIT ACCOUNTS

Aside from cash, the simplest way to break the paper trail from a practical point of view is to use transit accounts as more fully explained elsewhere under that heading. Briefly, a transit account is simply an account in a different name (perhaps a corporation), and in a country with bank secrecy. Funds are routed through two or three such accounts. Investigators usually can't be bothered to go through the legal procedures in foreign countries which can take an average of six months per account. Since most banks don't care much for bank robbers, drug-dealers or child-pornography peddlers they will usually give much faster, voluntary co-operation where evidence is given that the money comes from these illicit sources.

# F. HOW WILL MY HEIRS OR THE PERSONS I WANT TO INHERIT THE FUNDS BE ABLE TO GET MY MONEY [WHEN I DIE] WITHOUT KNOWING THE LOCATION OR BALANCE IN THE ACCOUNT DURING MY LIFETIME?

There are many possibilities. First, instructions about the existence and testamentary disposition of the account after your death can be given in a sealed envelope to a trusted third party. This person should probably live outside the jurisdiction of your home country. You can tell your kid or wife that she should see this person for a sealed envelope in the event of your death. The trusted third party should have some incentive to see that your heirs get the envelope – like being told that $2,000 will be delivered to him by the heir upon your death if he delivers. The envelope can contain a list of your assets, a will (properly witnessed) an assignment or death instructions. Banks in many countries accept death instructions, powers of attorney or assignment orders upon them signed before the death of the owner and do not require probates. This is true in Switzerland or Liechtenstein for instance – not however in most British Colonies or ex-colonies, where Common Law is in effect. There you need a will, probate and all that expensive bother. The Common Law idea is that it is too easy to forge a mere signature of a dead person and there should be a great deal of formality required to pass assets upon death. But as these "Estate" court proceedings have turned into a way to give lawyers, administrators, executors and appraisers and a grand assortment of politically appointed parasites a big chunk of your estate, people now go to great lengths to avoid probate. For advice on this subject there is a very good paperback book called (USA and UK versions) *How to Avoid Probate* by Norbert Dacey. But getting back to offshore banks, your bank will also be glad to have one of their own legal staff go over with you the various options you may have available to you with the costs, advantages, and disadvantages. One of my favorites is to simply have my heir sign all the papers to give him a joint account or signing power *during my lifetime as well as after my death,* but not to reveal the location of the account, except in the sealed letter to be opened upon my death. It is important to remember that some arrangements have to be made because if you do nothing, the fine print in your account opening papers usually provides that after some long period of inactivity in your account (like 20 years) the account becomes the sole property of the bank. Obviously, with this incentive, the bank is going to make absolutely no effort to find your heirs! In some countries, after periods of inactivity the State takes the money and the account earns no further interest for the holder, who must usually pay a 50 per cent fee to "heir-tracers" to get his own money back. In most of the states of the USA this period is only five to seven years! Moral? Make arrangements before you die unless you want the enemy to get your money.

# G. IF A SUBSTANTIAL SUM IS INVOLVED, HOW CAN MY HEIRS OR THE PERSON(S) I DESIGNATE GET MY MONEY WITHOUT A LOT OF PAPERWORK, PROBATES, AND SUCH UNPLEASANTNESS AS ESTATE, INHERITANCE AND GIFT TAXES?

The Swiss do not require the inheritance tax proceedings nor probate of estates to transfer to the next generation bank accounts of deceased foreigners. Other countries (including Switzerland) will honor a power of attorney giving another person signing power *even* after the death of the owner of the account. Thus, if you get the signature of your son (for instance) on a power of attorney form and leave this on deposit with your bank, when you die the son has signing power over the account. It is that simple. Just be sure you check with your bank to make sure that your testamentary instructions can be carried out as per your wishes and expectations. Then do the necessary paperwork. If you die with an account in your name and no instructions, your heir(s) will have to find out about the account. If he does, then any claim for it must proceed with the same formalities required in your home country plus similar proceedings in Switzerland. This may mean two probate proceedings! Based upon personal experience, this could eat up 20 per cent of the estate even before taxes, and introduce all sorts of complications and delays.

An arrangement favored by the wealthy (who may wish to put some time and distance between an heir and the money) is to form a Liechtenstein Anstalt or Foundation. A similar trust arrangement is also common on the Isle of Man. Both avoid probate. The trustees (named by the guy with the money) simply deal with the funds in any account as directed in a trust document executed before you die. No probate is necessary and the trustees are unconcerned with inheritance or estate taxes. You can have such a trust in the USA or England and it *can* avoid probate but it *doesn't* avoid estate or inheritance taxes that could eat up most of the estate.

Let's assume that your child or heir (like most of our kids) is a complete idiot. He will, if he has the power to do so, shortly after your death transfer your estate funds to his local bank in whatever high-tax country he lives. There, local authorities will no doubt confiscate all of your money for taxes. They will also demand still another sum for penalties, interest, and taxes that were evaded during your lifetime. If your heir had a brain in his head, he would leave your money where it is, take the advice of bankers and an independent lawyer he hires *in the country of the bank account.* **Never, never should he discuss offshore assets with any lawyer or accountant in his home country!** As a general rule, the heir should quietly spend or invest abroad – just as you did! **We cannot stress how important it is to have a talk with your potential heirs or beneficiaries on how to handle the funds you intend to leave them.** *Without such instructions, a multi-million pound or dollar inheritance could be nothing more than a major* **liability**.

In a real case, the widow of the richest man in Sweden in the mid-1980s ended up owing more to the government than two times the value of an inheritance she was stupid enough to honestly declare! She was forced into bankruptcy and narrowly avoided prison! May we humbly suggest that you buy your potential beneficiaries a copy of *PT 1* and *PT 2*. **Put a big red circle around this section!** Insist that they read it once a day for a year! If incomprehension is apparent you can be sure that your heir is too stupid to deal with your money in any rational manner. That is when you can and should set up a trust or foundation so that he gets only the income, or half the income for X years, and the funds are distributed only to **his** children. It is your money, and fortunately, you can still protect it against being thrown down the pan, even after you are no longer around personally.

What you do with your money is your affair, but look into how you may be able to protect your children against their own foolishness by means of trust arrangements. To set up a Liechtenstein Foundation, ask for the free brochure of Bank in Liechtenstein's Treuhand AG. Write: PO Box 683, FL-9490 Vaduz Liechtenstein. Any branch of any major bank will also have information and brochures on setting up trusts and foundations. We have found that the Royal Trust Company (any branch) is particularly knowledgeable and helpful in this regard. Bank trust departments are better than lawyers because they will assign an experienced staff lawyer to discuss your needs, offer suggestions and quote prices *without charging you anything.* They want your account and asset management business. As a result of this motivation, they will sometimes set up trusts and corporations at a discount from what you'd spend doing it on your own, in order to lock you into using their services. This may or may not be good for you. The only way to get good advice is to shop around and perhaps ultimately, hire an independent lawyer or accountant for a second or third opinion of your best options. **The only thing to** remember is NEVER discuss or set up anything intended to be secret or "offshore," with the aid of lawyers, accountants or bankers located in your own country of residence or citizenship! Dealing with local professionals who are obligated to keep records and/or report such arrangements to "authorities" defeats the whole purpose of the exercise.

## H. HOW DO YOU GET AROUND THE PROBLEM OF PROVIDING A "BANK REFERENCE" PARTICULARLY IF YOU ARE OPENING A FIRST ACCOUNT ABROAD IN A NEW BANKING PASSPORT IDENTITY?

Most bankers want a reference on you mainly "for the record". The world is full of swindlers and con men who pretend to be someone else in order to divert (i.e. steal) funds that don't belong to them. Bankers do not need the aggravation of being involved with customers who immerse them in litigation or unfavorable publicity. If you come in with a simple story, explaining why you want a secret account and if you plan no fancy and illegal financial shenanigans, **most banks in offshore banking centers will accept your account upon a mere showing of a passport**. Most individuals with tax or domestic problems do not want any foreign banks contacting any professionals or bankers in their home country. If you mention the common problems of possible divorce and the avoidance of confiscatory taxation, most "offshore" bankers will give you an understanding ear. None will ever want to be helpful to common criminals, terrorists, drug dealers etc. If they are hard-nosed or don't like your looks or smell, they may insist upon some sort of letter of introduction or reference. For a reference letter that will be acceptable everywhere, often it is possible to look up the name of an accountant or lawyer in the country of your banking passport, and to obtain a letter addressed "To whom it may concern". This letter says merely that "Mr. Curt Customer *has been a valued client for X years and is highly recommended"*. If you mention to your new banker that you wish to keep your new account a secret from everyone in your home country, the banker – if he has any sense of ethics, will never check your reference. You can point-blank ask him if he intends to call your reference giver, and if he says "yes", then say, you'll have to take your business elsewhere as you'd regard this as a serious breach of your confidentiality. Normally, your new banker has his document "for the file", and that is enough for him.

If your new potential banker does not like your looks, your attitude, or the fact that you are starting off by bringing in large sums of cash, he may reject your business. Thus it is best to make an appointment well in advance, come in to merely discuss the possibility of opening a substantial account. Then shut up and let the banker sell you! Perhaps you make the first deposit with a small amount of cash, say $25,000 to $50,000. If you need to deposit more, use checks you have purchased for cash or traveller's checks acquired at another bank in the same town, made payable to your new name or (once your account has been accepted) to the order of your new bank.

After an account is once opened, it is easier to feed it with cash (even in a country where cash deposits are monitored or restricted) by making a large number of smaller cash deposits in other branches of the same bank and also by depositing checks you have purchased for cash. Or you can make several cash deposits to new accounts at other banks and then consolidate by making bank transfers from other banks in the same town. You can simply ask at a branch if there are any restrictions or reporting requirements in that particular country in connection with cash deposits. We suggest you might have favorable answers in Andorra, Belgium, Luxembourg, Gibraltar, Germany, and Austria – to name a few names, but be careful in any EU country which since July 1992 has to report any amount over 15,000 ECUs (£10,000 or US $15,000) paid in or out in cash.

## I. ARE THERE OTHER INSTITUTIONS LIKE INSURANCE COMPANIES OR STOCKBROKERS THAT ONE CAN USE TO HAVE ASSETS SECRETLY DEPOSITED IN?

One can certainly open a stock brokerage account in a foreign country, and although these accounts generate a paper blizzard of statements, if they are sent to a mail drop far away from your home, you may be able to keep it a secret. Certainly you should not use a stockbroker from your home country – even via his branch offices abroad. Usually stockbrokers insist upon sending you a slip for every transaction. This is to keep your broker from churning your account without your knowledge. However, for privacy, I feel it is better to let a bank manage your stock deals because a bank can be instructed to hold all mail and statements until you call for them. You can always direct your bankers what to buy or sell from a public phone.

As to insurance companies, you will no doubt meet many a pitchman who wants to sell you an annuity, describing it as an "investment". There is no worse "investment" you can make. An annuity is simply money you give to a broker or salesman who takes a commission off the top. It can be as little as 5 per cent or up to 20 per cent. In the trade this is called a "front end load". It is always very substantial in the insurance business. What does the insurance company do with your money? Simple! The insurance company makes an investment in bonds or other securities that you could do just as well (and probably better) yourself. The insurance company then takes up to half of the return for itself, and pays you the rest spread out over your presumed lifetime. If you die earlier than they think you will, they get a huge windfall in that they keep the money. Your heirs get nothing. If you like the idea of having your liquid cash vanish at a stroke, then buy annuities. The big selling point is that an annuity can become more valuable because the currency (like Swiss Francs) will become more valuable over the years. That may be true. Currencies do go up, and down! But your investment return would be far better (and your losses if any would be smaller) if you simply bought some Swiss bonds yourself, and avoided giving a cut to the salesman and the insurance company. The other argument is that with an annuity you have protection from taxation and from creditor's claims. You get the same protection by investing offshore in an alternate identity or a secret account as we have been discussing in this section. There are zillions of variations on the annuity contract. They are all wonderful for the salesman who gets the front-end load, and for the insurance company who finds this is its most risk-free and profitable line of business. For you the investor, it is pure *merde*. You can look up that word in your French-English dictionary.

Insurance companies are OK. Pay them for health insurance or car liability insurance. But forget about using them for an "investment". Unless you are a complete numbskull, you can do better choosing your own investments, investing in any decent "no-load" bond or stock funds, or letting almost any banker do your money management. Annuities are for seriously retarded dumb mugs.

## J. DO YOU EVER RECOMMEND THE USE OF:

1) Asset protection plans of the sort marketed currently in the USA?
2) Guernsey, Isle of Man or other trusts?
3) Foreign corporations & Holding Companies
4) Liechtenstein Foundations
5) Owning your own bank

1. Asset protection plans established in your home country are totally worthless for tax avoidance. Only under the most far-fetched circumstances will they be any good at protecting you from the claims of plaintiffs, creditors or ex-wives. You will spend a lot of money and get nothing of any value. You will probably spend time in jail for contempt of court if you try to defend a case by saying "I no longer control my money, control is with a trustee in the Isle of Man – or in Liechtenstein!" Courts simply won't buy this and will send you to jail until you make the money being sought by your creditor (or the tax collector) appear. The best way, the only way, to protect your ass and your assets is to **make your ass and assets disappear.** You keep your mouth shut and arrange for the paperwork and passports to be in place. If the heat back home gets really serious, then follow your assets and make your arse disappear also – preferably before you are served with process in any serious lawsuit!

2, 3, 4. The problem with trusts, foundations, corporations and so on is that they involve other people in knowledge of your sensitive and personal financial affairs. If they are local people subject to the jurisdiction of a court where you are being sued, you can forget about any secrecy or protection. Thus, asset protection plans set up in your home country are going to be useless except under the most unlikely circumstances: Lloyd's of London once sold an insurance policy to *protect the insured against death from falling space debris*. The policy cost $25 and paid $100,000 if you were killed by a sputnik falling on you from outer space. The odds against cashing in were less than winning a couple million bucks in a lottery for a dollar "investment". As J.P. Barnum said, "There's a fool born every minute!" I would put lottery players in the foolish category. Asset protection plan buyers are in the same category. Why? Because the only thing they are protected against is an event that will probably never happen in just the right circumstances so that the asset protection scheme will really work when it is needed. Customers for these plans, or for lotteries will not quit gambling or doing what they are doing just because I say they are irrational and foolish. Some people will continue to set up corporations, trusts foundations and asset protection schemes for all the wrong reasons. They cost a lot to set up and run. Finally, they tend to tie you in with lawyers and accountants and reduce your flexibility and capacity for independent judgment. See my section on Banking Passports for a fuller discussion of this point. The only justification for using trusts, foundations, holding companies, etc. is if you are running an active business or professional practice and need them to insulate you from some types of business related lawsuits. This can usually be done more cheaply with liability insurance or secret offshore accounts. Or trust arrangements may be called for if you are getting on in years and you have heirs or beneficiaries that can't manage money on their own. Finally, you should shop around and get prices from several sources. The same exact "Asset Protection Scheme" that one attorney sells for $50,000, can be had from an offshore bank for $1,000.

If you are young and in good health, or if you have a child, wife or partner you trust, it is better to keep your offshore passive money in an individual "pen-name", making advance arrangements for disposition in the event of your incapacity or premature demise. Trusts, three-tiered holding companies Liechtenstein Anstalts and so on are just a bunch of baloney if all you want to do is have a safe place to keep passive assets!

5. Should you own your own bank or insurance company? Only if you are going into the banking or insurance business. Or if you are a swindler who will sell people worthless insurance policies, bogus bank letters of credit, loan commitments etc. A bank or insurance charter is less than worthless for merely handling passive investments. Why less than worthless? Because owning a bank always involves substantial annual running costs and annual taxes or payments in lieu of taxes, plus accounting, filing and domicile fees. For US tax purposes, a bank or insurance company owned by a US citizen and doing business abroad **can** accumulate tax-free profits abroad. This is the big selling point that a promoter uses to sell you a bank charter for $25,000 or more. He just bought the charter for $2,500 or less. But the problem is, to get this tax exemption, the bank must be a real bank (or insurance company) and not just a personal holding company for your assets. A real bank or holding company has **mainly outside customers** and **makes its money in banking** or insurance. Running a bank or insurance company is a full time job for anyone and usually involves the cost of many employees and multi-million dollar risks and loans. The typical charter buyer is much like the person who buys a noble title. You hang it on the wall and say "Mmmmmm, that's nice". Aside from admiring the certificate and impressing a few friends who don't know what it's all about, an offshore bank charter is quite worthless.

## K. HOW DO YOU ACCESS YOUR OWN [OFFSHORE] MONEY TO USE IT IN THE COUNTRY WHERE YOU NORMALLY LIVE?

This is the biggest problem! If you spend too much at home, this will attract the attention of local tax collectors who will do an analysis of your income and expenses and quickly discover something fishy. You can spend cash at home only if you do it low profile. You can bring back cash of the legally allowable amounts when you return from vacation trips. Or you can access your foreign cash via automatic teller machines and credit cards using a card in your new "alternate identity". For out-of-the-wall cash use banks at some distance from where you live. Never transfer funds from your offshore bank to your home country bank account. It will be considered taxable income unless you can show conclusively that it was a tax free gift from someone likely to make such a gift. There will be a tax due from the donor of the gift. If the donor is a foreigner, the local tax collector may be able to stick you for the gift tax. *The purpose of having a judgment proof nest egg abroad is not to bring it home to spend it, but to keep it abroad for the day you become a PT – or to survive a rainy day back home.*

If you get older and decide you may never use up your money before the rainy day comes, it is best (safest) to be a big spender only on vacations abroad. The game plan that will work for most PTs is to earn enough in your home country to build up offshore assets and then relocate comfortably abroad. Relocation can mean just moving abroad at a young age to turn over a new leaf, to get involved in a different line of work or activity, to wave bye-bye to ex-wives, tax collectors and bureaucrats. Or to retire and go fishing every day. Or to discover Sex Havens. Life can be great when you can go anywhere, do anything, have a large income and no records to keep. You ship your assets abroad in advance of your departure and then take your arse abroad to join your assets. Don't bring the mother lode home unless you want to create a very strong likelihood that you'll have to pay taxes on the whole shebang as ordinary income. Above all, don't spill the beans to any girlfriends, employees or anyone else in your home country. Keep your finances confidential, as most Continentals do.

## L. CAN YOU SUPPLY A LIST OF GOOD, RELIABLE, SAFE BANKS WHO KNOW HOW TO KEEP A SECRET? CAN YOU EXPLAIN HOW TO IDENTIFY GOOD BANKS?

Bankers and bank staff, like all people with mouths, are generally indiscreet. All but a very few countries are generally invasive of privacy rather than protective of it. Most governments (translate politicians) are ready, willing and able to confiscate your assets without giving it a second thought. So what does one do? The solution is to bank "offshore", in a country where your banker doesn't know anyone you know, and, as mentioned before, to bank under an alternate name. A small island or country like Switzerland or Luxembourg whose economy depends upon keeping it attractive as an offshore banking center is less likely to confiscate your money. Likewise, a few countries have a long tradition as banking centers.

We could use the "woman" example and say that banks are like women. We recognize too that our female readers could say the same thing about men! All men, women and banks have certain desirable characteristics and many have fatal flaws. Your favorite is not necessarily my favorite. But given what I have said up until now, and realizing that our readers want specific recommendations, here come a few.

### MAJOR WORLD CLASS BANKS

**Royal Trust Bank** is one of the three major Canadian banks. They are all good although I wouldn't put two cents into a Canadian (home office) bank if privacy was any concern. Foreign subsidiaries or branches are subject to local privacy regulations and thus offshore branches are reasonably secure. Still, I wouldn't use Royal Trust if I was a Canadian for reasons explained several times. For non-Canadian English speakers, they are a top choice. Royal Trust has locally established subsidiary banks in London, Zurich, Geneva, Barbados, Jersey, Isle of Man, Cayman, Singapore, Hong Kong, and a representative office in Tokyo. The home office stands behind them as to safety of your principal.

**Following are some of the biggest and best banks of the world. Most have branches abroad in every banking center. Recommended as indicated.**

Andorra– only has a few banks, see our *Andorra and Gibraltar Report* for the full story.

ABN (Algemeinliche Bank Nederlands). Use branches in Curacao or BonAire, Netherlands Antilles.

Banco di Roma. Use branch in Monaco.

Bank of Bermuda (Bermuda or Guernsey, CI) Bermuda has only three locally-owned banks, all are good. Try also Butterfield's Bank in Bermuda.

Bank National de Paris. (Use non French branches).

Barclays Bank. Big British bank, branches all over.

Edmond de Rothschild Bank. Good for Monaco.

Credit Suisse. Major Swiss bank. We *don't* like them.

Coutts & Company (Zurich or London). Classy bank used by Queen Elizabeth and other British aristocrats.

Grindlay's Bank (Jersey). Owned by ANZ (Australia and New Zealand) parent.

Hong Kong Shanghai Bank (owns British Bank of the Middle East).

International Westminster Bank (called Natwest in UK).

Jyske Bank. Copenhagen & Gibraltar.

Julius Baer Bank (Main Office Zurich), with branch in London. Has excellent record at handling investments.

Liechtenstein. Only three banks. All good. Bank in Liechtenstein, Liechtenstein Landes Bank, Private Trust Bank.

Lloyds Bank. British major player with branches all over the world.

Sarasin, Switzerland. Excellent investment performance in recent years.

Scandinaviska Bank. Use only branches outside Sweden.

Swiss Bank Corporation. Use branches outside Switzerland. Generally impersonal and uncaring.

Union Bank of Switzerland. Big Swiss bank. Use branch in Cayman Islands. Generally impersonal and uncaring.

Vontoble Bank. Zurich, Switzerland. Good investment management.

Westpac. Australian. Use branches only outside of home country.

We prefer not to make too many specific recommendations for fear that our recommendation may call attention of regulators to these banks and cause them to tighten up. Incidentally, we do not do business with any bank recommended here; we get no commissions nor kickbacks. We strongly suggest that you get hold of a directory of international banks (like the one published by Polk in the USA) at any public library. Then simply write off to the banks in places you'd like to bank in and see what they say. If you live in Big Brother land, get a mail-drop and use a pen-name for such correspondence. Best to open any account in person, and only with cash. Never open any account with a personal check or transfer from a bank in your home country if you want secrecy.

## DESIRABLE COUNTRIES FOR BANKING

**Austria:** Royal Trust Bank (owned by Canadian parent company), Rathausstrasse 20, (or PO Box 306, Austria 1010, Wien (Vienna). Phone: 43-1 43-61-61, Fax (43-1) 42-81-42. Our preferred contact there Peter Zipper, Senior Vice-President. Mention the Hill Reports and they will be glad to send you a packet of brochures in English about their services. Note: Because of local regulations, the services that banks offer tend to be similar in each country and any innovations that attract business are soon copied by competitor banks.

RTB offers asset management, their own stable of bond and stock funds, and all types of accounts in all currencies, plus multi-currency high-interest checking. You can write checks in any currency. Offers credit cards such as VISA without detailed application forms if a client keeps a balance in assets or cash of over US $30,000. Has many American clients. Most (if not all) officers speak perfect English. Bank charges in Austria are about half of Swiss charges. There is a 10 per cent government withholding tax on interest. This tax is paid by the bank out of your account without compromising bank secrecy, i.e. your name is never known to the government. Austria rates an A+ for bank secrecy in general. Withholding tax on interest is commonly avoided by holding long or short term bonds, or ''Fiduciary Accounts'' held outside of Austria which pay more interest and are not subject to this 10 per cent tax. Currency switching costs one-quarter of 1 per cent. They will accept instructions by fax or phone if a code word is agreed upon in advance. Numbered accounts are also assigned. They will also assist in the formation and administration of Manx or Liechtenstein trusts and foundations.

**Gibraltar:** Home to many banks and recommended as a place to form and domicile corporations cheaply. Letter to any of these banks at simply ''Gibraltar'' will be delivered.

Jyske Bank – Danish bank offers very liberal policy with regard to loans for currency speculation, and also many unusual services. A progressive and accommodating bank. Perhaps too unconservative for any mother-lode deposits, but good for doing business with and for use as a transit account. Does not require reference to open an account as of 1992. Offers multi-currency check writing and fast arrangements for credit cards.

**Guernsey:** Along with Jersey (the other Channel Island) is a major offshore banking center:

A letter addressed to any of these banks at St. Peter Port, Guernsey, Channel Islands, Great Britain, will get there. Note: This is only a selection of banks. There are many others!

Bank of Bermuda (highly recommended)
Guinness Mahon Bank (big British bank – pays highest bank interest rate on deposits of over £50,000)
Midland Bank
National Westminster

**Isle of Man:** A preferred location because they don't co-operate with any tax authority including Great Britain's and are well known for making life tough on creditors from abroad who seek to use Manx courts to collect anything from local investors or depositors.

A letter addressed to any of these banks at Isle of Man, Great Britain, will get there:

Anglo-Manx Bank
Barclays Bank
Lloyds Bank
Midland Bank (subsidiary of Hong Kong Bank)
Robert Fleming Bank
Royal Trust Bank
Tyndall Bank

**Jersey, Channel Islands, Great Britain.** If you plan to visit, Jersey is more charming, lively and interesting a place than Guernsey. But these islands are close together and you can see both by hovercraft from St. Malo, France in the same day. Jersey has a bit more class, and more banks than Guernsey.

Bank of Scotland
Bank of Wales
Barclays Bank
Cater Allen
Hill Samuel
Midland Bank

**Luxembourg, Duchy of (In Europe).** The Duchy of Luxembourg (one of the three original founding nations of the EC – Benelux) is said to be replacing Switzerland as the favorite banking haven of many wealthy individuals who desire maximum confidentiality, good service, and more reasonable charges – about 40 per cent off Swiss service charges. Accounts in Luxembourg may be held in any currency, and unlike Switzerland, there is no withholding tax on interest paid to foreign depositors. Thus, the use of fiduciary accounts to circumvent national withholding tax is not necessary in

Luxembourg. Luxembourg is both a city and a country. A complete list of all banks can be obtained by writing to Lucein Thiel, General Manager, Association of Banks in Luxembourg, Luxembourg. The biggest banks in Luxembourg are:

**Bank Internationale a Luxembourg (BIL)** and **Banque Generale du Luxembourg;** the two locally owned and operated banks. They are both very solid and like all banks have plenty of staff members who speak English. In fact, the general job requirement for any bank officer in Luxembourg is fluency in English and German. The other major players are the Deutsche Bank and Dresdner Bank, both German owned. But there are a total of 187 international banks which have opened offices in Luxembourg. Thus it is hard to name one major player which does not have a branch or wholly owned subsidiary there. There are no Spanish banks. However, you will find all the old standbys including Barclays, Lloyds, and Citibank. A letter addressed to "Name of Any Bank, Luxembourg" will get there. This comes in handy if you forget the address of your bank.

Luxembourg, like Switzerland, now has a "money laundering law" providing that any banker who knowingly or without checking properly on his customer handles criminal-source money faces five years in the Pokey. The practical effect of this is that most bankers are paranoid about new accounts materializing off the street. They want new customers to come to them with letters of reference from lawyers, accountants, bankers, or other customers.

Luxembourg bank accounts are insured by the government for up to Luxembourg Francs 500,000. In US dollars this is around $15,000 (or £8,500).

**Luxembourg Investment Funds:** Luxembourg is also home to a vast number (over 1,000) of investment funds. Many of these are sponsored by major banks. Some are "no-load" which means there is no front-end commission and most of your money goes into the actual investment, while others charge as much as 7 per cent commission to get in and up to 5 per cent per year off the top for management. Luxembourg is in fact the leader by a large margin of the offshore banking and financial centers with over £55 billion of other people's money held there. The second place in Europe is held by Jersey, with a mere £6 billion. One of the leading funds (performance-wise) in Luxembourg is Fleming. The Fleming Flagship fund, for instance has outperformed stock market indexes by about 80 per cent since it was started around 1989. But as of 1993, some fund managers express the fear that many stock indices are poised to follow Japan in a downward mode. I caution my readers that any fund that has been the leading performer in recent years is statistically more likely to be near the bottom next year than a consistent mid-level performer. Had I written this section last year, I'd have said that the top performer was the Gaia Hedge Fund, up almost 100 per cent every year for several years. But in the most recent year (1992) Gaia was down 67 per cent! Not so good for new arrivals who boarded last year. Performance like this is what makes many of our readers decide to let a bank manage their funds with the main objective being "capital preservation" rather than capital gains. The best and cheapest way to find out about investment opportunities is to request a free subscription to *The International*, Greystoke Place, Fetter Lane, London. EC4A 1ND, Great Britain. But remember this: any brochure or magazine you get for free is an advertiser supported sales tool. You can expect such a publication to say mainly nice things about their advertisers. *The International* is a very good little monthly magazine for investors and the price (free) is right! But don't expect them to pan their advertisers' products. When you pay a fairly hefty price for a Scope International Special Report (no advertising accepted) you can expect more objective and critical reviews.

**Switzerland** offers innumerable banks, dealers and brokers. If you require a full list please refer to: Publications Bancaires, Case postale 408, CH-1213 Petit-Lancy 1, Tel. (022) 792 93 78. The list is free but send a couple of International Reply coupons or a US dollar to pay for airmail postage.

**Basel: (Area code 061)**
**Baumann & Cle.** St.Jakobstrasse 46 271 30 22 Private banker
**Bank Clal** Marktplatz 13 261 80 33

**Bank Heusser & Cle.AG** Dufourstrasse 25 287 87 87
**Bank Ehinger & Cle. AG** Rittergasse 12 271 11 80
**Bank Sarasin & Cle.** Freie Strasse 107 277 77 77 Private banker
**Dreyfus Sohne & Cle. Ag** Aeschenvorstadt 14 286 66 66
**Gutzwiller & Cle.** Kaufhausgasse 7 272 88 33 Private banker
**La Roche & Co.** Rittergasse 25 271 15 00 Private banker
**Swiss Bank Corporation** Aescfhenvorstadt 1 288 20 20 Universal bank

**Bern: (Area Code: 031)**
**Swiss Volksbank** Weltpoststr.5 32 81 11 Universal bank

**Geneva: (Area Code: 022)**
**Banque Paribas (Suisse) SA** 2 Place de Hollande 787 71 11 All banking services
**Barclays Bank SA** 10 Rue d'Italy 28 65 50 All banking services
**Bordier & Cle.** 16 Rue de Hollande 317 12 12 Private banker
**Credit Lyonnais (Suisse) SA** Place Bel-Air 705 66 66
**Darier & Cle** 4 Rue de Saussure 21 41 11 Private banker
**Deutsche Bank (Suisse) SA** 3 Place des Bergues 739 01 11
**Hentsch & Cle** 15 Rue de la Corraterie 21 90 11 Private banker
**J.P. Morgan (Suisse) SA** 3 Place des Bergues 731 58 00. Classy American operation
**Lombard, Odier & Cle.** 11 Rue de la Corraterie 709 21 11 Private banker
**Merrill Lynch Bank (Suisse) SA** 7 Rue Munier-Romilly 47 11 11
**Mirabaud & Cle** 3 Bd. du Theatre 21 03 55 Private banker
**Picket &B Cle** 29 Boulvard G. Favon 705 22 11 Private banker
**Saudi-Swiss Bank** 10 Chemin de Rive 788 07 44
**Societe Bancaire J. Baer SA** 2 Boulvard du Theatre 20 13 33 All banking services
**United Overseas Bank SA** 11 Quai des Bergues 731 98 41

**Zurich: (Area Code: 01)**
**Adler & Co. AG** Claridenstrasse 22 202 78 11 Investment banking
**Arab Bank (Switzerland)** Talacker 21 265 71 11. Arab owned
**Bank Julius Baer & Co. AG** Bahnhofstrasse 36 228 51 11 All banking services
**Bank Leu AG** Bahnhofstrasse 32 219 11 11
**Bank Leumi Le-Israel (Schweiz)** Claridenstrasse 34 207 91 11. Israeli owned
**Bank J. Vontobel & Co. AG** Bahnhofstrasse 3 283 71 11 All banking services
**Citicorp Investment bank** Bahnhofstrasse 63 205 71 71
**Commerzbank (Schweiz) AG** Lintheschergasse 7 219 71 11 Investment banking, capital asset trustee
**Coutts & Co AG** Talstrasse 59 214 51 11 Private banker. Subsidary of Nat West London
**Credit Suisse** Paradeplatz 8 333 11 11 Universal bank
**Dresdner Bank AG** Utoquai 55 258 51 11. German
**Manufacturers Hanover Trust** Stockerstrasse 33 202 27 11
**Nomura Bank (Schweiz)** Bahnhofstrasse 71 219 91 11. Japanese
**Rothschild Bank AG** Zollikerstrasse 181 384 71 11 Capital asset trustee, corporate finance
**Shearson Lehman Bank** Stadelhoferstr. 22. 252 25 11 Commodities, Securities. American
**Sogenal Banque** Bleicherweg 1 220 71 11
**Standard Chartered Bank AG** Bleicherweg 62 206 91 11
**Swiss Cantobank** Baarematte, Zug, (042)33 03 30
**Union Bank of Switzerland** Bahnhofstrasse 45 234 11 11 Universal bank
**Yamaichi Bank (Schweiz)** Bahnhofstrasse 92 228 65 11

**Lugano: (Area code: 091)**
**Banca del Gottardo** Viale Francscini 8 28 11 11 All banking services. Beautiful architecture
**BSI Banca della Svizzera Italiana** Via Magaetti 2 58 71 11 All banking services

# CASH IS KING, LONG LIVE THE KING

In terms of privacy, cash is unrivalled – to a point. It is highly portable. It is accepted worldwide for just about any purchase (provided you have the correct local currency). And, best of all, it does not in itself leave behind a trace of you. Once issued, there are no records of transfers and it is defined as being a "bearer" instrument. This simply means "whoever holds cash is presumed to be the rightful owner of it". In most countries, this has led to a special "cash rule" law being passed which asserts that stolen cash tracked down should not be returned to its rightful owner *after* it has been spent. A merchant who, in good faith, accepts stolen cash for his goods or services from a bank robber does not risk being asked to return it.

The distinction is a crucial one. Let us say, for instance, that someone breaks into the Louvre Museum in Paris and steals *Mona Lisa* by Leonardo da Vinci. This, obviously, does not mean that the painting is now his – just as a bank robber does not automatically gain legal ownership of the loot the second he rushes out of the bank. If the art thief then sells the painting it does not follow that the buyer gains legal ownership of it – after all, it is still stolen property. No matter how many times a piece of stolen property is bought and resold, it legally remains the property of the owner from whom it was stolen. This means that if the property is ever recovered it will be returned to whence it was stolen – although certain countries, including Italy, make an exception to this rule if a buyer of stolen property acted 'in good faith'. This leads to some highly amusing international court battles where authorities in one country implore their colleagues in another to force the "good faith"-buyer of a stolen object to return it.

If you take 1,000 dollars, pounds or francs from your bank account and go spend it on something, there is no paper trail of what you did with it – only the fact that you signed a receipt for it and went away. You should, however, note that keeping purchase receipts for something you buy with cash is potentially culpable. A few years ago, the singer-cum-actress Barbara Streisand returned to the United States from a holiday in Japan. On examining her luggage (yes, celebrities are also harassed) two items of interest were found by the customs officials – a pair of fancy boots and a US $700 dollar cash receipt for said boots. As this exceeded the amount of foreign-purchased goods she could legally bring into the US without paying declaring it, good old Barb had to pay the duty and a fine. Needless to say, authorities issued a public statement informing the world press of their catch of a "celebrity-smuggler", presumably to inhibit others from perpetrating the same, crime.

Still, the fact remains that only cash may be handed over in exchange for goods or service without leaving anyone except the seller in a position to make a permanent record of it – and, again, watch out for what you do with any "cash receipt" given you. As a rule of thumb you may safely discard such receipts when the seller has delivered his end of the bargain *unless* you envisage later finding yourself in a position to prove that you are the rightful owner of whatever you bought. If you hold an absolutely top-secret meeting with someone you are not supposed to be seeing in a restaurant, for instance, someone finding the receipt may investigate by turning up at the restaurant and get you identified by showing pictures of you or your contact to the maitre d'. This may be highly damaging if, for instance, you are under a court order not to meet nor speak to a witness in a civil or criminal case. Golden Cash Rule number one: unless it is highly possible that you will be required to present them at a later date, discard immediately and safely (by burning, flushing out in toilet or similar) any cash receipts that you get. What should Barbara have done? Worn the boots and *mailed* that receipt to herself before leaving Japan, of course. Or paid the seven per cent duty!

## CASH. NEVER LEAVE HOME WITHOUT IT

You will find that it is folly to walk out of the door without having at least some cash on your person. Who knows – the local ATM (automated teller machine) may be on the blink. What if it refused to accept your credit cards? You may need to make a phone call. Carry small change, then you will not have to make an unnecessary purchase to have a banknote broken up. If you are actually on the receiving end of government surveillance, using cash only is doubly important.

Especially when travelling, you should take care to carry with you a sufficient amount of cash to pay or bail your way out of situations. This holds even more true when travelling to other countries. An example: let us assume, for instance, that you are involved in a traffic accident or merely get pulled over for some petty moving offence. Should this happen it is highly preferable to be able to pay the fine (or post bail) on the spot. In France, foreigners who pay fines in cash right then and there, only pay 33 per cent of the standard rate levied on locals: that is two-thirds off! And no, this is not a greasy-scheme. All foreign motorists are entitled to the discount from all French officers and you DO get a receipt. In any country you may be able to carefully negotiate a similar discount with the patrolman. If that is the case, then don't expect to be furnished with paperwork.

Some auto insurance companies offer an additional cover known as bail-bond insurance. In several Middle Eastern and Latin countries, notably Spain, authorities have the habit of holding foreign motorists in jail until bail is posted – or until the trial. This may mean wasting away in prison for weeks or even months.

If you have money to post bail yourself, it is better to have it in cold, hard cash. Cops won't let you go until the check clears. It is dangerous to access your Swiss bank account from the confines of a jail cell, as Spanish, Mexican, or other authorities may share the information on the whereabouts of your "mother-lode" with authorities in your home country.

## RATES OF EXCHANGE: MORE MILEAGE ON THE MARK

If you find yourself in a foreign country, you normally get the best rate of exchange in banks. Sometimes, however, post offices give you better value for your money if they are prepared to change foreign currency (France, for instance). Black markets can be even more profitable, but a wise PT is careful not to get cheated, nor to run afoul of the law. Apply commonsense and prudence. In Hungary or South America, you'll *always* get a fast shuffle from street money changers.

Large international hotels generally offer the worst rate of exchange. But they are open 24 hours a day and very seldom charge any commission. For a quick cash infusion in the middle of the night, they are better than the street people who whisper "change money".

Where to change money? As a rule of thumb, change your cash in the country where the currency you are carrying is stronger, worth more, higher esteemed and more stable than the currency you want. Günter is travelling to Istanbul from his home in Frankfurt. The German mark is a strong currency. The Turkish lira is not. Günter gets more mileage on his mark if he waits until he is in Turkey before exchanging it. The same is true between Switzerland and Italy. You get two per cent more changing Swiss francs in Italian banks. Normally, banks located in airports operate the same rates of exchange as those downtown. However, in some countries (Portugal, Morocco, etc) their charges and commissions tend to be much higher.

## HOW TO ELIMINATE ALL RISKS OF CASH

Is it "risky" to carry about serious money in cash? Not if you do it right.

First of all, when staying in hotels you may make use of the safety deposit box during the night. If no safety deposit box is available in the hotel, you may keep cash in your room with you at night, putting a wedge under the door to prevent night prowlers from entering. A makeshift wedge may be produced by slightly mangling a book. Simply travel with a plastic wedge, available in most hardware stores. In addition, put a couple of small coins on top of the door handle and place a glass or a plate underneath. This will wake you up if anyone forgets to knock.

Second, even if you carry cash on your person at all times, most pickpockets and muggers do not frisk their victims. You may carry several thousand dollars, Swiss francs or pounds sterling quite unobtrusively in e.g. a Velcro-fastened pouch around your ankle, thigh or in a money belt around your waist. Some currency has metal strips embedded and these can set off airport security alarms. If you are frisked after walking through a metal detector, security personnel may oblige you to show the contents of the pouches around your ankles or shins. You never know who may be watching.

In theory metal strips may show up but in practice there is so much other metal around in and on the human body, detectors are not really a concern. More worrying is the work of the US government agency which produces paper money and is researching a taggant added to the printing ink. This sneaky development could lead to chemical "sniffing" to detect the taggant and ignore other false factors.

A new style of underwear with money pouches has been dubbed "Kangaroos". These patented briefs by Portuguese inventor and underwear-designer Carlos Vieira have a pouch in front for storing money, credit cards and other valuables. They are somewhat hard to find but easy to have made yourself.

Other ways to thwart pickpockets and muggers: keep your bankroll in your toiletries. A Californian company makes a line of more than 150 camouflage safes. These are cans and bottles that look like the deodorants. But in reality, they are fake. The bottoms screw open to reveal hollow insides, perfect for storing money, jewellery and other important items. Designs include fake hairspray, fake soft drinks, fake jars of peanut butter, etc. Don't use them for smuggling as customs officers recognise them at a glance.

For keeping a few thousand dollars in your garage or in the boot of your car, there is even a fake tire inflater. The camouflage "safes" are between US $15 and $25 in most large department stores. Thieves in the USA are slowly catching on to them. But in the rest of the world, they are mainly unknown. The Corner Spy Shop, 56A Queensway (corner of Inverness Place), London W2 3RY has a small selection at £25 sterling per container. Call them at (+44) 71 243 0967 / (+44) 71 229 8350 or fax (+44) 71 792 9256. They do export. They also sell UV-ink, voice changers and other fun stuff, but at heavily inflated prices. Mail order buyers look to the USA for better selection and more realistic pricetags.

The one other thing you have to watch out for is currency controls. Some countries, such as Switzerland and Britain, have no currency import or export controls whatsoever for residents and non-residents alike. Other countries have strict controls for residents but not for non-residents – with the possible, added twist that non-residents may be obliged to declare the import of cash exceeding a certain amount in order to be allowed to re-export it on departure. Due to international concern about terrorists it is a lot easier to run afoul of these regulations when travelling by air, where you stand a high chance of getting frisked or even strip-searched (Pakistan is notorious for harassing departing travellers, residents and non-residents alike, to ensure that money, gold or diamonds are not smuggled out).

Even if there are no controls or regulations regarding the importation or export of cash in the country you are visiting you will be sure to raise some eyebrows if authorities discover a million dollars in cash in your carry-on luggage or in a suitcase in the trunk of your car. Warning: Many airports now require departing passengers to show that portable computers, cameras or hi-fis in carry-on luggage work – the legacy of the Lockerbie bombing. Do not rip out the intestines of your computer and replace with cash if you travel by air! At best, it may lead to nosey questions and waste of time – at worst, it may lead to you being detained until you can produce documentation that you came by the cash in a legal manner and are not a professional money launderer. Also remember that big stacks of money in a suitcase do show up on the sensitive X-ray machines now in use.

## HOW TO STAY INFORMED WHEN THE LAWS CHANGE

As laws change constantly you should either inquire with the local embassies of countries you plan to visit before departure or, at the very least, find some other way of getting the facts straight. A very useful publication is the *ABC World Airways Guide* (published by Reed Travel Group, Church Street, Dunstable, Bedfordshire LU5 4HB, England, phone (+44) 582 600 111, fax 582 695 230). The size of two phone books, this monthly guide lists not only all schedule arriving and departing flights, transfer connections etc. at all airports, worldwide, but also gives constantly updated information about not only currency control regulations (if any) in all countries but also useful additional information about social norms, ''do's and don'ts'' (never show the soles of your shoes in a Moslem country, for instance). Cost is about US $500 per year.

Cheaper yet is *TIM, the Travel Information Manual.* This volume omits airline schedules and the do's and don'ts. Because of this, it is far slimmer and thus far less expensive, too. TIM is a green A5-format paperback of about 400 pages, with a new edition every month. It lists currency rules, visa requirements, duty free allowances, etc. A free copy of last month's issue can probably be begged from your friendly neighborhood travel agent. Or subscribe to the 12 issues per year by writing to Travel Information Manual, PO Box 902, NL-2130 EA Hoofddorp, the Netherlands. At last count, a single monthly edition was NLG 22 (Dutch guilders). TIM is available in English only.

As long as you are able to convince authorities that you are merely a tourist you may get away with importing, carrying and exporting cash in amounts far bigger than those ''allowed'' by local law. It is always better to be regarded as merely an ignorant and slightly daft tourist than a local. Local citizens are always considered fair game for police and customs officials alike. Take the example of British comedian Ken Dodd. Dodd was indicted for tax-evasion after authorities got wise to the fact that he kept very large amounts of money in his house, in cash. Dodd's explanations that he quite simply does not trust banks failed to convince Big Brother-investigators. Fortunately for Dodd, he was able to convince the jury and was acquitted of the charges.

American authorities are notorious for flat-out confiscating large cash sums found in the possession of private citizens. In 1991, a woman in Florida was pulled over by a motorcycle cop on a minor traffic violation. When searching her purse for her driving license, the officer noticed that it was overflowing with large denomination dollar bills. She was immediately arrested on suspicion of being a drug dealer. Her money was confiscated. In reality, she was on her way to a real estate broker in order to close a property deal. The cash she carried was the intended downpayment. Only after several months of court battles was the money returned to her. No apology was offered, of course. Her lawyer probably got one third as his fee.

So, be smart. Carry more money than you ordinarily would need, and carry it right – on your person. If you need to transport large sums of money, avoid air travel if possible – even domestic flights. Americans get a particularly hard time from their government if found in possession of even relatively modest amounts in cash (about 1,000 dollars and up). If you need to move huge sums in cash OUT of your country, the absolutely most intelligent way of doing so is, if possible, to do so by boat. If you are worried about moving huge sums of cash out of the United States by plane, why not consider taking the Queen Elizabeth II to England? This way, at least, you will not have to explain the origins of the cash in plain view of US customs officials, as might be the case if the money was found in your car when crossing the border into Canada. Or, simply declare any reasonable sums you are going to export before you cross the border.

# TRANSPORTING YOUR OWN CASH ACROSS BORDERS

A final word on how to keep the cash "compact", as in non-bulky. Obviously you should strive to move large amounts around in as high denomination bills as possible. Until you reach your ultimate point of destination (your bank in Liechtenstein, for instance) make sure that you have kept spending money apart from the serious money. Have a smaller amount for airline tickets, gasoline and hotel bills in a money-clip, preferably in your trouser pocket, and even less-serious money – petty cash – for meals en route or even potentially violent beggars in a coat pocket. Never use a wallet, thieves love them. A wallet delivers everything from cash and credit cards to identification papers with a victim's home address in one, neat package. You may elaborate on this as a way of foiling robbers by having a seemingly bulging wallet containing nothing but small bills and expired or otherwise useless credit or similar plastic cards to placate a mugger. A nice touch is to include a piece of paper with the home address of your "favorite" congressman, cop or IRS-agent! Don't do this if you have ever been fingerprinted, though. The thief may hurt or kill the object of your ire during a break-in and if your fingerprints are found on any item the thief carries they may be traced to you.

Those who do not wish to leave any fingerprints anywhere always carry a small Tipp-Ex sized bottle of Beechams "Germolene NEW SKIN", available in British and stateside drugstores at approximately £1/$2 a pop. The 13ml jar even carries fingerprint-obscuring instructions and a clear drawing on how to use it on the outside of its packaging.

An alternative could be soft leather driving gloves or white dress-gloves of the kind used for black-tie affairs. Simpsons (Piccadilly, London), among others, carries an extensive stock. Some careful individuals often don their kid gloves to avoid getting their fingerprints on anything potentially incriminating including love letters.

To reduce bulk you may have to shop around for the right currency. Canadian dollars are available in 1,000-dollar denominations but these can be difficult to dispose of and if obtained from a bank are centrally registered. German 1000 Deutsche Mark bills are equal in value to roughly £260 sterling, but you may go one better: Swiss 1,000 Franc-bills are equal to about £400 Sterling (about US $700) and are also among the safest currencies. As opposed to US $-bills, Swiss Francs with their complex designs and colors are almost never a target for counterfeiters. If your bank hands you just one US $100 bill that turns out to be a phoney when you try to exchange or deposit it abroad you may come under some very unpleasant attention from local authorities. Far-fetched? Your author had this experience when exchanging dollars for lira in Ankara, Turkey a couple of years ago. After being questioned by a cop who – miraculously! – spoke English and also was positively disposed towards foreigners, the matter was solved amicably. On my return, I made sure to inform my Portugese bank that if they wanted me for a customer in the future they had better not give me any more fake $20-bills.

We are told that Singapore issues bills for 100,000 Singapore dollars (about US $50,000) but these are probably pretty rare outside South-East Asia. If interested in this exotic option check with the closest Singaporean embassy or consulate and with a bank – then commit to memory. Their 10,000 note is common.

All told, you may comfortably – if not necessarily legally – carry perhaps 50 Swiss 1,000-Franc bills in a pouch. With one strapped to each ankle, this equals 100,000 Swiss Francs or roughly £40,000 Sterling (about US $70,000) without the need for a double-bottomed briefcase.

Whatever you do, your physical person is the safest for carrying cash. To illustrate this, consider the Canadian retiree who a few years reported to the police in Stockholm that a suitcase containing his life's savings – about US $500,000 – had been stolen from the trunk of his rental car. Obviously not an insurance scam (insurance companies do not cover cash) the information was checked out with the Canadian authorities. Everything was kosher. The victim had, indeed, sold off his business a week earlier and had departed on a Europe-wide search for a place to retire – with his cash. Sad story.

So even if you are travelling with very large amounts of cash for any reason it is recommended that you keep it literally strapped to your person with ankle, waist and even arm pouches. This may make you as bulky in appearance as a bodybuilder with a history of steroids galore but it sure beats putting your stash in the trunk or glove box of a friendly Fiat Uno rent-a-car! Rental cars are a favorite target of thieves who usually get cameras and passports.

## THE BANKING PASSPORT

In the course of writing the *Passport Report,* we interviewed lawyers who used the term "Banking Passport". Until then, we had never heard of it. But after our initial rejection of the concept as something possibly illegal, and certainly unpatriotic, we have had a change of thinking. Especially for people who live in unfree countries, the concept of having a second *Banking Passport* now seems quite reasonable. For example:

Let's say that Mr. Smith is a citizen of the UNITED STATES OF ARRESTIA. As you know, ARRESTIA, hereafter called USA, or "A" for short, has all sorts of currency laws and restrictions. "A" makes the unreported transfer of cash abroad a major felony-crime of "money-laundering", punishable by 25 years in the pokey. It makes having a secret account abroad to preserve assets against government confiscation (by inflation or otherwise) a crime. Incredibly, failure to **file** detailed reports of all activities four times a year and pay one-third or more of your income to "the State" is also a crime. One can file all these reports and pay, but such disclosure defeats the whole purpose of most Arrestians – to have a nest-egg that is judgment proof, and above all, government proof. There are persistent rumors that the USA will follow the example of its mentor Russia and simply declare all banknotes over $20 to be null and void because cash is something only used by criminals and drug dealers. Confiscation of private property is the logical solution of bureau-rats to all conceivable civic problems. In our example, Mr. Smith is an Arrestian who has wangled the right to travel abroad freely. He also makes an occasional deal where profits could be paid into a foreign account. He would probably be glad to pay a reasonable tax on such profits. But if he did pay a tax and reveal the nature of his foreign business (or publicly report where he keeps his assets), he would never have anything squirrelled away for emergencies or retirement. So he stashes his cash and unwillingly accepts the risk of being a "criminal" by depositing his wealth outside of USA. Thus, Smith wants to be low profile.

"Offshore Financial Advisers" tell Mr. Smith that he can control, yet conceal, secret assets by means of trusts, holding companies, Foundations, and other expensive legal enitities requiring annual costs of £2000 or more to set up, and at least £1000 per annum for care and feeding. The disadvantage of such arrangements (necessary for active businesses, in our opinion, but a waste of money for mere asset management) is that not reporting such activities is illegal anyway. To make things worse, with offshore trusts or other vehicles,

A)    *Someone else knows your business!* Those persons are not necessarily:
       1) Discreet 2) Honest, nor 3) Cheap to feed.

B)    Your advisers (or new partners in crime) will say they "need" to be able to sign checks (to insulate you, they say) and control your funds. But all too often the adviser:
       1) Makes bad business decisions, 2) Makes mistakes 3) Is not available when you need him, 4) Steals, or at best 5) Gets into difficulties unrelated to you and to save his hide, gives you up. You can't sue anyone for telling your secrets without stirring up an even bigger can of worms!
       THE "BANKING PASSPORT" IS AN OPTION FOR ACHIEVING PRIVACY AND CONTROL.

The old alternative was setting up a corporation, foundation or trust. You create a separate "legal entity". Perhaps it is "offshore", which just means not in your native country. The corporate treasurer (not you) signs checks; you are supposed to control things behind the scenes. It works, sometimes. But what if you create another **person** with another nationality, and a full set of identification? Will this serve the same purpose more cheaply and effectively? Can this be done legally? For the person with "passive" investments, the answer is "Yes!" So let us now return to Mr. Smith.

Assume that a foreign country, The Grand Duchy of Freedomia will accept any (rich) person as a citizen and issue them a passport. Assume further that Freedomia (like most English-speaking countries) permits its citizens to use any name they like on their passports. Presto! Shazam! You have created something like a corporation or holding company or Foundation, but the difference is that *you have complete control.* The new person you bave created is the only completely reliable and trustworthy person in the whole world. Why? Because it is YOU, yourself!

Thus Mr. "P.T." Smith, instead of telling his lawyer "set me up with an offshore holding company", now says *"set me up with a new passport"* from a truly free country, or if none is available, then at least a country that does not care about its offshore citizens. That way, I won't have to serve in any Army to kill people. I won't spend half of my time filling out silly forms, about whom I went to lunch with and why. I won't pay any more income taxes or inheritance taxes, etc, nor allow myself to be treated like a 'resource', always exploited to pay for things I don't even believe in. Give me a new name and a new passport!" For a fee, that is exactly what many lawyers can do, If Mr. Smith read the *Passport Report* he might do it himself, for free! Either way, Mr. Smith, now, whenever he leaves Arrestia stops at his safe deposit box, just across the border. He deposits his A passport. Then, like Superman, he switches passports, thus changing identity to (for instance) "Sherlock Homes Acourt, Earl of Freedomia". The noble title is of course an optional extra, and for low profile purposes is definitely not recommended!

If Sherlock Homes Acourt, also known as Mr. Smith of Arrestia is a PT, he probably never visits either Arrestia or Freedomia with his new Freedomia passport. He keeps the two identities completely separate. When back in Arrestia for rare visits, Sherlock Holmes Acourt doesn't exist, at least not on any Arrestian computer. If any Arrestian spy should ever learn that someone named Sherlock has an account at the Terribly Secret Bank and Trust Company of Liechtenstein, the Arrestian investigator will ignore it. What does he care if some citizen of Freedomia has a secret account. Everyone knows that the Freedomia government is a bunch of anarchists who don't tie up their citizens with the heavy Arrestian ball and chain of taxes on worldwide income, currency restrictions, and long jail sentences for almost everything. (For those readers who haven't figured it out, Freedomia is every country in the world except the "Socialist Republics" and the Union of Socialist Arrestia – USA).

Getting back to Smith and his new passport, what has he accomplished? Smith has a new identity. With it he can judgment-proof his assets and do things that have no connection with Mr. Smith of Arrestia. He can even do things that are legal everywhere else, but might be slightly illegal in the eyes of the despots of Arrestia. Even if those dastardly secret snooper agents of Arrestia (planted in Swiss banks etc.) should intercept a communication or letter regarding "Sherlock Holmes Acourt" there would be no connection between Sherlock and Smith – unless Smith sent out a communication direct from Arrestia in his alias; or blabbed about his new arrangements.

As a dual Arrestian-Freedomian, it is possible that many countries would accept Smith as a tourist (without requiring a visa) or resident just because he was a citizen (and/or noble) of Freedomia. In any event, with two passports to choose from, he can usually travel or immigrate more easily in an emergency than most people. If you read *PT* or the *Passport Report* you know why having a second passport is such a good idea. The concept of a **Banking Passport** is simply that for a one-time expense and/or effort, one can become a "new person". This separates one from activities or assets best kept confidential.

# Chapter 7

# HOW AND WHY TO AVOID USING CHECKS

Whereas cash is virtually untraceable, checks provide investigating authorities with perhaps the most complete set of opportunities for finding out who paid what to whom, when – and, by asking around, perhaps also why.

Both the face and back of any cleared check is stored for posterity on microfilm, giving away the following information to those who may care to look:

Name and location of issuing bank,

account number on which check was drawn,

issuing date,

amount,

more often than not to whom the check was originally made out and

a nice copy of the signature of the account owner.

The back of the check will likewise show the signature of whoever cashed or deposited the check plus, if applicable, the signature of the original recipient of the check who later endorsed it and, lastly, either number of the ID (driver's license, passport) used to cash the check or the number of the account to which the check was deposited.

Now isn't that nice! If you write a check on an account later established to be owned by you, not only may any remaining funds in the account be seized, liened or attached but microfilm copies of all checks ever drawn on the account may be easily procured and investigated.

This is why, if you do not wish anyone to know where you live, you should *never* use a check to pay your rent – not even once! If the account is ever discovered to be connected to you then the police, tax authorities or a private investigator will have a direct lead to your landlord and, through him, to your physical whereabouts. Reversely, anyone receiving a check from you may opt to make a photocopy of it before depositing it and will in this fashion retain information about your bank account. If you use a check to make the first few instalments on, say, rent or a loan that you later fail to keep up, the clever creditor or landlord will be in a position to furnish a court with all the information that is necessary to freeze or seize your account and everything in it. If you pay for a maildrop by check, you have totally blown your cover.

To further elaborate on the problems this may cause you, suppose you are in another country and pay something by a check drawn on an account which, unbeknown to you, has been frozen in your absence. As a foreigner, you will most likely have to show your passport for the check to be accepted and your passport number will be noted on the back. When the check later turns out to be bad, the person on the receiving end of the bum check will be in a position to give local authorities your passport number – which may result in your being apprehended at the airport the next time you either enter or leave the country (the latter provided that computer checks are made of passport numbers on departing that country).

Now, you may not wish to live without checks although it is perfectly possible and much safer. But take all relevant precautions. You should fully realize that whenever you write a check, you implicitly give anyone in a position to investigate either your own account or that belonging to the recipient of the check, a veritable carte blanche to pursue the connection between you and him very thoroughly. The worst part of it is that it may not even be you yourself who needs to make a mistake – someone else may make the mistake for you, opening a Pandora's box of grief for you. Let us say, for instance, that you pay a lawyer for services rendered – by check. Unfortunately, the lawyer turns out to be crooked and in cahoots with parts of the underworld. Investigators poring over his financial records and bank accounts notice that you made a payment to their suspect (or defendant). This, in turn, may lead to your phone being tapped and your mail intercepted and examined to see if you, too, are a Mafioso.

## OUR SECRET: SOME CHECKS HAVE NO NEGATIVES

On the upside, however, you may still use checks to move money from A to B without a record of use to anyone being created by this. One example is that you may move money into a secret, offshore bank account a lot easier than going there in person by sending checks to the bank – as long as you use **cashier's checks** that you have obtained without disclosing your identity or presenting any ID whatsoever. One enterprising young man (who shall remain nameless) owns and operates a small chain of electronics stores in, well, a country somewhere in the Western hemisphere. He is able to save quite a bit of cash from the turnover of his business. This not only saves him a bundle on taxes but also makes his business seem "a-bit-less-lucrative-than-average". Thus it does not inspire the envy of his labor union employees and his local tax assessors.

Not being stupid, he does not keep the skimmed-off proceeds under his mattress nor in a bank in his own country. Instead, he maintains an ever-growing account with a bank in a country with strict bank secrecy laws. And about once a month, he travels a few hundred miles around his own country, walking into various banks and purchasing cashier's checks made out to a fictional person with a common name. He has one piece of ID to support this name, to be used only if absolutely necessary. This shows him to be a foreigner, resident in a very respectable (non-South American) country. He then endorses these checks twice, first with an indecipherable signature, then with his own and mails them to his bank which happily credits his account. In an attempt to throw anyone off the trail who might later claim that he has made both endorsements himself, he makes the first endorsement in black ink, using a fountain pen – and the second one, "his own" (the one his bankers will recognize, anyway), in blue with an ordinary, cheap ballpoint-pen. Reason: it is harder to compare two different signatures to see if they were by the same person if they have been made using writing instruments that differ in nature. Depending on the grip of the owner, the tip of a fountain pen takes on a certain angle with prolonged use by the same person (this is why you should never lend your expensive fountain pen to anyone lest the tip gets ruined) affecting the calligraphic characteristics of the writing. A ballpoint pen does not change its characteristics, regardless of who uses it.

This almost effortless exercise works to ensure that no record is maintained at the bank he uses for his business and private affairs to the effect that he has moved money out of the country. A number of banks in different cities in the same country will merely have microfilm copies of small checks made out to a Mr. This-And-That (This-And-That being a very common name in said country) that have later been cashed in a different country. The amounts are small – less than US $1,000 per check. Sounds like too little? It is not. Spend perhaps two or three hours walking into ten different banks with a wad of cash and the net result is cashier's checks worth a total of US $10,000. Do that once a month and the annual total comes to US $120,000. Or once a week for one year and you end up with a respectable US $520,000 moved anonymously, without a record of who bought the checks. Not as fast nor as good as going there in person – but cheaper. The only additional expense being a few buck's worth of envelopes and stamps.

An added bonus is that the exchange rate on a cashier's check is much closer to the "true" exchange rate than you will get for cash. You should routinely expect to be stiffed anywhere from 2 per cent to a whopping 7 per cent on small amounts of cash, calculating the span between what banks will offer you for cash as opposed to checks.

The trick for you now, of course, is to find out whether and where you can buy cashier's checks without having to present some sort of identification. Banking laws differ between countries and even within the same country, individual branches may have varying policies – sometimes even depending on whether the cashier is aware of any local, legal requirement that he ask to see some ID.

You may try this out for yourself the next time you have to renew a magazine subscription, repay a small loan to a friend or similar. Walk into any bank and ask to buy a cashier's check. See what they say. If you wish, you may do so at your "own" bank. If then asked whether you are a customer, you may truthfully answer "yes", then inquire subtly about the bank's policy. Will it make out cashier's checks to non-customers and, if so, on what conditions. "Is it legal or possible to buy a cashier's check without showing any ID?" and so forth. Work the angles and try different banks to find out the full range of opportunities open to you, the best being to buy a bank draft payable in the country of your bank in the currency you need, without being a customer and without showing any ID whatsoever. Also probe the limits to see exactly how big a check you can get at any one time without being a customer and with no ID. If you are going to move very large amounts of money, it is advisable to buy cashier's checks in a different city or even part of the country to minimize the risk of being recognized later (especially if you are a local hero or otherwise well-known). You do not need gossip from a bored bank clerk to her brother-in-law tax collector to set the IRS or the Inland Revenue on your trail.

*OUR BEST TIP: Use the American Express Bank or the American Express office in your country. Nearly every country has a branch. There, you can buy US-dollar cashier's checks and money orders. Each carries an upper limit of $200, so you may have to buy several (which is allowed and perfectly normal). None requires showing of any ID whatsoever, although this may change in the years to come.*

A couple of extra notes on checks – be they regular or cashier's. First of all, limit your own use of checks (save those darling cashier's checks – if you can find a way of buying them without showing any ID) and set it as a goal to cut all the way down to zero as soon as possible. Second, make sure that you – personally – have put yourself in a position to take advantage of the information offered to you on a silver platter by anyone paying *you* by check. As previously discussed you should take a photocopy of any check you receive before depositing it (except, of course, if you receive an awful lot of teeny-weeny little checks in the mail in response to a mail offer of some very cheap item.

# CLEARING TIME: HOW YOU CAN MAKE MORE MONEY SPECULATING AGAINST INTEREST RATES

Find out exactly how long it takes various types of checks to clear once you have deposited them and *also* exactly how much water has to flow under the bridge, so to speak, before your bank can no longer debit your account if the check bounces or turns out to be a fake.

Bank policies vary immensely from country to country, but here is a (very) rough guideline to how long it takes for a check to clear in most civilized (and computerized) countries:

| | |
|---|---|
| Personal check, same country (or state) | 1 to 3 days |
| Personal check, foreign origin, local currency | 8 to 10 days |
| Personal check, foreign origin, foreign currency | 2 to 3 weeks |
| Cashier's check, same country (or state) | same day |
| Cashier's check, foreign origin, local currency | about 3 days |
| Cashier's check, foreign origin, foreign currency | about one week |

The reason for the discrepancy between the clearing time for a personal and a cashier's check is, of course, that cashier's checks are considered a lot "safer" by banks. An individual or even a company may not think twice about passing bad checks, given sufficiently tight circumstances, whereas manufacturing and passing a bogus (fake) *cashier's check* is not only considered fraudulent – it is also classified as forgery and carries severe penalties for the perpetrator, if caught.

If you are (or expect to be) on the receiving end of a lot of checks you should huddle down with your bank liaison officer and get the low-down on local bank regulations and policies concerning clearing periods etc.

When you have taken a photocopy of a check you've received, file it in a place where you won't forget about it. If you are constantly on the move it may even pay to use a hand-held scanner and store an image of the check in the memory of a portable computer that you take with you on the road. The reason, if you call home to "touch base" with the office and learn that an important check has bounced, you will be able to take personal charge of the matter immediately with the image of the check on the screen before you. Unless you know that it's unadvisable to get too heavy-handed with the bum check artist (and, thus, prefer to coax him into paying up willingly) you may then immediately get in touch with your lawyer or even the police if need be.

If you learn about a check having bounced on you while on an extended stay abroad there are still things you can do: call up the customer's bank, for instance (or just threaten him with doing so) to ask whether there is any chance that the check might be honored if presented once more. In certain cases a delay of just a couple of days may mean that the account is totally depleted – but if you act immediately and decisively you (or your lawyer) may have the account frozen, sometimes overnight, and at least get whatever is left in the account even if it is not the full amount you've been stiffed on. At any rate, when stuck with a bad check it is definitely not the time to play Mr. Nice Guy. Rather, hit the perpetrator with the legal and financial equivalents of "the wrath of Gods". It may not win you a lot of friends but, then, friends are not what you are in business to make.

Lastly: if you truly have little reason to fear that your government (or anyone else) will ever subject your finances to scrutiny (as may be the case if, for instance, you live in a tax-haven) then you may find it more expedient to pay various bills by mailing a check. It may even be safe to do so if you have otherwise guarded yourself thoroughly against government intrusion on your privacy – such as, for instance, if you officially live in one country while in reality living and pretending to be a tourist in a second. There *are* legitimate and semi-safe uses for checks even if you are playing cat-and-mouse with the tax-collecting filth in your home country, **as long as you do not keep your main stash in a bank that can be linked in any way to your checking account.**

If you still want to simplify your life a bit by using checks, and if you have other safeguards in place, you might as well go the whole hog and get a checking account which allows you to write checks in any currency but still using only one checkbook. Many offshore banks in tax-havens like Andorra and the Isle of Man offer checkbooks to their customers **with no currency printed on the checks.** That's right. A typical offshore check will read "pay ........... , to ............ " and all you have to do is fill in the blanks – including the currency! The account itself, of course, will have to be maintained in one currency or another and usually this may be just about any one you want: US dollars, British pounds sterling or Japanese yen. This greatly simplifies your life if you need to pay bills in different currencies. Pay your subscription to *The Economist* by sending a check made out in pounds sterling, pay your subscription to *Cambio 16* in Spanish pesetas and your grocery bill in the local currency, whatever that may be.

When your bank gets your check from whomever received it, they will then simply convert, e.g. a check made out in Saudi Arabian Riyals will be calculated to its pound sterling equivalent before your account is debited. Such is the service extended by many offshore banks to customers like ourselves with neither title, fortune nor fame. But, again, do not keep too much moolah in any checking account – you never know who may get a peek at it.

*A NOTE OF CAUTION: All checks made out in US dollars eventually will be cleared through an American bank. If you entertain serious, well-founded fears that you may become the subject of harassment from the United States government, for any reason whatsoever, refuse to write out or accept checks in dollars. If you are in such a situation and still have to pay bills made out in dollars, either use cashier's (anonymously obtained or not at all!) or convert the amount into another, major currency. Do not forget to add the expected converting charges that the recipient may otherwise have to pick up. The USA recently has blocked the dollar accounts of foreign banks when it was established that one of the customers of the foreign bank was involved in an activity the USA considered illegal. if you are in a battle with the USA, to be safe, never keep so much as a dollar in a dollar account.*

## Chapter 8

# THE CREDIT CARD BATTLE
# FOR MORE PRIVACY

Credit cards offer the greatest risks to those in search of financial privacy.

The last of the three "major" money tools are credit cards. As with checks, you leave a number of traces behind for any detective (amateur sleuth or professional) to find when paying by plastic. These traces are the number of your credit card, expiry date, year of first card issued, the amount charged and where you used it. This, in turn, enables an investigator to not only track down the issuer of the credit card but also to obtain a copy of your card application (card applications are usually kept on file for five years, but don't count on such a short period. Your application may be kept forever or until the account is closed). Such an application contains all information that you were required to give before the card was issued to you, usually *at least* billing and home addresses, phone number (if any), employer (or name and address of business if self-employed). Also on file will be any change of information subsequently given such as change of billing address *plus*, possibly, a copy of any credit reports taken out on you by the card company. Information about everything that you have ever charged to a credit card is readily available from copies of past account statements. These may be used to piece together a picture of your movements, be it around the world or merely in your own country. A charge for gasoline in one city followed by another charge for gasoline and a hotel room in a second city will tell people that you drove from A to B – and also where A and B were. Depending on how and where you have used a card this information may tell a lot about you – your favorite restaurants and night clubs, what kind of magazines you subscribe to, stores that you frequent (including sex shops, escort agencies and the like), catalogs that you have ordered from etc. If you order by credit card after seeing an advertisement, a file may even be created showing in which issue of which magazine you saw the ad even if you do not explicitly state this to the phone operator. You may be asked to quote a reference number in the ad (unique to one issue of a particular magazine) or even because different phone numbers are given in all advertisements, telling the operator where the ad was seen before she even answers the phone. Keep that in mind if you have magazines mailed to your home address using a credit card can lead an investigator to you.

From this, you may realize that someone investigating you (and this may also be your bank evaluating whether your card should be extended for another period) will be able to deduce an awful lot of knowledge about you and your habits. You should assume that anything you ever charge to a credit card may, sooner or later, become as good as public knowledge and totally unconcealable. Therefore, do not use a credit card to order or pay for any goods or services that you wish to keep a secret. If you use a credit card to pay an escort girl agency, for instance, it may not show up on your statement as "Pussy Galore Escorts, Lausanne, Switzerland" but rather as "PG S.A., Lausanne, Switzerland". Working girls know that an uncompromised customer is a repeat customer. But then, an only slightly more thorough check will reveal just what the incurred charge went to cover.

## SHOP THE WORLD FOR HARD-TO-FIND PT ITEMS

On the other hand, credit cards are great for making long-distance purchases without having to write out and mail a check and wait for it to clear. You do not have to physically present your card in order to charge something to it. You may call up a travel agent or an airline and have a ticket mailed to you (or waiting for you at the airport) in a couple of minutes. If you need to buy something which is not available in your area or country, you may call up and have it sent to you just by quoting your card number. In the United States there are even specialized services that offer to locate just about any product not yet (or at all) available in Europe or elsewhere, buy it and ship it to you – and you may pay by credit card. Two of them are: SLEUTH USA, phone (+1) 410 992 5451 and "My American Connection", P.O. Box 22373, Cleveland, Ohio 44122, USA, phone (+1) 216 991 5565, fax (+1) 216 447 0933.

If in need of almost anything from England, the famous department store Harrods also takes credit card orders on (+44) 71 730 1234 – orders are taken around the clock (answering machine outside business hours). And, of course, you may send flowers by credit card anywhere in the world using the international Inter-Flora chain by phoning its British office on (+44) 529 304 545 (during regular business hours, 9 a.m.to 5 p.m.)

That said, be aware that this "easy ordering" is not possible in all countries. Some countries allow the use of credit cards only when they are presented in person. In some Scandinavian countries, for instance, it is actually *illegal* for businesses to let a customer charge something by giving his credit card number over the phone, by fax or even by a signed letter or response card. If you are a habitual credit card user then remember that things do not work the same way everywhere. Do not underestimate the importance of the discrepancies between countries in terms of which cards are accepted for what, how and under what conditions. Credit cards may have been big in the United States for a couple of decades but have only recently started to come into vogue in countries like Germany, for instance. In some countries, such as France, you may pay for everything, from gasoline to a Big Mac at McDonald's with your VISA-card but next to nothing with American Express. In other places, such as Switzerland, people will welcome a Mastercard but think you are a poor risk if you can't do better than Diners Club. The solution – cover your bases by having several different credit cards – and cash in the local currency as a backup.

Would you rather pay cash, then? You may use your credit card to get quick cash in the dead of night from an ATM (automated teller machine) – provided that you can find one that accepts your card. This may not be as easy as you think. In some countries, ATMs are only in place for certain kinds of cards. If you do not have the whole wide range of international credit cards on your person, you may be in for a rude surprise when it turns out that there is nowhere you may get cash with the particular kind of card you are carrying. Credit card companies and banks usually have small booklets listing the possible uses – or lack of same – in various countries. If you are going to a country for the first time you will be wise to check out the local situation, credit card-wise, *in advance* or you may find yourself wasting an inordinate amount of time.

## CREDIT CARDS: YOUR COLLECTION

A quick rundown of "major" credit cards and what they have going for them:

AMERICAN EXPRESS. Generally regarded as the most prestigious of cards (especially in the "Gold" and "Platinum" versions), AMEX is highly useful in North America but has a very, very long way to go in terms of being useful in stores and ATMs in most of Europe because of the higher percentages they make the businesses pay.

DINERS CLUB. Widely accepted in most of Europe, it is less-than-perfect in the United States. In the big eastern cities (New York, Washington) you may be able to scrape by with it but in the central and western states it is almost unknown and, thus, fairly useless.

VISA: The "most widely accepted" credit card, worldwide with millions of affiliated businesses and thousands of ATM-machines. Few stores that honor other credit cards do not also accept Visa. Also comes in a "gold" version known as "Visa Premier" or "Visa Preferred".

MASTERCARD: Not especially widespread outside the United States, it is often (but not always) accepted by businesses that also honor Visa, Eurocard and the lesser Access and JCB cards.

EUROCARD: Most European-issued Eurocards carry an additional Mastercard stamp, making the card acceptable wherever you find "Mastercard spoken" signs (and vice versa).

ACCESS (in Britain), JCB (Japan) and DISCOVER (USA) aspire to major league status, but have a way to travel.

On the subject of availability of ATMs you may find yourself confronted with misleading information when inquiring. If you ask a gas station attendant in Austria, for instance, whether there is anywhere you can get cash with your Visa card, he may nod happily and tell you "yes, yes, yes". Whereupon you may waste hours discovering that "yes", you can – but in banks – *some* banks, even – and only when they are open. As of this writing there is not one single ATM for Visa cards in Austria, same in the Netherlands. So if you inquire locally, be specific and make sure that people understand exactly what it is that your are asking about – show them the card, if need be. Be prepared to get a funny look if you ask about how to get cash with a piece of plastic in places like Germany. Traditionally very conservative in terms of plastic in general and credit in particular, people in Deutschland may shake their heads at this spectacular spendthrift idiot – **you** – who is asking about how to get "cash on credit!". If everything else fails, ask at a large, international hotel where concierges and receptionists generally know all there is to know locally about the subject. As a last resort, try asking at a change office – look for the signs announcing "Change – Cambio – Exchange – Wechsel". But again, it is preferable to make these inquiries *before* you depart rather than wind up trudging sullenly through the streets of St Moritz looking, searching . . .

As long as you keep in mind the inherent drawbacks of credit cards in terms of privacy and use them wisely, it is also crucial that you know the basics about *how* and *where* you go about obtaining one – and about the distinctions between various types of plastic, even those that carry the same "brand name". If you do not presently have any credit cards you may as well get the right kind – and the right way – while you are at it (chances are, sooner or later you'll need 'em). And if you already have one or more credit cards you may still benefit from either supplementing your collection – or switching one kind e.g. Visa with another and better version. Remember: credit cards are nothing but tools – and the better tools you use, the better the results are likely to be, in terms of privacy, freedom and lack of traceability.

With a major credit card such as American Express, Mastercard or Visa, most doors of the world spring open at your command. Those same doors remain forever closed if you are unable to produce a "major" piece of plastic.

Ever tried renting a car without a major credit card? In most places, this is an exercise in complete and utter futility. Even if you offer to plunk down a cash deposit of, say, £1,000, the young fellow behind the Budget Rent-A-Car counter will look quizzically at you if you shake your head solemnly when asked for your credit card. Nineteen out of 20 times, chances are that you will be turned down for even a one-day rental! This is especially true in some American states. In Europe and Asia, you should still be able to rent a smaller car with either a cash deposit or – even better – a voucher from your travel agency. Usually the voucher is prepaid.

When renting luxury cars (such as Maserati, Porsches, Jaguars and upwards), two credit cards are normally required.

Major credit cards are usually issued by banks and getting one used to be a relatively straightforward job where you would merely have to go through the motions: fill out a form, mail it to the bank or the card company. A rectangular piece of plastic would arrive in the mail a week or two later.

During the last few years, however, demands made in many countries on new applicants and in certain cases even for existing cardholders have been tightened considerably.

This is due to the unfortunate fact that banks and credit card companies alike have taken huge losses in the late Eighties and early Nineties due to an increasing number of delinquent accounts – in other words, some deadbeat card holders ran up enormous charges and overdue interest on cards during the mid- and late Eighties. When the recession hit, Amex took a hit as poor, dejected unemployed yuppies declined to keep on paying the monthly instalments.

Consequently, you now need to put in a lot more time and effort in order to qualify for a major credit card than that of merely filling out a form, ''moisten the edges, seal and mail''. Your credit-worthiness is really checked these days.

Generally speaking, most banks today require that an account is maintained in a proper and orderly fashion for at least three months and more often up to six or even twelve months before they will merely start to think about accepting your application.

Individuals with no visible means of support such as a steady job with a monthly salary being transferred to their account from an employer are having an increasingly hard time when engaging in the great plastic chase.

To make matters worse, even banks in tax havens have taken to using big, international credit agencies such as TRW to screen out irresponsible deadbeats and potential fraudsters. Details about thousands of mail accommodation addresses worldwide have been fed into computer databases, and a ''Hawk Alert'' is flashed on the screen if the address on your application (which must be the same as that of your account) is not your actual place of residence but just a maildrop. Be so advised, or you may find that months of preparation and nurturing of an account may turn out to be a total waste.

As always, a contraction in the number of suppliers of a commodity will eventually spur competition in the form of small companies to come up with creative solutions. In the case of credit cards, new options are emerging for the people who do not fit into the increasingly restrictive mould for being ''eligible'' for a major credit card.

## THE SECRET CREDIT CARDS

Several American corporations offer ''instant'' credit cards to all comers. Even a credit history resembling the financial equivalent of a Stephen King novel, or no credit history at all, is no impediment. Owe a cool £20,000 on your Barclaycard? Declared bankruptcy recently? Your company is in receivership or under chapter 11? Landlord says that eviction proceedings are imminent?

No problem: just say the word and regardless of your financial standing they will issue you with a new and shiny credit card – VISA, Mastercard or sometimes Diners Club. Even Gold Mastercards and gold VISA cards (Visa Premier) are available on request and are delivered immediately – you do not have to cultivate your account and pay your bills on time for a couple of years before being told that you are ''considered potentially eligible'' to go for the Gold.

Most of these companies require that you live in the USA. If you don't, this can be accomplished by obtaining a USA maildrop. Everything can be done by mail and there is no need to show up in person.

The information requested to OK your application is, to say the least, scant. Normally, a credit card application form is bursting with little boxes for you to fill out – name, address, employer, salary, previous addresses within the past five years etc *ad nauseam*. And, as you will do well to remember, all that information is readily available to authorities even years from now.

In comparison, for secured credit cards only three questions have to be answered : Name, address and desired type of card. No phone number, no references, no information about your employer, occupation or type of business.

Obviously, these companies are not run by a bunch of philantrophists with money to burn on people unwilling or unable to procure a credit card in the good, old-fashioned way by investing time in getting on a first-name basis with his or her friendly, personal banker. This should come as no surprise, considering the risk inherent in extending credit to anyone without first obtaining thorough knowledge of the character and financial standing of the individual in question.

Are the cards one may obtain on an "instant" basis the same as the ones available through ordinary channels? Yes – and no. There are, in fact, not only different "brand names" to choose from – but even cards carrying the same name may differ in nature. Many bankers are unaware of the distinctions, so perhaps some clarification is in order. Strictly speaking, a major credit card such as VISA comes in three varieties – even if most banks and card companies offer only one or two of them:

1) A **"credit, credit card"**. With an old-fashioned credit card, you charge to your heart's content and receive a bill at the end of the month. The credit card company hopes that you will eventually pay off the balance. In other words, the card company trusts you to pay.

2) A **"debit, credit card"**. Almost as tricky to get these days as the good old "credit, credit card", a debit card is directly tied to a bank account. Whatever charges the user runs up are debited to the bank account, and monthly account statements do not carry a remittance slip. The same account may have a checkbook tied to it as well. Credit as such, however, is not extended since you are not allowed to use the card in case the balance on the bank account wanders into the red.

3) A **"secured credit card"**. Here, there are two accounts : a frozen bank account the funds in which act as a guarantee for the card – and the actual credit card account. Statements are mailed only in the months when something is charged to the account, unless the balance for the preceeding month has yet to be paid off in full. But you are still obliged to make a minimum monthly payment of 10 per cent of the outstanding balance within a couple of weeks from receiving your statement.

Just as a card may be of the "credit, debit or secured" variety, there are different sorts of limits to how much one may charge on it. On an old-fashioned credit card, you are issued with a revolving line of credit and you may either pay off the balance in full every month or make a remittance of at least 10 per cent. If the balance is not paid off in full, a high interest rate (upwards of 18 per cent per annum or more) is levied on any balance left outstanding.

On a debit card, there is no line of credit. You may charge whatever you like, but the balance on the bank account to which the card is tied has to be kept in "credit" – in the black – at all times. In other words, letting the balance slip into debit constitutes an expensive and possibly even illegal overdraft.

On a secured credit card, you *also* have a revolving line of credit (just as with a "real" credit card) but this can never exceed a certain percentage of the balance on the frozen bank account needed to obtain the card. However, you still have the option of not paying off the balance in full every month and incur interest rates that approach usury – just like with a "credit, credit card". The balance on the frozen bank account remains unchanged (except for interest that is eventually earned on it) unless you fail to pay your bills and the credit card is revoked. If that happens, the funds in the frozen account are applied towards the oustanding balance on the credit card account.

Since "credit, credit cards" and debit cards alike are issued subject to a number of requirements that must be met, including spending some time maintaining a regular bank account with the issuing bank or otherwise building up a good credit rating, a secured credit card is the easiest, fastest way to have a VISA, Mastercard or Diners Club card issued in your name. Only essential questions (name and address and desired type of card) are asked and a bare minimum of two requirements must be met (furnishing a notarized photocopy of the first two pages of your passport and providing the funds to go in a frozen bank account to secure the card). But absolutely no credit check is made.

So what kind of cash do you have to come up with for the frozen bank account in order to be issued with a secured credit card? We recently investigated one of the more typical operations. For a regular Mastercard, VISA or Diners Club card, you need to put at least US $1,500 in the frozen account. For a Gold Mastercard or a VISA Premier, the figure is US $6,000. This provides sufficient guarantee for the card to be issued, with no credit check whatsoever.

As far as credit limit goes, this is directly tied to whatever you put in the frozen bank account – of course, you may increase your own credit limit by depositing more funds in this account. You are not able to withdraw funds from the frozen bank account or use it to pay down the balance on your card account – but if the card is cancelled by yourself or the card company for any reason, the credit card balance is debited to the frozen account and remaining funds, if any, are returned to you in full.

The credit limits for the cards are as follows: for a standard, no-frills card the limit is 80 per cent of the balance in the frozen account – that is, US $1,500 (the minimum) in the frozen account gives you a credit limit of US $1,200.

For a Gold Mastercard or a VISA Premier, the corresponding figures are 83.33 per cent – that is, US $6,000 in the frozen account gives you a credit limit on the card of US $5,000.

Secured credit cards have been popular for years in the United States among people who cannot, for some reason, qualify for a regular credit card or a debit card. This owes in part to the American obsession with credit histories – elaborate point systems have been put into place by banks and card companies, making it all but impossible to obtain anything but a secured credit card if the applicant gives the wrong type of answers to questions such as "employed or self-employed", "married or single", "previous addresses with the past five years", "have you ever declared personal bankruptcy", "annual salary", "company position" etc.

Individuals without any credit history at all, such as people who have lived their lives on the otherwise recommended "cash basis", have been turned down for credit cards and debit cards in droves. Since the United States is a pretty miserable place to live in if you carry no kind of plastic whatsoever, the obvious solution is to get one or more secured credit cards.

So how to get one? For a fee, each company processes your card application. As long as the funds for the frozen bank account are forthcoming and a name and address furnished, the application is guaranteed not to be turned down. The success rate in obtaining a card for clients providing these details is not 90 per cent, 95 per cent or even 99 per cent – but 100 per cent, period. This makes it a bit of a joke referring to the papers you have to fill out as an *application* – "order form" would be more precise. The fees charged for processing an application are usually in the US $100 to US $500 region. If asked for more, you may be dealing with a con man.

This, of course, if the biggest risk of all.

Unfortunately, some companies in this business are out-and-out frauds taking advantage of people's need for financial privacy or taking advance of someone else's bad credit history. Behind several small classified ads have lurked fly-by-night operations. Usually, these are operated by a fraudster who takes your security deposit and runs. With each client paying in several thousand dollars, this can be a profitable business. The last such caper pulled off was by ICC, International Card Corporation, supposedly a subsidiary of Wellington Capital Trust. This later turned out to be a fictitious entity, non-existent and not registered anywhere. The man behind the fraud, a "Hunter B Andrews" in Costa Rica, disappeared as fast as he came into being. This person is not in Costa Rica anymore, but is carrying on with this very same flim-flam using a different name, a different company and a different address in a different country. For the latest report on reputable and disreputable companies and how best to deal with them, write to Inter-Europäische (attn Julie Terrell), P.O. Box 2462, CH-1002 Lausanne, Switzerland. Enclose a $50-note or £30 cash and ask for their latest printout of Report #7, "Secured Credit Cards". This report is updated twice monthly and goes into greater detail than this chapter. Several well-heeded warnings are listed as well as addresses and price comparisons. It spans not just the USA but other countries as well, with a chapter on working with more than one country at the same time. Also, a special chapter is devoted to showing you how you can obtain secured credit cards without putting up a penny in security. When ordering, ask for a list of other reports as well. Several are quite interesting and within the scope of this book.

What you need to consider is this: *Whether* you need a major credit card, be it in the form of a "real-credit", "debit" or "secured" rectangular piece of plastic – and, if so, *which* of these to get – and *how* to go about using and obtaining it. From a privacy point of view, the very best cards are obviously the above-mentioned ''secured'' cards, as you have to give an absolute bare minimum of information to get them – *if*, that is, you decide that you want any plastic at all. Do you? Consider the following example:

An acquaintance of ours, a budding young entrepreneur from Hampstead, London, recently got a call from an business associate in the US, informing him that a deal he had been negotiating for months was finally ready to be closed. Could he fly out to sign the contract? Fly into Kennedy, stay in Manhattan and drive out to New Jersey the next morning? Sure, no problem . . . Packing a bag in a jiffy, he headed to Heathrow and plunked down cash for a ticket on a British Airways flight to JFK, New York. Nothing to it, airlines will gladly accept cash – in Europe, anyway, they do. Still.

Once safely landed in New York, he went straight to the Avis desk to rent a car. ''No credit card? Sorry Sir, we need a major credit card for deposit.'' After checking with every single rental company in the terminal, he went back to Avis. Would it be possible to rent a car from another Avis location without a credit card? ''Not anywhere in New York State, sorry, Sir'' Outside of New York State, then? It turned out that the closest place to rent a car without a credit card was in Hartford, Connecticut – about 100 miles north of New York City.

As all planes to Bradley Airport in Hartford were booked solid for the rest of the day, he wound up spending three hours and US $30 on an uncomfortable bus going to the Bus Terminal in central Hartford, from whence a taxi took him to the Avis counter at Bradley. To rent the car, he had to not only prepay for three days rental and fork over US $500 deposit – he also had to leave his return ticket to London behind, to be collected when the car was returned. By then it was rush hour, and the trip back to Manhattan took a good four hours. The hotel, too, required prepayment plus a several hundred dollar deposit.

Once the contract was signed, it was another four hour drive back up north to Hartford – drop the car off and pay US $90 for a one-way ticket on the American Eagle shuttle to Kennedy.

The mere fact that he did not possess either a credit card, a debit card or even a secured credit card wound up costing him almost one full day of driving back and forth – plus about US $300 in bus and plane tickets, additional mileage on the rental car, gasoline and so forth. Golden Credit Card Rule number one: Get the plastic *before* you need it.

One thing you should keep in mind when deciding on the type of card you want is that there is a problem with ''credit, credit cards'' and debit cards: they are issued on faith – that is, they are issued because your credit rating is found to be sufficient to warrant issuing the applicant with a card.

But just as nuptial vows are often broken, faith may be revoked. Credit card companies do not stop checking the financial standing of their clients after issuing the card. When renewal time comes around, the companies will routinely review the account and obtain an updated credit report – and if new and less savoury details show up, not only is a card not renewed but the existing card may even be revoked prior to the expiry date printed on the card. Written notices are not given on this, but the files are quietly altered so that any merchant checking the card will be asked to confiscate the card immediately.

Horror stories abound. An especially unlucky Spanish entrepreneur found his ''favorite'' credit card being revoked while he was away on holiday in a location where, as a cardholder for years, he carried almost no cash and relied almost exclusively on the card. Only luck and good fortune prevented him from being stranded thousands of miles from nowhere in the middle of a four week vacation, with £200 in cash and a return ticket to Madrid. Reason: the card company questioned his creditworthiness due to a recent string of cash advances.

A few months later, the same man had another card confiscated when attempting to pay for a business dinner. Reason: the card company had received a tender inquiry about the account from the Spanish tax authorities. Needless to say, the resulting loss of face with his business acquaintances eventually wound up costing him literally tens of thousands of pounds in lost profits.

What is most disquieting about this is the fact that in both cases, all monthly statements had been paid in full and on time for at least two years prior to the cards being revoked. But the mere shadow of doubt about the cardholder led to cards being revoked and in one case even confiscated without any attempt being made on the part of the credit card company to inform the customer in advance.

So unless you plan to live the rest of your life on Elm Street and never, ever leave suburbia, it is sheer foolishness to believe that you will at no time need a piece of plastic with a "major" name on it. Since it is hard to forecast anything (particularly the future), it makes a lot of sense to get at least two cards well before you actually need them. Without plastic, you can never claim to be very well prepared for harsh or inconvenient eventualities. For car rental, plane and hotel reservations a major card is all but indispensable. Even if obtaining an old-fashioned credit card or a debit card is no problem for you, you still ought to consider adding a secured credit card to your collection if privacy and peace of mind register anywhere on your list of priorities, as they rightly should.

If you do have an alternate identity and/or a banking passport, a driving license and matching credit card is almost essential to complete the package. The secured credit card is quite good and probably the only plastic you can get under this circumstance – a "new individual" being created, with no credit history, no job and no address. As a general rule, the new ID and credit card should be obtained abroad and never used in the home country.

# Chapter 9

# REVIEWED: OTHER MONEY TOOLS

Besides using the three "major" forms of money – cash, checks and credit cards – there are other means which you can use when you either need to pay a bill or to move funds from A to B. It is important to be aware of these additional possibilities. They may all be put to very good use as a supplement to the "majors".

You are probably aware of some of these already. But consider the following, then sit back and think whether perhaps changing your habits (and perceptions) just a bit may be a very efficient way of improving your privacy and enhancing your freedom.

## MONEY ORDERS

It is far from certain that you wish to use checks or credit cards at all to settle the bills and charges for a whole, wide range of goods and services. Especially if you are in the early stages of distancing yourself from the world at large in general and creditors and authorities in particular, it makes good sense to limit your reliance on cash and credit cards to pay for anything that may, ultimately, be connected to you.

Let us state, for instance, that you are contemplating moving from your home country because of ruinous taxes, pending litigation, a divorce battle, fears about a criminal case being built against you or anything similar. As far as the latter goes, let me yet again ever so gently remind you that the mere fact that something is called "criminal" by no means should be automatically taken to mean that it is a real "crime". A crime presupposes a victim, and a victim worthy of protection at that. An example is a cheating business partner who seeks to take over the business for himself by alleging that you are guilty of embezzlement in order to drive you out without paying – don't laugh or shrug it off, this is a very common tactic. Likewise, women seeking a divorce and child custody in the era of "no fault" commonly accuse their spouse of the crime of child abuse. To avoid imprisonment and disgrace, a speedy exit with your ass and assets intact may be called for.

In any event, you may need to purchase something without running the risk of anybody else finding out about it – perhaps this "something" is the ticket you need to get out of the situation gracefully. If you have even the tiniest inkling of suspicion that ominous forces will soon be snapping at your shins, this means that your bank and credit card accounts are under surveillance. It is always wise to assume that someone may be looking over your shoulder to get clues about your plans from watching what happens on your bank and credit card accounts.

Fred Familyman was about to be declared bankrupt. He wished to pay for the services of a mail drop where he could receive certain information in absolute privacy – for example, to receive personal mail without it being intercepted by the estate managers. Marvin Merrymoney needed the mail drop in order to receive balance statements relating to the offshore bank account he was about to open. You can surely think of many more examples yourself. The world is a place where a careful man is always doing better than his careless brother.

Now, all of these cases call for an absolutely dead-secret mail drop somewhere far, far away – in ''Neverland'', as it were. You want no one but yourself to find out about it. But since mail drops cost money, you have to come up with some. You do not want – or cannot – go in person. Sending a check will be a dead giveaway and cashier's checks may prove impossible to come by without showing ID when buying them – or altogether unavailable in your country, whatever. One solution is to walk into the nearest American Express office, same as with cashier's checks, and purchase a money order, then mail it to whomever you need to pay off. You do not need to show ID and the money order is made out on the spot. American Express money orders are available at a nominal charge in just about any country and are accepted for clearance by banks anywhere. US-based readers can also buy MOs from post offices or supermarkets and convenience stores. Not one single trace is left of the transaction. True, you will be asked for your name to be put on the money order when you buy it, but no ID of any kind is necessary. If, as in the case of our example with the mail drop, you use a name differing from your own, do not let the operator of the mail drop in on this little detail. Money orders are insured against loss if you keep the carbon copy.

A few years ago, one client used money orders galore. He was about to expatriate himself from the socialist worker's paradise of Sweden and was actively seeking information about how and where to open foreign bank accounts, how to get passports from other countries – precisely the sort of books that are not exactly easy to come by in a quasi-communist country.

In order to obtain this information, he first rented a mail drop in nearby Copenhagen, Denmark where he could receive mail in complete privacy and anonymity. Whenever he wished to order books with subjects ranging from passports to ''Swiss-bank-accounts-for-beginners'', he travelled to another city from the one in which he lived, went to the local American Express office, bought money orders in a make-believe name and mailed them to various publishers in England and the United States – giving his Danish maildrop address *in lieu* of his real one. And it really *did* turn out to be a very worthwhile precaution. He made it safely and passed the ''exodus-advice'' on to a friend who was having some problems with the local tax vultures. But his friend, unwisely and foolishly, did not go to such great lengths to guard himself against being found out. He freely ordered books and magazines of a freedom-loving nature, and paid by his Swedish-issued credit card over the phone. Planning to leave everything save his money behind, he made no obvious preparations to move his personal belongings – in short, there was no physical movement of furniture, hints to family and friends or anything else that might have tipped off the authorities. Two days before his planned expatriation, he was arrested and summarily charged with tax evasion and planning to flee the country. During his later trial (he was acquitted, but not before spending almost one year in jail ''on remand'') it was revealed that police and tax investigators had been monitoring both his bank and credit card accounts for over two years, looking for clues that might indicate that the man was, indeed, ''conspiring'' to leave the ''workers' paradise''. His arrest was arranged so that he wouldn't be tempted to leave a huge tax bill behind.

# INSTANT TRANSFERS: WESTERN UNION AND THOMAS COOK COMPETE

Both Western Union and Thomas Cook offer similar money transfers. It may take less than an hour to several days or even more than a week, depending on how much you are willing to pay for their services.

We have found Western Union to be best. It is big in the USA and is expanding its European net. It is located in the capitals of all EU-countries (and more) and is busy signing up banks, hotels, small storekeepers and other associates in all provinces.

Its charges are steep and there are limits on the amounts you can move. But head offices are open 24 hours a day and so are several of their associates/agents. This means that you can pay in or retrieve money around the clock.

For a transfer to work, however, a mere computer in the other end is not enough. You need somebody to actually go to Western Union in the sending country and pay in the sum you want to retrieve where you are . . . or vice versa. When Western Union national HQ (or Thomas Cook, if you are using its organization) is notified that the money has been deposited, it sends an OK to wherever you want to withdraw the transfer sum, then the money can be paid out, less charges. All very fast and efficient. You pay in cash, you take cash out at the other side of the world.

You can even get your money without showing ID. Werner Braun did this recently. He called up Western Union and told them he'd had his wallet and all his money plus credit cards stolen. Thus he didn't have any ID. He then arranged for a friend to transfer US $1,000 across borders via Western Union. It all took less than an hour. And instead of asking for Werner Braun's ID, the Western Union agent merely asked Werner "what is your mother's maiden name". This was a code agreed upon. Any code would have been sufficient. So for privacy and secrecy in financial transfers, these transactions seem hard to beat. The only disadvantage is that Western Union has rather stiff charges. One reader complains that a wire transfer of $250 to his son in Senegal, Africa, cost him $150!

## POSTAL MONEY ORDERS

At post offices in most countries, you can buy postal or giro money orders. These are either just post office to post office money orders or money orders exactly the same as "normal" MOs.

In addition, in the UK, a postal giro account holder can usually be supplied with *international giro checks*. Ask your post office giro bank for a promotional leaflet on these giro checks. **When travelling, you can walk into any European post office with checks from any other European post office and withdraw hundreds of pounds sterling – in local currency – with these instruments.** The operation is fast and payout is instant. There is no waiting to see if the account back in your home country actually has funds in it to cover the transaction. These international giro checks are the post office's answer to traveller's checks. You yourself write in the amount you want to withdraw (up to a preset maximum limit which differs from country to country). Anyone, even foreigners, can open postal giro accounts. In most countries, anyone can get the international checks, too. They are strictly personal to the account holder and cannot be transferred.

## TRAVELLER'S CHECKS

Almost everywhere when you travel, cash is preferred over traveller's checks. In most third world countries you can only cash traveller's checks at large international hotels and banks in the capital. Traveller's checks are fast becoming less and less attractive as commissions go up when cashing them. Often you end up paying far more than the original one per cent (when buying) for the safety that goes with these checks. Ask the exchange office what commission it deducts before signing your checks as there are some real rip-offs. The plus-side is that in most countries, traveller's checks are accepted at a slightly better rate than cash – though not, usually, at a rate as good as for other checks.

Thomas Cook traveller's checks are not recommended as Thomas Cook offices charge one per cent commission to cash their own checks! American Express offices charge no commission to cash their own travellers checks but Amex and Thomas Cook give exchange rates worse than banks. A cheeky sign posted at American Express offices worldwide reads: "There's no reason for it: *it's just our policy.*" If you are changing over US $20, you are usually better off going to a post office or bank and paying the standard one per cent or two per cent commission to cash checks there.

Keep a record of which checks you have cashed in case the remaining checks are stolen and you have to make a claim. To report stolen American Express traveller's checks, ring 273-571 600 in England (country code +44), reverse charges from anywhere or – if you can't reverse charges – quickly give your number and ask them to call you right back.

The Eurochecks – shortened EC – are related to traveller's checks but have the added advantage that you write in the amount you need and thus use them exactly like personal checks. With an EC card – similar to the British check guarantee card – you can use Eurochecks as an international, pre-guaranteed personal checkbook whenever you see the "EC"-symbol displayed. Disadvantages? Price and the fact that each new year you will have to start over again with a new set of checks in a new book. But they are very flexible and beat traveller's checks in many ways.

To get Eurochecks, you will need some sort of relationship with a bank. Thus, they do not offer much in the way of secrecy. They do leave a trace for anyone to follow "back home". Ordinary traveller's cheques, on the other hand, can be purchased by anyone walking in off the street. Only when cashing them will you have to show ID (normally, at least). Of course, Eurochecks obtained in a banking passport name, at a bank outside of your home country do offer a confidential way of dealing with money, if done carefully.

## WIRE TRANSFERS AND THE TRANSIT ACCOUNT

Moving money between countries by wire transfer is immensely useful, especially if the amounts in question are larger than what you would feel comfortable about carrying around on your person.

As with checks and credit cards, a wire transfer leaves a number of traces behind. Not only does the bank from which the transfer is initiated retain records of the transaction, but the bank on the receiving end will be able to dig up at short notice details about who ordered the transfer and from where, right down – in some cases – to the account number from whence the funds originated.

That said, you may simply have no other option than to make a wire transfer when paying for something. If conducting business abroad, for instance, even cashier's checks may take uncomfortably long to clear and cause costly delays. A wire transfer, on the other hand, is irrevocable and the party receiving the funds will normally feel confident about releasing goods for shipment as soon as he gets a call from his bank to the effect that the money is in his account.

Some ways exist to shield who made a wire transfer.

One of them is known as the "P-T" or "passthrough", commonly referred to as a transit account.

Here, the transfer is routed through several banks. At one or more points along the way, either the manager of the branch or an employee will act as "recipient" of the funds, legally signing his name to the account. Thus, if you need to put obstacles in the way of investigators, you would arrange for a "passthrough account" to be set up before wiring funds to it. It will cost a bit of money and may also necessitate that you go in person to wherever the bank in question is located to arrange the matter. Don't count on being able to do it from behind your desk.

Once the money has been wired from your bank account to the "passthrough account", you visit the receiving bank – or have a friend do the honors – and withdraw the funds, in cash. Whereupon you quite simply take the money – in cash – to another bank in the area, from which you will wire the funds to the ultimate destination.

You may do this fairly easily in countries with liberal banking regulations, but usually in the USA at least personal or one bank reference will be required to open the second account no matter where you go plus some valid ID, of course. Needless to say, this should not be the bank you enlisted for the "passthrough" account, unless you want to take the chance that they lead investigators to your new bank. Don't forget that banks *do* keep records not only of your account transactions but also of any enquiry ever made about you. Some – in fact, many – banks have been known to studiously keep *even Christmas cards* mailed to them by satisfied customers!

If you are moving large amounts of funds in this way you should be aware that it is likely to cause raised eyebrows when you walk into a bank where you are not known with a suitcase full of cash that you just collected from Bank Number One (the "passthrough account"). The degree of this interest will vary according to the jurisdiction in which you conduct such business, of course. In some countries, "large amounts" are anything above £5,000 and upwards, in cash! These countries tend to be the ones co-operating with the USA's so-called war on drugs. They are a party to all sorts of liberty-threatening treaties. These would not be our first choices for banking, but sometimes you just don't have a choice if you are doing business in, say, Britain or the United States.

If you make a habit of cash-depositing "large amounts" then you may soon find yourself a better-known character in the local banking community than you wish to be. Bank employees may frequent the same restaurants and bars, for instance, and you do not need Mr Lee, your friendly teller from Bank Number One chatting to his friend, Mr Yu, the lovable, huggable clerk from Bank Number Two about how one customer – you – took out US $6,000,000 in cash the same morning. It *might* just set Mr Yu thinking – and talking – about, "how odd, I had someone deposit that same in amount in cash just before lunch". That sort of talk is all that is needed to establish a trail – and precisely why it would be very nice indeed if more people would remember the signs put up in public houses by the British Government during World War II, saying "Loose lips sink ships!".

Swiss banks routinely sign all foreign transfers "on behalf of a client" without revealing who. Nor is the account known, as all transfers are normally routed through one of the bank's own accounts for such purposes. Swiss bank secrecy, however, is only as good as the Swiss. More on this shortly.

A final, interesting note on wire transfers. If you travel a lot, consider opening one or more bank accounts in each and every country you habitually visit. Not necessarily a secret account (though that is always preferable), but just a standard, "foreign" account. All you need to open it is your passport and a maildrop address. The reason? When and if you go back to the country in question, you don't have to exchange money at the low rates usually offered for cash by banks and exchange kiosks. Instead, you simply wire whatever you figure you'll need to your local account from your "main" bank. The exchange rates for wire transfers are normally far better than cash exchange rates. As soon as you get over, say, £1,000 or so, the wire transfer charge will be less than what you would otherwise have lost on the inferior cash exchange rate.

Don't let the transit bank in on your reasons. Banks generally try to avoid customers who have no intention of eventually building up to a respectable deposit. But if you walk into a bank (preferably a large one with a widespread net of retail offices) and state that you wish to open an account, you don't have to give a reason, and a small opening deposit is accepted. You may need to try a couple of banks, one where you will get information as to whether the local laws require that account holders have an address in the country or not, how to make withdrawals when you need them (passbook, checkbook, etc.) and another one where you may walk confidently in through the door, armed with this knowledge. For obvious reasons, a banker will take an immediate dislike to you if he realizes that you will only use his services for your occasional transit of funds and not on a regular basis. In Britain, many banks will refuse to open accounts for foreigners if the "expected length of stay" is less than, say, a year or even 18 months – "too much hassle", they say. If you get that sort of reply, just say "thank you" and walk into another bank around the corner and say that you plan to stay in old Blighty (or France, Germany, Australia, whatever) forever.

It can be great fun to play the sleuthing game and get information this way. Ashley, a career woman of our passing acquaintance for years has maintained accounts with perhaps 20 different banks in as many countries with as little as £100 in each – just for the convenience of having a "local" bank when she visits on business or holiday. But she will still get excited about the prospect of spending her first morning in a new country by questioning bankers and adding to her "account collection". Does it work? Sure. Whenever she darts off on an extended business trip, she will instruct her local bank to transfer appropriate sums to her, care of foreign banks along her itinerary. She claims that, even with perhaps 10 trips abroad every year for the past 30 years, she has not set foot in an exchange booth for about a decade. As some travel writers explain, merely changing money can cost up to 10 per cent of total vacation expenses. Bank to bank transfers or credit card usage can lower this to around two per cent.

# LOOK CLOSELY AT BEARER SHARES AND BONDS

By definition, a share or bond issued as "bearer" may be freely bought, sold, traded or given away without any paper trail. Being "bearer", the share or bond is legally owned by whoever has it in his or her physical possession. No central registration exists of who owns it, meaning that for all intents and purposes, it is as good (i.e. untraceable) as cash.

Bearer shares are issued by most non-USA offshore corporations, in countries where no legal registration requirements exist. Only the registered managers (or people holding a power of attorney from them) can gain access to bank accounts or other assets belonging to the corporation. We will look at offshore corporations in more detail later. And show just how you can use bearer securities to insulate yourself and your finances from prying eyes.

Bearer bonds are considered by many personal and privacy-conscious investors to be the best invention since sliced bread. Issued not only by corporations, bearer bonds are also used by banks, insurance companies and even countries, states and municipalities to raise cash. The giant Ford Motor Corporation is among the corporations that issued bearer bonds, and just about every nation on the planet does so – including the United States. Bearer "T-Bills" were only recently discontinued as part of the "drug war".

The reason you should be concerned with bearer bonds is that such a bond is a **monetary instrument** – and the one that offers the absolute maximum in terms of both privacy and *denomination*. Both cash and gold have their limitations. Let us say, for instance, that you wish to move £100,000 from England to Switzerland. A lot of money, right? In banknotes that would be a sizeable stack, no matter what currency you opt for. You could fit it into your luggage or even onto your person with little trouble, but you might not wish to be stopped and questioned by security at London Heathrow when grabbing a flight to Basel because of funny-looking bulges under your clothes. Putting it in your carry-on briefcase wouldn't work, either, since the bundles would be visible during the X-ray check. And you most likely wouldn't want to put it in your checked luggage lest it got lost or stolen. Now, you might of course drive to Switzerland instead. But there, too, is a slight problem: You would have to drive either through France (and the French still oblige travellers to declare cash in excess of approximately £2,500) *or* through Holland and Germany to reach the Swiss border.

Did you assume the Swiss love foreigners with suitcases full of cash? Those days are long gone. Today, they ask a veritable dungload of questions to shield themselves from accusations of assisting so-called "money launderers". Thus, *large* sums are better transported by first converting them into **bearer bonds**. Getting back to the example of how to get £100,000 from England to Switzerland, the best (if not cheapest) way to do it is to visit a bank or a stock brokerage house which will sell them to you. Take your time and visit several banks and brokers, depending on how much money you have to convert. When done, put them in your briefcase, with a lot of other junk – books, magazines, computer printouts or whatever – and you are ready for the X-ray machine (and a pat-down, if it comes to that). Fly to a nice, quiet, civilized country where the yodelling locals make cheeses with big holes.

One caveat about bearer bonds (and shares): as there is no central registration of bonds, you could accidentally buy stolen shares. As stolen bearer shares can be cancelled, you can then kiss your money goodbye. The easiest way to avoid this is to buy bearer securities only from a major bank or broker. They supply you with a receipt and guaranty the paper is *bona fide*.

Con artists love everything that has a tad of a mystic aura about it, whether this "mystique" is earned or not. Every year, both banks and private investors are duped into either forking over money for worthless, *cancelled* bearer bonds (and shares) – or into extending large loans, taking physical possession of the bonds as collateral. The way it works is by a crook obtaining, usually by theft, a number of bonds that have been redeemed but never quite made it to the incinerator. Sometimes it will be obvious to someone who knows what to look for – one or more tiny holes or perforations on the bond . . . in a corner, for instance. But those little holes, if undetected, may mean that the piece of paper you just paid £10,000 for is about as valuable as a piece of toilet tissue. On other occasions, bonds have been peddled that have previously been redeemed but for some reason or other never got perforated. Be careful. Bearer bonds really *are* very valuable as a monetary tool, but you should guard yourself against hoaxes by buying *only* from a bank or a large, thoroughly reputable brokerage house. Don't be satisfied just because you have seen an ad for a brokerage house (or even a bank) in a newspaper and thus reckon that the outfit must be legit. Two decades ago, an unknown individual referred to by investigators as "Dr No" placed ads in several, international bank registers for The Bank of Sark, **a bank that never existed**. Not to attract customers or any business, but merely to make the name linger in the memories of bank managers everywhere. After buying and placing these ads for three consecutive years, he managed to pull off an international swindle with cashier's checks and bearer bonds based on the *mere perception* created as to the bank's existence. He got away with more than US $100,000,000 – a cool one hundred million bucks. Both Interpol and a lot of banks and investors are still wringing their hands over the affair. Dr. No is still at large.

So when you go to buy bearer bonds, check the scene out carefully and gather as much information as you possibly can. Place calls to good, old brokerage houses and merchant banks such as Manufacturers Hanover, Prudential Bache, Merrill Lynch or Goldman Sachs.

## THE ABC OF BEARER-BONDING

It is essential to understand basic terms pertaining to bearer bonds. They come in two versions: "coupon" and "non-coupon". The former is a bond with a number of coupons attached to it. At specified intervals, these coupons may be cut out and redeemed for cash, either at a bank or by mailing it directly to whoever issued the bond in the first place. Rules vary, but will be stated on the back of the bond. This cash will usually be interest payments, the bond itself being redeemable at face value upon maturity.

On a non-coupon bond, there are no coupons. This means that interest is not *paid out* as long as you hold the bond but is simply "added to the value" of the bond until it matures.

Let us say, for instance, that a bond is issued in the amount of £100,000. The interest rate is set at 10 per cent p.a. and the date of maturity (the date when the bond may be redeemed at full face value, i.e. £100,000) is seven years from issuing date. Obviously, no one would pay £100,000 for a bond just for the pleasure of owning it for seven years, then get the same amount back – in effect, that would mean getting no interest. So what happens is that the bond is sold at a **discount to face value**. For the purpose of this example, an interest rate of 10 per cent p.a. and a running time of seven years is set because an amount will double in seven years (plus a few weeks, anyway) if an interest rate of 10 per cent is left to be compounded upon – the good old "interest on interest". Now, when the bond is first issued it will have a face value of £100,000 but be sold for £50,000 – a 50 per cent discount on face value. No one in his right mind would pay the £100,000 face value before maturation date, seven years hence. Remember, yet again, that there are no coupons on such a bond. In fact, interest for the entire seven years will be paid in a lump sum of £50,000 after seven years – plus the £50,000 originally paid for the bond. Strictly speaking, one does not "buy" a bond but rather *lend* money and receive the bond as *collateral* for the loan. So what happens if you need or want your money back – recall the loan, as it were – before maturation date? No problem. You just find someone who wants to buy it. That is exactly the sort of thing banks and brokerage houses do for a living. They make surprisingly small charges for their services. Of course, if a low-quality junk bond is involved, there may be no buyers. After one year, you will be able to sell the bond in the example, for which you paid £50,000, for £55,000 – the original outlay plus 10 per cent interest (£5,000). And, no, as long as your bearer bonds are not counterfeit or damaged, you will have no problem selling them. Just walk into any bank or stock brokers office with your bond and they will happily buy it from you at the prevailing price.

It should be noted, of course, that bearer bonds are *investments* – as places to put your money and earn interest. They can be just as fickle as ordinary bonds. If the interest rate quoted on your bearer bonds is e.g. 10 per cent and the general interest rates suddenly skyrocket to 20 per cent, then the price of your bond will naturally slip by 50 per cent. If, on the other hand, general interest rates plummet to 5 per cent, your bearer bond will double in value because it promises a rate of interest – 10 per cent – that is double that obtainable elsewhere.

## THE UNBEATABLE BEARER BOND

As a conduit for converting your cash and transporting it in the least conspicous way, bearer bonds are *unbeatable*. You can convert £1,000,000 into perhaps ten pieces of paper (ten bonds of £100,000 each) and carry them on your person. A border guard has the legal authority to confiscate any cash you carry in excess of that you can legally import without declaring it (why would any country even ban the importation of cash in the first place?) Yet, he will not give a second glance to £1,000,000 or US $2,000,000 as long as it is in the form of bearer shares or bonds. But as government regulations may require some reporting to transport these papers over a border, you may wish to mail them by registered mail.

Are bearer bonds safe? If you lose them, kiss your money goodbye – just as with cash.* So guard them closely, and preferably either keep them in a safety deposit box or on your person only as long as you need in order to get them to the bank where you wish to stash your "motherlode". It may be possible to insure bearer bonds in case of theft, fire or loss if you have photocopies of them – ask an insurance company if you dread the risk. A very few bearer bonds do come preinsured.

On another note, bearer bonds may not be safe – from *legislators*. In 1992, the National Bank of Pakistan carried a number of full-page ads in *The International Tribune,* touting the issue of a new series of bearer bonds – and proudly proclaiming that buyers would not be questioned as to origins of funds used to buy the bonds. What a bummer! The US government, acting as self-elected "World Cop", felt that this was a punch in its eye, being as it is that the very nature of bearer bonds make them interesting to those elusive "money launderers". In the opinion of the US government, the Pakistanis went way too far in promoting this factual reality. The USA threatened to summarily arrest and prosecute all Pakistani bankers living or working in the United States for "aiding and abetting" drug dealers and money launderers, current and prospective. Talk about Nazi methods! But it worked. A short, three weeks later, the National Bank of Pakistan ran a new series of ads to the effect that the bearer bonds on offer had been withdrawn. Big Brother struck another blow against freedom.Pakistan then went on to sell its bearer bonds more discreetly as almost all nations and corporations do.

Finally: *Be aware that you really **do** need to start thinking about how you intend to move large sums at some future date*, unless you have your mind set on spending your entire life in your present country no matter what. Bearer bonds exist now – use them before that door closes. Cash is great but bulky: £1,000,000.00 doesn't buy what it used to, but it still takes up a lot of room. Even in Swiss 1,000 Franc notes we are talking about roughly 2,500 bills. In US $100 bills, the equivalent number is about 18,500 greenbacks. In terms of keeping cash on your person, I reckon that you can get away with carrying 600 or perhaps even 1,000 bills of any denomination strapped to your legs and in a money belt – but that's about the limit before you have to start carrying a brown paper shopping bag. This is the preferred method of transporting large amounts of cash, low profile style. How does gold compare? Not well.

---

* There is a way to get a duplicate bond to replace one that is lost, stolen or destroyed. You will need a "lost instrument surety bond" from an insurance company, costing about 12 per cent of value, and you will have to wait about six months after you prove the paper was lost or destroyed.

Gertrude Stein would say that "a pound of gold is a pound of gold is a pound of gold". Fine, but an ounce of gold is still only about US $360 – making a pound of gold a measly US $5,500. With a bit of effort, you may be able to drag a Samsonite filled with 50 kilos of gold (and the Samsonite may hold), but that is still "only" a bit more than US $550,000. And then you have to transport the stuff. The last time we moved a mere million dollars in gold it broke the axle of a heavy-duty baggage cart at Zurich Airport. It took three porters to lift our suitcase. When leaving New York there was no reporting requirement at the time for gold and, likewise, Swiss Customs doesn't care if you import 20 tons of the stuff.

Bearer bonds were born in a pre-computer world. Now that the world has got hooked on silicon, the days of the bearer bonds may be numbered. Get yours and lock them in a box.

# Chapter 10

# BANKS

If you are like most of us, you have a bank account. Why should you have more than one bank account? Simply put, because you should never put all your eggs into one basket. Something may happen to prevent you from using the bank that you presently use. A strike, for instance. OK, we agree, bank employees usually do not strike. When they do, they usually do *together*, in all banks at once. That is why your second bank account should be in a different city and another should be in a different country. But let us examine in detail why it is wise to have **at least** two different bank accounts – and in at least **two different banks.** To start off, you are sure to use your bank for various things – like receiving your pay, cashing and writing checks and the like. You may even own a business which is financed with a loan from the bank. Nothing wrong with that, even though we fail to understand how a lot of people will pay huge interest on personal loans and still spend money on vacations, television sets and new cars before paying off their loans.

But let us pretend that you have a small business (all big businesses started as small businesses, so that doesn't mean you are not a potential tycoon) and a loan to go with it from your friendly, neighborhood bank. In a separate account, you keep your personal savings. When obtaining the loan (or credit line), you will probably have had to sign a personal guarantee to the effect that you will personally assume liability for the loan if your business goes bust. That is the "standard procedure" adhered to by most banks for small and medium-size, commercial loans.

What few businessmen realize is that your own bank may cause your business to "go bust", or at least get in severe difficulties, at hours' notice – by *revoking* a revolving line of credit, for instance. Why would a bank do that? Well, if you suddenly get into a little legal fight with an ex-business partner, or with the local authorities, or even happen to have an eye-opening "letter to the editor" in the local rag about, say, abortion or a similarly explosive issue, the manager of your bank may suddenly forget that it is the customer – you – who ultimately pays his salary. He turns against you. You may be in the right. He may be in the wrong. That is a small consolation.

When a bank suddenly recalls a loan or revokes a line of credit, that means that you will be personally liable for payment if your business does not pay up immediately. And this is why some bankers will get the idea in their heads of *freezing your personal account* immediately, without notifying you – as a "down payment" on the liability that you **will** occur if your business does not make good on its debts within the required time.

## THE CASE OF JIM HUGHES

Jim Hughes relates how he got into a heap of trouble. He opened a business in Houston, Texas. One day, a local "Gay Rights" march caused quite a stir. A photo on the front page of one local paper clearly identified him as one of the marchers. His bank manager happened to recognize "Gay Jim" as one of his customers. He – the bank manager – also happened to be a bit of a redneck. Two days later, poor Jim received a short, tersely worded letter to the effect that since his $50,000 credit line was overdrawn by a few hundred dollars, it had been revoked for "breach of contract". He immediately drove down to his bank and demanded a full explanation, which he duly got – "we cannot have a customer overdrawing his account without prior acceptance from us" and a lot more bull in the same vein. Various slurs and insults were traded. At the conclusion of the meeting, the customer proceeded to the counter to withdraw his personal savings. Wouldn't you just know that this had been frozen, to "ensure" that he would "live up to his personal liability" a few days hence! This caused him no end of trouble, when trying to establish a relationship with another bank on the basis of what was, to all intents and purposes, the banking equivalent of a "dishonorable discharge". In the meantime, he was unable to finance his ongoing business by drawing on his personal savings – something he would have avoided had he had the good foresight to keep these, or at least part of them, in another bank. You may not be gay but similar freezing of all accounts happens when a tax dispute, divorce, or lawsuit is involved.

## THE CASE OF "KING MAILORDER"

Another individual, this one a client, used to operate a small mail order house, selling a range of gadgets through classified ads. Being self-financing, he maintained a bank account for the sole purpose of clearing checks quickly and inexpensively – something to reckon with, considering that he made perhaps US $12,000 worth of business per week and about half that was paid to his business by check. Along the way, he had added a couple of extra "company names" to his collection, trying to boost sales by doing the time-honored, mail order "compete with yourself" concept. Awareness of a product is raised – and potential competitors discouraged – by running ads for essentially the same product under several different corporate names and addresses. As it happened, he maintained his bank account in the name of "United Gadgets, Inc." but soon found himself receiving and clearing a much larger number of checks made out by customers to "International Gizmos, Inc." than to the original business. Without a hitch, he cleared checks to "IG, Inc." through his "UG, Inc." account for several months. Nobody ever asked any questions, he was well-known in the bank, having been a steady, no-problems customer for well over two years.

One Friday afternoon, he went to his bank with a stack of checks as usual. When he came to make a withdrawal on the account, however, he was told that he would "have to see the manager". This turned out to be a distrusting, somewhat aggressive individual of the male gender, with bad breath and gum disease, who asked for an "explanation" of what all those checks to "International Gizmos" were doing being cleared through a bank account belonging to "United Gadgets". The customer patiently explained that he owned both companies, and that he merely thought it expedient to maintain only one bank account since the two businesses were really being run as one. To which the manager replied: "Well, we can't have that. If you wish to deposit 'International Gizmos' checks we want to have a look at the incorporation papers to make sure that you are authorized to handle the affairs of that company. We cannot have customers clearing checks made out just any old way unless we know they are properly authorized to do so". The client quietly said that this would be all right, but could he at least clear the checks he had brought with him now, make a withdrawal and then come back on Monday. "No," came the answer, "until we see the papers from 'International Gizmos', we can allow you to do no such thing."

There was one, slight snag to this . . . the client was not a great believer in credit cards (clever bugger!) and, consequently, had none. He also had to go on a business trip in another state over the weekend and needed cash – of which he also had none, since he was unable to draw on his account before furnishing the documents required by the bank. In other words, unless he could convince the suspicious bank manager, his trip would be derailed. You don't get very far on US $50 and change.

And this is where he turned out to have made a wise move. A few months in advance, he had opened an account with a different bank in the same town – this one in the name of "International Gizmos, Inc." Why? Because, because, well . . . , "because, just in case". To make sure. In case his main bank should suffer a bank robbery and be put out of business for a couple of days – or something like that. He had not quite realized it, but on the basis of an unrationalized wish to give himself a second option, he had gotten wise and established an alternative account through which he could clear his incoming checks, should the need ever arise – which it did.

To sum it up, your attitude towards banks should be as follows: banks are essentially shops that make their profit both from the spread in interest rates between deposits and loans, and from various charges on wire transfers, exchange of foreign cash, selling travellers' checks, issuing credit cards etc. *And that is it*. Banks do not exist to "help", "assist" or "tide over" their customers. Just like any other business, a bank has as its only claim to existence the need of shareholders to somehow earn a return on their invested capital. Never tell a banker that he ought to have a "social conscience" or that he has a "duty" to further the interests of local businesses. Such claims should be left to the looters and moochers of the left wing, who believe that just because someone happens to be sitting on a stack of (other people's) money, then he is automatically obliged to lend it out to "deserving causes". Balderdash! IBM has no obligation whatsoever to give away computers free to college students, and shareholders would be right to demand the ousting of any CEO or chairman of the board advocating such "noble" ways of wasting the paid-in capital.

Therefore, be prepared to think of banks as mere tools of convenience that will let you write checks, *sell* you the use of a credit card and receive and keep your funds for you. Then take the next, logical step and realize that since banks are often the targets of swindles and scams they need to put certain safeguards in place to make sure they are not duped or victimized. Bonnie and Clyde, when asked why they robbed banks, looked at the reporter incredulously and replied: "Well, because that's where the money is at."

Maintain at least one, second bank account in a different bank. Not only is it okay for starters, but also in the long run. After all, someone else may just decide to take hostages or put a virus in the computer of "your" bank on the day you have to make an urgent withdrawal or order a quick, necessary wire transfer. Offshore banks are fine (in fact, they're a necessity) but keep a "back-up bank", or two close to where you live – just in case.

All banks pay lip-service to the idea of customer confidentiality. But the reality is far different. In Europe the situation is expected to become worse after 1 January, 1993, when European Community rules on money laundering come into effect. Under the umbrella of seeking to prevent the disguise of proceeds of "drug trafficking and other criminal activities", EU banks will be entitled to lift secrecy where money laundering is suspected. Financial institutions and relevant authorities will co-operate in reporting "suspicious" transactions. Most importantly, records will be kept to identify customers and their transactions. The identification procedure will be triggered if anyone walks into a bank to deposit more than Ecu 15,000 (about £10,000) at one time or makes several cash deposits in what appears to be "linked operations". As of early 1993, a majority of the countries of the EU decided they were not ready for this planned integration. The dismantling of border posts and broader financial co-operation was "postponed indefinitely". But some EU countries are operating this rule. You should assume they all are now.

## A MINI-GUIDE TO CONFIDENTIAL BANKING

The prudent capital-preserver spreads his assets in different countries, never more than 10-15 per cent in any one bank. To avoid currency fluctuations, he has maybe 10 per cent dollars 10 per cent pounds, 10 per cent D-mark, 10 per cent Yen, and so on. Plus, of course, a little heavy metal (like gold or platinum) here and there.

He prefers countries with banking secrecy and no currency regulations. Using a banking passport he keeps his assets registered in at least two different names.

## SWITZERLAND. LESS THAN MEETS THE EYE?

Is Switzerland all that its cracked up to be? Many Swiss banks are leery of taking on American clients. Also there is a recent American-Swiss treaty agreement to penetrate the veil of secrecy of numbered accounts and to require banks to reveal information about an account holder if the USA authorities demand it claiming that the owner is involved in organized crime. Such claims can be made and they are hard to disprove, either in the United States or Switzerland.

We know of one private bank in Switzerland which is still the essence of confidential banking. It is efficient, very safe and behaves the way Swiss bankers did 20 years ago. This bank, is willing to take on substantial clients and NOT disclose anything to anybody EVER. The assets required are at least $500,000. We have worked with them in the past and find them reliable. But accounts must be set up in a very special way.

## LIECHTENSTEIN: THE STATE GUARANTEES ALL DEPOSITS

Little Liechtenstein is a mini-Switzerland in terms of banking. Local banks are all modelled on the Swiss Example. But the Swiss have lately come under the thumb of Big Brother (USA). The US Department of Justice says "Organized Crime" and the Swiss authorities often (without any notice to the accused) say "Freeze the Account!" Liechtenstein has, so far tried to be independent. A claimant against a Liechtenstein account holder seeking to grab any assets, must already know all details of the account and then bring an action that would result in a recovery to the plaintiff just as if he were a Liechtensteiner suing another Liechtensteiner. Thus, there have been several actions where a foreign wife was able to claim an account of her husband where she had full knowledge of the account including the number and balance. A Liechtenstein court will award spousal and child support against a runaway husband. Of course when a lawsuit is started, the defendant gets notice, and in most cases, this allows for sufficient time to withdraw and move all funds.

Secrecy in Liechtenstein and the client's interests are thus more well respected than in Switzerland, Also, the IRS does not (as yet) have undercover agents inside the three banks of Liechtenstein. If such moles were ever strategically placed, they would be guilty of several criminal offenses under Liechtenstein law. The same is true in Switzerland of course, but as the banks there are much bigger and employ far more foreigners as officers with access to most information, and because they have offices in most countries abroad, one can assume that Swiss bank secrecy is like Swiss cheese, full of holes. The major bank in Liechtenstein does unfortunately, have a small New York and London office, but the other two banks are strictly local. The tiny "Furstentum" is difficult to get to. There are no major airports nearby. It is an hour's bus or combination train and bus ride from Zurich. This inconvenient location is one disadvantage of doing business in Liechtenstein. But if you rent a car at Zurich airport, it is a pleasant, scenic hour on the freeway.

In Liechtenstein, ALL deposits (no limit) are guaranteed by the state itself. Of course, this guarantee is only as good as the country. And Liechtenstein is one of the twenty smallest countries on Earth. It is also one of the five richest in per capita income and personal wealth. We have reason to believe, however, that Liechtenstein could cover any local banking test with flying colors. The Prince who is the sovereign and the major stockholder in the conservative Bank in Liechtenstein might have to sell a few art works from his collection of several hundred old masters, but at 50 million dollars a pop, we prefer him as our guarantor of last resort in preference to the USA Treasury. The Prince is debt free and has lots of assets. This is more than we can say for what is allegedly "the greatest nation on Earth".

# AUSTRIA, HOME OF THE SPARKASSENBUCH

In Austria, to get a ''Sparbuch'', no ID is needed. This Austrian bearer saving account comes with a little passbook that entitles the bearer to withdraw whatever is in the account. To safeguard theft or loss of the passbook, you can have a ''merke'' or a ''losungswort'', an optional code that you'll have to give verbally to the bank when you present the passbook.

The ''Sparkassenbuch'' is one of the ultimate weapons you can have in your fight for bank secrecy. Local confidentiality laws mirroring those of neighboring Switzerland are very tough. Revealing ANYTHING about a client's affairs automatically leads a bank employee to the pokey. Since Austria is not a hotbed of tax evaders, deposed dictators and drug criminals, USA authorities give it little notice. As far as we know, the IRS does not have any undercover agents assigned to work in Austrian banks.

One of the best guarded secrets in the international banking community right now is the Austrian Sparbuch. For privacy purposes, it beats flat-out any type of account offered by any bank or financial institution in any country anywhere on the planet.

It frees you from worries about obtaining alternative ID, mailing addresses in other countries, references and whatnot – you don't even have to ''create'' one single ''professional reference'' to open it.

The Austrian Sparbuch is an institution almost as old as banking itself. As German-speaking readers will know, Sparbuch literally means ''Savings Book'' or what is generally known as a passbook.

Physically, a Sparbuch is a small 14 page booklet, or really just a folded piece of cardboard, with the name of the bank and a computer printout of the most recent transactions pertaining to the account.

You may remember this benign looking contraption from the days before checkbooks and VISA-cards conquered banks everywhere and changed people's habits forever.

In order to open a Sparbuch account, an Austrian quite simply walks into any branch of any bank in Austria, deposits an appropriate sum (which should be no less than the equivalent of £25 sterling) and walks out five minutes later with the Sparbuch.

The Sparbuch has a number of huge advantages over any other type of account offered by banks outside of Austria.

For one thing, the account does not need to carry a name! That's right: the account may be either in the name of an individual or of a corporation, including offshore-corporations – or it may be in no name at all, a so-called ''Ueberbringer'' account or ''bearer-passbook''. As the term implies, whoever physically holds the passbook is presumed to be its legal owner!

Anyone who has ever leafed through literature about offshore corporations will know that certain countries allow company stock to be issued in the form of bearer-shares. An Ueberbringer-Sparbuch is the bank account equivalent of bearer-shares.

Secondly, Austria has full and complete banking secrecy on a much better scale than Switzerland. No ID whatsoever need be shown on opening an account, and the owner of the account does not even need to provide an address. In other words, there is no paper trail whatsoever such as references, letters etc. to give away the true identity of the owner of the account,

And in the nature of things, no account statements are mailed to the owner of the account – EVER! If that sounds like an odd ''advantage'', think of the kind of damage all too frequently inflicted on unwary individuals when statements and letters from banks are intercepted by spouses, tax-authorities, police or other despicable privacy-invaders.

Instead of regular statements, the Sparbuch is updated automatically and any accrued interest added whenever it is presented at a branch of the issuing bank.

It is absolutely, unquestionably impossible to establish just who opened the account (and who owns it) by means of checking available records – since no records have ever been created except the physical Sparbuch itself and the account number in the bank's computer-system. No forms to fill out, no ID to show, nothing!

Thirdly, it is entirely legal to transfer a Sparbuch from one person to another without giving the bank or anyone else notice about this. In certain countries it has been made a (victimless) crime to sell or even give away a passbook, This, of course, stems from Big Brother's tasteless wish to collect as much knowledge and as much data about bank account owners worldwide as possible. If necessary, a Sparbuch may be sent in the mail to pay back a debt – left in a sealed envelope with a will to beat immoral probate taxes – or even donated to Greenpeace, if the owner is so inclined!

Furthermore, it is completely safe. Even though it is not strictly necessary, a Sparbuch will usually be issued with a code which is needed whenever withdrawals are made. This code is not one of those horrendously forgettable four-digit codes issued by credit card companies, but is actually chosen by the customer himself. The way it should be, really – who better to know what combination of letters and/or digits is the easiest to remember than the individual who actually owns the account?

If the Sparbuch is lost, one quite simply applies to the bank, gives the name (if any) of the account, the account number and the code – the so-called Losungswort – and a new Sparbuch is issued. Usually, no charge is made for this.

Being, in reality, a ''bearer-passbook'', a Sparbuch account does not as a rule offer a very high interest rate. Expect interest to be in the order of 3-5 per cent annually at most, even if a slightly higher interest may be available by changing the account status to e.g. 12-months' notice.

A Sparbuch account may only be denominated in Austrian schillings, which are not in the EMS, the European Monetary Snake, Indirectly, however, the schilling has for the past few years been tied to the Deutschmark, and is therefore a remarkably stable and reliable currency. In the real world, this offers a greater degree of stability than the Swiss Franc.

In order to make a deposit, one will either need to walk into a branch of the bank in question and plonk down cash in any currency (which will be converted into schillings before being credited to the account). Similarly, one may freely mail checks denominated in Austrian Schillings made payable to the bank or the fantasy name of the account, if you decide to have one, to any branch of the relevant bank, enclosing a note advising the bank to credit the checks to the Sparbuch, quoting the account number. And of course, SWIFT-transfers may be made to a Sparbuch in exactly the same way SWIFT-transfers are usually made – naturally, one does not need to indicate the ''bearer-passbook'' nature of the account when ordering the transfer!

It is not possible to make SWIFT transfers from a Sparbuch account – thus, you or someone you trust will have to go to Austria to visit a branch (any branch) of your bank and make the appropriate withdrawal.

However, if you send the Sparbuch by registered mail to the bank with an enclosed note stating that you wish to make a withdrawal and including the Losungswort the code – the bank may do so, provided that you pay applicable charges to have a check made out and mailed back to you with the Sparbuch.

Since the point of the Sparbuch exercise is to ensure complete and unquestioned privacy without leaving even a shred of paper trail behind for government snoops or others (disgruntled ex-spouses, bankruptcy lawyers etc.) to follow, one has to take great care about exactly how a Sparbuch account is opened.

It is not possible to open a Sparbuch by mail, unfortunately, so someone has to physically appear in Austria in order to open the account. Needless to say, this ''someone'' should not be an acquaintance or relative who may one day blurt out the details of your secret Austrian bank account in a drunken stupor or, God forbid, under interrogation by authorities hell-bent on stealing your money.

Even if you are not averse to the idea of a couple of days in Austria, and even if you have mastered German and are sufficiently versed in the art of pursuading bank clerks to do what they really ought not to be doing, think again.

If the purpose of having a Sparbuch is to fully and completely avoid leaving any clues that may eventually lead to yourself, including fingerprints, why show up at the bank in person? Bank employees have, on occasion, been known to have frightfully good memories. So why not consider letting someone else do the job for you – it does not have to be expensive.

At least one lawyer that we know of offers to open a Sparbuch account for you with no hassle whatsoever. You do not need to show any ID, no photocopies of passport or driver's license is needed. These Sparbuchs are delivered "off the shelf" as anonymous (Ueberbringer) accounts, complete with an easy-to-remember codeword (Losungswort). They come, as standard, with an opening balance of 100 Austrian schillings, roughly equivalent to £6 (about US $10). Please send £250/$400 to Scope international and your Sparbuch will be sent by return. If you require the account to be in a particular fantasy name, please add £25/$40 and allow one month for delivery.

# THE ROLLS ROYCE OF ULTIMATE PRIVACY: THE WERTPAPIERBUCH

Let me describe this absolutely ultimate banking tool: the Wertpapierbuch looks like an ordinary Sparbuch, but in essence contains two very different accounts in one book – a deposit account and a brokerage account.

The deposit account works much like a settlement account for securities transactions, while the second account is a brokerage account, through which the holder can buy any type of stocks, bonds, options and even futures contracts. All transactions are anonymous and can be placed with a secret code word, Losungswort, by phone or fax worldwide.

Now . . . think of the possibilities . . . worldwide anonymous, secret banking! There are no other forms to be filled out, no references to be given. Nor is there a limit on the amount which can be deposited in the account. Included in your package is the easy to remember Losungswort which will allow you to trade from anywhere in the world, simply by faxing or calling the appropriate numbers at the securities trading department of the issuing bank. Your funds are being held safely and anonymously at the Austrian bank and protected by Austria's stringent secrecy laws, while your order is executed with one of the largest German brokerage firms.

You may call or fax the bank for immediate details on the execution of your order. No statements are mailed out because that would create a papertrail to your disadvantage. With your Wertpapierbuch you will receive a detailed information brochure regarding deposits, withdrawals, bank charges for various transactions, swift transfers etc., including special tips and hints on how to utilize your Wertpapierbuch for maximum profit and privacy protection. All the other procedures such as withdrawals, deposits etc, are the same as with the Sparbuch.

One difference – these accounts can only be held in DM as they are the innovative product of a few clever banks in an Austrian/German customs enclave, where Austrian secrecy laws are valid. Notable to mention is that these banks are subsidiaries of the largest Austrian banks.

**THE BEST, SAFEST AND EASIEST WAY.** Time is money, and letting someone else go through the bothersome motions makes sense in more ways than one.

The cost for obtaining your Wertpapierbuch is £400/$600. The book is delivered with an opening balance of DM50, ($35). However, the issuing banks request initial deposit of DM25,000 (£17,000) to fully operate the account for stock, option and futures trading.

The Wertpapierbuch offers an additional deposit account and all the options of a full brokerage account, anonymously and secretly. This explains the higher service charge compared to the Sparbuch. However, if you are looking for a long-term solution for your privacy and asset protection, the Wertpapierbuch is the right choice.

Worldwide delivery can be arranged by DHL courier at an additional charge of US $25, otherwise they are despatched by airmail post.

Think about it. Whether you do it yourself or leave the job to a competent professional, which we would recommend, how often are you presented with such a clear-cut, easy-to-use and ready-to-roll solution to taking the first, practical step towards true privacy in banking?

To obtain your Austrian Wertpapierbuch please send the appropriate remittance to Scope International Ltd and we will advise you how to proceed.

# YUGOSLAVIA: STAY CLEAR FOR NOW

Quasi-Communist Yugoslavia is now Serbia, Bosnia, Croatia, Hertzogovina, Moslem Enclaves, Hungarian Enclaves plus a few other bits and war torn pieces). Officially, most of these new countries have bank secrecy, But unless you are a contrarian or have an inside track, you probably shouldn't touch any Yugoslav investments even with a proverbial a ten foot pole. It may be blown away tomorrow. For daring adventurers among our readers, if you speak the local lingo and want to follow Lord Rothschild's advice about investing when there is blood running in the streets, try talking to some of the Yugoslavian banks in other countries. There, they are bound by local deposit insurance schemes. Of course, a fixed interest rate deposit is hardly the kind of investment Rothschild was talking about. To make big returns on your money in a war situation, you must buy a business or property for a song, and then, keep your fingers crossed that peace and prosperity will return. Sometimes, perhaps usually, it does. In places like Lebanon however, the wait has been many years. Probably a total outsider would not be able to make intelligent investments even with the help of foreign branches of the large Yugoslavian banks abroad. No harm in trying to make a few contacts: POSLOVNE JEDINICE UDRUZENE BEOGRADSKE BANKE, Urania Strasse 34, CH-8001 Zurich and POSLOVNE JEDICINE JUGOBANKE, Talstrasse 82, CH-8001 Zurich, Switzerland are both solid Yugoslav banks owned abroad. They are probably not too busy and might enjoy a drop-in visit from a potential investor. If you had visited Kuwaiti bankers during the recent Gulf War, you might well have made killing on one thing or another. In fact, Kuwaiti currency for a time, was selling at a 98 per cent discount. US $20,000 or pounds invested would have made you a millionaire three months later. Lord Rothschild was right about a great many things. On the other hand, 20,000 in USSR roubles at the time of the hard-line coup in '91 would barely buy you a copy of this book at press time!

Yugoslavia is coming apart. With political instability and large pro-Communist elements gaining power, we fear overnight confiscation laws or coercion of some sort. Local depositors may be forced to sell or exchange their dollar-deposits into local "confetti" currency. We point out that where there is crisis there is also opportunity, but the opportunity is for very well informed, well placed people. Unless you are in this category or have partners who are, we view the risk of buying into most of the former Yugoslavia as not worth running.

# HUNGARY, NEW HAVEN FOR DIRTY DOLLARS

Another former East-bloc country, Hungary, is interesting for PTs. We are aware that Hungary recently attracted hundreds of millions of dollars by guaranteeing a state secured 20 per cent interest rate in **hard currency,** with bank secrecy. Mostly, the deposits were said to have come from bureaucrats in Russia, and other countries of the former East-bloc.

Customers are people wary of Switzerland and vice-versa. Hungary is a "no questions asked" country. In many banks, you do not even have to show any ID to open an account. English and German is spoken in most banks catering to foreigners.

Many "dirty" marks, dollars and other currencies are crossing the border into Hungarian banks these days. So far, few "investors" have tried to withdraw any cash. No problems so far. Yet we well remember the period around 1979 when Mexican banks offered a government guaranteed 19 per cent interest rate on dollar deposits when the going rate was closer to nine per cent. After attracting many millions of dollars, the rules of the game were changed so that funds could only be withdrawn in pesos. These were worth a small percentage of the original dollar deposit. Hungary is possibly more honorable than Mexico, but unless its economy gets into high gear, it won't be able to pay the interest back in hard currency.

Cautious investors will stay clear of deals that may give them a pocket full of worthless forints. Still, emerging markets are where the action is , and if you could get into a deal to import, export or pioneer the manufacture of some product or service in Hungary, you could do a lot worse.

## BAHAMAS AND OTHER SUNNY PLACES FOR SHADY PEOPLE

The Bahamas Islands, like several other Caribbean pleasure domes, has attracted its fair share of offshore deposits. This island, with the Caymans, is known to be a favorite financial hideaway and vacation spot for some of the big time crime barons. Also, Americans attracted by the convenience factor, are said to bury much of their loot in the sunny Caymans, Bermuda, Bahamas and Nassau banks. Panama is also a top choice.

Bermuda is a better place for serious money. Insistent upon several verifiable references for new customers, they say that they try to attract and keep only "good clean business." In Bermuda you only have a choice of three locally owned and operated banks! These are, Butterfields, Bank of Bermuda and one other. In the Americas, we feel that places like the Dutch Antilles (north of Venezuela) and Panama are probably the best places for PTs to go to right now. The Antilles is home to many respectable international banks including ABN, the giant bank of the Netherlands . . . Dutch ways still rule many aspects of island life. The Caribbean banks are said to have more funds on deposit than all the banks in America put together. An interesting statistic if true for the population and gross national product of these islands couldn't be much more than five per cent of the USA's. This says something about how depositors view the all-round desirability of American banks. With substantial account balances in the USA now being seized without court order just "on suspicion" of laundering or tax evasion, few knowledgeable people are using American banks any more.

Panama, with 115 of the world's largest banks represented, is nowhere near as bad as its reputation. It is a corrupt country, but the banks are surprisingly, way above the general slime. The country plays host to some of the most efficient banks and financial advisors in the Americas. Yet beware of the many crooks and con-men based in Panama. Some own "banks" that are no more than mail-drops! Beware in Panama, but beware everywhere. Deal only with banks, lawyers and financial advisors of known respectability.

## THE BRITISH OFFSHORE HAVENS IN EUROPE: JERSEY, GIBRALTAR, ISLE OF MAN AND GUERNSEY

Jersey and Guernsey in the English Channel, Isle of Man in the Irish Sea and Gibraltar on the southernmost tip of Spain are all in the Sterling area. Accounts can be held in any currency, however.

Their banks are mostly British. Local legislation is modelled on that of the United Kingdom, with one major change. In the locations mentioned no taxes on interest are withheld. Also, there is bank secrecy. Sort of.

We do not hold most British banks in very high esteem, as (especially outside of London) we have found them to be relatively clumsy and restrictive. Plus, the staff, often tend to be blabbermouths. Never do British offshore banks come anywhere close to the Swiss banks in terms of efficiency, confidentiality and range of services offered. Then again, they are cheaper. If you are not into active trading, they are perfectly OK for long term deposits.

If you can live with silly rules (imposed by the banks themselves!) on minimum deposits, maximum number of checks to write, special surcharges for more than 80 withdrawals a year, funny ways of calculating the interest and the like, then you can live with British banks. At least pounds, the interest rate you will get is a good point higher (net) than you'll get from non-British banks.

They usually offer great interest on sterling. For years it's been between 12 and 15 per cent per annum – naturally with no tax deducted at source. In 1993, the rates dropped to just below seven per cent. But compared to 4 per cent on dollars from USA banks, even a paltry seven per cent looks good.

Sark: This island sports two one-room banks with access to stockbrokers all over the world and bank secrecy. Sark "residents" with mail drops established via Scope International can use some of the world's safest banks. Consult *The Channel Island Report* published by Scope for more info. But beware of certain providers of services on Sark *formerly* recommended by us. Ask us about recent developments on this island.

# ANDORRA: OUR FAVORITE MOUNTAIN RETREAT

Nestled in a hidden valley in the Pyreness, tiny Andorra offers bank secrecy and efficiency surpassing that of Switzerland. This little country has no taxes and the lowest prices in Europe on almost everything.

Native Andorrans all have one other thing in their favor: they know and recognize that nobody owes them a living. No Andorran gets any subsidy or free ride. These mountain people work hard, study hard and to try to get ahead, Result: without any big fuss or fanfare they now have a privately-owned, thriving local service economy. Their unregulated banking system is safe, sound, prosperous, computerized, streamlined, discreet and very customer-oriented.

Banks in Andorra offer a personal and personable service, i.e. friendly but respectful.. Bankers are generally competent and positive thinking. Many speak English. The local lingo is Catalan, but French and Spanish is commonly understood. We have been fortunate enough to discover a local organization that (for a small fee) will provide maildrop services, help the newcomer find a property to rent or buy, open a bank accounts, get local residence permits, and so on. While more information is in our Andorra report, you may wish to contact: SERVISSIM, [SIMON BINSTED, Manager] – Roc Escolls 3-4 A. Av. Meritxell, 20; Andorra la Vella, Principat d' Andorra; ph: (33) France+ (628) 604-14/61148; fax:63 797

Anything you want to accomplish or do, just ask. They try hard to make it happen. If they cannot manage it, they are genuinely apologetic. Servissim or Andorra banks will even receive telex messages and mail for you. Banks will rent you a little private PO Box in their vault for your mail! Local banks will serve you well in Spanish, French, Catalan, English, German or Italian. Banking in Andorra is very straightforward. You walk in the door, ask about opening a new account, show any ID, letter of reference from a local customer or your present banker and you will be given an account number. Then you can place current or long-term deposit balances in all freely convertible currencies with no further ado. No sub-account or multiple account foolishness, no lengthy forms to fill out, no minimum balances, no references, no humming and hawing. Once known, you can bring **in** a mixed bag of foreign bank notes in any amount and deposit it all to your account UNCONVERTED. There is no "counting charge" of up to two per cent as you get in Switzerland. Or else you can use your cash to buy francs, pesetas, US dollars, pounds, Deutschmarks, Swiss francs or whatever is your fancy. The exchange rate for customers is close to interbank rates.

USA-style reporting requirements and restrictions are simply unheard of in Andorra where banking is not subject to endless rules, regulations or red-tape. You can earn very respectable interest rates on passbook savings accounts or deposit balances in any currency. You can elect (at slightly lower interest) to have a no-notice, no-penalty 100 per cent withdrawal of your entire account at any time. Interest is calculated on a daily basis and posted to your passbook twice yearly. Further, your Andorran bank will also invest your money in CDs, time deposits, stock and bond transactions – or on most major bourses. You can do gold, silver or platinum bullion transactions. Arrangements for loans and margin are practically identical to Swiss set-ups including Swiss type arrangements to avoid sales taxes on delivery of physical gold or silver bullion. They do not yet trade for you in futures and options but probably will be able to handle more complex trades by the time you read this. Andorra is highly recommended.

In Andorra, unlike Switzerland, you can have a current account that pays interest on checking accounts instead of charging negative interest to keep your money.

To reiterate: Andorran banks offer banking secrecy, accounts in ANY currency, secret numbered accounts, many different currencies in one bank account. **There are no restrictions whatsoever on cash or other money movements in and out of Andorra.** However, getting large amounts of cash through French or Spanish customs requires knowledge of the rules and a bit of finesse.

**For more information on Andorra, read** *The Andorra & The Secret Enclaves Report* and *The Gibraltar Report* from Scope International.

PART TWO

# USING MAIL DROPS
# FOR FUN AND PROFIT

# Chapter 11

# HOW AND WHY TO USE A "DEAD DROP"

For some individuals, getting and using an address other than one's own can seem stressful. Especially if the address is a mail drop. This is because the term "mail drop" comes from the spy literature. Sensitive communication is left by a spy for the intelligence agent responsible for "running him" in a so-called "dead drop". This is a hollow tree, a trash bin or similar.

While interesting enough, dead drops are not feasible for information which you need to receive with the help of the postal service. This author personally doubts if the Royal Mail would deliver a letter addressed as follows:

> *Tape This Envelope Under Cistern Top,*
> *Third stall,*
> *Men's Room,*
> *Paddington Tube Station,*
> *London,*
> *ENGLAND.*

Indeed, the letter might be delivered – but more likely to the police rather than in the manner indicated on the envelope.

To get at the nuts and bolts of how and why to use a mail drop it is necessary to develop a full understanding of the reasons why these services exist.

A commercial mail drop operation basically consists of a physical address recognized by the postal service – either a post office box or a street address where the mailman may deliver a letter or parcel. This physical address is occupied or otherwise controlled by individuals who, for a fee, offer to receive and keep or forward mail according to the wishes of the customer, who does not physically reside on the premises.

These services all operate as businesses. They are, of course, strictly legal and must comply with all requirements of the country in which they operate. They advertise, often in classifieds under headings such as "business services" or "business contacts". You can even look some of them up in the Yellow Pages under serviced offices, accommodation bureaux, secretarial services, or mail forwarding. In France, mail drops are listed under "Domiciliation, Servicede".

Postal services in different countries have various terms under which they accept delivering a letter. In Britain, for instance, a letter will be delivered as long as a post office box number or a street address is indicated on the envelope – regardless of the name of the addressee.

In some other countries, however, the postal service will refuse to deliver a letter unless the name of the recipient corresponds with the name on the door. This is an important point. Even if the individual(s) or company occupying a given address are quite prepared to receive mail addressed to a certain name, the mail may never be delivered to the address in the first place unless the mail man finds that particular name on the door or mailbox.

Should you decide to use a "pen name" for some purpose, e.g. when requesting information, you should make sure that the mail drop is informed of this *before* you expect the letter to arrive. If you ignore this the letter may either be returned to sender by the postal service or delivery may be refused by the mail drop.

# WHY DO COMMERCIAL MAIL DROPS EXIST?

To make money. A fee is charged by the operator of the mail drop for receiving mail. So the reason is obviously a desire on the part of the operator to cater to people willing to pay for the privilege of being able to use the address belonging to the commercial mail drop, as opposed to receiving the mail at the individual's own home address.

*Now **why would anyone pay** for such a privilege?* Conventional wisdom has it that it is the sender, rather than the recipient, that has to bear the cost of using the postal service to deliver a letter. Right? Nevertheless, a significant number of people still shell out money to receive mail at an address different from their own humble abodes.

The reason most often quoted for this is "privacy considerations".

Many people are quite willing to pay a commercial mail drop operation money in order to have a place where mail may be received away from home – wherever "home" may be. For example: an individual wishes to receive information from a company about, say, an insurance scheme. He (or she) does not, however, enjoy receiving unexpected and irritating visits from insurance salesmen who invades his (or her) privacy.

Mail is usually shoved through a slot in the front door or stuffed into a mail box. Whoever gets to that door (or the mail box) also gets to look at the envelopes – and the return addresses – and may thus be able to get an idea of the nature of their contents without opening them. This may result in unwanted consequences for the recipient of the mail if it falls into – or passes through – the hands of someone with whom a (potential) conflict exists.

Henry, a hardworking dentist, wants to obtain a divorce. There may be a great number of very good reasons why he does not want his spouse to learn about this in advance. He may not even be sure that he wants a divorce, but merely wants to learn about the financial and other considerations before taking the necessary legal action. In this case, he has two options if he wishes to keep his wife from seeing letters from his attorney. He can either make absolutely sure that he gets to the mail first or he can instruct the attorney to write to him at an address where his wife (or colleagues, or boss) will not see the correspondence. The former is playing with fire, the latter is an intelligent decision brought on by concern about keeping his intentions secret for as long as possible.

Another very good example is "Frank F. Reedom", a cunning individual who has enough good sense to keep his life's savings in a bank outside his own country. He has several reasons for this. First, to obtain gross interest with no tax deducted (by keeping the account in a tax haven). Second, to avoid the existence of the bank account becoming known to his local tax man. In the nature of things it is quite easy for Big Brother to intercept mail, either to open it or merely to observe (and perhaps photocopy) the envelope. This has happened over and over again in most countries in this world. The most "civilized" countries are the worst. Citizens have their mail opened as a matter of routine **just because the stamp on the envelope shows it to come from a tax haven**. Citizens in the USA, Britain, Scandinavia, Germany, Japan and a host of other nations have had such experiences even though they were **never under any investigation of any kind** and never had done anything wrong. This is the way Big Brother operates. We are way beyond "1984". It is high time to take precautions.

Any individual under either open or clandestine surveillance owing to suspicions about tax irregularities will, without knowing it, often be under "mail surveillance". If and when the Inland Revenue (or the IRS) decides to open a criminal tax case against him, it will know the name of the bank(s) in which the defendant-to-be has assets. Again, it is much easier to slap a lien on an account, even in a tax haven, if the tax people have advance knowledge of the name of the bank – and the name on the account. Unless, again, the individual has wisely chosen to instruct his bank to mail all statements to a mail drop, preferably in a more neutral country, as opposed to his place of residence. As long as he takes care not to divulge this address to anyone, he will stand a much better chance of keeping knowledge about the account to himself.

Quincy O'Rourke, too, decided to use a maildrop – but for a different reason. He was "wanted" by a pack of bloodthirsty lawyers and process servers. He didn't want to let them know his true whereabouts. O'Rourke was unable – and unwilling – to pay alimony and child support to his ex-wife. He shielded himself behind a mail drop, unwilling to let creditors know where he physically lived. Others in similar circumstances have used mail drops to keep secret where they receive most of their mail, as in the case of an undischarged bankrupt whose mail is redirected to the receiver handling his bankruptcy case.

The fourth reason for using a mail drop is as a means of establishing a "branch office" or even a "head office" as cheaply as possible for a company or a corporation. This is quite legal and there is nothing odious whatsoever about it. Usually mail drops also provide telephone answering and fax forwarding. No countries have laws stating that a corporation has to have an office with a full time employee in residence, somewhere rented by or belonging to the corporation to itself and not shared with anyone else. An agent is all that is required. On the other hand, it is imperative that some sort of address is given when incorporating a company. In some countries it is not legal to give merely a post office box number as the address of the corporation, a street address is required.

As even the smallest of offices costs more to rent than charges of a commercial mail drop, it usually makes good sense to obtain the use of the required address by paying a fee for this. Why sign a lease for an expensive office? Especially if the company is still being run from the kitchen table of the owner! As a rule of thumb, the monthly fee charged by a mail drop equals about five per cent of what one would have to pay for a very modest office in the same area. Every businessman knows that efficiency and strict cash-flow control are two of the most important factors if you are to succeed with any new company. So it is only prudent to use the address of the mail drop as the corporate address until enough business is generated to justify renting physical accommodation for the enterprise.

To sum up, there are four basic reasons why anyone would use a mail drop:

1) To receive mail in one's own name in a discreet fashion;
2) To receive mail in a "pen name";
3) To put distance between one self – or one's "pen name" – and the people and companies from whom one receives mail;
4) To incorporate a company without renting a "real" office;
5) To avoid personal visits and drop-in calls by clients, salesmen and other correspondents.

We are not concerned with the morals or motives of the individual (or company) wishing to use a mail drop – but quite simply HOW to go about using it in such a way as to maximize the chance of success of the above objectives. In this context a mail drop is to be considered as a means to an end – whatever that end may be.

Some may be tempted to view the existence of mail drops as potentially valuable tools for criminals. Perhaps, but so are telephones (for fraudulent salesmen), cars (for getting away after pulling a bank heist) and planes (for skipping to Brazil with the loot). The mere fact that a product or a service *may* be used by criminals – and sometimes will be – cannot justify forbidding any product or service.

As PTs we are participating in and creating a better, happier world order. We are people who respect, enjoy and promote individual freedom, the sanctity of private property, equality, opportunity, social justice, unlimited prosperity, vibrant good health. Bringing freedom and happiness to everyone in the world starts with you. If government disagrees, keep a low profile and escape the tentacles of Big

Brother. If his army of bureaucrats won't let you lead the life YOU want to live – a happy and truly free life – you can drop out. Move your ass and your assets out of his greedy grasp. This way you put limits on BB. Using a mail drop as the first step in becoming a PT is one of your most effective, and most cost-efficient, tools.

## TODAY, MORE THAN EVER, HONEST PEOPLE NEED SECOND ADDRESSES

A great many people are unaware of the fact that mail drops exist. When made aware of it many Boy Scout Johns quite often react along the lines of "honest people don't need mail drops".

Not true! The world that we live in is far from ideal and complete honesty and integrity does not immunize anyone from the annoyances or dangers of it.

Thus, it is wise to put some distance between you and those who pose an existing (or future, potential) threat.

Unless you are very brave – or very stupid – you would not drive a Cadillac into Bronx, New York without locking the doors. You would not stop at a red traffic light in Rio de Janeiro at night. If you are seriously interested in minimizing the dangers presented to you by other drivers. You would not drive in a car without making sure it was a heavy Land Rover and without using seat belts.

In other words, be smart. Protect yourself. Do not make it easy for anyone who might wish to harm you, physically, financially or otherwise. Take prudent counter-measures well in advance. Whatever your concerns, commercial mail drop operations provide you with an excellent vehicle for protecting yourself by giving you an alternative address to use when your intelligence suggests that giving out your real address – the place where you sleep, so to speak – is inadvisable and/or potentially dangerous.

Having a second address is no more dishonest than having an unlisted telephone number . . . But even an unlisted telephone number may be traced, legally or otherwise, by government, creditors, private investigators or anyone else. A recent survey shows that more than 50 per cent of the entire population of Los Angeles have unlisted telephone numbers. Would so many people bother ever so slightly about this unless a real and valid reason – apprehension – existed?

Again, if you value your privacy and your time – not to mention your money – you are better off not only having an unlisted telephone number but also having an "alternative" address with a mail drop.

So how to deal with a mail drop? The first consideration, of course, is to set yourself up as a customer with the service. This implies that you must, in some fashion, undertake communication with the operator of the mail drop and establish yourself as a client. The following is a breakdown of the procedure in which to go about it:

Step 1) Find out where you wish to receive your mail – i.e., what country, town and, if applicable, which street.
Step 2) Find out in which name – or names – you wish to receive mail.
Step 3) Establish how you will physically obtain the mail after it has been received by the mail drop.
Step 4) **DO NOT GIVE THE MAIL DROP YOUR REAL ADDRESS OR TELEPHONE NUMBER! GIVE THEM A HOTEL ADDRESS**
Step 5) Undertake communication with one or more mail drops to inquire about prices, terms etc. Then settle for the one which offers the best combination.
Step 6) Get yourself established as a client with the mail drop.
Step 7) Test the mail drop.
Step 8) Use it.

Let's now cover these eight steps in more detail, one by one, and in the right order.

# WHERE SHOULD YOU HAVE YOUR MAIL DROP?

Your actual needs and concerns determine where you should receive your mail. Also give thought to the future. Anything can happen out there. Future, potential needs and wants should not be forgotten.

The more intricate your personal present and future concerns, the lower profile you want.

Consider very carefully the potential damage, financial and otherwise, you will suffer either if the contents of your mail is made known to someone – such as the tax people – OR if someone is able to find out about your actual place of residence (where you sleep) through your mail drop.

Since you DO know what your present situation is (or at the very least what it may be, at worst) and since you are hopefully intelligent enough to assess the nature of (potential) trouble that the future may bring, USE this knowledge. The more urgent the reasons why you do not wish people to know where you live (or what sort of mail you receive), the greater the need to put as much distance between yourself and the mail drop and you as possible. Assess the dangers, then choose accordingly. The precautions that you need to take vary vastly according to whether you are concerned about annoying personal visits from the proverbial insurance salesman or, whether you are wanted by the state's social workers for, say, abducting your own children in violation of a court decision.

Generally speaking it is never very advisable to use a mail drop in the same town or city where you live, unless it happens to be a very big one – in which case you may be alright simply using a mail drop on the other side of town. If, for instance, you are a single woman worried about annoying visits from your "ex", this will do.

There are several "security levels":

SECURITY LEVEL A. Use a mail drop in the same small town – or in the same part of a city – where you actually live. If you have any direct, personal contact with the operator of the mail drop then they will get to know you – and may, one day, recognize you as you enter or leave your home. This knowledge may then, at a later date, be divulged to the wrong person.

SECURITY LEVEL B. Use a maildrop in a different town. This implies that it will be more of a hassle to collect the mail yourself since you will have to travel further to get it. On the other hand, it may also throw people looking for you a bit off the track, since conventional wisdom has it that most people are too lazy to drive substantial distances to get their mail. If you live in central London but drive out to Oxford to retrieve your mail then you stand less of a chance of your actual address being accidentally found out than if you use a mail drop in your own neighborhood. But remember to park far away from the mail drop so that your car license plates are not observed nor recorded.

SECURITY LEVEL C. Use a maildrop in a different country. You may live in Germany but receive your mail in Paris, France – or live in the USA but receive your mail in Canada. Anyone looking for you will now be thrown way off the track since the search will be located in an entirely different jurisdiction. Someone looking to sue you, for instance, may give up the idea if you are thought to be living in another country on the basis of your mailing address – since it is always more costly to bring a suit against someone in Country A for a claim originating in Country B than bringing the same suit in the country where the claim originated.

If you have reason to believe that someone – a government agency, for instance, is either already keeping you under surveillance or might start doing so then you should definitely resolve to receive all mail that might result in raised eyebrows (or give away "critical" information) in a country different from your own.

SECURITY LEVEL D. Use a mail drop on another continent. If you live in the USA receive your mail in Australia, for instance – or if you live in Europe, receive your mail in Singapore or in Hong Kong. This will make it all but impossible for anyone looking for you to find out where you may receive mail – and it will add a very significant layer of protection to your situation. Obviously it will also add to the cost of actually retrieving your mail. More on this subject shortly.

# IN WHICH NAME (OR NAMES) SHOULD YOU RECEIVE MAIL?

This ties directly into your present situation and apprehensions about the future. As long as you are not seeking to defraud anyone it is absolutely legal to call yourself anything you wish. Opening a bank account anywhere but Austria almost certainly means that you will have to provide some sort of ID – or at the very least one or more professional references – to the bank. If you plan to use the address for banking purposes it will almost certainly be necessary to use your own name. Or your banking passport name in case you have been clever enough to get alternate identifications and open a foreign bank account in a different name. If the name (or names) in which you receive mail also happens to be on an account somewhere in which you maintain a sizeable balance, then you should make certain that the mail is received in a different country – or on a different continent – from where you actually live: go to Security Level C or D. Better yet, instruct the bank to "hold all mail until personally called for". Government agencies operate with relative impunity and are highly alert to mail coming from offshore banking centers such as the Isle of Man, the Cayman Islands, Switzerland.

It is a very good idea to use a "pen name" for mail that you receive in the country where you actually live – information you request, for instance. If you use a mail drop in your own country and you are concerned about privacy then do not give away your "real" name to anyone. Just use a "pen name". Especially if you are in the habit of requesting literature or information of a sexual or political nature, and if you wish to receive it in the town where you live, then you should do your utmost to make sure that this mail is addressed only to your "pen name". Anyone who might take a fancy to investigating you based on the nature of your mail (as adjudged either by opening it or by an "interesting" return name and address printed on the envelope) will have a much harder time finding out who you are. Say that your name is John Smith. Assume you wish to order what is generally termed "sexually explicit literature" (or gadgets). If you want to keep this perversion to yourself then don't let anyone know that it was ordered by you, John Smith. Throw them way off the track by ordering in the name of, say, "Clifton Scumbag". Giving away your real name will make it a lot easier to track you down by way of telephone registers or utility companies records since you will almost certainly have given your real name to these.

As PTs we are free to govern our own lives. Each person should have the right to decide for himself whether or not to pray, eat, drink, sleep, smoke, have children, live or die. In this world, people who attempt nothing more than this with their own lives are very often harassed or prosecuted by government officials. A low profile is paramount if you want to avoid harrassment by petty government officials. Each and every citizen today can become a victim when some bureaucrat presses a few buttons to summon up their computer files. Armed with this information, they can, if they wish, apply pressure or build a legal case against you for many victimless crimes from adultery to tax evasion. PTs make sure they get OFF the computers and OUT of the sight of government. One way to HIDE from Big Brother is by keeping a maildrop or two and using pen names whenever necessary. Even better, this is a perfectly legal way to play hide-and-seek with Big Brother.

## HOW DO YOU WISH TO RETRIEVE YOUR MAIL?

This can be a touchy subject and is, in many ways, the area where the most people make the most (and the worst) mistakes. You wish to retrieve something (your mail) with a minimum risk of putting yourself in a hot spot – that is why you use a mail drop in the first place. Consider this analogy: kidnappers usually demand ransom for their hostages. Hostages can be released almost anywhere with a low level of risk. But they also need to take physical possession of the ransom money. And it is at this stage that a kidnapper is most likely to be apprehended, since he not only has to announce in advance where and how he wants to collect the money, he also has to put himself or an agent in this place and take physical delivery. Some kidnappers have been known to ask that ransom money be thrown from a moving train within a few seconds from the time that radio instructions are received. It is doubtful that you will be able to find a mail drop operator who will follow these instructions. If a maildrop operator would co-operate, the costs would be high and it would raise awareness of you to an astronomical level.

Bear in mind that all maildrops can forward your mail to your home address. But you should give serious thought as to whether you want to oblige them! We think you shouldn't. Unless you move very frequently and have no problem changing your place of residence in no time flat, you should avoid giving away the whereabouts of your nest at all cost.

Yes, mail drop operators – almost to a man – insist that they offer "confidential service" and that they "protect their clients' privacy". This is probably true, if nobody asks. They do not take out newspaper ads listing their clients' names and home addresses once a month. But that's about it! All private investigators know that a US $100 tip gets a maildrop employee to give up any information they need.

Keep in mind that the reason you use a mail drop is to protect yourself – or to retain a very high level of privacy. The main goal is to keep secret the places where you physically live. From this naturally follows that since you do not give out your home address, but give your mail drop address instead, then you should not inform your friendly mail drop operator of your real home address, either.

Why? Because mail drop operators are PEOPLE. And people may, regrettably, be convinced by someone else to "forget" all their golden promises of "confidentiality" etc. A bad mail drop will give out your address if anyone asks. Thankfully there are not a lot of those around – they tend to go out of business about as fast as their clients' expectation of confidentiality go out the window!

Still, any shrewd private investigator may get your address – that is, the address to where your mail is forwarded – quite easily. Investigators use several ruses. One of their favorites is pretending to be searching for you since you are the missing heir to a fortune! If that doesn't work, another investigator comes back claiming he is with the narcotics squad, undercover, looking into an international ring of which you are presumed to be the leader. Private detectives always have credentials closely resembling government law enforcement ID. You'd be amazed at the stories private sleuths sometimes dream up to earn their keep. And you'd be even more amazed at the number of mail drop operators who oblige them: giving out your address, either thinking they had done you a great favour (in the case of the heir-scam) or that he is helping rid the world of baddies. Instead, he just handed over your home address to some investigator working for one of your creditors or for your ex-spouse.

Even the most thoroughly conscientious mail drop operator will very quickly own up and deliver your address if approached by "the proper authorities". Many mail drop operators have a healthy disdain for the tax-man (especially if the tax-man is from another country), but a request from the local police must be answered if the maildrop expects to stay in business. In certain countries the authorities do not hesitate to cook up, or allege, completely bogus charges against an individual – such as trafficking in drugs or child pornography – in order to "break down" any resistance from your mail service or get a court order of disclosure to put your mail drop under pressure. It is a distinct possibility that the authorities will lie about the real reason they want your address, which may be that they want you to testify against an alleged criminal. They may invent charges against you (you are a big-time heroin dealer) just to retrieve your home address.

It follows, then, that since such a thing exists as a "magic word" (e.g. "drugdealer") to make your mail drop operator waive all his supposed commitments to you, then you must put space between yourself and the mail drop, just as you put the mail drop between you and the rest of the world. Therefore, be very careful if you decide to give out your true home address to your mail drop. We think you shouldn't. A reader says:

"Never, ever give out your home address to your mail drop operator. Many years ago I did this – and was shocked to one day discover my address, and those of other clients, easily accessible in a Rotadex prominently displayed on the reception desk. Needless to say, I cut all ties with this mail drop immediately."

How, then, do you retrieve your mail? You can either go and collect it in person, send someone else or have it forwarded.

If you choose to **go and collect your mail in person**, it means that you, yourself physically go to collect your mail at the maildrop. Depending on which security level (A, B, C or D) you have chosen this will range from driving across town to flying (or driving) to a different country – or continent – every time you wish to retrieve your mail. Depending on your level of apprehension about security, it may be advisable to arrive irregularly without prior notice – walk in the door, pick it up, walk out. It is usually a good idea to park your car several blocks from where you pick up the mail so as not to have it noticed by employees of the mail drop. One of our readers received a ton of mail from his ex-wife's lawyers at his mail drop. The envelopes, of course, carried the return address of a big law firm; in other words, it was obvious to the mail drop that their customer had some sort of legal fight going on. Thinking that she was acting for the good lord and justice and the American way, the owner of the mail drop jotted down the name of the (rental) car he was driving when he casually parked it on the street outside one day. Several months later, investigators working for the shrewd lawyer of his ex-wife tracked down not only the name of the car rental company but also the number of the credit card used to rent the car. This credit card, in turn, was issued on a foreign bank account which was subsequently seized – to the tune of a loss to the client of about US $250,000.

Also remember that mail drops may be staked out not only by the police (e.g. in the case of a criminal tax fraud case under way) but also by a private investigator. So act accordingly whenever you go anywhere near the place where you receive your mail. One noted tactic is to mail a big parcel then follow the individual carrying it out – the parcel screaming like a billboard ''Here I am''. If you receive large, bulky items which you have not ordered and which do not carry return addresses that you know of, then it may be advisable to let it stay behind and work out how to get it another day. Better safe than sorry!

As a final note on personal pick-up, you may consider this: before visiting your mail drop for the first time – even if that is to be the only time – tell the mail drop that the person collecting your mail (or paying for their services in untraceable cash) is not you but rather ''a trusted friend''. If possible, send a friend or bellboy from a hotel to collect your mail. In this fashion your mail drop does not know you ''as you'' but rather as a friend (or associate) of yourself. This may very well be advisable if your situation dictates that your mail drop should not know what their client – you – actually looks like. If anyone ever contacts the mail drop to ask if they have seen the client – you – they will automatically say ''no''. When choosing a maildrop, it is better to deal with a large outlet, like CITIBOX in London, if possible. The larger places furnish clients with a separate 24-hour-access lockable mailbox that can be accessed by anyone with a key. If no personal contact is involved, you will be harder to identify. A stake-out by an investigator armed with your photo can be thwarted if someone else makes the actual pick-ups. Naturally, if you send someone else for your mail at irregular intervals, as much as a month apart, a stake-out becomes prohibitively expensive for your enemies. If your picker-up does not know where you live but simply remails to still another address, like general delivery (*poste restante*) in a different country, you have effectively buffered yourself.

You can also **have your mail forwarded by the maildrop**. People who take an active interest in protecting themselves – and their own remaining lifetimes – will usually ask that anything received by the mail drop be either remailed immediately (to another mail drop) or that all mail be held pending further instructions.

## USE A HOTEL

We have already discussed why you should never give out your home address to your mail drop. The absolutely safest way to go about remailing is not to give your mail drop any address AT ALL. Reason? You are travelling. If, for instance, you give a bogus address that is really a hotel or empty lot, then your mail will be lost or returned to sender if a fumbling blockhead remails to this non-existent (or fake) address, forgetting that mail should be HELD. This is an important point to remember. If your mail drop insists that you give an address, not only should you never, ever give them your home address – you should also never give them a fake or non-existent address lest, by mistake, your mail gets sent there and subsequently lost. A second maildrop is best.

It follows that you should either have your mail remailed to a place closer to where you live or, even better, to the place that you would like anyone breaking down the first barrier (forcing or coercing the mail drop to give out your supposed address) to THINK that you live. Let us say that you live in New York City and receive your mail in Canada, from whence it is forwarded to Los Angeles. Now anyone who gets your address in Los Angeles from the mail drop in Canada, for instance by lying about you and stating that you are a wanted criminal, will automatically think that you are in Los Angeles and not in New York. The trick now is to get the mail from Los Angeles, on the other side of the continent. Depending on the urgency of mail you may either pick it up yourself if you go to LA often enough. Or you may contract with yet another service in LA to go and pick up the mail for you and hold it. If security is a real concern, your picker-up can mail it to you care of a hotel in New Jersey (south of New York City). You make a reservation at the hotel saying you will be "flying in from Colorado on business". Unless you really are a fugitive felon (in which case you stand a hefty chance of being hunted down sooner or later – which is a good reason to stick to the straight and narrow) a really tenacious investigator will now think that you live in Canada, then that you live in Los Angeles – and then, finally, that you really live in Colorado and sometimes have business in New Jersey. In this fashion, it will take a pretty massive operation to track you down to New York City, especially if you also make a deal with the hotel in New Jersey to hold all mail for you until you come and pick it up in a "quick in, quick out" fashion (with a nice tip to the receptionist, of course). The hotel could also be instructed to send mail to another hotel or general delivery address.

The more links you put in the chain between you and the address you quote to the world at large as "yours", **the better the chance that you will have advance knowledge** from one of the links in case someone starts "leaning on" your mail drop(s). We have found that maildrop operators usually will tell a client that someone has dropped by to look for them, without any prompting.

## NEGOTIATING WITH MAILDROPS: THE GOOD, THE BAD AND THE UGLY

Depending on your situation you may need to take any number of precautions when you inquire about the services of one or more mail drops in the area(s) that you have chosen.

One mistake that you should never make is to ask the maildrop to send you information about their services, prices at your home. This information is likely to be filed and kept – and even if it is not you will risk giving away your secret maildrop if your mail is under surveillance, be it from your spouse, the police or just your friendly, nosey mailman.

The very best way to inquire about the services of a mail drop is by phone. In this way, the mail drop operator does not know where you are, and no initial "paper trail" is generated leading from the mail drop to you – or even to the general area in which you live.

Again, it is always advisable to be as careful about phoning your maildrop. The careful PT always assumes his 'phone and fax is tapped. Use a pay phone! The phone systems in many countries are rigged to store and file away information about the numbers that have been called from any given phone – as in itemized phone bills. If, for instance, you are looking to get a divorce and want to use the services of a mail drop to put distance between yourself and your spouse when the break comes, it is pretty stupid to risk this information reaching your spouse when the phone number of your mail drop turns up on your phone bill. Your spouse and everyone else has easy access to phone records.

When you do phone, do not call from your home or from your office. These phones may or may not be tapped but there is a better than fair chance that someone may later learn which numbers you have called by obtaining copies of your bills from the phone company. Big hotels often have nice, quiet lounges where you may make calls even if you are not a guest. Needless to say, you should never make the call from a hotel if you are paying by credit card since the credit card bill will lead straight to the hotel which, in turn, will have a copy of your itemized room bill on file, with a complete listing of the numbers you have called. You would be surprised how many otherwise astute businessmen get into marital trouble when the spouses call up the numbers dialled from the room (and indicated on the hotel bill later found somewhere) and find that they belong to escort services! So when you do make the calls, use a public pay phone. Resist the temptation to put the call on your credit card. Remember that the only tracks that may lead someone to your maildrop and subsequently to you are the paper trails that you accidentally (or stupidly) create.

As for the terms of the mail drop(s) you have chosen it is usually a good idea to initially opt for a minimum three-month service. You may save by entering into a one-year deal, but it is generally a good idea to see how reliable it is before committing yourself to any long term deals. Also try to deal with a maildrop that has a three-year or longer business history. No use contracting for a year with a fly-by-night outfit that folds up in a few weeks. There is no reason why you should pre-pay for one year if things quickly turn sour and you have to make a switch. Minimizing your potential losses is what any reasonably intelligent individual would do in all matters of life, and dealing with a mail drop should be no different.

In the world of mail drops, some are good, some are bad and some can be downright ugly.

You may find that your mail drop will want you to sign a contract. It is preferable to avoid this. Your contract will be kept in a file. The insistence on contracts vary from country to country, but you may well find that even a mail drop that initially insists on a contract will relent if you simply pay your bills but ignore requests to return the contract. The nicer you behave on your phone or in any correspondence with your mail drop, the less the likelihood that the operator will keep pestering you for a contract. Be smart, and use psychology to achieve what you want.

Some mail drops also insist that you provide some sort of identification, while others could not care less as long as they get their money. If the mail drop has had bad previous experiences with clients then it is all but certain that you will be asked for identification if you show up to negotiate in person. In many countries citizens are required to carry some sort of identification. If you both look and act as the tourist that you are – or are pretending to be – you may still be asked for a photocopy of your passport. Again, this should be avoided. The easiest and best way to negotiate with a mail drop is to do it by phone. Even if your mail drop is in the country where you actually live it is as easy to call up and negotiate the service as if you were living in another country. If you are living in Spain, say, and you want a mail drop there, you call up the mail drop and pretend that you live in, say, England. When asked, as you surely will be, for your home address you may quite simply give the address of a mail drop in England, then ask that nothing be forwarded there, offering a probable excuse such as "my friendly, local mail man seems to lose some of my letters pretty often". Just to make absolutely sure, it may be a good idea to contract for a month or so with the mail drop in England to receive anything that your Spanish mail drop may send. This mail drop should have a standing order to forward all mail to you – in another envelope – to your Spanish service. If you find that your mail drop has forwarded anything against your standing orders you should immediately get on the phone and implore them not to send you anything – by explaining, for instance, that you are "currently travelling in the Far East" or some such. People are creatures of habit and just as with Pavlov's dogs you may need to "train" your mail drop to forward your mail – or NOT to forward your mail – according to your specific instructions. As running a maildrop is not highly remunerative, you should not expect a high degree of intelligence on the part of these operatives.

A final note on identification. Even if a mail drop in a given country is required by law to demand proper identification of clients (e.g. for taxation purposes) then these demands are usually waived for "foreign" clients. If a country has laws on the books demanding that people identify themselves to mail drops, then the general (and ignorant) assumption will be that such laws exist in other countries, too.

In other words, let us presuppose that you are living in such a country and that you are looking to establish a mail drop there. If you show up in person then identification will be demanded of you. What to do? Call them up instead, explain that you are living (and calling from) another country and be prepared to give out an address in that country as your "home" address. This address, of course, should merely belong to another mail drop – but the mail drop in the "problem country" will assume that you are who you say you are since you "must" (according to their line of thinking) have identified yourself as such to someone at the address you give as your "home" (or office) in a foreign country.

## WHEN AND HOW TO ESTABLISH YOURSELF AS A CLIENT

You will, obviously, need to pay for the services of your mail drop. The safest and least cumbersome way in which to do so is to pay first for, say, three months and thereafter one year in advance depending on how expensive the mail drop is and how likely it is that you may need to cut your ties to it before the paid-for time has run out. This means that you have a few months in which to test the mail drop for security and efficiency – and if it passes this test then you prepay for one year, thus minimizing the time you have to spend on payment considerations in the future. Mail drop operators like money (as do we all) and look more favourably at a client who pays one year in advance than at a client who constantly needs to be reminded to pay his monthly (or quarterly) bills.

When you do pay the fee, remember why you are using a mail drop. What are your concerns and your apprehensions? The more space you need to put between yourself and your mail drop, the more elaborate the precautions you have to take when making your payments.

One thing is certain: you shouldn't pay your mail drop by credit card or by a personal check unless these lead either to accounts that cannot be traced to your name (or dwelling) or to accounts that are all but emptied. If you opt for a mail drop through which to carry on correspondence with the lawyers representing your spouse in a drawn-out alimony battle, then it would be folly to pay your mail drop with a cheque drawn on the secret, Swiss bank account in which you have stashed the "mother lode" that your spouse wants to get at. Be smart. Pay either in cash – in the event that you show up in person – or by a postal money order. Of course, you may ask your mail drop in one country to buy and mail a money order on your behalf to your mail drop in another country. The variations on this theme are infinite.

Needless to say, the mail drop may make a mental note about the nature in which you made your payment, especially if it does not conform to the story they have heard you tell. If you pretend to be living in London then the mail drop should, ideally, receive the payment from this country. Precaution is the name of the game and should never be forgotten. Remember that one ounce of preparation is worth a ton of cure.

Generally speaking the least traceable way to move funds is by way of the postal service, which means either by postal money order or by cash. In a few countries it is "illegal" to send cash funds abroad in the mail – but it is also a victimless crime. If you wrap the cash in two pieces of ordinary writing paper and mail it to your mail drop looking like an ordinary business letter, the risk of the cash disappearing is virtually nil – as long, of course, as the mail drop does not take the cash and pretend never to have received it. To minimize the risk of this happening you may send several letters, each containing a portion of the total payment. Even a full-fledged conman will have a tough time trying to explain that he did not receive a single one of the five or ten letters you mailed him!

Beware, however, of sending cash by courier services such as DHL (TNT, Fedex or UPS). They will do it, especially if you do *not* tell them that your shipment of "documents" contains cash, too – but in countries with currency restrictions the shipment may be opened either by DHL or by the customs service in the country where the shipment originates (or arrives). One client let his account with a mail drop in the United States get badly in arrears, then attempted to send US $500 in cash by DHL in order to retrieve the mail that had been steadily accumulating. He sent it by DHL from Paris, France, but the sealed and taped envelope in the pouch was opened by French customs and the cash was confiscated. It is far better to plan ahead, not to have your account slide into the red and to pay either by postal money order or, if you must, by cash sent in what looks like an envelope containing ordinary business (or personal) correspondence. A very thin letter or packet is less likely to be opened by either customs or thieves in the postal service.

When the matter of payment has been prudently taken care of then you have completed the process of establishing yourself as a client. It is vital that you constantly remind yourself of the reasons why you are using your mail drop. What are your fears? Your apprehensions? Your concerns? These, present and potential, are what determine the manner in which you should choose your mail drop and set it up. Using your common sense and your intelligence always works, and so does choosing a higher level of privacy – or security level – than you may actually need right now.

Who is to say what the future may bring? In the words of New York builder Donald Trump: "If you take care of the downside, the upside will take care of itself." Translation: if you choose a mail drop and operate it in a fashion that is geared towards a much higher level of safety and privacy than what you need, you will suffer less of a blow if things turn unexpectedly worse. Things have a way of going sour for people who are unprepared. If your marriage is shaky you will want to have a lawyer and a mail drop lined up when the bubble finally bursts. If you are fiddling with your income taxes, the same thing goes. And at the very least you are well advised to obtain as much relevant knowledge about any subject that bothers you – or may bother you in the future – as you possibly can.

An individual of intelligence seeks knowledge about how to handle potential problems before they surface. Let us illustrate: a client of ours had a longstanding and mutually beneficial relationship with a mail drop which suddenly came under fierce attack from the tax people in his home country. He did not really have a whole lot of knowledge about the workings of a mail drop and was totally unprepared to set himself up as a client somewhere else, as the mail drop he was using had initially been procured by his lawyer. One day he phoned his mail drop and was told, in so many words: "We expect to be served with a court order within one or two days telling us to hand over your mail to the authorities. If you do not tell us where to send it by tomorrow then it may be too late. Now, can you give me an address where I may mail the letters we are keeping for you?"

The client was shocked and devastated. He had previously received mail in hotels, forwarded there from his mail drop, but now he needed to establish a new service immediately. He hung up, promising to call back later. Frantically, he picked up a copy of *The International Herald Tribune* and called up the number of a mail service advertising in the classifieds. He introduced himself, obtained an address and immediately called back his "old" drop and told them to send it to "his new home", giving the address of the new service. Whereupon he crossed a nearby border to a different country to pay for the services of his new mail drop from another country to deflect attention from the city (and country) in which he was really living.

He would have been well advised to simply use a big hotel in a major city once. He should also have on file a master plan of strategic withdrawal involving a number of mail drops. This would have saved him the terror of "feeling stuck", without an address to give in order to save his accumulated sensitive mail from being turned over to the enemy.

It is a point well worth repeating that it is especially in times of unexpected trouble that advance planning and preparation are better to have done early A cornered rat's mind is clouded. It will not hurt you to contact one or several of the mail drops listed here right now. It is better, and highly preferable, to use your intelligence to think ahead about where and how you may, at some future point, want to deal with your mail than to have to make such arrangements when events suddenly conspire against you with ominous speed.

## WHY TESTING YOUR MAIL DROP IS SO, SO IMPORTANT
Your mail drop – present or potential – is to be looked upon as a business partner. It will provide you with a service in exchange for funds. It is always wise to check out your business partners as well as you can (without drawing undue attention to the fact) before starting to rely heavily on them.

Depending on the services that you will need from your mail drop, you should make a number of "dry runs" on each. Which means, arrange to make sure that your instructions are carried out to the letter and with due diligence. Say, for instance, that you are establishing yourself as a client with a mail drop because you expect your marriage to go down the tubes in the not too distant future. Let us further suppose that when it does you will want to move to another location without giving this away to your spouse.

Establish yourself as a client with the mail drop now *as if* you already had a bloodthirsty pack of lawyers at your heels. Test it to make sure that the mail you may be getting will actually be forwarded to you as per your instructions. If you intend to pick it up personally, you should carry out the procedure in advance as a "drill". How to do it? Mail yourself some letters at your new mail drop, then either pick it up or have it remailed in the fashion that you expect to employ when push comes to shove. This serves two purposes. First of all, you get to know about any pitfalls in the level of efficiency of your mail drop *ahead of time*. This enables you to discuss any problems or concerns with the operator now, before any other (and more serious) problems surface. Second, you will become known as an "active" client to your mail drop and, if you are not too lacking in social graces, the people working at your mail drop will start to "like" you. It is always a good idea to be on a good standing with your business partners. Get to know their employee's names and so on. Small gifts such as candies or a bottle of wine may buy you a little more loyalty or information when your adversaries come knocking. The operator of a mail drop used by one of my clients collects stamps. After finding out about this, he now clips and saves any overseas stamps from his mail and gives them to the operator who is beaming like a child at Christmas at this courtesy. Needless to say, he does not hand over stamps originating in the country where he maintains his "major" bank account (the account statements from this make a "soft landing" at another mail drop) – quite to the contrary, he actively requests information from various companies in a well-known tax haven on the other side of the earth. If anyone ever breaks through the significant layer of protection generated from goodwill towards him by the happy operator they will, at worst, be looking for his bank accounts in Switzerland, not in the Cayman Islands. Of course, we stress again, your mother lode account statements should never be floating around in the mails. If your bank won't hold your mail, get another bank.

## USING YOUR MAIL DROP: LITTLE-KNOWN SECRETS

After going through the motions of establishing yourself as a client and testing the mail drop you are ready to use it to maximum potential, whether this be of a protective (privacy) nature or in a professional function.

Whatever you do, make sure that you pay your bills on time. Always make sure that your instructions are delivered and properly understood. Do not "expect" the people working at your mail drop to be clairvoyants – or even to always remember what you have told them orally.

If, for a long time, your mail drop has had a standing order about where to forward mail to you, things may change. You may want to have your mail kept for personal pick-up in the future or you may want it forwarded to a different address. If, for instance, you send a fax to your mail drop with new orders you should also be clever enough to follow this up with a phone call to make sure that the instructions have been received and properly understood. Do not "expect" your mail to be forwarded on the day that you have instructed your mail drop to do so. Follow up with a phone call to **confirm** that it has been done. The operator of your mail drop will recognize you as a precise client who is trustworthy and expects his business partners to be so, too. He (or she) will not only take greater care to follow your instructions to the letter, but will respect you – the client – for insisting on this.

Most people do not know that they can use a mail drop for a lot more than just receiving mail.

Once you are an established and valued client, your mail drop will do almost anything for you. Standard services include secretarial work of all kinds, accounting, simple banking and running your business for you. Most mail drops have phone, fax and telex services on offer as well. If the price is right, and if you have no objections to people being able to call up your mail drop, you should consider opting for the phone and fax services in addition to basic mail. It does make you look more credible to your customers.

More often than not, you can also ask your mail drop to order a personal phone line for you. You can even have them install your own fax line, so you have two numbers for your use only. The cost will usually just be the telephone company line rental charges. There will rarely be any outgoing calls, just incoming. For dealing with calls you can install a telephone answering machine, a fax, a voice mail system, an all-in-one computer or a call diverter. Baffled? We will cover some of these technobits in detail in the chapter on communications.

Renting shelf-space at your mail drop is usually very cheap indeed. An answering machine takes up very little room. Even a computer can usually sit and hum for less than £100 a year.

These tools, in turn, can make you more money. Which brings us to . . .

# Chapter 12

# MAKING YOUR MAIL DROP PAY

How to turn your maildrop into a pot of gold?

As you now know, the services offered by a mail drop basically consist of receiving mail on your behalf and then either forwarding it to you (in a new envelope) somewhere else or keeping it for your personal pick-up.

However, many mail drops offer more than this basic service. Many of which may be used to increase your earning power by saving you time and trouble.

Most also offer to receive faxes and phone messages for you, either on their own phone number or on a line installed specially for your use. In the case of the latter, you will (naturally) have to pay the phone installation and service charges but it may be worth it depending on your situation. Many services also accept that their address is used when incorporating a company, with the mail drop acting as ''registered office''. In some jurisdictions this may require various forms to be filled out with proof of the identity of corporate directors and officers.

You should understand that the people operating your mail drop are in it only for the money, which is the way it should be. It is to the best interests of the operator of the mail drop that clients are kept happy and their demands and wishes are catered to. Many mail drops actively encourage clients to use them not only for mail (and fax and/or phone message) reception but also for secretarial services such as typing, translation, incorporating companies and even errands. You should, of course, be prepared to pay the standard hourly fee for any services you require that are above and beyond the basic services for which you have contracted. It may be a bargain. You should never be afraid to ask your mail drop to get you information about services you may need, to buy products for you, or do small errands as long as you are prepared to pay for their time. If you make it very clear and plain that you are willing to pay for it and that you are not just trying to obtain a ''freebie service'' or a ''friendly favor'' then you may easily talk your mail drop operator into doing research work for you or to ship out your products or information brochures. If you are looking for a product you cannot obtain in your own country, ask your foreign mail drop to get it for you. Needless to say, you should make sure that there are sufficient funds in your account to cover the costs of such services. Simply stick a banknote of the proper denomination in a letter and send it to your mail drop, thanking them in advance for their services.

Do not expect to get credit from your mail drop. It is customary that all fees are paid in advance. It works to prevent apprehension about your skipping out on a large bill – something that will certainly make the forwarding of your mail grind to a sudden halt.

## REMAILING
A service that is in great demand by people not wishing to give away in which country they actually live

is remailing. Remailing means that you address your letters, then stuff them in a larger envelope and send it to the operator of your mail drop with instructions that the letters be stamped locally (if you have not already done this yourself) and mailed from the area where your mail drop is located, rather than from the area in which you live. In this fashion, the letters are stamped and postmarked in the city, country, continent, in which you wish the letters to "originate". Say that you have decided to move to sunny, southern Spain but do not wish to be bothered by annoying relatives or creditors (or worse). You establish a mail drop in, say, London from whence your mail is discreetly forwarded to Spain. But since you may still need to write to people, it would be a give-away if all letters from you arrive bearing Spanish stamps and postmarks. In this case, you would simply send all your outgoing correspondence to London with instructions that the letters be stamped and stuffed in any red, London post box. Now those on the receiving end will take one look at the envelope and think "well, he (or she) really IS in London". We know of one service in Singapore which will do remailing for anyone, even non-clients. This service is operated by an American expatriate, who does not ask any questions nor keep any files. Need a letter mailed from Singapore? He will send your 10 gram, or less, letter airmail to any worldwide location. Just put your letter in a sealed addressed envelope, put the letter into another envelope with US $3.00 cash or the equivalent in any currency or by money order and mail to: E.W. Special Services, P.O. Box 1341, Raffles City, Singapore 9117. Scope will also do the same for you in the UK for £2/$3.

Whereas some mail drops are merely that – mail reception facilities and little else – others have gone the whole hog and offer just about any service you may ever need.

A London-based operator, The Leyton Office, has a comprehensive service on offer ranging from letter collection and live telephone answering to office administration such as wordprocessing and photocopying. Mail collection costs £35 for three months, £60 for six months and £100 for one year. For £5.00, you can have 50 re-direction labels, allowing your mail to be sent anywhere in the UK or Europe at no extra postal charge, using one label per letter. An alternative for £10 is to buy 20 first class stamped strong brown envelopes in which your mail can be sealed and sent out the same day. Letters can be posted from The Leyton Office at a minimum charge of £5 for 1-100 letters and £5 per hundred thereafter.

There are two live telephone answering services offered by this company. For a regular service, covering up to 70 calls a quarter, the cost is £35 a quarter, £60 for six months (120 calls) or £100 annually (200 calls), giving office hours' cover plus answerphone back-up. An exclusive line can be bought which will be answered in your personal or company name. Again it operates office hours and costs from £200 for three months to £500 for a year. Fax reception services are available. Wordprocessing, typesetting, laser printing and photocopying are offered to produce letterheads or similar.

The Leyton Office is at St Georges House, 31A, St Georges Road, Leyton, London E10 5RH, telephone (+44 international) (0)81 556 2979, fax (0)81 539 2862 and is highly recommended.

You should note that if your personal situation necessitates the utmost in discretion then you should not succumb to the temptation of giving out your home address to *anyone*, not even the most trustworthy maildrop. This is mentioned since some books and operators give the idea that a truly trustworthy mail drop may be relied upon to safeguard your home address. Suffice it to say that if you are wanted by serious gangsters (or by a vicious government agency somewhere) then you should keep your home address to the only one person in this world that you may safely trust – yourself. Disregard this at your peril. Another consideration is that some mail drop services are high profile. Most mail order merchandisers and law enforcement agencies recognize these at once as mail drops.

## OTHER PRIVACY CONSIDERATIONS

A PT does not shoot himself in the foot. If you fear that the taxman is about to get up close and personal any day now, do NOT reach for the phone in your home or office. Why not? Because it may be bugged

Big Brother is everywhere nowadays. If you are facing a personal bankruptcy and want to make use of the services of a mail drop for mail that you do not wish to pass through the hands of the receiver, remember that your phone records may be subpoenaed later. This may give away the fact that you have acted to receive certain mail in a "clandestine way". Whatever your situation and the future facing you, it is up to you and no one else to act in such a way as to minimize your risk – or to maximize your gains, as the case may be. If it is worth doing, it is worth doing right. Contemplate, be rational, deduce from what you know that which you need to do, then do it – and do it right.

## USE YOUR FRIENDLY PHONEBOOK

It is also a good idea to get photocopies of the Yellow Pages listings of mail drops and secretarial services in any city or country that you visit when travelling. This way, you will rapidly be building a file of information for future reference on mail drops that do not advertise internationally and may thus be more low profile.

## LET A LAWYER DO IT

This is the most expensive option but most lawyers will receive c/o their firm sensitive mail such as passports or important contracts. Consider using an offshore lawyer on a one-time basis for holding your most valuable documents.

## RUNNING YOUR OWN AD

One additional and interesting (but rather time-consuming) way of locating mail drops just about anywhere is to run an ad in a local newspaper in the designated area, looking for a company (a small office, shop or store, for instance) that will provide mail and other services for a "(foreign) company seeking to enter the (local) market".

You WILL get a lot of replies. We know. We have tried it. Most are from small businesses seeking to make a few extra dollars a month helping you out. They are NOT normally in the mail drop business. You will perhaps be their only client in this area. They are amateurs and will not have a lot of expertise. But probably they will give you good service and attention. You will be able to bargain over price. You will probably even be able to work with them in some sort of a contingency fee arrangement. No profit for you means no profit for them. Or an arrangement where they are paid a percentage of net monies. Receipts, a fixed fee for each letter forwarded or some other such deal. Use your imagination. Then haggle.

## THE CHEAPEST MAIL DROP OF ALL IS NOT A MAIL DROP

Finally, large international hotels will generally receive and hold mail marked "please hold for arriving guest" if you notify the hotel ahead of time. Needless to say this method is viable only for a very limited amount of mail at each hotel, but you may wish to give it a try just to get the experience.

The safest and cheapest form of security is no mail, no messages, and no communications. Having spent all this time on mail drops, we must add that if someone serious is out to kill you or jail you for life, the only way to be almost 100 per cent secure is to:

1) Break all ties with your past, especially contacts with relatives or friends;

2) Discontinue all activities, businesses and hobbies you were identified with;

3) If you must communicate with anyone from the past, call them at a pre-arranged public phone, from a public phone in a city that you will never visit again. Never use the same city twice;

4) Never send or receive mail, faxes or any other communications from old contacts;
5) Completely change your identity;
6) Move yourself and your assets to places seldom frequented by your former friends, adversaries, or any countryman who might conceivably know any of them;
7) Change your physical appearance and never use your old language.

# PART THREE

# BETTER LIVING
# THRU' TECHNOLOGY

**Chapter 13**

# HOW SECURE ARE *YOUR* COMMUNICATIONS?

Keep the enemy confused; use diversity when you communicate.

You should get yourself at least one maildrop. And, preferably, several – in different countries.

Mail is not the only way to go. The RIGHT way to communicate is to be determined by your particular situation.

Communication is the sending, receiving or exchanging of data and information, mainly verbal, written or electronic form. The exact purpose of "moving" data dictates the way in which it should be done, especially as far as privacy is concerned.

When seeking to reach a goal (in this instance, communicating in privacy and security), it is essential to be aware of a few new options, with the old standbys.

In the following four chapters, we shall cover all the do's and all the don'ts of using mail, telephones (with mobile phones and the so-called superphones as well), faxes and plain, verbal face-to-face speaking.

---

### CASE HISTORY:
### BANKER WITH TERMINALLY HIGH PROFILE

A fugitive financier said to be worth $100 million was nabbed in 1992 only because of his high profile.

Tom J. Billman, former president of Community Savings & Loan in Bethesda, Maryland, fled to Spain after a jury in the United States entered a $112 million judgment against him in October 1988 in the collapse of his thrift. He was indicted in January 1990 on federal charges alleging he defrauded depositors of $106 million. Maybe he did; maybe he didn't. Either way, he'll be convicted.

In Spain, Billman was able to support himself regally on funds allegedly drained from his failed savings and loan and secreted in Switzerland. He kept a lavish mansion in the southern Spanish port of Estepona and owned two luxury yachts – a $318,000, 44-foot motor launch with a two-member crew, and a $102,000, 45-foot sailboat. After setting up house in Spain under the alias George M. Lady, Billman established a yacht brokerage business. He retained a set of lawyers in Gibraltar to handle his business affairs.

Yachts, a high profile business and a lavish mansion was too much visibility for fugitive Billman. The US Marshalls soon got word of his Spanish high life. The Marshalls placed large ads in the *Herald Tribune* (with his photo) offering a $200,000 reward for information leading to his arrest and extradition. We suspect that they already knew exactly where he was, but the ads were placed just to get the Spanish police to co-operate by making Billman out to be a high-level desperado, and letting them get a share of the reward being funded by USA taxpayers. Billman was quickly apprehended in Estepona, Spain. He should've read *PT*. High profile is never a good idea, even if you are not a fugitive. If you are wanted by the Law or by others who'd like to do you harm, it is fatal.

# Chapter 14

# LOW PROFILE MAIL TIPS

If you need to communicate or do business and want to minimize the risk, mail drops are the *numero uno* basic safeguard that you can implement. Put some distance between yourself and the rest of the world. If you are still unconvinced you may be deluding yourself on the level of your actual willingness to reach the PT goals you have by now set out for yourself.

Above all, mail implies "receiving or sending someone a letter" – or receiving or ordering something else, such as goods (books, magazines, gadgets or computer disks). The shipment may be intercepted and either inspected or photocopied *en route* to its destination, i.e. the intended recipient. This is especially true if the person, corporation or bank that you are mailing something to happens to be under mail surveillance. This happens in cases of divorce, bankruptcy/receivership or other investigations. Thus, if you have reason to protect the interests of the recipient of your shipment (as well, of course, as your own) then, if at all possible, arrange to send mail in a fashion that carries the least degree of risk to recipient. If, for instance, you are mailing an overdue check to someone you know to be in dire, financial straits, it is a nice touch to inquire beforehand by phone whether the address is accurate or whether arriving mail is known (or suspected) to be diverted and get alternate instructions if need be. If you have not spoken to someone for a long time, it will reflect very favorably on you, in his opinion anyway, if you do your bit to ensure that a check you mail winds up with him and *not* with his enemies. Incidentally, if you have recently received payments from someone now embroiled in litigation, you may be required to return such funds to the estate – which is another reason to be very circumspect. Be careful not to say too much when communicating with people who are in this sort of "trouble". Your mail may fall into the wrong hands.

Secondly, when sending something, determine what you wish to happen when the shipment is either received or intercepted, which means, what impression do you wish to give the recipient and/or investigators? It is easy to make people believe that you are in a different country – or on a different continent – by quite simply using a **remailing service**, as outlined in the previous chapter. Put whatever you wish to send in an addressed (but not stamped) envelope, then stuff this into a larger envelope and mail this to wherever you wish the letter postmarked. Include with the "sensitive" letter instructions to the "intermediary recipient" (mail forwarder) to remail. If you already have a maildrop in another country and this is known to the recipient or suspected by investigators who may also know you, it is easy to officially (or unofficially) ask your "known" mail drop operator if you have recently (or ever) requested remailing. The same goes, of course, even if your mail drop actually *is* super-secret in the event that it later *becomes* public knowledge.

The way to get around this is to have such mail remailed by someone else to whom you will never be connected – either a separate mail drop (use a different name) or a hotel. A client being chased by unsavoury characters recently wished to give the impression that he was in Rome, Italy. As he only needed one single letter remailed, he put this in an envelope with a few thousand lira (US $3.00) and mailed it to a large hotel in the capital with a letter that read something like this:

*"Dear Sir, I recently visited Rome and was enthralled by your beautiful city. I received an absolutely outstanding service from your staff and will not hesitate for a moment to recommend your hotel to friends, family and business acquaintances. I trust that they will be treated as well as I was. However, I have a slight problem. I forgot to mail a promised letter to my dear old Aunt from Rome before leaving. I am burdened by a bad conscience over this forgetfulness of mine. Could I ask you to please be so kind as to affix local Italian postage stamps to the enclosed envelope and drop it in a mailbox? I would be very grateful for this, and also enclose 10,000 lira (or a £5 note) to cover postage and the trouble. Thanking you very much in advance and looking forward to staying with you again soon, I remain yours sincerely"*, etc.

Did the hotel oblige? Of course they did. In effect, the hounds on his tail spent several weeks and a small fortune travelling around Italy looking for him, giving him more than enough time to sell off some assets that they would otherwise have located and seized. He is currently living in great comfort in "Neverland". We still get nice Christmas cards from him every year – remailed, of course. The man is not stupid!

Quite obviously, you should expect to be able to use this ploy with only one or two letters per hotel – and not with too many letters at one time so as not to test the patience of the concierge. Always address such requests as well as the actual, physical envelope not merely to the hotel but to "concierge", "concierge desk" or "reception". Do *not* put a name on the outer envelope as this may mean that the shipment is thought to be for an arriving guest and never will be opened.

The only possible risk with this is if the hotel uses a postmarking machine instead of a stamp when doing you this little favour – this may lead investigators to the hotel (postmarking machines print tell-tale numbers in addition to date and place, allowing one to pinpoint the owner of the machine) – who may remember your letter and little "story". However, judging from scores of cases, letters like this are usually mailed with a regular stamp. The cost? Figure the price of the stamp, then add somewhere in the order of £5-£10 (or US $), preferably *local currency* as a tip, cash.

It is, of course, a nice touch if you already have stationery and envelopes from the hotel in question and use these with your request – as long as they are not so old as to probably having been later replaced with a new design, which would nullify your explanation of having stayed with the hotel "recently".

Remember that if you have ever stayed at a hotel and either do not wish to give this fact away at all, or if you have paid with a credit card that ties in to one of your main (or undisclosed) bank accounts, then you should not use stationery or envelopes from such a hotel *at all*. Most hotels keep written records or even "guest profiles" of everyone who has ever stayed with them. These records may include either credit card numbers or other details about how you paid for your stay, including which travel agency (if any) you used to book the room. But generally speaking, hotels are highly useful for a number of purposes (see "hotels" chapter later in this book). You can get hotel stationery, usually just by asking for a few sheets and envelopes at the concierge (front) desk – even if you don't stay there.

If you don't know the address of any large hotels in the city from where you want your letter mailed, call the international telephone operator and ask. Or check travel guides and international hotel directories. Ask your travel agency or enquire with a local branch of a large international chain. Every big hotel in your city probably has a display of brochures of "sister hotels" around the world.

# MAKE LIKE A SPY: THE ART OF INVISIBLE INK

A nice little touch on how to include messages in a letter that are hard for outsiders to spot. Arrange, preferably face-to-face and not by phone, a code that may be included either with the address or in the letter itself. Let us say, for instance, that you would usually start off a letter to a friend with the phrase "Dear Nick". Now, say that you wish to include something – a phone number, for instance – that you do not wish someone intercepting or later finding the letter to stumble on. You may then arrange with Nick, that in this case you will instead start off with spelling out his name in full, i.e., "Dear Nicholas".

If Nick receives such a letter, he will know that sensitive info is included somewhere. How to avoid detection of such info by a third party with prying eyes?

By writing it in the modern equivalent of "invisible ink"! Visit a large stationery store or a graphics tools supply house and get a UV-marker. Anything you write with the UV marker (a phone number, address or other secret message) will be invisible to the naked eye. For "Nicholas" to read your sensitive info, he will have to use a hand-held UV (ultra-violet) lamp of the sort commonly used by stamp collectors. UV-lamps are freely and cheaply available in photo stores or stamp emporiums, for instance. Price, about £5 for the marker and less than £10 for the UV-lamp.

As an aside, UV-lamps are what leads to the capture of most people travelling on false passports. When examining a passport, the customs or immigrations official will put the passport under a UV-lamp to check whether the original photo in the passport has been removed or altered after being treated with fluid solvents. If it has, the passport is immediately established as being a fake without having to resort to checking with the issuing embassy or even Interpol listings of stolen, blank passports. Most countries mark passports with UV codes. Fake or altered passports show up under UV light.

You can obtain cheap UV-pens by mail order if you ask for "Edding" UV-Security markers and enclose £3/each incl P&P to Bennett & Sterling, Windmill Hill, Enfield, London, England. Tel (+44) 81 367 0777). Another brand is manufactured by the Austrian company Trodat, and it also supplies UV stamp pads and UV ink for use in fountain pens. Mailorder division is based in Milan, Italy (via E Breda 146, local tel 02 2551392). Trodat UV pens are sold at all large stationery stores. You can also buy UV ink and use it with stamp pads and ordinary rubber stamps.

One minor problem with UV pens and ink is that the products have only a short shelf life so you need to buy fresh to ensure efficiency. Ultraviolet pencils in various base colors have infinite shelf life. UV ink as used on passports usually is sealed airtight and has longer life than ordinary ink.

An excellent source of ultraviolet inks, powders, lights and much other surveillance, intelligence, security, privacy protection and paramilitary materials is Mr Jeff Davis at Shomer-Tec, PO Box 2039, Bellingham, Washington 98227 USA, telephone (206) 733-6214, fax (206) 676-5248. His 94-page catalog is extremely comprehensive and of value to PTs, who should mention a referral from Steve Uhrig of SWS Security (1300 Boyd Road Street, Maryland, 21154-1826, USA, telephone (410) 879-4035, fax (410) 836-1190). PTs seeking maximum privacy can order Shomer-Tec products through SWS Security for a small premium.

A useful item available from Shomer-Tec is an "envelope privacy protector", consisting of standard letter-sized sheets of paper completely coated with magnetic ink on one side and colored ink on the other. Short of physically opening the envelope, these sheets should protect post communications from almost any attack, including electronic scanning and envelope compromise spray.

# MODERN MAIL MANNERS

Apart from the mere logistics of getting a letter to someone, you should evaluate the possible ramifications for your own interests if the recipient later turns out not to be "your friend" – or if investigators either open the letter or photocopy the envelope (the latter being quite legal, even without a court warrant, in many countries – including the US and England).

Even if you do not expect the recipient to be under mail surveillance, bear in mind that a later conflict of interest may mean that "whatever you wrote may be used against you at a later date".

In fact, you should follow the same procedure with letters that you write as you should with credit cards or checks. Never put anything in them that you would hate seeing plastered all over the front pages. Take great pains to structure and phrase the letter in such a way that a stranger reading your letter would think you are pure as the driven snow, and have the morals and ethics of Santa Claus and St Peter combined. If your low-down brother-in-law is seeking to use his knowledge of e.g. your tax evasion to blackmail you into giving him a loan, write him a letter (and keep a copy) that does not mention your own affairs but rather is a "negative" to his proposal of an insurance scam, a major fraud or similar. This may cause him to think twice about pursuing the matter further. Especially in an age when most people, including public prosecutors, have been sold on the idea that "where there is smoke, there is sure to be fire", such false allegations are useful to deter people from harassing you – the best part being that efficiency is 90 per cent guaranteed even if you never even imply that you "might" go to the authorities. A sample letter might read:

- "Dear Jack. At lunch the other day, you suggested that we work together on bilking the First Interstate Bank by lending against phoney IOUs and cancelled foreign stock certificates. I feel compelled to repeat yet again that I absolutely deplore your highly illegal suggestions and your attempt to make me part of your conspiracies. I will have nothing to do with them. I suggest you think about an honest way to get the money you need for your gambling and womanizing. Do not try to involve me in your criminal conspiracies. Your brother-in-law, John."

If Jack values his own marriage, my guess is that he will back down from using his knowledge about your Swiss bank account against you. I also recommend that you move any such account to another country, just in case he is too dense to get the drift.

Should you file letters that you receive? **The golden rule on files is not to file anything incriminating and in general as little as possible** or at least as little as possible. Only file letters (and faxes) that you receive plus copies of those you send yourself if there is any *real* possibility that you may later need them to prove a claim against someone – or disprove a claim or allegation made against you. Even if you make a legally binding offer by letter, you may freely throw away the original since anyone wishing to use legal means to compel you to honor your offer will have to produce a copy. If information is involved, just clip out the informative bits, and file in a place with other such information. Better yet, scan or re-input the info and only keep it electronically in your computer.

A lot of people file away everything they receive – like little children who are still thrilled at getting "their very own mail". Don't! Non-essential files are a pain in the butt to store and in the course of our lives can cause problems. One woman I lived with came across old love letters and had a jealousy attack over things that happened before I met her. Do you need all your files? How often do you refer to them? As with other belongings and possessions, files can tie you down. If you have not looked at a particular folder or referred to a piece of paper during the last year or so, you ought to junk it.

Files are bulky, take up room and weigh a lot. You may want to keep your Army discharge papers but most other mail should go straight into an incinerator or the shredding machine the second you have read and digested it.

Incidentally, paper shredding machines provide not only peace of mind but also some very real security, especially if you use them religiously. Former US defense minister Caspar Weinberger was indicted by a special prosecutor on several alleged felonies in the arms-for-hostages-scandal. These allegations did not involve Weinberger taking part in the scam, but, rather, alleged destroying of personal notes *after* they became of possible interest to prosecutors. If you can prove that you do not keep any files, and that you keep copies of letters only until you have achieved your purposes (i.e. getting paid for a job done) and point to the fact that you own a well-used shredding machine, you are much safer. During the hostage-taking at the US embassy in Teheran, Iranian students thought they could beat a shredding machine given sufficient time and manpower. They could! The little darlings called a press conference and announced to the world that they had "pieced together a secret CIA-document", which was true. Investing what must have been thousands of man-hours, they had succeeded in beating security technology. Just a pity for the little misfits that the "secret CIA-document" turned out to be *a requisition for 12 cartons of ball-point pens!* Boy, that really made the guys sweat up at Langley, Virginia. If that's all a dedicated group of loonies can come up with after months of work, you should not worry about the IRS or anyone else being able to use shredded documents for anything useful. Do you have a shredder? If not, get one. They are cheap, selling from about £200 (about US $360) and upwards. Depending on your resources and how much you travel, get either a portable "spaghetti-shredder" to put on top of paper bins in your home, office or hotel rooms – or a "cross-shredder" that cuts both ways. Some more expensive models will make absolute flour not only of documents but also of video tape casettes and even *coins*. Did we forget to mention that shredders kill fingerprints, too? Get one! If you travel a lot, consider one to take with you on the road and use in hotel rooms for bills from strip joints your wife shouldn't know about, travel agencies you have visited on the way and so forth. Do not wait until you come home. There is no reason to take one non-essential piece of paper through customs – as Barbara Streisand found out a little late. Why use a shredder? Is it not safe to leave crumbled-up documents in a hotel paper-bin which is emptied daily? Let us merely say that if your situation and actions require the utmost in discretion then, "no", you shouldn't.

One final, added benefit when you own a shredder. Your desk will be a lot less cluttered up by useless junk and you'll get more done.

Even if you use remailing services, you may give away your hand. A slightly different paper size is used in Europe and the US, for instance. The same goes for envelopes. If you are looking to give the fake impression that you are on another continent, make sure that you use letters and envelopes the sizes of which are consistent with the scenario you are creating or trying to inspire.

Preferably, they should even be obtained in the alleged countries of origin. Forensics is an extremely exact science. When investigators have the ability to pinpoint the "DNA-fingerprints" of a suspect by analyzing *dried saliva in a cigarette butt* left at a crime scene (as happened after a Mafia bombing in Italy) then rest assured that it is not hard to establish where a simple piece of paper originated – and perhaps even where it was sold – and possibly even to whom, as in the case of special custom-printed stationery.

Fingerprints, too, are easy to find on the back of sealing tape, inside envelope flaps etc.

These precautions are probably unnecessary in most cases, but you never know. If, for instance, you are writing yourself a glowingly positive reference letter (in the course of establishing a second identity, for instance) then your fingerprint on the reference could give away this cute little tactic – even if checked years later. Of course, this works in reverse, too. One client had his offices burgled and vandalized during the night. The burglar left behind a load of filth on the walls and a couple of empty spray cans on the floor. These were subsequently turned over to the police who initially could not identify the fingerprints. But *four years later*, the client was contacted by the police who had finally matched the prints on the empty spray cans with those of an individual who had been arrested in a serious fraud case. It turned out that the perpetrator of both crimes was an employee whom our client had fired one year before the burglary.

Finally, a couple of more mundane details concerning mail. Besides not incriminating yourself by committing questionable details and subjects to paper and making sure that you use mail drops and remailing as required by your circumstances (and, preferably, a bit more religiously than "strictly necessary", just in case), make sure that your letters arrive intact and unopened. Use high-quality envelopes (if possible) that will not come apart during transfer, write using an electric typewriter with a disposable daisy wheel and never use handwriting on either letters or envelopes. If at all possible, use address labels or envelopes with see-through windows and print everything, including labels, using an ink-jet printer or a laserprinter which can never be traced to you personally. Avoid writing anything by hand, even if it means going to a little trouble. If you do not have any self-adhesive labels handy, type the address on a small piece of paper, then tape this onto the envelope. Wrap contents either in one or two pieces of heavy, dark colored paper – or use tin-foil, carbon paper or even a newspaper clipping, beware that the origin of the newspaper should be consistent with the impression you are trying to create. Put the inner wrapper around the contents in order to foil X-ray machines and anyone who may try to use clear-fluid to take a peek. See earlier reference to envelope privacy protectors.

If you wish to give the recipient the best possible way of knowing whether his mail is being tampered with, then seal flaps and put a number of pencil or pen marks over the flap edges *before* taping with Scotch tape. You may want to mention that you did so in your letter – or in advance, by phone.

Just in case it wasn't stressed enough. We suggest that you never, never sign by hand any sensitive letters. Also, to avoid a letter being used against you, don't even type your name, or any of your pen names. Your correspondents will know it's you if you start closing with "funny" names of one series: for instance, dog, cat rabbit, monkey. Or Stalin, Lenin, Trotsky.

## Chapter 15

# TRIED AND TESTED TELEPHONE TACTICS

Ever heard this one: "Don't you just love telephones? They're easy, cheap and so much more *personal* than just writing a letter"?

Or how about this one: "Reach out and touch someone". Yup, and you just need to do it the wrong way *once* and someone may "reach out" and touch you – by laying a heavy hand on your shoulder.

Everybody has heard about phones being tapped by the police in "criminal cases" and yet very few people realize that they, too, are already on the receiving end of a bugging by authorities. Installing bugs are no big problem for the boys in blue – a search warrant will immediately facilitate a tap being connected on any phone. How to obtain a search warrant? Just say "drug enforcement". This works, for cops at least, every single time. If you are in the habit of complaining about your local "establishment", either verbally or in writing, you may just as well consider your home phone as bugged for any conversation that you would rather keep confidential. Yes, you may get "anti-bugging" equipment, the problem is that the device you buy will only detect "unauthorized" bugs. In most countries, authorities can install taps in switching centrals. It is impossible to detect those.

These days all international calls are recorded for later use by several government agencies from a wide variety of nations.


## UNAUTHORIZED EAVESDROPPERS AND WHAT TO DO ABOUT THEM

If unauthorized bugging would bother you, consider this. It is extremely easy to install a bug on your telephone. A ten-year-old can do it. If someone is dedicated to eavesdropping on your conversations, it is easy to install miniature or even sub-miniature microphones either in your phone itself, or in the rooms of your office or home, which will not be detected when doing a regular sweep of your phone lines. For this reason, American embassies worldwide are equipped with switchboards that have been manufactured in the United States and escorted by marine guards all the way to the foreign embassy before being installed by personnel with security clearance.

The truth is that even with countermeasures, it is all but impossible for amateurs to detect eavesdropping. Competent countermeasures experts, such as those employed by SWS, 1300 Boyd Road, Street, Maryland, 21154-1826, USA, tel (410) 879-4035, fax (410) 836-1190, can find virtually anything, at a price.

Satellites in orbit around the planet can pick up just about any electrical or electronic communication. In theory, it is quite possible for satellites and earth-based listening stations to pick up every telephone conversation being conducted worldwide and relay this back to the ground. Here, supercomputers can record and break down all conversations, determine the languages they are being conducted in, search for "key words" (such as names and places) and spew out transcripts complete with information of who called whom from where and about what. An example: who called from Washington, DC to Zug, Switzerland and used the expression "wire transfer" a minimum of three times and the expression "secrecy" at least once? Currently, the United States National Security Agency (NSA) is doing this – it claims to be tracking down terrorists and drug lords rather than wanting to bust you for fiddling with your taxes.

At present, this is not a practical threat to PTs but it is wise to be aware of all possibilities and the vast amounts of data accumulating certainly will be used against private citizens for other purposes in the future. However, today, unless you are involved with terrorism or the drug business, there is little reason for you to fear that such drastic measures are being levelled to monitor you and your business/investment activities. On the other hand, it always pays dividends to prevent rather than to repair. An Italian restaurant in Little Italy, New York, once favored by the local mob, even has a sign on the pay phone in the men's room, saying "Warning! This phone is bugged!".

We suggest that to avoid monitoring you either do not have a phone in your home at all or that you scrupulously refrain from using it for conversations about anything that you would not like to discuss in detail with your local tax authorities, the police, a private investigator or your wife and kids. It is "stupidity squared" to call your mistress from your home or office. An Arab wanna-be PT was married, had a business and worked in an oil-rich nation in the Middle East. He also was having an affair with a young stewardess. He showed us pictures of the gorgeous creature. He intended to sell his business in secrecy, transfer his assets abroad, abandon his wife and obtain a non-consent divorce in the Dominican Republic. He planned to marry his mistress and move with her to a nice quiet suburb of Madrid, Spain. At least, that was the plan. However, he made two ultimately very expensive mistakes: one, he called his mistress daily from his office (but never from his home); two, he had forgotten to tell his mistress that he had been married throughout the course of the three years he had known her.

So what happened? Well, one day he brought his briefcase home from the office, forgetting that he had absentmindedly thrown some business mail, including his office phone bill, in it. During the evening, he received an emergency call from a customer and left in a hurry. A bit suspicious about the great number of "weekend business meetings" in another city, his wife had been unable to check on him since women do not have the right to travel alone by car or plane in that country. She now looked through the contents of his briefcase and noted that a great many calls had been placed to the same phone number in Spain, starting from about the time when the mistress quit her job and moved there to wait for her lover and supposedly soon-to-be husband. On a hunch, the wife picked up the phone and dialled the number – and got our friend's mistress on the phone. In very rapid succession, the man found himself in great legal trouble as his wife sued him for divorce and his mistress, furious at being lied to, undertook a number of highly successful actions to destroy his business in the oil nation.

When we met him, there was little damage control left to do. Most of his funds had been seized, either by US courts acting on the behests of his wife's lawyers, or by the local authorities who also sought to wring his neck for committing adultery, the latter being illegal and punishable by death in the country where it had taken place. Only by going to some very great trouble did we finally manage to save enough funds to enable the client to make a modest start in a different country.

It is quite possible that someone finds his (or her) marriage to be so unbearable that he is willing to do almost everything to get out of it. Some people may even see it as noble to obtain a divorce in secrecy and not inform their new spouses about previous marriages. In any event, we think this particular chap has learned his lesson about the dangers of itemized phone bills. Rule? Dispose of them immediately.

Itemized phone bills? Not available everywhere but phone companies in many countries (including the US, England, France and many Middle Eastern nations) offer not only to invoice the client but also provide a listing of all numbers called from the telephone in question. This, of course, saves phone companies from some of the hassle otherwise occurring when irate customers claim that they "could never have used the phone that much". It also allows business owners to track employees' calls.

Spouses can check on each other. Tax authorities and police can always obtain copies of the records from phone companies and, going over them carefully, search for clues such as calls to secret business partners, banks or mail drop operators in other countries.

Even if your particular telephone invoice may not be itemized, details of your calls, including calls received, are still recorded in a central data bank if you switch through a digital central (as compared to old analogue exchanges). Readers with inside experiences are invited to write us on these subjects. We will reciprocate for good stories we use in future editions with a free book or special report. And we will, of course, include this information in the next revised and updated edition of this book for the benefit of all. PTs are like a family. No matter where we go, we help each other lead better, freer lives in an unfree world.

## PHONE SECRECY SHORTLIST
Our three-step suggestion on how you should deal with telephones:
1)    Do not have a phone in your home;
2)    If you must, do not use it for *any* even *remotely* sensitive conversations;
3)    Make *all* sensitive phone conversations from public payphones.

Do not use phones in your hotel room, for instance. Most hotels automatically obtain and keep a record of every call made from their rooms. They charge anywhere from double to five times ordinary prices, at that. Even if you check in under a different name and settle your bill in cash, you had better be very, very careful that someone is not following you around or later learns, by way of eavesdropping or similar, that you have stayed at a hotel from whence you have made sensitive calls. It is easy to get copies of old room and phone bills from the night porter – or even the general manager! – of a hotel, provided sufficient cash is offered (anywhere from £10 up). Once again, use only *public* pay phones of the kind operated by either coins or over-the-counter phone cards. Never pay for a sensitive call by a credit card, unless you do not mind that an investigator will be able to later con or pressure the card and phone companies into divulging *whom* you called *when* and from *where*.

Wish to know how? For example, it is quite possible for an investigator to call up the hotel (or phone or card company in question) and *pose* as the customer on whom information is sought, then ask for a *copy* of the bill being mailed "for tax purposes" since the original has been inexplicably "lost" and then have it mailed to a different address, because "I/we *have moved*". If you think it cannot be done, try it !

## RECEIVE INCOMING TELEPHONE CALLS SAFELY
So what if you have to *receive* **sensitive phone calls?** Again, you may want to work with a mail drop to take your messages. Or install an answering machine at their premises. A call diverter is one possibility if you just want to throw people a bit off track. They are sold through phone companies or electronics stores. Cheapest are through advertising sheets such as the UK's *Exchange & Mart* or Sunday supplements. You put a call diverter in one place. Any incoming calls can be diverted to any other phone in the world.

If a call is of a nature that you don't want to let it inside your four walls, incoming calls are normally not monitored at hotels (or cheap motels). But an even better tactic is to walk around *in advance* and copy down the call numbers of a number of public phone booths. Do not forget to make some indication to yourself of where the box is. Use a simple and easy to remember numeric code to scramble the numbers lest anyone find your notes (see the chapter on codes). Then simply inform people to call you (giving a specific, exact time) at one of these numbers. You need not even tell them it is a public phone booth. Best places and times to receive such calls are when the risk that someone else is using the phone is low. This means at night or the very early morning. As far as locations go, opt for somewhere with little or no background noise, such as the lobby phone of a hotel that you are **not** staying at, a booth in an airport at night or even one in the street provided it will be reasonably quiet with minimal traffic noise at the time when you expect to receive the call.

Interestingly enough, in some countries you can still receive free *collect calls* (billed to receiving phone) at phone booths. However, defrauding the phone company is illegal since you have no right to evade charges rightly due them. So even if it is possible in your area and the call goes through, you may also find a couple of boys in blue at your shoulder five minutes into the conversation if the local phone company has finally gotten wise to this little scam.

## PERSONAL PHONE PROTOCOL, ADVANCED

In addition to the three steps mentioned above, here is some additional, "privacy-correct" wisdom to add to your own, personal phone protocol:

1) Never make or accept collect phone calls if you worry about someone tracking you down – no matter what the excuse;
   If you have kids who may need to call collect if they get in trouble, arrange for them to give a special name or code word which the operator *must* say or you will refuse the call. Obviously you should not *make* collect calls, either, since the person you speak to may later call back to the operator and learn the location (even of a phone booth) where the call originated.

2) Even if you are home, why not let an answering machine pick up the phone. This will let you screen out calls from people you do not wish to speak to. You either ignore the caller, call back later or pick up the phone if it happens to be someone you actually wish to speak with.

3) The *message* on your answering machine is important. If you are wary that someone may recognize you from your voice, get someone else to record it. If you are woman living alone, ask a male friend or co-worker to record the outgoing message, including a line about "one of us will get back to you". If you are a well-known bachelor (or gay), ask a woman of your acquaintance to do this little favour for you. If you feel diffident about having the machine greeting callers with any voice *at all*, simply record a short piece of music before the beep comes and don't forget to let people who have your number know about this.

4) Even if you can save a few bucks on cheap equipment, get an answering machine which will allow you to retrieve messages (and change your own, outgoing message) by remote control. Some units allow you to do this without a hand held remote control, from a touch-tone phone. If possible, buy a top-of-the-line model which you can also turn *on* as well as *off* from a distance. This is especially useful for giving the impression that you have either left or entered your home and fiddled with the machine, without you having to go anywhere near the place. However, you should be aware that almost all remote pickup capable answering machines can be hacked and compromised. Technology soon will be available to thwart the eavesdroppers but for now you should change entry codes on the machine frequently.

## ROAMING WITH MOBILE PHONES

Cellular or mobile phones (car phones) are nice in that you may receive calls at them without giving away your location. You should be aware that since the area of each "cell" serviced by individual transceiver stations is limited, car phones also emit a non-audible, so-called "roaming" signal that will give away the area in which the phone is whenever the phone is active – which means *turned on*, not just when you speak on it. This, in turn, may put authorities in a position to put an APB (All Points Bulletin) on the user and the type, description and license plate number of his car (if known). Calls *made* from cellular phones are always itemized on the bill, which is also a good reason to be careful.

Professional cellular intercept systems are available but of limited use, partly because cellular phones change channels frequently at random. Amateur snoopers with ordinary consumer scanners are ineffective. The US cellular system has 832 channels available at present and 1232 in the NAMPS systems being introduced. It won't be long before the systems go digital then eavesdropping will be even more difficult. If a government agent wishes to listen in, he can go straight to the cellular system provider and make a connection through its computer, virtually a direct wiretap. This method requires full co-operation with the cellular service company and, technically, in the USA an intercept cannot be made without a court order.

If you are important enough, such as Prince Charles and Princess Di, someone *may* be able to tap into a personal conversation with a paramour and sell your secrets to the gutter Press. In which case, it's still safer to use public phones.

## SUPER PHONES

A third option exists for making calls and even though we mention it, we shall once more firmly advise you to make sensitive calls *only* from public payphones.

"Super phones" consist of two units. One, the base unit, has to be professionally installed on a telephone line and the other is a mobile unit you carry around with you, either on your person or in your car. The principle is exactly the same as that employed in ordinary home cordless phones, except that both head unit and the handset are larger and heavier. Both carry high-wattage transceivers to increase range but that makes them more liable to interception. In most areas of the world, there are no clear frequencies available where these devices could operate and such frequencies are used heavily by government agencies.

The range is highly dependent on the terrain and territory, lower in cities and mountainous areas, somewhat higher in flat, deserted areas or at sea. A major problem with a super phone is that you cannot use it unless you have the base unit plugged into a regular phone line somewhere, which in its turn may be bugged. In other words, people who can *call you* on a super phone will be able to locate the whereabouts of the base unit since this must be installed wherever the corresponding number is. Of course, you could use a call diverter.

"Super phones" are freely available in most mid- and far eastern countries, in many parts of the US and in France. Prices (not to mention legality of use) vary *very* widely but expect having to pay anywhere from £300 (US $480) for standard 20-km (18 mile) equipment and up to about five times that on ultra long-range equipment. But contrary to what some manufacturers and salesmen may pitch, these are not simple plug and play machines.

## ADD-ON GADGETS FOR YOUR PHONE

As stated, we think that if you are a privacy freak, you should not have a home phone to begin with. For communication privacy (and personal safety) it is always preferable to go out and use a public phone.

If you have to have a phone, get an answering machine. Use it to screen out crank callers and obnoxious salesmen and those you would rather not speak to.

Also: **DO** get an unlisted phone number. If your home phone is currently listed in your own name, get it changed to an unlisted number. Have the name on your phone bill changed to a company name – and, if possible, get your bills sent elsewhere than your home or office. Be careful about the latter: no mail drop operator should *ever* know your home address, but if you use a different name and *only* use your maildrop to receive your phone bill – fine. This is an area where extreme compartmentalization is required in terms of mail drops. If anyone ever locates your "phone-bill maildrop" because you slipped up and gave it away as an exception, then that someone can visit your maildrop (at night, if need be), intercept your mail and obtain your home address from the bill. Be careful.

Building onto that, give out your home phone number on an extremely strictly followed "need-to-know" basis.

Scramblers are best purchased in the United States, where selection is the best in the world and prices are second only to the Far East. The person at the other end of the conversation needs a similar scrambler as well. They are NOT 100 per cent secure. If somebody records your end of the conversation, then steals or borrows your scrambler, he or she will be able to decipher the tape. This depends on how advanced your scrambler is. It also depends on the technical prowess of whoever is bugging you. They can also unscramble a taped conversation with a digital decoder.

Our opinion: Do not use scramblers. A telephone company employee scanning the lines will immediately know that something is up if he hears scrambler-noise. Before you know it, you may attract all kinds of unwanted heat. Criminals use scramblers and if you do, the law may assume that you are a criminal. Better just to use coded language or don't use the phone at all. Scramblers provide privacy not secrecy. There are techniques for privacy protection over telephones that do not require all parties to have compatible equipment but this is a specialist – and expensive – option.

Additional gadgets? Cordless phones for use around your home or yard are fine as long as you do not receive nor make any calls that are sensitive *in the least* where you live. They are, however, fairly practical and very, very easy to bug with a simple ham receiver unit.

If you can get caller ID in your area, GET IT. If available, this service from the phone company (or gadget from elsewhere) that will not only display the calling number on the screen *during* calling but also maintain an erasable *memory* of who called in your absence. In many countries, caller-ID service is not presently available from phone companies but advertised by independent merchants. Be aware that some of the people selling "caller ID units" are, in reality, selling a machine into which you can code the numbers from which you will accept calls – and then oblige the caller to punch in his number (to flash on your display) before your phone will ring. Obviously, this is really a pretty fake product in that the caller will have to punch in only a number he already has – and not necessarily the one from which he is calling.

As an alternative, a simple "code box" is available and standard on some faxes. It can be programmed with a number of three or four digit codes. When someone is calling, he or she will be told "please enter your code now". Unless he does this, the connection will be cut off. If you can, get one of these babes with both display and memory. They are better than the fake caller ID gadgets as they are easier to use, fewer digits have to be punched in. In addition, if the machine will show the code that has been punched in this will allow you to give different codes to different people. Thus you find out if someone has given out your phone number – as in the case when the code indicated on the display is the same as that given to only one, single person with strict instructions *not* to give it out. In such case you may wish to annul this code and cut off contact with your loose-lipped friend immediately . . .

Remember, virtually anyone with the technology to monitor communications properly will be able to decode cheap scramblers. The real things are restricted by, and for, governments' use. It is almost easier to traffic in illegal arms than in true communications security equipment.

# AT&T'S BRAVE NEW WORLD

If speed and efficiency is more important to you than privacy, consider using some of the more advanced services offered by US telecommunications giant AT&T.

Even if you do not live or have a place of business in the US, you can get a phone number with any mail drop number in the US. You may put a "local call only" block on the number to prevent the mail drop operator from misusing your private number, just in case.

Then, apply for an AT&T credit card. As long as you have a major credit card to guarantee payment, it will automatically be granted.

The reason WHY a US phone number may be valuable, even if you do not live in the US, or even if you never visit, is that AT&T offers some services that are not, to my knowledge, presently available from any other phone company, anywhere.

These include, among other things, *voice mail* and *fax reception without you having to have a fax machine installed.*

**Voice mail** means that someone calls your number and is asked to leave a message. This message is then automatically digitized and put into a voice mail bank. Whenever you feel like it, you dial your US number *from anywhere in the world.* If you use your AT&T credit card for this call, even if you make it from the hotel, you are billed at the "normal", low rate for a call to the US – not the ruinously exorbitant rates usually charged by hotels. You then enter a special code and all your messages are played back to you.

The same goes for faxes. If you do not feel particularly comfortable having certain faxes reach you at your place of business, mail drop, a hotel or even in your home, you merely give out your "US Fax number". All faxes transmitted to this number are then automatically stored in a vast data bank. Whereupon you phone a special number, dial a secret code and the faxes are transmitted to any phone number, anywhere in the world. Which, of course, just might happen to be a phone booth on the streets of Alice Springs, Australia where you are standing in wait with a trusty, portable fax machine. Almost every copy shop in the world now offers fax transmission and reception. For those still living in the Stone Age, a facsimile machine (fax) will transmit or receive any message or image on a piece of paper, via telephone, to or from any other fax machine. The message or picture can also come from or go to a computer screen if linked to a telephone.

Another special AT&T service is that you may record a message to be relayed to one or more phone numbers, anywhere on Planet Earth . . . *later.* Let us say that you are in Tokyo and about to depart for Argentina, but wish to give certain people a little "greeting" to put them on the wrong track or just not wake them up at an odd hour for them. Call a special, fully computerized AT&T number, punch in the relevant codes – including your AT&T credit card number – record your message and punch in the numbers to which it should be relayed, and when.

Needless to say, you should be careful how you use these services. Uncle Sam can easily check with AT&T and find out whom you called, from where you did it and, if applicable, the number of the credit card that you use to pay for your AT&T bills. This, in turn, will lead directly to the bank that has issued the credit card and either to assets in your accounts with that bank, *or*, by no means a stretch of the imagination, to the glowing references originally submitted to *that* bank from *another* bank where you still keep sizeable amounts stashed.

Still, you will be able to not only play cat and mouse with nosey competitors and ex-wives or girlfriends, but also to simplify the way you get messages and faxes without physically "having to be anywhere you might be found". Use AT&T if you can profit or otherwise benefit from such advanced services. It may sound outlandish, at first, especially if you never set foot in the US – but since that's where the services are on offer, and since you can get them without having to go there, well, at least consider it.

Further information about AT&T overseas services are available from freephone numbers in almost every country in the world. For a full up-to-date listing, check AT&T's daily ad in every issue of the *International Herald Tribune.*

# TELEPHONE CALLS: LONG DISTANCE

### DISCREET CALLING

These days, both local and long distance calls will be recorded on computers. The information on the numbers (who called whom) will be available to investigators for many years to come. For those who want to be discreet, it is wise to assume that a digital, compressed recording of every phone call exists and can be retrieved by Big Brother. The information that a call was made or received, and nothing more, has put many people in hot water. There is such a record of every call made from a private residence, office, public phone, hotel, or government office.

Using cash (coins) and anonymous public phones are one way to insure that there is no *useful* record of any call having been made once you've made it. But if the phone you are calling to or from is tapped, the public phone from which you are calling can normally be identified within a few minutes, if not instantly. Naturally, if you are calling from a foreign country, it would be easy for private detectives or law enforcement authorities to arrange for you to be harassed, murdered, kidnapped or arrested in the course of a single call. However, if you call from the same booth on a regular basis, you could be creating a dangerous situation for yourself.

"Pomeroy", a client we advised *not* to kidnap his own child, did it anyway and took the kid on a PT-style life, ending up in the lovely tourist-filled island of Ibiza, Spain. He made it a practice to call (from a public phone) another child he had left behind every Christmas and birthday. On the occasion of the third call, the wife he left behind had a trace set up with the aid of the FBI. The phone rang on schedule. As the kidnapped child jabbered with his sister, the police determined the exact location of the call box. The father thought he was immune from trouble, being in a foreign country (legally). Besides, he felt that it would take weeks to get the local cops to take any interest in him and he planned to leave in two days. He wasn't aware of the speed and sophistication of modern electronics. The local Spanish police were alerted while he was on the phone. Another ten minutes and they would have nabbed him at the phone booth, but by sheer luck, he was gone when they arrived. But the police, armed with a faxed photo of Pomeroy and son, asked in the neighborhood about this particular tourist. Like most of us, he was lazy and used a booth not far from where he lived. Even if he hadn't been this sloppy, because Ibiza is a relatively-small island, the rented apartment would soon have been staked out. But he had made it easier. The cops went from the grocer who informed on Pomeroy directly to his apartment. A day after he made the call, the child was in the custody of a representative of the Embassy and on his way home to Mamma (against his will). It turned out that Spain, while not very helpful when it came to many other offenses, didn't like childnappers and was party to a treaty of co-operation in such matters. The father was in for a long and expensive legal battle that he lost when his money to pay Spanish lawyers ran out. He reportedly got a ten-year sentence after being expelled from Spain (not extradited) and placed on a plane bound for his home town.

Moral of the story: Don't assume that public phones insulate you absolutely. They can insulate you if calls are made irregularly and from a country where you don't live. An island is the worst place to be targeted for someone who is being sought by police or anyone else who wants to do them harm. Make calls from a busy place, and talk for under two minutes. Then get far away.

## CREDIT CARD DIALLING

Many airports and other public places all over the world are now equipped with special telephones that accept Visa or Master Charge Credit cards to make local or long distance phone calls. Also, many of the American telephone companies issue credit cards usable abroad to dial the USA. By using these cards the cost of phoning the USA is often reduced by half or more. To charge calls to the USA, to an outfit like AT&T, you dial an access number (on your credit card) wherever you are and then punch in your credit card number on the phone. Bills can be sent to the address you have given the phone company, debited to a USA phone subscriber, or paid direct by your bank. Most European countries now have many of their phones equipped to take special debit phone cards or "telecartes." These are usually purchased at newsstands, tobacco stores or post offices. You pay in advance buying a card for your, local or long distance calls. These "smart cards" use up your money as you make the calls from public phones. For privacy, these are the best way to go. Why? There is no record of who made the call or where it came from.

## HELPFUL HINTS

On my first trips abroad, when I had to make a long distance telephone call, I simply called the hotel operator wherever I was staying and he or she handled everything. But when you become a PT and start renting apartments instead of staying at full service hotels, you must learn to do many things all by yourself. Calling unassisted on the phone is one of these things. Just as an apartment may be rented for about 20 per cent of the cost of staying in a comparable hotel suite, the cost of telephone calls made from your own phone is much cheaper than using hotel operators. When you direct dial yourself from a public phone (or your own apartment) you save the hotel's add-on charges of up to 100 per cent over the basic rate. For the first calls you make, it's probably a good idea to head over to the local telephone company and make your first calls from their central office. While there, pick up a booklet (usually available in English) explaining about all the services offered and their cost. Note too that in most places the local telephone company is a part of the (government-owned) post and telegraph system. England and the USA are the only countries having private telephone companies. Naturally, these privately owned companies are cheaper and more efficient than their publicly owned counterparts. Faxes: you can usually send a fax from any post office considerably more cheaply than from a hotel or copy shop. At some post offices you can also receive faxes c/o general delivery. But remember this: if you get anything at a post office, you'll usually have to show identification to prove you are the person to whom a letter or fax is addressed. In a copy-shop they don't care.

## DIRECT LONG DISTANCE DIALLING – HOW TO DO IT

Fortunately, the telephone companies have made a few worldwide simple rules for long distance direct dialling. Learn them once, and rest easy. These days phone systems are compatible all over the world. If you forget the rules, or if you need an access code, country code or a local area code quickly, this book will serve as a handy reference,

## INTERNATIONAL ACCESS CODE

To direct dial a number outside of the country you are in, you must first dial an ''access code'' which gets you onto the international circuits. The access code is usually ''00'' or ''010'' after which you hear a buzz (dial tone) and can dial the rest of the number. Some countries have a different access code and we are including them all here.

## ASSISTANCE & INFORMATION

Usually you can simply dial the operator, ''O''

There are always special numbers for services to foreigners in their own language. If you arrive in a city and stay a few days in a hotel before getting an apartment, it is a good idea to copy these numbers down from the phone information card found in every hotel or just take this handy card with you. You will probably need these instructions later on. You will need to know whom to call for collect calls abroad, weather information, bedtime stories, accurate time, plane and train arrivals and departures, etc. Usually if you have only the number of the international operator, she will give you leads to the others. In England, for instance, the number to get an international operator is simply ''155''. To have the operator look up a number outside of UK, dial ''153'' for international inquiries. In France international directory inquiries go to ''19-33-13''. The international operator is ''19-33''. To make a collect call you need operator assistance. Getting through to an operator is a major problem in many countries – particularly in the Third World. Getting one who speaks English can also be a problem. Thus is it better to direct dial when you can. In later editions we will try to have all the information numbers and special assistance numbers listed for all countries. Please send us appropriate booklet(s) or information from your part of the world. It would be appreciated! Reader contributions make each edition a better reference book than its predecessor.

# HERE IS HOW TO DIAL WHEN ABROAD

To get an outside line from hotels or offices

Usually dial "9" or "0"

Then, Access Code – Usually "010" or "00"

+ Country Code (see list following)

+ Area Code (normally when calling abroad you drop the first zero,

if any in this code)

+ Local Number

Every country has a direct dialling code. Here they are:

**Albania:** To Dial Out: 00; To Dial In: 355 + Area Code + Local Number. Automatic direct dialling is theoretically available in or out, but the Albanian telephone system tends to be unreliable. Reduced rate periods available. No collect calls.

**Algeria:** To Dial Out: 00; To Dial In: 213 + Area Code + Local Number. Collect calls OK.

**Andorra:** To Dial Out: 19; To Dial In: 33 628 + Local Number (5 digits). Do not use international codes when calling to or from France. To dial to France, dial 7 plus 1 for Paris) and then the local eight-digit number. To dial from France, dial (16 from Paris) and 628 + the local five-digit Andorran number. Reduced rate periods available. No collect calls.

**Anguilla:** To Dial Out: 011; To Dial In: 1809. You will get an operator to whom you will give the local number you want, no direct dialling. No collect calls.

**Antigua + Barbuda:** To Dial Out: 011; To Dial In: 1 809 + Local Number (7 digits). Do not dial international code from the US. Collect calls OK.

**Antilles (Netherlands):** To Dial Out: 00; To Dial In: 599 + Area Code + Local Number. (For Aroba: 297. You will get an operator to whom you will give the local number you want). No collect calls.

**Argentina:** To Dial Out: 00; To Dial In: 54 + Area Code + Local Number. Omit 0 from beginning of area code if it has one. Reduced rate periods available. Collect calls OK.

**Ascension Island:** To Dial Out: 01; To Dial In: 247 + Local Number (4 digits). No collect calls.

**Australia:** To Dial Out: 00 11; To Dial In: 61 + Area Code + Local Number. Reduced rate periods available. Collect calls OK.

**Austria:** To Dial Out: 00; To Dial In: 43 + Area Code + Local Number. Omit 0 from beginning of area code if it has one. Reduced rate periods available. No collect calls.

**Bahamas:** To Dial Out: 011; To Dial In: 1 809 + Local Number (7 digits). Do not dial international code from the US. Collect calls OK.

**Bahrain:** To Dial Out: 0; To Dial In: 973 + Local Number 6 digits). Reduced rate periods available. No collect calls.

**Bangladesh:** To Dial Out: 00; To Dial In: 880 + Area Code + Local Number. Omit 0 from beginning of area code if it has one. No collect calls.

**Barbados:** To Dial Out: 011; To Dial In: 1 809 + Local Number(7 digits). Do not dial international code from the US. Collect calls OK.

**Belgium:** To Dial Out: 00; To Dial In: 32 + Area Code + Local Number. Omit 0 from beginning of area code if it has one. Reduced rate periods available. Collect calls OK.

**Belize:** To Dial Out: 00; TO Dial In: 501 + Area Code + Local Number. Collect calls OK.

**Benin:** To Dial Out: 00; To Dial In: 229 + Local Number (6 digits). Reduced rate periods available. Collect calls OK.

**Bermuda:** To Dial Out: 011; To Dial In: 1 809 + Local Number (7 digits). Do not dial international code if calling from the USA. Collect calls OK.

**Bhotan:** To Dial Out: Operator assistance required, no direct dialling; To dial In: 975 + Local Number (5 digits). No collect calls.

**Bolivia:** To Dial Out: 0; To Dial In: 591 + Area Code + Local Number. Omit 0 from beginning of area code if it has one. No collect calls.

**Botswana:** To Dial Out: 00; To Dial In: 267 + Area Code + Local Number. No collect calls.

**Brazil:** To Dial Out: 00; To Dial In: 55 + Area Code + Local Number. Omit 0 from beginning of area code if it has one. Reduced rate periods available. Collect calls OK.

**Brunei Darussalam:** To Dial Out: 01; To Dial In: 673 + Area Code + Local Number. No collect calls.

**Bulgaria:** To Dial Out: 00; To Dial In: 359 + Area Code + Local Number. Reduced rate periods available. No collect calls.

**Burkina Faso:** To Dial Out: 00; To Dial In: 226 + Local Number (6 digits). Reduced rate periods available. Collect calls OK.

**Burma:** To Dial Out: Operator assistance required, no direct dialling; To Dial In: 95 + Area Code + Local Number. No collect calls.

**Burundi:** To Dial Out: 90; To Dial In: 257 + Area Code + Local Number. Reduced rate periods available. No collect calls.

**Cambodia:** To Dial Out: 00; To Dial In: for Phnom Penh: 855 + Local Number, for outside Phnom Penh: 33855. You will get an operator to whom you will give the local number you want. No collect calls.

**Cameroon:** To Dial Out: 00; To Dial In: 237 + Local Number (6 digits). Reduced rate periods available. No collect calls.

**Canada:** To Dial Out: 011; To Dial In: 1 + Area Code + Local Number. Reduced rate periods available. Collect calls OK.

**Canary Islands:** To Dial Out: 07; To Dial In: 34 + Area Code + Local Number. Reduced rate periods available. Collect calls OK.

**Cape Verde:** To Dial Out: 0; To Dial In: 238 + Local Number (6 digits). No collect calls.

**Cayman Islands:** To Dial Out: 0; To Dial In: 1 809 + Local Number 7 digits). Do not dial international code if calling from the US. Collect calls OK.

**Central African Republic:** To Dial Out: 19; To Dial In: 236 + Area Code + Local Number. Reduced rate periods available. Collect calls OK.

**Chad:** To Dial Out: 15; To Dial In: 235 + Local Number (6 digits). Reduced rate periods available. Collect calls OK.

**Chile:** To Dial Out: 00; To Dial In: 56 + Area Code + Local Number. Omit 0 from beginning of area code if it has one. Collect calls OK.

**China:** To Dial Out: 00; To Dial In: 86 + Area Code + Local Number. Reduced rate periods available. Collect calls OK.

**CIS (Community of Independent States):** To Dial Out: 810; To Dial In: 7 + Area Code + Local Number. Some areas require operator assistance. Reduced rate periods available. No collect calls.

**Columbia:** To Dial Out: 90; To Dial In: 57 + Area Code + Local Number. Omit 0 from beginning of area code if it has one. Reduced rate periods available. Collect calls OK.

**Congo:** To Dial Out: 00; To Dial In: 242 + Area Code + Local Number. Reduced rate periods available. No collect calls.

**Cook Islands:** To Dial Out: 00; To Dial In: 682 + Local Number (5 digits). No collect calls.

**Costa Rica:** To Dial Out: 00; To Dial In: 506 + Local Number (6 digits). Collect calls OK.

**Côte d'Ivore:** To Dial Out: 00; To Dial In: 225 + Local Number (6 digits). Reduced rate periods available. Collect calls OK.

**Cuba:** To Dial Out: 119; To Dial In: 53 + Area Code + Local Number. No collect calls.

**Cyprus:** To Dial Out: 00; To Dial In: 357 + Area Code + Local Number. Omit 0 from beginning of area code if it has one. Reduced rate periods available. Collect calls OK.

**Czechoslovakia:** To Dial Out: 00; To Dial In: 42 + Area Code + Local Number. Reduced rate periods available. Collect calls OK.

**Denmark:** To Dial Out: 009; To Dial In: 45 + Local Number (8 digits). Reduced rates periods available. Collect calls OK.

**Djibouti:** To Dial Out: 00; To Dial In: 253 + Local Number (6 digits). Reduced rate periods available. Collect calls OK.

**Dominica:** To Dial Out: 011; To Dial In: 1 809 + Local Number (7 digits). Do not dial international code from the US. Collect calls OK.

**Dominican Republic:** To Dial Out: 011; To Dial In: 1 809 + Local Number (7 digits). Do not dial international code from the US. No collect calls.

**Ecuador:** To Dial Out: 00; To Dial In: 593 + Area Code + Local Number. Omit 0 from beginning of area code if it has one. No collect calls.

**Egypt:** To Dial Out: 00; To Dial In: 20 + Area Code + Local Number. Reduced rate periods available. No collect calls.

**El Salvador:** To Dial Out: 0; To Dial In: 503 + Local Number (6 digits). No collect calls.

**Equatorial Guinea:** To Dial Out: Operator assistance required, no direct dialling. To dial In: 240 + Local Number. Reduced rate periods available. No collect calls.

**Ethiopia:** To Dial Out: 00; To Dial In: 251 + Area Code + Local Number. No collect calls.

**Falkland Islands:** To Dial Out: 01; To Dial In: 500 + Local Number (5 digits). No collect calls.

**Faroe Islands:** To Dial Out: 009; To Dial In: 298 + Local Number (5 digits). Reduced rate periods available. Collect calls OK.

**Fiji:** To Dial Out: 05; To Dial In: 679 + Local Number (5 or 6 digits). No collect calls.

**Finland:** To Dial Out: 990; To Dial In: 358 + Area Code + Local Number. Omit 9 from beginning of area code if it has one. Reduced rate periods available. Collect calls OK.

**France:** To Dial Out: 19; To Dial In: 33 + Local Number. France does not have area codes. For Paris City and Greater Paris, the eight-digit local number should be preceded by a 1. For the rest of the country just dial the eight-digit local number. Reduced rate periods available. Collect calls OK.

**Gabon:** To Dial Out: 00; To Dial In: 241 + Local Number (6 digits). Reduced rate periods available. Collect calls OK.

**Gambia:** To Dial Out: 00; To Dial In: 220 + Local Number (5 digits). No collect calls.

**Germany:** To Dial Out: formerly West: 00; formerly East: 06; To Dial In: formerly West: 49 + Area Code + Local Number. Omit 0 from beginning of area code if it has one. Formerly East: 37 + Area Code + Local Number. Reduced rate periods available. No collect calls.

**Ghana:** To Dial Out: 00; To Dial In: 233 + Area Code + Local Number. No collect calls.

**Gibraltar:** To Dial Out: 00; To Dial In: 350 + Local Number (5 digits). Reduced rate periods available. Collect calls OK.

**Greece:** To Dial Out: 00; To Dial In: 30 + Area Code + Local Number. Reduced rate periods available. Collect calls OK.

**Greenland:** To Dial Out: 009; To Dial In: 299 + Local Number (5 digits). Reduced rate periods available. No collect calls.

**Grenada:** To Dial Out: 011; To Dial In: 1 809 + Local Number (7 digits). Do not dial international code from the US. Collect calls OK.

**Guam:** To Dial Out: 001; To Dial In: 671 + Local Number (7 digits). It may not be possible to dial directly. Collect calls OK.

**Guatemala:** To Dial Out: 00; To Dial In: 502 + Area Code + Local Number. Omit 0 from beginning of area code if it has one. No collect calls.

**Guinea:** To Dial Out: 00; To Dial In: 224 + Local Number (6 digits). No collect calls.

**Guinea-Bissau:** To Dial Out: Operator assistance required, no direct dialing. To Dial In: 245 + Local Number (6 digits). Operator assistance may be required. No collect calls.

**Guyana:** To Dial Out: 001; To Dial In: 592 + Area Code + Local Number. No collect calls.

**Haiti:** To Dial Out: 00; To Dial In: 509 + Local Number (6 digits). Reduced rate periods available. No collect calls.

**Honduras:** To Dial Out: 00; To Dial In: 504 + Local Number (6 digits). No collect calls.

**Hong Kong:** To Dial Out: 001; To Dial In: 852 + Area Code + Local Number. Reduced rate periods available. Collect calls OK.

**Hungary:** To Dial Out: 00; To Dial In: 36 + Area Code + Local Number. Omit 0 from beginning of area code if it has one. Reduced rate periods available. No collect calls.

**Iceland:** To Dial Out: 90; To Dial In: 354 + Area Code + Local Number. Omit 9 from beginning of area code if it has one. Reduced rate periods available. Collect calls OK.

**India:** To Dial Out: 900; To Dial In: 91 + Area Code + Local Number. Omit 0 from beginning of area code if it has one. Reduced rate periods available. Collect calls OK.

**Indonesia:** To Dial Out: 00; To Dial In: 62 + Area Code + Local Number. Collect calls OK.

**Iran:** To Dial Out: 00; To Dial In: 98 + Area Code + Local Number. No collect calls.

**Iraq:** To Dial Out: 00; To Dial In: 964 + Area Code + Local Number. No collect calls.

**Ireland:** To Dial Out: 16; To Dial In: 353 + Area Code + Local Number. Reduced rate periods available. Collect calls OK.

**Israel:** To Dial Out: 00; To Dial In: 972 + Area Code + Local Number. Omit 0 from beginning of area code if it has one. Reduced rate periods available. Collect calls OK.

**Italy:** To Dial Out: 00; To Dial In: 39 + Area Code + Local Number. For Vatican City 39 66982 is complete in itself and requires no further digits. Reduced rate periods available. Collect calls OK.

**Jamaica:** To Dial Out: 011; To Dial In: 1 809 + Local Number (7 digits). Do not dial international code from the US. No collect calls.

**Japan:** To Dial Out: 001; To Dial In: 81 + Area Code + Local Number. Omit 0 from beginning of area code if it has one. Reduced rate periods available. Collect calls OK.

**Jordan:** To Dial Out: 00; To Dial In: 962 + Area Code + Local Number. Reduced rate periods available. No collect calls.

**Kenya:** To Dial Out: 00; To Dial In: 254 + Area Code + Local Number. No collect calls.

**Kiribati:** To Dial Out: 09; To Dial In: 686 + Local Number (5 digits). No collect calls.

**Korea, PDR (North):** To Dial Out: 99; To Dial In: 850 + Area Code + Local Number. For Pyongyang dial 2 for area code and then local number, for all other areas dial international operator. No collect calls.

**Korea, Republic (South):** To Dial Out: 001; To Dial In: 82 + Area Code + Local Number. Reduced rate periods available. Collect calls OK.

**Kuwait:** To Dial Out: 00; To Dial In: 965 + Local Number (6 or 7 digits). Reduced rate periods available. No collect calls.

**Laos (R.D.P.):** To Dial Out: Operator assistance required, no direct dialing. To Dial In: 856. You will get an operator to whom you will give the local number you want. No collect calls.

**Lebanon:** To Dial Out: 00; To Dial In: 961 + Area Code + Local Number. Reduced rate periods available. No collect calls.

**Lesotho:** To Dial Out: 00; To Dial In: 266 + Local Number (5 or 6 digits). Collect calls OK.

**Liberia:** To Dial Out: 00; To Dial In: 321 + Local Number (6 digits). No collect calls.

**Libya:** To Dial Out: 00; To Dial In: 218 + Area Code + Local Number. No collect calls.

**Liechtenstein:** To Dial Out: 00; To Dial In: 41 + Area Code + Local Number. The area code should be 75 and the local number will have five, six or seven digits. Reduced rate periods available. Collect calls OK.

**Luxembourg:** To Dial Out: 00; To Dial In: 352 + Local Number (5 digits). Reduced rate periods available. Collect calls OK.

**Macao:** To Dial Out: 00; To Dial In: 853 + Local Number 5,6 or 7 digits). No collect calls.

**Madagascar:** To Dial Out: 16; To Dial In: 261 + Area Code + Local Number. Reduced rate periods available. No collect calls.

**Madeira:** To Dial Out: 00; To Dial In: 351 91 + Local Number (5 or 6 digits). Reduced rate periods available. Collect calls OK.

**Malawi:** To Dial Out: 101; To Dial In: 265 + Area Code + Local Number. No collect calls.

**Malaysia:** To Dial Out: 007; To Dial In: 60 + Area Code + Local Number. Omit 0 from beginning of area code if it has one. Collect calls OK.

**Maldives:** To Dial Out: 00; To Dial In: 960 + Area Code + Local Number. Area code and local number should have six digits. Collect calls OK.

**Mali:** To Dial Out: 00; To Dial In: 223 + Local Number (6 digits). Reduced rate periods available. Collect calls OK.

**Malta:** To Dial Out: 00; To Dial In: 356 + Local Number (6 digits). Reduced rate periods available. No collect calls.

**Mauritania:** To Dial Out: 00; To Dial In: 222 + Local Number (6 digits). Reduced rate periods available. Collect calls OK.

**Mauritius:** To Dial Out: 00; To Dial In: 230 + Local Number (7 digits). Reduced rate periods available. Collect calls OK.

**Mexico:** To Dial Out: 98; To Dial In: 52 + Area Code + Local Number. Reduced rate periods available. Collect calls OK.

**Monaco:** To Dial Out: 19; To Dial In: 33 93 + Local Number (6 digits). Do not use international codes when calling to or from France. To dial to France, dial (16 + 1 for Paris) and the local eight-digit French number directly. To dial from France, dial (16 from Paris) and 93 + the local six-digit Monaco number. Reduced rate periods available. No collect calls.

**Mongolia:** To Dial Out: Operator assistance required, no direct dialling. To Dial In: 976. You will get an operator to whom you will give the local number you want. No collect calls.

**Montserrat:** To Dial Out: 011; To Dial In: 1 809 + Local Number (7 digits). Do not dial international code from the US. Collect calls OK.

**Morocco:** To Dial Out: 00; To Dial In: 212 + Area Code + Local Number. Local numbers should all have six digits, in most cases beginning with old area codes. Callers for Western Sahara require operator assistance. Reduced rate periods available. Collect calls OK.

**Mozambique:** To Dial Out: 00; To Dial In: 258 + Area Code + Local Number. No collect calls.

**Myanmer:** see Burma

**Namibia:** To Dial Out: 09; To Dial In: 264 + Area Code + Local Number. Collect calls OK.

**Nauru:** To Dial Out: Operator assistance required, no direct dialing. To Dial In: 674 + Local Number (4 digits). Collect calls OK.

**Nepal:** To Dial Out: 00; To Dial In: 977 + Area Code + Local Number. Omit 0 from beginning of area code if it has one. No collect calls.

**Netherlands:** To Dial Out: 09; To Dial Inn: 31 + Area Code + Local Number. Omit 0 from beginning of area code if it has one. Reduced rate periods available. Collect calls OK.

**New Caledonia:** To Dial Out: 19 00; To Dial In: 687 + Local Number (6 digits). Reduced rate periods available. Collect calls OK.

**New Zealand:** To Dial Out: 00; To Dial In: 64 + Area Code + Local Number. New Zealand is currently undertaking a major renumbering program, if you encounter problems contact the International Operator. Reduced rate periods available. Collect calls OK.

**Nicaragua:** To Dial Out: 00; To Dial In: 505 + Area Code + Local Number. Omit 0 from beginning of area code if it has one. No collect calls.

**Niger:** To Dial Out: 00; To Dial In: 227 + Local Number (6 digits). Reduced rate periods available. Collect calls OK.

**Nigeria:** To Dial Out: 009; To Dial In: 234 + Area Code + Local Number. No collect calls.

**Norfolk Island:** To Dial Out: Operator assistance required, no direct dialing. To Dial In: 672 + Local Number (4 digits). No collect calls.

**Northern Marianas:** To Dial Out: 010; To Dial In: 670 + Area Code + Local Number. No collect calls.

**Norway:** To Dial Out: 095; To Dial In: 47 + Area Code + Local Number. Omit 0 from beginning of area code if it has one. Reduced rate periods available. Collect calls OK.

**Oman:** To Dial Out: 00; To Dial In: 968 + Local Number (6 digits). Reduced rate periods available. No collect calls.

**Pakistan:** To Dial Out: 00; To Dial In: 92 + Area Code + Local Number. Omit 0 from beginning of area code if it has one. No collect calls.

**Panama:** To Dial Out: 00; To Dial In: 507 + Local Number (6 digits). No collect calls.

**Papua New Guinea:** To Dial Out: 31; To Dial In: 675 + Local Number (6 digits). No collect calls.

**Paraguay:** To Dial Out: 002; To Dial In: 595 + Area Code + Local Number. No collect calls.

**Peru:** To Dial Out: 00; To Dial In: 51 + Area Code + Local Number. Omit 0 from beginning of area code if it has one. Collect calls OK.

**Philippines:** To Dial Out: 00; To Dial In: 63 + Area Code + Local Number. Collect calls OK.

**Poland:** To Dial Out: 00; To Dial In: 48 + Area Code + Local Number. Reduced rate periods available. No collect calls.

**Puerto Rico:** To Dial Out: 35; To Dial In: 1 809 + Local Number (7 digits). Do not dial international code from the US. Collect calls OK.

**Qatar:** To Dial Out: 00; To Dial In: 974 + Local Number (6 digits). Reduced rate periods available. No collect calls.

**Rodriguez Island:** see Mauritius

**Romania:** To Dial Out: Operator assistance required, no direct dialing. To Dial In: 40 + Area Code + Local Number. Reduced rate periods available. No collect calls.

**Rwanda:** To Dial Out: 00; To Dial In: 250 + Local Number (5 digits). Reduced rate periods available. No collect calls.

**St Helena:** To Dial Out: 00; To Dial In: 290 + Local Number (3 digits). Reduced rate periods available. No collect calls.

**St Kitts and Nevis:** To Dial Out: 011; To Dial In: 1 809 + Local Number (7 digits). Do not dial international code from the US. For St Kitts numbers start with 465 and for Nevis numbers start with 469. Collect calls OK.

**St Lucia:** To Dial Out: 00; To Dial In: 1 809 + Local Number (7 digits). Do not dial international code from the US. Collect calls OK.

**St Vincent and the Grenadines:** To Dial Out: 0; To Dial In: 1 809 + Local Number (7 digits). Do not dial international code from the US. Collect calls OK.

**Saipan:** see Northern Marianas

**Samoa (USA):** To Dial Out: 1; To Dial In: 684 + Local Number (7 digits). No collect calls.

**Samoa (Western):** To Dial Out: 0; To Dial In: 685 + Local Number (5 digits). Calls available to Apia only. No collect calls.

**San Marino:** To Dial Out: 00; To Dial In: 39 549 + Local Number. Reduced rate periods available. Collect calls OK.

**Sao Tome and Principe:** To Dial Out: Operator assistance required, no direct dialling. To Dial In: 239 + Area Code + Local Number. No collect calls.

**Saudi Arabia:** To Dial Out: 00; To Dial In: 966 + Area Code + Local Number. The working week runs from Saturday to Thursday in Saudi Arabia. Reduced rate periods available. No collect calls.

**Senegal:** To Dial Out: 00; To Dial In: 221 + Local Number (6 digits). Reduced rate periods available. Collect calls OK.

**Seychelles:** To Dial Out: 00; To Dial In: 248 + Local Number (5 digits). No collect calls.

**Sierra Leone:** To Dial Out: Operator assistance required, no direct dialling. To Dial In: 232 + Area Code + Local Number. Operator assistance may be required. No collect calls.

**Singapore:** To Dial Out: 005; To Dial In: 65 + Area Code + Local Number. Reduced rate periods available. Collect calls OK.

**Solomon Islands:** To Dial Out: 00; To Dial In: 677 + Local Number (5 or 7 digits). No collect calls.

**Somalia:** To Dial Out: 16; To Dial In: 252 + Area Code + Local Number. No collect calls.

**South Africa:** To Dial Out: 09; To Dial In: 27 + Area Code + Local Number. Reduced rate periods available. Collect calls OK.

**Spain:** To Dial Out: 07; To Dial In: 34 + Area Code + Local Number. Area code and local number should be eight digits. Omit 9 from beginning of area code if it has one. Reduced rate periods available. Collect calls OK

**Sri Lanka:** To Dial Out: 00; To Dial In: 94 + Area Code + Local Number. Omit 0 from beginning of area code if it has one. No collect calls.

**Sudan:** To Dial Out: 00; To Dial In: 249. You will get an operator to whom you will give the local number you want. No collect calls.

**Suriname:** To Dial Out: 002; To Dial In: 597 + Local Number (5 digits). No collect calls.

**Swaziland:** To Dial Out: 0; To Dial In: 268 + Local Number (5 digits). Collect calls OK.

**Sweden:** To Dial Out: 009; To Dial In: 46 + Area Code + Local Number. Omit 0 from beginning of area code if it has one. Reduced rate periods available. Collect calls OK.

**Switzerland:** To Dial Out: 00; To Dial In: 41 + Area Code + Local Number. Omit 0 from beginning of area code if it has one. Reduced rates available. Collect calls OK.

**Syria:** To Dial Out: 00; To Dial In: 963 + Area Code + Local Number. Reduced rate periods available. Collect calls OK.

**Taiwan:** To Dial Out: 002; To Dial In: 886 + Area Code + Local Number. Reduced rate periods available. No collect calls.

**Tanzania:** To Dial Out: Operator assistance required, no direct dialing. To Dial In: 255 + Area Code + Local Number. Operator assistance may be required. No collect calls.

**Thailand:** To Dial Out: 001; To Dial In: 66 + Area Code + Local Number. Collect calls OK.

**Togo:** To Dial Out: 00; To Dial In: 228 + Local Number (6 digits). Reduced rate periods available. Collect calls OK.

**Tonga:** To Dial Out: 09; To Dial In: 676 + Local Number (5 digits). No collect calls.

**Trinidad and Tobago:** To Dial Out: 01; To Dial In: 1 809 + Local Number (7 digits). Do not dial international code from the US. Collect calls OK.

**Tunisia:** To Dial Out: 00; To Dial In: 216 + Area Code + Local Number. Reduced rate periods available. Collect calls OK.

**Turkey:** To Dial Out: 99; To Dial In: 90; + Area Code + Local Number. Omit 9 from beginning of area code if it has one. Reduced rate periods available. No collect calls.

**Turks and Caicos Islands:** To Dial Out: 0; To Dial In: 1 809 + Local Number (7 digits). Do not dial international code from the US. Collect calls OK.

**Uganda:** To Dial Out: 00; To Dial In: 256 + Area Code + Local Number. No collect calls.

**United Arab Emirates:** To Dial Out: 00; To Dial In: 971 + Area Code + Local Number. Reduced rate periods available. No collect calls.

**United Kingdom (UK):** To Dial Out: 010; To Dial In: 44 + Area Code + Local Number. Omit 0 from beginning of area code if it has one. Reduced rate periods available. Collect calls OK.

**Uruguay:** To Dial Out: 00; To Dial In: 598 + Area Code + Local Number. Omit 0 from beginning of area code if it has one. No collect calls.

**USA:** To Dial Out: 011; To Dial In: 1 + Area Code + Local Number. Reduced rate periods available. Collect calls OK.

**USSR:** See CIS (Community of Independent States)

**Vanuatu:** To Dial Out: 00; To Dial In: 678 + Local Number (4 digits). Collect calls OK.

**Vatican City:** See Italy

**Venezuela:** To Dial Out: 00; To Dial In: 58 + Area Code + Local Number. Omit 0 from beginning of area code if it has one. Reduced rate periods available. Collect calls OK.

**Vietnam:** To Dial Out: 00; To Dial In: 84 + Local Number (6 digits). No collect calls.

**Virgin Islands (UK):** To Dial Out: 011; To Dial In: 1 809 + Local Number (7 digits). Do not dial international code from the US. Collect calls OK.

**Virgin Islands (USA):** To Dial Out: 01; To Dial In: 1 809 + Local Number (7 digits). Do not dial international code from the US. Collect calls OK.

**Wallis and Futuna:** To Dial Out: 19; To Dial In: 681 + Local Number. Reduced rate periods available. No collect calls.

**Yemen:** To Dial Out: formerly Arab Republic (AR): 00; formerly People's Democratic Republic (PDR): Operator assistance required, no direct dialing. To Dial In: formerly AR: 967 + Area Code + Local Number. Reduced rate periods available. Formerly PDR: 969 + Area Code + Local Number. Operator assistance may be required. No collect calls.

**Yugoslavia:** To Dial Out: 99; To Dial In: 38 + Area Code + Local Number. Omit 0 from beginning of area code if it has one. Reduced rate periods available. Collect calls OK.

**Zaire:** To Dial Out: 00; To Dial In: 243 + Area Code + Local Number. Reduced rate periods available. No collect calls.

**Zambia:** To Dial Out: 00; To Dial In: 260 + Area Code + Local Number. No collect calls.

**Zimbabwe:** To Dial Out: 110; To Dial In: 263 + Area Code + Local Number. No collect calls.

# WHAT TIME IS IT IN THE PLACE YOU WANT TO CALL

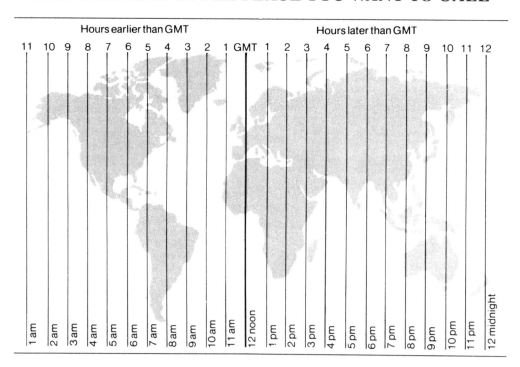

# SECRET EURO PAGER

With a UK billing address, or just a mail drop, you can order a Hutchison Telecom pager with a Euromessage facility. It's the only pager that keeps you in touch all over the EU, main cities in France, Germany, Italy and Switzerland, and so far, the only form of mobile communication that works outside the UK, since the GSM mobile phone network is not yet covering all of Europe. Paging is billed at standard UK rates no matter where you are. All the caller needs to do is ring your number. He will never know where you are, although messages sent to pagers can be monitored through specialist equipment. The phone is answered in your name or with any greeting of your choice, a message is then taken and transmitted seconds later to your pager. This service operates 24 hours a day, 365 days a year. The Euromessage facility is only available from Hutchison at UK freephone number 0800 282826. Or write to Hutchison Telecom, Freepost CV 1037, Stratford-upon-Avon, Warwickshire CV37 9BR, UK, for more info and their free guide to mobile communications. The Euromessage Pager costs £112.32 for initial connection, thereafter £33.50 monthly for the personalized answering service.

Mercury Worldwide Telecommunication Ltd (MWT), being a PT company means that PT needs are understood and met. The first is that your local telephone exchange isn't aware of traffic sent through MWT, so neither is your local jurisdiction. All precautions are taken to ensure the customer's privacy, including, if so desired, non-billing card to further avoid the snoops. Also sophisticated PT-style international information buffering ensures further privacy. What is more, as your supplier is a PT, nobody can oblige it to reveal anything about its customers (they have to find it first!). The company is called **Mercury Worldwide Telecommunication** and the service it provides is called "I'm Glad You Called". You'll be able to call countries that are hard or impossible to call from the country you're in, quickly and without operator intervention. Other privacy concerns, such as scrambling and encryption can be addressed by MWT's personnel.

This small company has big (but Practically Transparent) ideas and is committed to support the PT in his venture for economy, privacy, value and service, and, we are told, is currently developing an international fund transfer system aimed at servicing the PT. Mercury Worldwide Telecommunication Ltd, c/o Scope International, Forestside House, Forestside, Rowlands Castle, Hampshire PO9 6EE.

# Chapter 16

# A MOST IMPORTANT TOOL: FAX

Transmitting documents by facsimile (fax) allows you to get them from A to B without sending an original and allows you to cut the time involved from several days for mail to a minute or so for a fax.

Sending a fax may even be cheaper than mailing a letter. Certain phone companies in the United States bill phone calls in six-second increments, meaning that a domestic fax that takes about half a minute to transmit winds up costing about a dime (10 cents). And it certainly means vastly increased possibilities for speeding up negotiations and other business procedures. All in all, the fax machine is possibly the device that will prove to be the most profoundly cost-efficient change in the way people do business since the telex.

If you use a fax to transmit business documents, it may be wise to check with a local lawyer whether a signed document transmitted by fax carries the same legally binding implications as that of either a (mailed) letter or a telex. For years, offers and statements made by telex have been considered legally binding for contract purposes – but in most countries, a certain confusion still surrounds the question of whether the same holds true for, say, an "offer to buy" made exclusively by fax. It makes sense to get the low-down on this from your lawyer, lest you find yourself in the process of being tricked into placing an unmerited value on a faxed offer as you would on a letter. Different jurisdictions have different rules.

When it comes to receiving faxes you will have to be able to physically receive them one way or another, i.e. by a fax machine somewhere that is connected to the phone system. Just as with mail, you may wish to receive faxes at a different location from the one in which you are physically present.

The thing to remember if receiving faxes elsewhere is that any document ticking in over your trusty Panasonic is an open letter. Unless you, and you alone, are on hand to grab the document as it emerges from the machine, anyone else with access to the machine may intercept and read it. Thus, if you opt to receive faxes at a hotel or a maildrop, make sure to inform people to whom you give the number that any fax they send will be read by someone else before it reaches you. This means, instruct your correspondents not to use obvious code language nor to divulge sensitive details about yourself.

Your enemies can intercept and make photocopies of any and all incoming faxes if they know your number. So whatever you do, be extremely careful of how you undertake to receive faxes that have anything *at all* to do with your personal finances or physical whereabouts.

On the other hand, it may be necessary for you to receive faxes quickly. You may not be willing or able to wait for even the fastest mail drop operator to mail or transmit them to you. Should you keep your fax in your home or office instead? Not if you want to maximize your privacy.

There are two ways how you may receive faxes without giving away your whereabouts:
1) Receive your faxes at a mail drop, then phone the mail drop operator from a public phone and have him or her read your faxes to you over the phone. If possible, instruct people to whom you give your fax number to use some sort of code language that ties in nicely with whatever story (if any) about your particular line of business you have fed your mail drop operator. This tactic enables you to check for faxes and other messages as often as you wish, even if hourly or bi-hourly. The limitation is that you can only check for faxes in this fashion during the opening hours of the drop, which usually means nine-to-five on weekdays only;

2)      Have your own fax machine installed at the mail drop. You may either pay the drop operator to buy
        a fax for you, or you may go yourself – or send a friend – to buy and install it. This fax machine
        should be hooked up to a separate line used only by you. The machine used for this purpose should
        have so-called mailbox and 'polling' features. This means that incoming faxes will not be printed
        out – i.e., the mail drop operator will only hear the phone ring but will have no way of knowing
        what sort of faxes you receive. To retrieve faxes, you quite simply use another fax machine to call
        up the fax at your mail drop, punching in a code telling the fax that keeps your incoming faxes
        stored electronically to "download" these to the machine that you call from. Sounds
        complicated? It's plain and simple as dirt. Let's say that you have your own fax-machine with an
        electronic storage mailbox installed at a New York maildrop. During the day, this machine has
        received and electronically stored (but *not* printed out) a number of faxes from your various
        contacts. You now take the fax machine you keep in your home city, say London and call up your
        New York fax number. When the New York fax answers, you punch in a code – say, "1234". This
        tells the New York fax to transmit everything held in its memory to the fax on the other end – i.e.,
        the fax machine you are playing around with in London. And this machine – not the one in New
        York – will now start printing out all your faxes. This is the technique known as "polling", where
        a fax is waiting to be transmitted through one machine, the process being set off by another
        machine calling up and giving a code.

        The only risks involved in having a fax somewhere else to receive transmissions and hold them for
you till you call up yourself are:

1)      The "known" fax may be on a line that is bugged but it is very difficult to intercept normal fax
        transmissions;
2)      it may be confiscated, with your message inside;
3)      or analyzed while in place for contents of memory (hard but not impossible to do);
4)      finally, incoming calls (including those from you) may be traced in a matter of seconds if local and
        a few minutes if from abroad

# WELCOME TO THE WONDERFUL WORLD OF THE PT-PC

The third, existing possibility as far as privacy-oriented fax reception is concerned is well worth
considering. This solution consists of having a computer, generally a PC, meaning a machine compatible
with the IBM "PC" models, installed somewhere for the sole purpose of receiving and relaying faxes
and even voice messages.

        Quite a few PTs already use this fantastic little gambit. Here is how it works. First, one obtains a
mail drop somewhere and pays not only for mail reception but also for "shelf space", in other words, for
having one's own computer on the premises. This computer is then connected to two separate phone
lines, the installation and service charges for which one also reimburses the mail drop. Then, one either
sends an associate or a trusted friend (or oneself, posing as one of these) to the mail drop to install the
computer or it may, after installation of the software, simply be sent by freight or otherwise with the
simple instruction that the mail drop operator plug the machine into the mains and the two phone lines.
Turn it on, taping the power switch securely into the "on" position.

        The machine is left to run 24 hours a day, seven days a week. One phone line acts as incoming link
for faxes, E-mail (electronic mail) and even voice messages. The other line is used when the computer
dials up another number to relay these messages to the user. The user may, himself, dial up this number
from a public phone if he is sufficiently clever to remember that he should never give away his
whereabouts by having anyone, not even a machine, calling him up at his home or office.

        Installed in the machine will be a special fax card and "modem" which automatically detects
whether an incoming call is a fax, E-mail or a regular phone call. Your computer selects the applicable

software program to deal with each of these and store messages, even spoken messages, in electronic form on its hard disk. The system may be programed to remove all previously stored messages after uploading them elsewhere by overwriting them with electronic "garbage" as opposed to merely deleting files. An average computer whiz, acting for authorities or other investigators, might otherwise be able to retrieve deleted files because most computers will store them in "limbo".

To further ensure against curious mail drop operators trying to find out the exact nature of incoming faxes, E-mail and voice messages, no keyboard nor monitor need be installed with the machine. For maximum security, the video display may be removed and the keyboard plug blocked or removed. The cabinet itself may also be sealed off hermetically. A hardware switch (with internal battery back-up) can automatically erase all data in memory and on the hard disk if tampered with. To guard against accidental power failure, the machine may be configured to automatically restart once mains electricity supply is resumed, or supplied with a back-up battery.

A solution like the one just described offers a vast array of possibilities. The user may give out one of the numbers to which the computer is connected as his "home phone and fax number". All incoming calls will immediately be detected as being either fax (or E-mail) or a regular phonecall. Incoming faxes will be received. The machine can be set up to answer back with a completely false and misleading ID. For instance, if the number and the machine are both in London, England, a fax reception may be acknowledged by transmitting back a phone number and company name in Athens, Greece. This may cause an American investigator to believe that the London number is merely hooked up to an ordinary call diverter. He may move his investigation to the Greek capital without bothering to check out the London premises.

If a person calls up, a synthesized (digitized) and possibly altered voice may answer "please leave a message and I'll get back to you". The message left by the caller will be automatically digitalized and stored on the hard disk for later transmission, either automatically (by the machine calling up its owner) or by the owner calling up from a phone booth and either playing back messages – or downloading them into his portable computer for later playback (through the speaker built into the computer). At the caller's public phone, a hand-held acoustic coupler pressed against the handset of the phone can be used for data transmission.

A system like this is not cheap, but not too expensive, either. The hardware – the computer itself with all necessary cards and connections – may run as low as US $1,000 to 1,500. A complete software package offering the above mentioned functions may be delivered and installed at a charge ranging from about US $ 2,500 including additional hardware, cards, etc. One inexpensive and easy to use system recommended by SWS Security, of Maryland, is called Bigmouth and is manufactured by Talking Technology, 1125 Atlantic Avenue # 101, Alameda, California 94501 USA, telephone(510) 522-3800, fax (510) 522- 5556.

## HOW BEST TO TRANSMIT FAXES

You may freely send a fax from the privacy of your home or office if privacy is not a consideration. But, as explained, modern electronics can tell the fax recipient the number you are calling from, even if this number is not printed on your fax message.

All fax machines are equipped to identify themselves by a name and possibly even a number both when receiving and transmitting faxes. If you have your own fax machine, why code it with your name or home fax (or phone number)? Regrettably, only a limited number of faxes will leave the "ID" line completely blank and offer nothing in the way of identification when transmitting or receiving. Most will identify the machine as, say, a Xerox 321, much as a clothes designer insists on putting a label on the outside of garments.

When someone receives a fax from you, the top of the paper will usually bear a line with a text saying something like "from XXXXXXXXXX", the X's being a name and/or number that have been coded by the owner of the machine. The important part here is to be aware that it is possible to establish the type of machine that has transmitted the fax since manufacturers use different character sets and formats, e.g. where, and in which order, information about sender ID, time, date and year are placed in the ID-line. If you have received a fax from someone and saved it, you may at a later date compare the ID with other faxes received in order to see if the same person is faxing you under different names and pretenses.

Especially when faxing from a hotel – or any other business – it is important to remember that the owner of the fax more probably than not has had his fax coded with his name and phone number. If you are trying to conceal the fact that you are in, say, Gibraltar, this all but rules out using anyone else's fax machine to contact someone whom you'd rather have think that you are in Tokyo. Even if the name of the owner and his country or area code are not given away in the ID-line, it is usually fairly easy to establish this merely by looking at the way the numbers are sequenced. For instance, someone receiving a fax with an ID line saying merely "from 12 34 56 78" is certain to center his search for you in countries with such four sets of two digit phone number configurations. If, on the other hand, the ID-line reads "Gibbons 123 4567", the fax would likely have originated in England or the United States – but certainly not in Denmark, France or any other country with 8-digit, four-sets-of-two phone numbers.

If time permits, you may send a fax by first mailing it – routing it via one or several remailing services, if need be – to a mail drop or someone else who will then transmit it from their fax machine. Don't assume the recipient of a fax can't determine the location of the transmitting station. With the proper equipment, he can.

## OUR FAVORITE FAX IS AS PORTABLE AS WE ARE

In our qualified opinion, for lowest profile, the very best way to transmit faxes is to invest in a portable, battery-powered fax machine. These little marvels will both plug into any phone jack you might come across. They also use acoustic couplers, enabling you to send a fax from a phone booth. That's right, step into a phone booth, unzip the carrier bag and insert the letter you wish to transmit. Then dial the number you wish to fax. Fasten the acoustic coupler connected to the fax to the handset by way of a Velcro-strap and fax away from a location that does not lead anyone to your office or bedroom.

This practise of using portable fax machines is getting very widespread indeed. We recently received (in the mail) the following from a *Financial Times* correspondent who happens to be a friend, philosophizing on faxomania:

*FAX WARS WREAK WIDESPREAD HAVOC. From our correspondent in Europe: Faxes whirr and hum around the clock across the continent, the lack of explosions and other accoutrements of conventional warfare belying the fact that this is serious business. Come twilight, expats entrenched in Pas de la Casa (Principat d'Andorra) make especially daring sorties, transmitting anti-establishment or sometimes just plain funny stuff across unstable phone lines (at considerable risk of transmission errors) to associates all over Europe. Most transmissions take place at night when rates are lower but distinct beeping sounds are heard during the daytime, too, in locations as diverse as Trondheim (Norway) and Gibraltar (vis-a-vis La Linea, Spain). No phone is safe, it seems, from high-tech equipment in the hands of operators who hold the term of "dedicated lines" to be a joke, although a good one. A number of combatants have adopted tight fisted, no-holds-barred tactics to squeeze the absolute maximum of information onto every transmitted page, at the same time using the most outrageous antics to achieve priority attention from intended recipients. Examples include quotes and classified ads from* The Economist *crudely pasted into every available margin. This correspondent personally received two pages containing no less than eight different examples of exotic typefaces, no doubt generated by an advanced Postscript laser printer somewhere in time, and all of this in a transmission just shy of one hundred lines. It is every man and his battery-powered, highly portable fax equipment for himself. Zip onto the Autobahn and you can fax your biz from a roadside tollphone. Lightweight faxes are making their way onto commercial aircraft and trains, ready for use immediately on the public telephones now found in planes and streamliners or express trains.*

If you have to communicate in writing with the rest of the world – don't forget that a £1 fax will often say more than a £10 phone call – then you should get a fax. While you are at it, you might as well get a portable one that you can use anywhere in the world, without accidentally giving away your whereabouts.

Why not get a portable fax? After mail drops, it is the second most important investment in goods or services that you can make to enhance your privacy. If you must, a quick fax is faster than a letter, cheaper than a phone call and harder to trace than either of them. Use this option for your own benefit.

Which fax to choose ? The market is bursting with offers. Olivetti, AEC and Nissei carry more or less similar portables. All can be had with an optional 12V car battery, converter and a chip for connecting to mobile phones. In late 1992, Japanese office-machine giant Ricoh introduced a new, battery powered, portable fax called the PF-1. Labelled "the lightest, most portable fax in the world", it weighs in at under 4 pounds. Prices are likely to drop further, but the PF-1 was introduced at US $1,500 – which means that by the time you read this, you can probably get one at less than US $1,000.

Shop around. The cheapest places to buy fax machines, or just about any sort of electronics, are in Singapore or in New York (hint: electronics prices are generally better in stores on 7th Avenue than on 5th due to lower rents). Check the market thoroughly before you buy. Things to consider are: does the fax run on battery plus both 110 and 220 volts? If not fitted with an internal, automatic switching mechanism (the way an electric razor normally is), can you get an external transformer; is an acoustic coupler included (remember that Velcro straps are best for attaching handset to coupler)?; what is the battery capacity? Can you plug into wall mains or your car cigarette lighter for a recharge.

Remember that a portable fax machine ideally should be as easy to use and recharge as a video camera. Even if the price is higher, you may want to get a fax with an easy-to-*replace* battery that can be changed on the spot. As battery capacity is generally about five pages (and rarely more than nine), it may be useful to be able to bring an several fully charged batteries if you go to a phone booth to fire off a large number of faxes. Better to change battery on the spot and carry on, rather than having to retreat to your home (or hotel room) to recharge.

A final note on portable faxes. Battery life may tend to be very short unless you completely discharge the battery at least once a month before slowly recharging. Be aware that not all portable faxes have a built-in regulator to prevent you from overcharging – and ruining – the battery.

Do you want to travel even lighter? A built-in fax/modem card can be hooked up to your notebook computer and attached to an acoustic coupler (between $75 and $160 if purchased separately). This will perform in exactly the same way as a portable fax, save that you can only fax documents from your hard disk. If you want to fire off paper from the "outside" world you have to first figure out a way of digitalizing them into the computer. This will at least mean one extra step, scanning. Handheld scanners with software included can be had for about $150 upwards. For text or computer generated material you won't need a scanner but for pen and ink drawings you will.

For notebook-toting travellers, an internal fax/modem card will save you lugging a printer along. Just fax that report by free call to the fax machine in the hotel where you're staying and you will have an instant "hardcopy" print. Most hotels don't charge guests for incoming faxes. Quality is often better than normal faxes and certainly no worse. Good hotels usually have plain paper faxes so your reports will appear to have been printed on a high-quality lazer printer. US-based monthly magazines such as *"Mobile Office"* and *"PC Laptop"* write on these matters. Check newsstands or send $3.95 + $1 P&P to L.F.P. Inc., 9117 Wilshire Blvd Suite 300, Beverly Hills, CA 90210, USA for a sample copy of these newsletters.

**Chapter 17**

# GETTING PERSONAL: CODES AND CONDUCT

People from different cultures have different ways not only of expressing themselves through body language but may also pick up signals from you that you inadvertantly display. In certain Moslem countries, a man who sits with his legs crossed is thought to (willfully) indicate that he is gay. Likewise, you should never show the soles of your shoes to an Arab or to most other Moslems. This is considered gravely insulting. Finger-signs may also mean different things depending on where you are: making a circle by putting your forefinger and thumb together means "Perfect" or "Thanks" in some countries, whereas in Greece, for example, it is a symbol meant to invite homosexual advances. The two-finger sign meaning "I don't believe you" in the US is used in Italy to mean "someone is sleeping with the wife of the person you are communicating with".

## IS SOMEONE SHAFTING YOU?

If you wish to establish whether a conversation partner is being honest, body language is not difficult to read. Pick up a couple of books on the subject if you are often involved in conferences where reading clues as to your partner or opponent's mindset (nervousness, aggression, defensiveness etc.) may be of help. Fidgeting implies nervousness, standing – and especially sitting – with arms crossed over the chest belies a negative or defensive attitude (premature protectiveness) and so forth. A bit of personal study and reading books on the subject is advisable.

Reading "face language" is a bit more tricky. People are usually more self-conscious of their facial expressions than about their body language. Some people make their livings by putting on a poker face to the world at all times. One hint that you might find useful, however, is that someone who is not quite truthful will let his (or her) facial expression of surprise or astonishment at an accusation, for instance, last *too long*. An example: if you tell someone "I think you had your fingers in the till", then watch the reaction. If a look of astonishment lasts more than about one second before being supplanted by one of disbelief or indignation, you may have hit the nail on the head. Take a mirror and try it out on yourself – the difference between an expression that lasts too long and one that doesn't is quite obvious once you are tuned in to watch for it.

You may be thinking of using a lie-detector, either the polygraph or voice stress analyzer. But lie-detector technology is extremely suspect and not to be relied upon. In many instances, the "test" will merely intimidate the subject and not be of any help. Most of the equipment on the market is of dubious value. If a PT has a genuine need for such a device or similar, he should contact SWS Security, 1300 Boyd Road Street, Maryland 21154-1826, USA, telephone (410) 879-4035, fax (410) 836-1190.

## CHOOSE YOUR WORDS WITH CARE

Always be careful to keep a low profile no matter who you talk to and what you discuss.

One risk against your interests during a face-to-face conversation lies in surveillance by third-party individuals. In theory this may take the form of bugs (radio-frequency microphones), direction-sensitive microphones or laser beam recording bugs. The latter two methods are only likely to be effective in laboratory conditions, not real life, despite salesmen's hype.

Someone may also pick up a conversation between yourself and someone else – without either party's knowledge or consent of this – by lip reading, although this is unlikely. Someone with an audio and video tape recording of a conversation conducted in a noisy place may obtain a better transcript of the conversation by enlisting the services of a lip-reader.

And it *does* happen. In the United States, federal snoops will engage in such tactics if bugging or direction sensitive microphones fail to do the trick. So will a whole host of intelligence agencies if the stakes are high enough. During pre-arrest surveillance of mobster Henry Hill (on whose story the movie *Wise Guy* was based), investigators noted that Hill would habitually cover his mouth during clandestine conversations to guard against exactly these tactics. Besides covering your mouth, counter-ploys involve moving your head frequently and switching between different languages at random to foil a mono-lingual listener. A good reason to learn a second – or third – language . . .

# CODES (AND SAVOIR-FAIRE)

The use of codes will serve greatly to enhance your privacy and keep others confused about your whereabouts, activities, assets, goals, hopes, fears and apprehensions. Keeping your mouth shut whenever you do not absolutely, positively have to say something is better than any code.

Codes are not just for spies, drug dealers and organized crime "personnel", they are also an extremely valuable tool for the privacy and freedom-seeking individual.

The extent to which you can make codes work for you depends largely on the nature of the people you are dealing with. You probably should not try to talk your friendly, local bank manager into dividing the balance on your bank account by the temperature in Atlanta, as listed by some obscure statistical publication before divulging the figure to you over the phone. No need to attract unnecessary attention to yourself by being *too* insistent on codes or secrecy where ordinary people are concerned – especially in a day and age when the majority of all people have been brainwashed into seeing drug peddlers everywhere. A DEA-agent was quoted in *Time* magazine a few years ago as saying that: "The best way for someone to operate a drug wholesaling ring inconspicuously out of middleclass suburbia is to give the neighbors the impression that they are God-fearing people who dig Donny and Marie Osmond" (note to younger readers: "The Osmonds" was a Mormon pop group notorious for pouring sticky syrup all over the airwaves back in the Seventies).

If you are dealing with kindred spirits who enjoy a good battle of wits with Big Bore for the sake of avoiding theft by taxation (or just for the sheer fun of it), you should be on safe ground. The same applies if you are involved in business dealings where a great degree of due diligence must be exercised to avoid giving plans away to snooping competitors. In fact, American businesses lose billions of dollars every year due to idiot employees – and even managers and CEOs – who freely blabber out the most privileged of information on regular phone lines or even (ouch!) on cellular phones. If you are self-employed, keep the cards close to your chest – at all times! This is essential if you wish to prosper. And if you are an employee, being a model of discretion will, sooner or later, bring you an awful lot of goodwill from your superiors. If you help protect the interests of your employer even far beyond the call of duty, you will further your own goals in the process.

There are any number of ways in which you may use codes. As already explained, it is always best to do it as low-key as possible. One New York dope-dealer thought he was "safe" by referring to cocaine as "golf balls" over the phone. Big mistake (especially because golf balls usually are not sold by the gram or even the kilo!). Any jury listening to his supposedly "innocent" conversations would take about two minutes to reach a "guilty" decision.

The best way to use codes is to arrange with your contacts and business associates for certain words and phrases to mean something else than they would to an eavesdropper. An example: let us say that you call someone to arrange a meeting at noon. When you make the call (or send the fax), indicate that the appointment is scheduled for midnight. If you want to meet in the lobby of the nearest Holiday Inn, say ''at the Sheraton'' instead, if the other party understands you.

If you are serious about codes, remember that if they are simple enough to memorize, they are simple enough to break. Most people think in a similar way. Codes cannot be relied upon if you are dealing with a government agency which employs professionals in code-breaking

Several friends have developed the use of codes to an artform. This confuses outsiders – and it's great fun, too. One stockbroker signs himself Wyatt Earp or another famous gunslinger.

Another PT drives a grey BMW, which he consequently refers to as ''my white Mercedes convertible''. Whenever possible, he will refer to himself and the person he is speaking to (or faxing) in the third person – and not just change the names but also occasionally reverse the sex. Thus, he may refer to himself as ''red-headed Rhonda''. When communicating with one particular associate, the two will send faxes to each other's mail-drop and have them read to one another over the phone. The mail drop operators think that their clients are in the music industry, or at least that is what the pre-set code words suggest.

Funny ideas. Why not refer to US dollars as ''Uncle Suckers'' – and Spanish pesetas as ''Piratos'' – and British pounds sterling as ''(big) Bens''? Be careful which codes you use about currency, however. If you refer to it as ''Funny Money'', a wiretapping FBI agent might think he had stumbled on a counterfeiting operation.

You might start using codes, especially with people you know and trust – and also with new contacts whom you are testing for dependability. If you prearrange with someone to always refer to, e.g. Luxembourg as ''Louisiana'' when speaking on the phone, you may then sit back attentively and observe whether he or she is capable of helping you protect your interests – and, thus, his or her own – or if there will be a lot of moronic, tell-tale giggling whenever a code word is about to be uttered. Should that happen, use the first personal encounter with the individual in question to sternly admonish him that codes are there to deflect attention and mislead the enemy – and are *not* to be given away just because some fool thinks it is a great joke to ''play James Bond''.

Think up codes easy for you to remember. Then start prearranging their use with your various business and personal associates and acquaintances by discussing the subject during face-to-face encounters. If anyone hesitates or wavers, quite simply remind him why your mutual relationship exists in the first place – and that you appreciate not only privacy but also place a higher value on people who know its worth than on standard-issue morons.

Your inner circle will quickly adjust and find that codes become second nature, especially after they start realizing some of the benefits. And whereas the material benefits will inevitably take some time to materialize, the psychological benefits are immense and immediate. You will enjoy a tremendously increased peace of mind. In addition, you will find that when you no longer spend a lot of time worrying about whether someone will discover something at an inopportune moment (because you will have prevented this from happening in the first place by using impenetrable codes) you will find your thoughts focusing more clearly on practical matters – like enjoying life more or making money.

Also be discreet. One of the best ways, bar none, to get ahead in life in general and in business in particular is to shut up and listen. The less you shoot your mouth off, the more you will hear – and learn from and about your friends and business and personal acquaintances. Make sure that people in your life observe a certain code of silence, too. This is not to say that you should promise your secretary a ''Colombian necktie'' if she reveals the name of your dog to a journalist (much less deliver on such a promise!) but that you will do very well by starting to practice a personal sort of ''Omerta'' *yourself*. Just as no good husband will discuss with others whether his wife uses Tampax or old-fashioned sanitary napkins, so you should not let on what you know about the little quirks and pecularities of your employer (or employees), your business partners and associates or even your personal friends and acquaintances. Shut up! Sooner or later, the information is bound to find its way back to the person you described in less-than-flattering terms. Think of the "Dennis the Menace" cartoon, in which a bratty kid will constantly embarrass his parents by asking them about guests in their presence, along the lines of "Dad, is this the man who is always sitting on his wallet?"

If you *do* have to say anything, be positive or non-commital. Do not say, "so-and-so is a dishonest arsehole" even though you think he is. It will reflect badly upon you and make people wonder about your motives. If hard pressed, be like the banker who will not say "no way in Hell would we loan one penny to that deadbeat", but rather "at this time, we feel that the interests of the customer in question will be better served by a bank or other financial institution that has a more progressive outlook which is in better keeping with what we perceive to be said customer's present circumstances." In other words: Blah-blah-blah. If possible, do not say anything, but if you cannot evade it, *say nothing by being euphemistic and diplomatic to a fault.*

Finally, the downside on codes is that if they are obvious and over-used, you may attract unwanted police or other attention to perfectly legal activities. Our ex-stockbroker was a believer in the conspiracy theory (everyone was conspiring to know what he was recommending to clients). Instead of speaking normally on the phone, his conversations always involved angels, black eagles, big Bens and Cayman pirates. These were code names for his favorite stocks. But the SEC thought he was "up to something" and mounted an investigation. Certain minor irregularities were discovered and he was fired. When you use codes, the eavesdropper should not be aware that you are using them. A good code sounds or reads like innocent conversation, perhaps with a lot of slang or pet names.

# PART FOUR

# MOVING ABOUT:
# THE A+A EXPANDED

# Chapter 18

# PLANES, TRAINS, AUTOMOBILES . . . AND MORE!

It pays huge dividends to keep your wits about you when it comes to going about from A to B. One Dutch expat of our acquaintance recently "felt the need" to go back and see his "family and friends".

Relishing the fact that he was now an expatriate and owned a big, expensive tax-free car on Swiss "Z"-plates, he drove into Holland from Belgium. On this particular day, Dutch customs officials just happened to decide on a little "raid" at the border. Usually, one can take the motorway straight from Belgium into Holland without stopping but on this day, the red lights were flashing.

Pulling the car to a halt, he merrily flashed his Dutch passport. The customs official gave him a funny look and asked where the car was registered.

"In Switzerland," came the happy reply.

"But you are a Dutch national?"

"Yup, but I live outside of Holland and am only going back for a few days to visit," replied the lad.

Most countries do not allow their own citizens – or even foreign residents – to drive foreign registered cars inside their own borders. The young man in question knew this, but surmised that since he was living outside Holland, and could document this, he was not breaking the law. Only one tiny snag, after leaving Holland, the Dutch tax authorities had gotten the idea in their heads that he owed back taxes (a criminal offense in Holland). When a computer check was made on his return, due to the fact that he was driving a foreign registered car, his right as an expatriate to do so having to be verified – the delinquent tax debt was discovered. In due course he was arrested and carted off to jail. His expensive Lexus was confiscated.

So, if you are an expatriate, never drive a foreign registered, tax-free Flashmobile back into your own country. You never know what sort of silliness – not to mention theft – the government in your old country cooked up for you in your absence. Especially in countries with high automobile taxes where the appearance at the border of an expatriate with an expensive set of wheels will give rise to much envy in the minds of petty civil servants.

No matter in which countries you drive, always take care not to draw any undue attention to yourself. A banal, little accident may set the ball rolling and draw attention to you in the place where you are living, perhaps as a non-registered, transient alien. What's worse, a serious accident that results in your being hospitalized will automatically mean that your embassy is informed, with a view to the embassy contacting your family "back home".

In one noted case about 15 years ago, a Belgian white collar criminal and fugitive living in Argentina was involved in an automobile accident in which his wife got severely injured. Accompanying her on a flight back to Brussels, he was unaware that the Belgian embassy in Buenos Aires had been informed of the accident and evacuation. They, in due course, had notified Brussels where authorities to their surprise discovered that the woman was registered as the wife of a known fugitive. On touch down in Belgium, the plane was met by a small army of police officers with submachine guns. The fugitive (who had never anticipated this) was promptly taken into custody.

If you have to drive, do it right. Drive safely, responsibly and defensively. Yes, most motorists may have oat bran for brains. But no matter how tempting it may be to assert your "right of way", resist that temptation. There's always a slight chance that a minor fender-bender can blossom into something far more sinister.

When you travel by car, always be prudent. This matters especially when driving in other countries, no matter how friendly the natives seem to be. Do bring not only a valid (and preferably international) driver's license but also the car's registration and insurance papers. A "green card" certifying the international validity of your third party insurance is essential. Very rarely these days do you need a *carnet de passages en douane*. However, get this document in case you need it. A handful of backward third world nations still require it.

When stopped, always be as stupid and foreign as you can. If you cannot point to the fact that you are staying at a hotel (perhaps because you are staying in a rented house or apartment that you would rather not mention), also carry your passport AND a packed suitcase with everything a "tourist" would carry through the country. The latter is important if you are staying unofficially and un-registered for longer periods of time. You do not wish to have to explain to a Swiss policeman how it has come about that you are driving around Zürich with only various valid papers, the clothes on your back and no luggage whatsoever – and still claim to be neither in a hotel, nor being able to name a local address that you are currently occupying.

Standard safety concerns aside, you should also take care to prevent yourself from being easily followed, identified or coming under traffic cop scrutiny due to the physical appearance of your car.

Always choose a non-conspicuous car that fits in with your image. Don't make it easy for others to spot it as yours. Fox tails dangling from the antenna, an assortment of bumperstickers, fancy spoilers or vanity plates for that matter – all are to avoided. Even if you drive a Rolls Royce, people will tend to notice it less if the license plate reads "G 581 HS" than if it says "RICH 1" or "SUCCES". Likewise, even the most self-effacing clunker may stand out in a parking lot if fitted with an odd or just plain funny stickers or plates. And, lest we forget, more than one woman has been raped because she absolutely had to have a license plate reading "TINA" or "CHERRYL", telling a sleazy nightprowler that breaking in and hiding in the backseat for the owner to arrive might be worth a bit of panty-ripping and throat-slitting.

So what kind of car *should* you drive? The obvious answer is anything that "comes thirteen a dozen" wherever you are. In the United States, a mid-range Chevy is great and will provoke little hostility from demented followers of the "Buy American" doctrine. In Europe, get a Ford or an Opel for maximum invisibility. In Britain, a Rover is OK – so is a smaller Mercedes in Germany, France, Switzerland and Austria. The point is to get something common that will not draw attention to you. If you crave more, you can always fit the largest engine available, spruce up the interior with leather seats and all optional extras and even decorate the outside with original, run-of-the-mill alloy rims. But apart from that, keep the car as inconspicuous as at all possible. You do not need to draw anybody's attention to you by virtue of stupid bumper stickers or one of those incredibly daft suction-cup Garfields dangling from your rear window.

Make sure that the address to which the car is registered is either a mail drop or, if need be, your business. If someone notices you speeding through the city at night, a call may be placed to the cops informing of a "possible drunk driver". In the United States of Albania, a group fittingly enough called MADD (Mothers Against Drunk Driving) encourage all and sundry to call the cops with the registration numbers of cars seen speeding at night. This enables the boys in blue to greet the owner when he arrives home – or even break into the house and force him to take a breathalyzer test *after* he has left the vehicle in the garage and gone to bed. It happens! If you wish to escape this sort of Gestapo-like tactics, make sure that any search for your vehicle is at least initially diverted towards a mail drop and not towards your nest. Needless to say, never risk driving when drunk or stoned.

## WALT THOMPSON'S STORY

The tale of Walt Thompson is a "worst case scenario" of what may happen if one **parks** in the wrong spot. Walt suspected his wife of cheating on him. He did not really have any hard evidence or even any rational reason to suspect infidelity – he merely had what women call "an intuition" and what men call a *hunch*.

During a business trip abroad, he phoned home to "touch base" inquiring about his wife's plans for the evening (he wasn't scheduled to come back for another week). For some reason, he was not quite satisfied with her explanation that she was "off to see a girlfriend". Unfortunately, he was unable and, indeed, unwilling, to go back to check on her.

He phoned a friend in his home town and asked him to drive around his house to see whether his wife's car was in the driveway. An hour later, the friend called back and told him, "no". Having established that his wife at least had left their home – and thus, probably, was not fouling their common bed with a lover – he was still nagged by suspicion. It was getting harder for him to concentrate on the business at hand. He didn't really have any idea whom his wife would be seeing in the event that the story about a girlfriend was untrue. But, well, there *was* this business associate of his, a charming young wolf about ten years his junior . . .

So in short order, he called up a mini cab (taxi) service in the area where the business associate was known to live. Having gotten his address from information (not all people have unlisted numbers), he instructed the dispatcher to send a car to the home of Walt's business partner, then call back when he was in place. The call came in about half an hour later, and with quivering voice the client told the dispatcher to ask the driver whether a mint-green Toyota Celica Convertible was in the driveway next to the Mercedes owned by the young devil. You guessed it. Yes, the Mercedes was there – and so was the wife's ridiculously green Celica.

Two days later, Walt's unfaithful wife came home from work to find the house completely emptied of furniture. Even the phones were gone. She turned to run out and call the police from a phone booth. On the inside of the front door, she found an ugly letter from her husband nailed to the mahogany, icily informing her that she had better hang on to her car as the only asset she had left. Their joint bank accounts had been closed, the funds transferred, attempting to use her credit cards proved futile as Walt had withdrawn his co-signer guarantees by certified letter to the card companies.

The cheating business partner in question received a surprise delegation of determined-looking IRS auditors a few days later, courtesy of some snitching by an anonymous Walt-soundalike. As they say in the American Bar Association: "When you want a divorce, do it right and forget everything about playing Prince Valiant. Instead, beat your spouse to the game and have some fun."

## THE IDEAL AUTO ALARM SYSTEM

If you are serious about protecting what is yours, here's a list of the functions that should be incorporated with any auto alarm.

Arming and disarming. This is best done with the use of a tiny handheld *radio* transmitter. Infra-red transmitters are a no-no as you will have to point the transmitter in the direction of the vehicle for them to work. A radio transmitter, on the other hand, will work even if you keep it in your coat pocket and press the switch from 50 feet away. In some countries, radio-controlled auto alarms are hard to come by due to stupid airwave regulations (kudos to the FCC-people in the US who have a progressive outlook on this).

When arming and disarming, the alarm should acknowledge this by flashing headlights or marker lights, with an optional audio signal (''chirp'') to go with it. There should be a special indication, such a higher number of flashes and 'chirps' if the alarm has been activated during your absence.

An additional, ''panic'' feature should be included that will enable you to set off the alarm from a distance by keeping the transmitter button depressed for a couple of seconds – either to scare off thieves about to smash your windows, or in the event that you are being harassed or threatened while approaching your vehicle.

It is a great convenience if the alarm is interfaced with the central door lock system in the vehicle, automatically locking and unlocking doors when arming and disarming. In addition, the whole thing may be wired up to automatically roll up all power windows and even close an electric sunroof when you arm the vehicle. It will make it faster for you to get out of the car and into a phone booth (or shopping mall) on a hot summer afternoon, without tempting you to leave the car exposed with open windows. A ''starter disable relay'' is essential. This, more than anything else, will serve to prevent a thief from running off with the car.

For the alarm to be set off, you should insist on additional 'trip wires' in addition to just the doors being opened. Options include an adjustable microphone to detect smashed windows and even a miniature microwave device that will detect a hand being stuck through an open window or someone cutting through a convertible top. Infra red sensors are obsolete and will lead to more false alarms, as they may be tripped off by sharp light or even dramatic temperature changes.

With most, good alarms you can also get a pager which will alert you if the car is broken into from a distance of up to a few thousand feet. It costs about the same as the alarm itself (US $3,50) but may be worth it.

In some countries, you may even get a ''passive alarm'' that will let a thief hi-jack your vehicle – only to disable the ignition a few minutes later and alert the police with the whereabouts of the vehicle. Cute stuff. Cute price, too, about £1,000. Available from, among others, AutoSeeker Limited, 2 Carlton Court, Fifth Avenue, Team Valley Trading Estate, Gateshead NE11 0AX, England. Phone (091) 487 5573, fax (091) 482 6493.

But be slightly wary of ultra-sophisticated alarms if they give off too many false alerts, they are worse than useless.

Oh yes, how does one beat most auto alarms? Easy, by smashing either a headlight or a marker light, then inserting a screwdriver in the bulb socket. When the alarm goes off, it will be short-circuited and blow its fuse, leaving it useless. If you are still wondering how to prevent someone from circumventing your alarm in this way, it's easy, too. Merely have your installer insert a fuse in the wire running from the alarm ''head unit'' to the marker lights. Bet they didn't teach you that in driving school . . .

How low can you go, ''automotive profile''-wise? This may give you an idea. In one of our playgrounds, a next-door neighbor – who lives about a mile down the road – owns a benign little BMW. No one ever gives it a second glance. The ''318'' sign on the trunk lid seems to tell a tale of someone who wanted a ''Beamer'' but couldn't (or wouldn't) quite pay the price and thus settled on getting a pedal-powered version (just kidding). He parks it anywhere – no one would steal a bottom-of-the-line BMW, especially not there. But a closer look provides a revelation of sorts. Enlisting the assistance of Hartge, a German ''auto-tailor'' firm, the standard engine has been replaced with BMW's 5-litre V12 engine – the same found in the top of the line 750 limousine model. It took some shoehorning but they managed nonetheless. Before installation, even this ''motive power'' was found inadequate and consequently tuned and ported and God only knows what. When turning on the flow from the big, blue NOS (nitrous oxide) bottle in the trunk, the measly-looking Krautmobile packs in excess of 600 horsepower and will, theoretically, cream a Lamborghini Diablo at top speeds of over 200 mph.

For good measure, he also had the thing bullet and bomb proofed, bringing the weight close to two tons. At a total cost approaching £90,000 (US $160,000) for the entire thing, this is one expensive "sleeper". But, as he says, "not letting people know what you have until you choose to show them is the whole point, both in business, with the opposite sex and with cars". Many of our readers get powerful 16-valve engine cars and then remove the manufacturers' badges which say to thieves "steal me, I'm hot". Low profile, as always, is best.

# AIR TRANSPORT, GOOD MANNERS AND BAD

When travelling by air, you might as well realize from the outset that you have little or no control over the checks and searches to which you will be subjected. On all commercial flights, you will have to wander through a metal detector. And not only will your carry-on luggage be X-rayed and possibly searched, many airlines now X-ray check luggage as well. Any sort of commercial air transport necessitates extreme caution not only in what you bring along but also in how you get to and from the plane – as when making reservations, checking in and clearing customs (on international flights).

Airlines keep extensive records, including passenger lists. This offends every PT principle. If you are as opposed to all forms of centralized registration as we are, do make sure that the airline will register you on the passenger list under a name that is just different enough from your own to make it hard to make the connection (pardon the pun) to you.

When booking a ticket, do so from a public pay phone and spell at least your surname and preferably also your given name wrong to the reservations clerk. If your name is Robert Brown, for instance, make sure you spell it something like "Wobert Bowen", for instance. Since you know that your name is misspelled in the computer reservations files, it will be easy enough for you to pick up your ticket. Leave the incorrectly spelt name on the ticket when you pick it up. If you have to show identification when checking in – or even at the gate – it is unlikely that you will encounter any problems. After all, everybody knows that telephone reservations clerks cannot spell – right? Yet this will serve to ensure that someone looking for you as "Brown, Robert" is unlikely to come up with the connection to "Bowen, Wobert" even though the two sound very much the same.

Airline tickets are nice! As a matter of fact, a bunch of business class tickets may very well be worth a small, non-declarable fortune that you can later redeem for cash. Most airlines allow both business and first class tickets to be purchased with or without reservations (open tickets) and will even accept a ticket from another airline as payment in whole or in part when selling you a ticket between completely different destinations.

To illustrate the point, here is a little story a reader sent us: *"Not long ago,"* he writes, *"I found myself in Istanbul, Turkey with a business class ticket for London, England, issued by Turkish Airlines (not as good as British Airways but sure beats both Olympic Airways and even SAS in the quality department). On arriving at Kemal Atatürk Airport, I found to my distress that some of the good people at Türk Hava Yollari (Turkish Airlines) wanted more money for less work and that management disagreed. In short, a strike had been called. Further to my irritation, I had to change my itinerary and go to Stockholm, Sweden instead of London. The obvious solution would have been to take an SAS flight instead but it was way overbooked. Somewhat miffed, I approached the Lufthansa counter and plunked down my Istanbul-London, THY-issued ticket as part payment on an Istanbul-Stockholm ticket (with a one-night layover in Frankfurt, Germany). What the heck, I couldn't stay in Minaret Heaven forever. Still not quite content at the prospect of wasting a day, I took my new Lufthansa ticket and strolled over to the Swissair counter. And, lo and behold, they had a nice flight to Stockholm via Zürich, Switzerland – but with no layover! My Lufthansa vouchers were not yet five minutes old when I exchanged them for this new, more convenient ticket."*

Flexibility is exactly the reason why business class tickets are so great. You may buy one without needing to make a reservation at the same time (or with an open return), then not only change reservation dates but also exchange them *ad infinitum* between just about any airlines. Usually, a business class ticket may also be redeemed, in cash, at any branch office, worldwide, of the issuing airline. Depending on your own itineraries, you may benefit mightily from grilling your travel agent on these possibilities. If you need to convert some liquid cash into almost-impossible-to-trace "monetary instruments", consider airline tickets. A bundle of ten JAL New York-Tokyo round-trip, first class tickets is a lot less bulky than the roughly US $50,000 they will cost you to buy. As long as you make sure to have reservation dates on all of them (later to be changed or cancelled when you redeem the tickets for cash), you will not give the game away to an inquisitive customs official. You are merely a hard working executive whose job entails constantly peddling between the US and Japan, right? The best part is that **airline tickets are not considered one of those notorious "certain monetary instruments"** that you would otherwise have had to declare on entering and leaving the US and a lot of other countries. As long as an airline ticket is of the fully convertible, fully redeemable variety (meaning, in effect, business or first class) it is as good as cash and a lot less conspicuous. It can be a great ploy to defeat currency controls or restrictions on how much cash you can take out of the country.

Yes, there are some intricate regulations governing tickets sold by travel agencies or charged to credit cards – but if you do a bit of shopping around with airlines themselves, you may find that the London-Los Angeles ticket you bought from the British Airways counter in Shannon, Ireland may be converted to cash at the BA office in Gibraltar. Rules *do* change. Certain airlines will adamantly insist that "you can only have a ticket redeemed where you bought it". Find out the rules. Airline employees of any description are usually the nicest, friendliest people you can find anywhere outside of hotels (and the US congress, at election time).

If you are very safety-conscious, how to buy your ticket if all you have is too much black cash that you would have a hard time explaining away? By using the "step-up" routine, that's how. Let us suppose that you have US $3,000 in cash and need, say, a round trip ticket from New York to London. Obviously, you do not want to plunk down that kind of dough in front of a zit-faced, "civic minded" kid sitting in the Manhattan TWA-office. What you do instead is shop with various airlines, buying first a fully convertible, US $ 500 ticket to anywhere in the United States. You then take this ticket to another office (or come back another day, depending on how much time you have) and buy a new ticket for a more expensive route, paying partly with the unused ticket, part cash. Then you repeat this procedure anywhere from two to six times, each time putting down a business class ticket and a few hundred bucks, cash – never forgetting to fret about how you "stupidly" left home without your Amex.

Another way to get airline tickets, either by paying cash *or* in a hurry when your wallet has been stolen (or your bank accounts and credit cards frozen . . .) is to enlist the services of a travel agency.

Travel agencies love to cater for "the business traveller in search of superior service" and whatever incredibly conceited slogans their ad agencies dream up. They try to convince people that it matters whether you buy your tickets from Wagon Lits or from American Express Travel Agency. To plan ahead, you would first of all scout out a reasonably large travel agency in your area where you establish a corporate account – using, for instance, the name and mail drop address of the offshore corporation that no man should be without. Then you gradually build up a credit balance in the account on which you may draw quickly and unnoticedly should the going ever get tough. Do not make payments by cheque or credit cards, rather go to a post office and send them postal money orders or transfer the amount to the agency's bank account from a bank account belonging to your offshore corporation.

Then, when and if push comes to shove, you need merely call up the travel agency and say "This is Herbert Hooligan from British Soccering, Inc. We have an employee, Jonathan B. Phree, who needs to go from Houston, Texas to Zug, Switzerland tomorrow. Our account number is EZ4-U2BA123-PT. Could you get him a reservation on a United flight and have it waiting for him at the counter when he checks in?" Of course they can. Their "aim is to please".

## HOW TO COPE WITH HIJACKERS

Once you are on a plane, having obtained your ticket with care and foresight and the little darlings of the skies are falling all over themselves, offering you the choice between "coffee, tea or me?", a couple of unkempt semi-humans with profoundly distasteful body odour start waving around guns and plastic explosives, insisting that a Libyan desert is a better place to spend a Saturday night than Athens.

What should you do in such a situation – apart from recanting any atheist convictions you might have acquired over the years? Well, there actually are a few things you *can* do. Quickly but quietly get rid of your Armani tie, expensive crocodile-skin belt, Gianni Versace suit jacket, Bally ostrich-skin loafers and Rolex gold watch. Then, if you happen to carry a US or British passport, get it out of the way (chuck it into the in-flight magazine, for instance, which no one reads anyway).

The reason, aircraft hijackers, as a group, are not benevolently inclined towards succesful-looking businessmen – nor towards citizens "belonging" to those two stalwart bulwarks against international terrorism: the US and Britain. In a number of hijackings, terrorists have threatened to start shooting US citizens, then continuing with the British once the former have run out. You will make yourself much less of a target in a hijack situation if you keep dead quiet, look like a dishevelled and slightly demented tourist. And, of course, carry anything but a US, British or (especially) Israeli passport.

Admittedly, your chance of being caught up in an airline hi-jacking is even less than that of being killed in a crash (about 1:300,000). But if you are serious about doing something to protect your life in a truly ugly situation is high on your list of priorities (it should be), you will be carrying a **camouflage passport.**

Camouflage . . . what? Yes. If you carry a passport that identifies you as a citizen of the US, Britain, Israel or even some less-than-generous-with-the-PLO Arab states (Egypt, for instance) it may be a smart move also to carry a passport identifying you as an innocent dork. Like a Dane, for instance. Or an Icelander. Or a Canadian. Or, even better, a citizen of Ceylon, the New Hebrides or British Honduras.

The difference is that whereas no Danish, Icelandic or Canadian will give or even sell you one of their passports just because you are worried about being victimized for your current citizenship, you may get passports from the three latter nations for a few hundred bucks. Okay, not *real* passports – after all, these countries no longer exist: Ceylon is now Sri Lanka, the New Hebrides became Vanuatu and British Honduras changed its name to Belize years ago. But few people are aware of this (most immigration officers not included, alas). That has paved the way for some enterprising people to legally issue anyone with a "passport" from one of these three, no longer existing countries for use as "life-savers" in hi-jack (and other) situations.

Terrorists will routinely collect passports from their hostages to identify those whom they will want to kill first, usually on the basis of nationality. As the object of all plane hijackings is to attract publicity, it makes more sense (or less nonsense, at any rate) for a "heroic, Islamic martyr" to blow out the brains of an American than a Hebridian. Or a Ceylonian, as it were. Since it is pretty useless to speculate on whether or not you will ever find yourself in such a situation, suffice it to say that if you *are* American, British or Israeli or otherwise think that your nationality or name may put you at special risk, perhaps it will be wise to get one of these camouflage passports (available for £370/$550, contact Scope International at fax +44 – 705 591975 for more information or read the special chapter on Camouflage Passports in W.G. Hill's *THE PASSPORT REPORT*. Order form at the back of this book).

If a camouflage passport is found on your person on arrival at your destination, the name, birthdate and other information in it should closely match those in your "real" passport, or a customs officer may start asking rude questions far beyond the usual astonished or suspicious look you will be getting in any event. Do not attempt to leave or enter any country using a camouflage passport as the attempt is 98 per cent likely to fail (in fact, keep it on your person at all times and show only if obliged to empty your pockets). You can get your camouflage passport in any name you like. People have used these for banking, too, especially in countries where the banks are less efficient and apparently not very alert as to where foreigners claim to be from.

A somewhat cheaper way to obtain an official-looking document for use in a tight situation is to get a passport from the so-called "World Service Authority" organisation. Founded by a certain, very idealistic Garry Davis (self-declared "World Coordinator"), WSA issues both "passports" and even "world identity cards" that may come in handy for, well, anything but passing international borders. Available from The World Service Authority, Suite 1106, Continental Building, 1012 14th Street NW, Washington, DC 20005 (phone 202 638 2662, fax 202 638 0638), US $180 gets you a renewable, 15-year WSA "passport". If you have only one passport, at least do yourself the favor of contacting WSA just to get current information for your "alternative ID" files.

Once you land safely, an international flight obliges you to clear immigrations and customs. The former is merely a time-consuming annoyance, the latter may be lethal to your health if you happen to carry something you are not supposed to – such as drugs, guns and excess cash in most countries and even printed matter in some. For example, a copy of *Playboy* magazine or any newspaper with a Page 3 Girl may get you thrown in a deep, dark hole in Saudi Arabia and many other Moslem countries. Venezuela prohibits the import of any printed matter from the Dominican Republic – and so on. In Singapore, chewing gum is contraband and its illegal importation can get you free accommodation in "The Hole". Check before you go to avoid delays or unwelcome investigations into your identity if the latter may prove delicate (you should know if it does).

## HOW A PT COMBATS JETLAG
Jet-lag can be overcome.

When travelling by jet to the East or to the West, you pass through several time zones within a short space of time. This upsets your biological rhythms. Result: jet-lag.

Travel from north to south or vice versa does not affect us in the same way. Why? We remain within the same time zone.

It has been established that travelling from east to west is less strenuous than from west to east. It is more natural for the body to extend the day than to shorten it. The body finds it easier to adjust to a later bedtime as opposed to an earlier one.

We can easily adjust our biological clock to one time zone change every day. This means it could take six days to adjust to New York time after flying in from mainland Europe.

Sleeplessness can be one problem of jet lag – especially if the time of arrival is early in the day. Those who sleep for a few hours after arrival can find it difficult to sleep when night falls. Those who don't sleep on arrival wander round extremely tired and achieve nothing constructive out of their next few days.

Remedy? If possible, try to adjust to the new time zone a few days prior to departure. If practical, go to bed earlier if flying east and later when travelling west.

If it is possible to choose a flight which arrives at local bed time, so much the better. Starting your trip with a good night's sleep will also help considerably. If it is possible to get a few hours sleep during the flight this will also help.

Don't eat or consume too much booze on the plane – even if it is free. Remember to drink plenty of water or soft drinks. Walk around the plane to maintain your circulation and do some isometric exercises.

## AIRSICKNESS OR MOTION SICKNESS
Finally, though it is not a directly related topic, if you are affected by airsickness or motion sickness during a flight or while zig-zagging up a mountain road, there is a new product – not a pill – that works very well for most people. It is an elastic band or bracelet with a 1 centimeter wide metal stud or rivet (usually stainless steel) that sticks out a bit. You follow the directions on the box and position each rivet (one on each hand) so that it pokes you in the place where your pulse is taken. Presto! No motion

sickness. Please write in if this suggestion helps you and if you have any other cures to recommend to readers.

# A TIP: CROSSING BORDERS WITHOUT A PASSPORT

Smugglers and criminals have used this method for years, now honest PTs can, too. How to cross borders without a passport.

In most countries, there are usually one or more routes into the neighboring country that HAVE NO BORDER STATIONS. These unmanned crossing points are usually small backwater roads. Sometimes they are no more than dirt roads used by local farmers.

In Europe, such crossings abound. Recently *The Economist* ran a story on how one correspondent managed to sneak on such back roads into all 12 EU member countries WITH NO PASSPORT AT ALL. All he did was to arm himself with the Goodyear road map of Europe. It shows all roads. Those with the symbol of a small flag on them have manned border crossings. Those without the flag are roads without surveillance or customs posts.

It is not illegal to use these border crossings points. But of course, officials of the countries involved have the right to ask for proper travel documents in the event that you are unlucky enough to be apprehended or stopped in a spot check. The usual penalty for improper entry is simply deportation. In a typical motorist case, the driver would be asked to return to the country he came from and possibly be given police escort in that direction.

This could lead to a "domino effect" where the prior country illegally entered is informed of your situation, and they in turn send you back to your country of origin.

Unpleasant incursions into the freedom of EU citizens to travel are ever-increasing. For example, Customs and Excise authorities regularly exchange data on vehicles or persons moving through the now notionally borderless Europe with their counterparts in other countries. Even travel agents are not immune. There is an agreement between travel agents throughout Europe to report the travel plans of people who they find suspicious to a freephone number. The British travel agents' association, ABTA, has sanctioned an agreement for its 700 members to become unpaid informants to HM Customs. Travellers should be wary of alerting travel agents' staff in this way if they wish to avoid being reported on the freephone.

# HOW TO FILE A POLICE REPORT OF LOST PASSPORT

Here is a sample -

Start off by stating your name and address after "Filed By". Also state the date filed.

Sample wording:

"On 14 February 1993, at Heathrow Air Terminal No. 1, after clearing passport control, but before customs, I found it necessary to use the bathroom, at around 9:30 a.m. A leather money pouch that was attached to my belt must have, at that time, slipped off my belt onto the toilet floor. I did not notice the loss at the time because of my rucksack also being in the stall. However, shortly after departing the airport, I noticed that this pouch had gone missing. I returned to the airport asking the lost and found official to check the toilet I had just left. [I was not allowed to go because it was in the restricted area]. He reported back that it was not there and had not been turned in. Later that day, I filed a loss of property report at the airport, and have checked back several times. My belt and contents were not turned in. I believe that in my belt was about £250 in cash, various identity cards, air tickets, and most importantly, my CANADIAN PASSPORT, number unknown, issued about two or three years ago, in London and in the name of DONALD DUCK. Inside the money belt was an offer of reward for the return of the belt and contents. I had hoped that it would be mailed back, but after one week it has not been returned. I do not believe the belt was stolen and my passport, but I could be wrong. This report is being filed with the Metropolitan Police because the person at the Canadian Embassy in London has told me that filing such a statement is a pre-requisite for obtaining a duplicate or replacement passport.

POLICE REPORT NUMBER: 78/5643/91, STATION: WEST END CENTRAL.''

# PUBLIC TRANSPORT

The most inconspicuous and least traceable way to travel is by tourist bus – or by train, if need be. Passengers on tourist buses are usually waved through borders with little in the way of formalities. Even on a train, you are fairly unlikely to be hassled.

Especially if you are carrying something small that you would rather not take on an airplane, making a long journey by bus or train is preferable to going by car. There are no security checks and rarely any passenger manifests where ground transportation is concerned. You get a chance to catch up on your sleep when you don't have to drive yourself. Trains are more secure than buses as far as accidents go, but a bit less so when it comes to being ignored by authorities. But if you have your paperwork well in order and are not breaking any laws by virtue of the contents of your luggage, trains still allow you to get up and walk around once in a while – or even to have a shower on many long-distance routes.

Many high speed trains in Europe are extremely comfortable. And the fastest way of travelling, too. If you calculate check-in time and getting to/from the airport, going by train is often speedier for journeys less than 500-600 km.

# LOW COST TRAVEL PASSES WORLDWIDE
## RAIL & BUS TRAVEL
Below is listed a selection of some of the numerous travel passes available on bus and rail networks worldwide. The passes listed are valid for the whole national system unless otherwise stated. A more comprehensive listing can be found in a book called *Travel Passes Worldwide* (from Hippocrene Books), which is a comprehensive guide to most air, rail and road passes worldwide. Buy the book at specialist travel bookstores. In general, passes are purchased from travel agents. Thomas Cook and American Express would handle most of them. Prices are not listed because they change rapidly. Some passes are better deals than others. Rule of thumb is that if you take the longest journey possible on two days of a five day pass, you get your money's worth.
## EUROPE
THE RAIL EUROP SENIOR CARD. Valid for one year, for purchasers over 60. Gives reductions up to 50 per cent all over western Europe.

RAIL EUROP FAMILY. One adult member of the family pays full fare for tickets, and up to two of the other adults travel for half price. Children aged 4 to 12 pay half-fare and one child under 4 travels free.

INTER-RAIL. For the under-26, Inter Rail pass allows one month travel of unlimited distance in western Europe plus Czechslovakia, Hungary, Morocco, Romania and Turkey.

INTER-RAIL + BOAT. Adds free travel on many Mediterranean, Scandinavian and Irish Sea ships – for 10 days, or one month.
## ARGENTINA
ARGENPASS. Valid for 30 days; 60 days; 90 days. Under-26 receive 20 per cent reduction.
## AUSTRALIA
AUSTRAILPASS. Valid for 14 days; 21 days, 7 day extensions.

KANGAROO 'ROAD AND RAIL' PASS. For extensive travel, Greyhound coach routes and rail for 28 days. Also passes for individual state networks.

GREYHOUND BUS PASS. Valid for up to 60 days' travel, with a break of up to 7 days permitted. Must be bought before reaching Australia.

DOWN-UNDER COACH PASS. Valid for 9 days' travel on Greyhounds in Australia and Mount Cook Lines in New Zealand.

ANSETT PIONEER AUSSIEPASS. Up to 60 days' travel on Ansett Lines.

**CANADA**

CANRAILPASS. For state-owned VIA rail system and associated buses only. 15-30 days, 20 per cent discount for under-24s. Also 8-day Eastern, Western and Marine regional passes,

**INDIA**

INDRAIL PASS. Seven days; 15 days; 21 days; 30 days, Passes also available for longer periods.

**ISRAEL**

EGGED ROUND ABOUT BUS TICKETS. Seven days, 14 days, 21 days, 30 days.

**JAPAN**

JAPAN RAIL PASS. Valid for 7 days, 14 days, 21 days.

**MALAYSIA**

MALAYAN RAILPASS. Valid for 10 days, 30 days.

**MOROCCO**

CARTE D'ABONNEMENT. Valid for I month.

**NEW ZEALAND**

NEW ZEALAND TRAVELPASS. Also covers inter-island ferries and some coaches. 8 days; 15 days; 22 days. Down-Under coachpass, see Australia.

**SINGAPORE**

THE MALAYSIAN-SINGAPORE RAIL PASS. Covers Singapore, Malaysia and Thailand and lasts for 10 days.

**USA**

AMTRAK NATIONAL RAIL PASS. Valid for 45 days, Regional passes available.

GREYHOUND AMERIPASS. Thirty days' use of Greyhound bus network. Must be bought before arriving in the US. Contact: Compass Travel, tel. UK 0733 51780. Remember, buses and trains in the USA are not nearly as clean, safe and comfortable as their European equivalents.

TRAILWAYS USA PASS. Valid for 5 days' minimum travel on the trailways bus network throughout the United States.

# MOTORCYCLES

Even if you have no intention of ever getting on one, bear with me for a brief outline of this often neglected option. Motor cycles are great for low-profile transport, *especially* if you are travelling to other countries. True, they are thoroughly lacking in creature comforts, although models are available that sport built-in, eight-speaker radios with a CD changer in the sidebags. One of them is the Honda Goldwing Aspencade. With six cylinders, 1500cc and over 100 horsepower, it's a house on two wheels. Only the sauna and the fireplace are missing, though it does come with a powerful heater.

For quick. efficient border crossings a motorcycle may very well turn out to be far better than a car. Why? Because anyone crossing a border on a motorcycle is automatically thought to be a very harmless tourist, whether young or old. In all my years, I have never seen or even heard of one, single biker getting harassed by customs officers for anything but stupid forgetfulness pertaining to insurance and registration papers – the kind of thing a well-prepared person like you or me would never let happen. People are also *nice* to bikers, in most places anyway. As long as they are on holiday and don't have elaborate gang "marks" sewn to the back of their leatherjackets, bikers on holiday are sometimes even treated with a bit of pity. I mean as in "too bad you can't afford a car".

Another reaction you are likely to get when driving a bike instead of a car in another country is usually one of "Oh, you're travelling around our country on your motorcycle? Wow. I wish I could do that."

Well you can. All you need is the bike and the stamp in your driver's license allowing you to drive it – plus a helmet and suitable set of safety leathers (figure £100 for the helmet and perhaps £600 for a top-of-the-line outfit consisting of leather jacket, pants, boots and gloves).

But it's dangerous, right? Probably it is in a head-on collision with a Land Rover. Still, if you dress right, it may in some accidents be safer than a car as long as there's no snow or sleet on the road. An old friend of mine has totalled his bike not once, nor twice but *thrice* (I never said he was careful). He hasn't even got a broken limb or a scar to show for it. This is especially true with high-speed accidents. In a car, even strapped in your seatbelt, rescue workers may have to get you – or your remains – out of the car with drills and blowtorches after you did a salto in your Opel Astra. But with a motorcycle, you merely hit the ground from a low altitude and graze along the asphalt (this is where the leather comes in). You may break a couple of dozen bones but at least you will never be crushed between the steering column and the back seat.

If you don't already have a license to drive a motorcycle, get one. It's cheap. In most countries, even with a bit of driving eduction, it is unlikely to cost more than a few hundred pounds. It is an interesting second option: if you need to make a fast move – or merely need some transportation that is easy to park and hard to spot as "your wheels" – then you can quickly get a decent, used bike for perhaps a thousand pounds and drive yourself across a continent in a few days, with everyone back home wondering where the heck you went. It is also good for off-road travel to a high mountain camp where you can lay low if the need arises.

## HOTELS: PT ONE-STOP SHOPS

Hotels deserve special mention while we are on the subject of moving about. After all, most people – even though they rarely leave their home town – will spend at least a couple of nights at one sooner or later.

The first thing to realize about hotels is that they are essentially *sleeping machines* – that's it, nothing else. Unless you book a suite because you need a quiet place for negotiations, chances are that you will only find yourself in one to begin with because you need a place to sleep. That being so, choose your hotel in a rational way, asking yourself the question: "What do I need?" If you are not incredibly spoiled, the answer is likely to be "a bed with some walls around it, a sink and a shower, preferably with at least lukewarm water." Why splash out £300 per night on a suite in Mayfair when you can get the same, basic facilities – even if less attractively packaged – for one tenth of the price in Harrow or Ruislip or at less than half the price of Kensington? We can give you one very good reason why cheap hotels are better, they have fewer employees and a higher staff turnover. Which means, they are much more likely to forget your name and face than a marble-and-brass palace. A couple of years ago, British actor Richard Harrison neatly summed it up in a CNN-commercial for one of the "leading hotels of the world", by saying that: "You don't have to tell them what your requirements are. They know it before you come." Right. And if you come often enough, they may even start taking an active interest in your habits, visitors, phone calls etc. Forget expensive hotels! As far as privacy goes, they are pure death if they know you.

That said, there are a lot of ways how you may use hotels – even when you are not staying in them. To begin with, hotel employees are, by and large, the most service-minded people you can find anywhere. They know that the only things they have to offer besides bed and bathroom facilities for rent by the day are *themselves* and the services they offer. If they convey a good image to the general public, they will be recommended – and stay in business. If not, they fold.

Just about any hotel will happily let you use their phone or send a fax for you, even if they make an exorbitant charge. Never mind. If you are not a guest, they will quickly forget about you and have no records to show that you were ever there. In fact, one may sometimes save the rent of an office or a suite by quite simply conducting business negotiations in the lobby of a hotel. Few people realize that by no means do you have to *stay* at a hotel in order to *be* there. We have held more than a fair share of three-hour meetings in the lobby of the Concorde Lafayette hotel in Paris and in the Tropical Bar of the Sheraton Skyline at Heathrow, London without spending a night at either place (not on the same occasions, anyway). Cost: Nada. A few Perriers or cups of coffee from the bar, perhaps, but that's about it. You can stay there for almost as long as you want, in complete relaxation and comfort. No one will question you about what you are doing there, as long as you dress well enough not to look like a bum. A PT-guru arranges all of his meetings at hotels. He does not like strangers to know where and how he lives.

Walk up to the concierge or receptionist in any hotel worth its salt, anywhere, and ask for "some paper and envelopes". You'll get it, no questions asked – and for free. If ever asked if you are a guest, truthfully answer "no", then add, "I'm still waiting for my party, but I guess he hasn't arrived or checked in yet and want to leave them some messages" – then walk back and resume your work in the bar or lobby.

Another way to get value from a hotel without paying a dime for it is when you ask directions or even advice on local customs, norms etc. If you find yourself in need of a respectable barber, most hotels have one on the premises. If you need to have a pair of trousers laid up, down, in or out, a hotel will either do it for you while you wait or they will tell where to have it done locally. Same with dry-cleaning, flight reservations etc. Hotels should be considered **one-stop shops** for everything the PT needs in terms of not only telecommunications (and post offices) but also for the most arcane, local information.

To illustrate just *how* friendly hotels can be, consider this little tale from real life. Once, we undertook to drive from London to Lausanne. With us, we brought (among other things) a letter which I needed to fax on the way. For certain reasons, sending it before I left, or using my portable fax to send it from a phone booth *en route* was out of the question. It had to be faxed from somewhere inbetween those two points, with my being able to later verify this, just in case. Circumnavigating Paris, I headed due east on the toll-free Route Nationale 5 in the direction of Strasburg and Montpellier, dodging opposing trucks during takeovers like Mad Max on amphetamines.

The time was just right as I entered the small, picturesque town of Didier – which just happens to have a hotel belonging to the two-star French IBIS chain, conveniently located close to the road. I entered and asked the receptionist to transmit the fax, when it hit me, I had forgotten to put some vital information in the fax! True, I had my computer in the car, but, somewhat out of the ordinary, I had brought my big, bulky laser printer along instead of my portable Canon. I sighed inwardly, theorizing on the hassle of dragging an 80-pound laser printer into the lobby and setting it up. Handwriting the additional information on a separate piece of paper was not an option. So, with an embarassed grin, I asked the receptionist if he happened to have a typewriter I could borrow for a few seconds. "Sure, monsieur, no problem" came the reply, and seconds later I was frantically typing away on an ancient IBM behind the counter. A few minutes later, the "extra-info" fax was well on its way, courtesy of France Telecom and IBIS. A note to readers who have perfected the ten-finger system, in many European countries, keyboards are not of the QWERTY-type (referring to the six letters in the uppermost, left corner of the keyboard) that is generally used in Britain and the US – so study the layout carefully before you start, or use the two-finger system for a change.

Another example of hotel helpfulness? A friend in Portugal tells us that he found his beautiful, penthouse apartment with the inspired help of a young lady working the reception of the hotel he stayed at when first arriving in the country. Promising to pay for a night on the town for her and her boyfriend, he had no problem getting her to peruse Portuguese newspapers in the search for an apartment priced for the natives, and not at the same exorbitant prices generally charged in local, English-language papers. This tactic in itself saved him perhaps $5,000 in rent money during his first year in the country. So don't tell us that hotels automatically "have to cost money". They may very well pay for themselves and cost you nothing.

As has briefly been touched upon in the chapter on mail drops, you may enlist the services of a hotel when it comes to *receiving* faxes and packages. While they will not generally agree to sign for registered deliveries except for guests, they will be happy to do almost everything else for you, provided you tip generously once in a while. Another ploy is to make a reservation a month in advance but pick up your mail and cancel the reservation before your scheduled arrival date. Such changes of plan are common and will not cause ill will unless you pull that same stunt too many times at the same hotel.

The best way to establish such a service is not to do it out of the blue but to first stay for a couple of nights at the hotel, inquiring daily about "faxes or messages for me?" You may even send a letter, fax or phone a message to *yourself* just to make them remember that you are a guest with communication needs surpassing those of most tourists.

Then, when checking out, ask them to keep anything that might arrive for you "until your next visit". Of course they'll do it – hotels love repeat customers, it's their bread and butter. By now, you are well on the road to setting yourself up with a full-service mail drop where you may receive letters, faxes and even messages 24 hours a day, seven days a week. This is something you will learn to appreciate the first time you have to receive an urgent fax during the weekend when your mail drop is closed! All it takes is a bit of tipping. Assuming that you start gently and don't receive *too* much mail at a hotel (never ask banks, especially local, to mail account statements to you at a hotel) then we guess you can get a service like this in most towns, and in most countries, for something like £20 per month. The arithmetic boils down to checking for mail and messages perhaps once a week, tipping £5 (or £10, if they start giving you a surly look) every time, whether or not anything is waiting for you.

## THE PACKED SUITCASE

In the event of the sudden need to exit your home, due to earthquake, flood, fire, riots, war, fiscal or legal problems, etc., I advocate you keep a packed suitcase ready. Everyone will have different needs, ideas, preferences, so this is a rough outline which you can adjust. It should have three lists on top: add these items if you have 3-5 minutes; add these if you've 5-15 minutes; add these if you've over 15 minutes. Once each six months, review contents and revise, update, modernize. Don't use matching, attractive luggage, it's a target. Possible contents: current passport with visas, 1 Krugerrand, 1 Mexican gold, 1 Maple Leaf, 2-3 rare coins (in toto: your 'collection'), 2-3 rare stamps, cash in 3-4 currencies, credit cards (one in a pen name?), address book, drivers license, sports gear so you appear as a tourist, 1-2 books worth re-reading, mini-dictionaries (2-3 languages), 1 light suit, 1 sweater, 1 heavy jacket (same for women), 4 shirts, slacks, ties, underwear and stockings, tough shoes, I crushable hat, various weight scarves, complete toiletry case, battery/windup razor, torch, Swiss knife, photos, (and press clips of ID) from past to show new friends who you are, wood matches, candle, blow-up pillow, space blanket (weighs nothing), small coin for phones, trench coat, nylon string, toilet tissue, tampons, tissues, vitamins, coded list of bank accounts, medical record, essential medication, pens/paper, maybe a light sleeping bag, hand warmers, insect repellant, water purifying tablets, salt, sunburn lotion, compass, safe deposit key, spare glasses and prescription, extra medical prescriptions, fold-up brolly, maybe camera and film, candy bar or quick energy food, checks, nailfile, notebook, wind-up alarm clock?, small plastic bags, maps, extra keys, business cards, three brandy miniatures, pocket shortwave radio, first-aid kit, scissors. Add or subtract to suit. Put items on top which you may remove to carry on your person, Keep suitcase in a closet with lots of boxes that look messy, not tempting to steal. Always leave money on a table, so a thief gets something easy, so he is happy and non-vindictive.

# DRESS FOR SUCCESS

When you travel, be a self-contained unit as much as possible. Even if only going to the corner shop, but especially on trips. Be prepared for the unexpected. Some people dress DOWN for errands and trips. Why? A friend just visited me. His luggage didn't arrive. Had he been in sweat pants and jogging shoes, how embarrassing to have met me, gone to dinner in a best restaurant in such travel clothes! Being bright, he dressed UP to travel

(as everyone should; the days when you got dirty travelling went out with steam locomotives and dirt roads). Dress to travel as though you'll never see your suitcases again. You may not. At least for 2-3 days. Going through customs (or with local police) is often smoother if you are well-dressed. Scruffy clothes get stopped. Dressing sloppy is also bad for your morale. Going a step further, hand carry what you need to be kidnapped in, caught in an earthquake, flood, fire, riot or arrested, held up in customs, robbed or just running into a VIP or old friends. Carry: a lot of cash (small and large bills ), credit cards, home and car keys, address and phone numbers for a lawyer, doctor, key friends. Never use a wallet! Thieves love them; they get all your valuables in one neat packet! Carry items loose in shirt pocket (safest) and both front slacks pockets (never rear) and jacket pockets. Carry blank checks, a passport, driver's license, fresh handkerchief, coins for phone booths, foreign currencies, some ID that shows your credibility, business cards, gum or breath freshener, pen and paper, a letter of reference from a VIP (e.g. a banker or Congressman), an item to read when you are delayed unexpectedly. Wear a belt! ) A small penknife and police whistle are optional/recommended. All of this on your body, not in a briefcase. Harder for women (who can use handbags, pockets, pouches inside jackets). Overdress rather than underdress; if the weather gets warm you can remove something; if it gets cold you are helpless. Summary: dress attractively and dress for emergencies when you step out of your front door. It'll soon become a habit. Don't wish you had done this when it's too late.

# QUIET INTERNATIONALIZATION OF SELF

Not all people relish the idea of travelling abroad merely to protect their private and business interests. But whether or not you like the idea, you should at least put yourself at ease with it.

If you are already an accomplished world-traveller – fine. But if you are not, start getting into the habit of quietly slipping in and out of your own country without telling a living soul. If you have a flourishing business in, say, Charlotte, South Carolina and are worried about the IRS, do *not* tell anyone about your trip to the Swiss Alps or the sunny beaches (and banks . . .) of the Caribbean. Keep quiet!

Instead, merely mumble something to your employees (or employer) about having to visit a sick aunt in Providence, Rhode Island and take a plane (or drive) to Niagara Falls, New York, then walk across the border and make your way to Switzerland from Canada. Bring cash or plenty of traveller's checks and do not phone home just to tell your wife and kids how overwhelmed you are at the beautiful, clean city of Zürich. Just go there, get the information and/or open the bank accounts that are the object of your trip, then quietly slip back into the US by the same route you left and go back to your life.

It is very important to keep q-u-i-e-t about your foreign trips, especially if the people around you are down-to-the-ground, common folk. If you have to travel a lot to protect your interests, not only should you get used to the idea of doing it – and doing it right – but also to the idea of keeping the fact that you are a bit of a globetrotter to yourself. Always.

# WORLDWIDE WEATHER GUIDE PT MEANS ''PERFECT TEMPERATURE''

For a lot of us, choosing where to live depends to a great extent on the weather. Personally, I think lots of sunshine is great and I don't like skiing as much as I used to. Of course sunshine is not the only thing that counts. Good looking available girls can make the difference between a good trip and a bad trip. We went to The Philippines last year and found the climate in Bagiuo City nothing short of ideal. The hostesses at the Swagman Hotel couldn't have been friendlier, prettier- or more eager to please. And the prices were peanuts. So why did we leave? Brown-outs, low levels of sanitation, totally corrupt cops and officials with their hands out for a bribe at every level, pollution, high crime, stuff like that! Still, sunny days and a warm, pleasant climate makes life more enjoyable for many of us and climate is a starting point.If you like invigorating cold, this chart will help you pick out the right split too. To make it easier for you to plan ahead, and choose where to be at what time of the year, we've included this information detailing temperature and humidity at major cities throughout the world.

Temperature: Average daily maximum and minimum temperatures are shade temperatures, Maximum temperatures usually occur in early afternoon, and minimum temperatures just before sunrise. Humidity: Measured as a daily figure at one or more fixed hours daily. It is normally lowest in the early afternoon and highest just before sunrise. High humidity combined with high temperatures increases discomfort. Rain (precipitation) includes all forms of moisture falling on the earth, mainly rain and snow. Average monthly.

| | *J* | *F* | *M* | *A* | *M* | *J* | *J* | *A* | *S* | *O* | *N* | *D* |
|---|---|---|---|---|---|---|---|---|---|---|---|---|
| **Accra** | | | | | | | | | | | | |
| Temp. F | | | | | | | | | | | | |
| Max | 87 | 88 | 88 | 88 | 87 | 84 | 81 | 80 | 81 | 85 | 87 | 88 |
| Min | 73 | 75 | 76 | 76 | 75 | 74 | 73 | 71 | 73 | 74 | 75 | 75 |
| Temp. C | | | | | | | | | | | | |
| Max | 31 | 31 | 31 | 31 | 31 | 29 | 38 | 38 | 38 | 29 | 31 | 31 |
| Min | 23 | 24 | 24 | 24 | 24 | 23 | 23 | 22 | 23 | 23 | 24 | 24 |
| Hmdty. % | | | | | | | | | | | | |
| am | 95 | 96 | 95 | 96 | 96 | 97 | 97 | 97 | 96 | 97 | 97 | 97 |
| pm | 61 | 61 | 63 | 65 | 68 | 74 | 76 | 77 | 72 | 71 | 66 | 64 |
| Rain mm | 15 | 33 | 56 | 81 | 142 | 178 | 46 | 15 | 36 | 64 | 36 | 23 |
| **Amsterdam** | | | | | | | | | | | | |
| Temp. F | | | | | | | | | | | | |
| Max | 40 | 42 | 49 | 56 | 64 | 70 | 72 | 71 | 67 | 57 | 48 | 42 |
| Min | 31 | 31 | 34 | 40 | 46 | 51 | 55 | 55 | 50 | 44 | 38 | 33 |
| Temp. C | | | | | | | | | | | | |
| Max | 4 | 5 | 10 | 13 | 18 | 21 | 22 | 22 | 19 | 14 | 9 | 5 |
| Min | -1 | -1 | 1 | 4 | 8 | 11 | 13 | 13 | 10 | 7 | 3 | 1 |
| Hmdty. % | | | | | | | | | | | | |
| am | 90 | 90 | 86 | 79 | 75 | 75 | 79 | 82 | 86 | 90 | 92 | 91 |
| pm | 82 | 76 | 65 | 61 | 59 | 59 | 64 | 65 | 67 | 72 | 81 | 85 |
| Rain mm | 68 | 53 | 44 | 49 | 52 | 58 | 77 | 87 | 72 | 72 | 70 | 64 |
| **Athens** | | | | | | | | | | | | |
| Temp. F | | | | | | | | | | | | |
| Max | 55 | 57 | 60 | 68 | 77 | 86 | 92 | 92 | 84 | 75 | 66 | 58 |
| Min | 44 | 44 | 46 | 52 | 61 | 68 | 73 | 73 | 67 | 60 | 53 | 47 |
| Temp. C | | | | | | | | | | | | |
| Max | 13 | 14 | 16 | 20 | 25 | 30 | 33 | 33 | 29 | 24 | 19 | 15 |
| Min | 6 | 7 | 8 | 11 | 16 | 20 | 23 | 23 | 19 | 15 | 12 | 8 |
| Hmdty. % | | | | | | | | | | | | |
| am | 77 | 74 | 71 | 65 | 60 | 50 | 47 | 48 | 58 | 70 | 78 | 78 |
| pm | 62 | 57 | 54 | 48 | 47 | 39 | 34 | 34 | 42 | 52 | 61 | 63 |
| Rain mm | 62 | 37 | 37 | 23 | 23 | 14 | 6 | 7 | 15 | 51 | 56 | 71 |

|  | J | F | M | A | M | J | J | A | S | O | N | D |
|---|---|---|---|---|---|---|---|---|---|---|---|---|
| **Auckland** | | | | | | | | | | | | |
| Temp. F | | | | | | | | | | | | |
| Max | 73 | 73 | 71 | 67 | 62 | 58 | 56 | 58 | 60 | 63 | 66 | 70 |
| Min | 60 | 60 | 59 | 56 | 51 | 48 | 46 | 46 | 49 | 52 | 54 | 57 |
| Temp. C | | | | | | | | | | | | |
| Max | 23 | 23 | 22 | 19 | 17 | 14 | 13 | 13 | 16 | 17 | 19 | 21 |
| Min | 16 | 16 | 15 | 13 | 11 | 9 | 8 | 8 | 9 | 11 | 12 | 14 |
| Hmdty. % | | | | | | | | | | | | |
| am | 71 | 72 | 74 | 78 | 80 | 83 | 84 | 80 | 76 | 74 | 71 | 70 |
| pm | 62 | 61 | 65 | 69 | 70 | 73 | 74 | 70 | 68 | 66 | 64 | 64 |
| Rain mm | 79 | 84 | 81 | 97 | 127 | 137 | 145 | 117 | 102 | 102 | 89 | 79 |
| **Bahrain** | | | | | | | | | | | | |
| Temp. F | | | | | | | | | | | | |
| Max | 68 | 70 | 75 | 84 | 92 | 96 | 99 | 100 | 96 | 90 | 82 | 71 |
| Min | 57 | 59 | 63 | 70 | 78 | 82 | 85 | 85 | 81 | 75 | 69 | 60 |
| Temp. C | | | | | | | | | | | | |
| Max | 32 | 33 | 34 | 35 | 34 | 33 | 32 | 32 | 32 | 31 | 31 | 31 |
| Min | 14 | 15 | 17 | 21 | 26 | 28 | 29 | 29 | 27 | 24 | 21 | 16 |
| Hmdty. % | | | | | | | | | | | | |
| am | 85 | 83 | 80 | 75 | 71 | 69 | 69 | 74 | 75 | 80 | 80 | 85 |
| pm | 71 | 70 | 70 | 66 | 63 | 64 | 67 | 65 | 64 | 66 | 70 | 77 |
| Rain mm | 8 | 18 | 13 | 8 | 0 | 0 | 0 | 0 | 0 | 0 | 18 | 18 |
| **Bangkok** | | | | | | | | | | | | |
| Temp. F | | | | | | | | | | | | |
| Max | 89 | 91 | 93 | 95 | 93 | 91 | 90 | 90 | 89 | 88 | 87 | 87 |
| Min | 68 | 72 | 75 | 77 | 77 | 76 | 76 | 76 | 76 | 75 | 72 | 68 |
| Temp. C | | | | | | | | | | | | |
| Max | 32 | 33 | 34 | 35 | 34 | 33 | 32 | 32 | 32 | 31 | 31 | 31 |
| Min | 20 | 22 | 24 | 25 | 25 | 24 | 24 | 24 | 24 | 25 | 22 | 20 |
| Hmdty. % | | | | | | | | | | | | |
| am | 91 | 92 | 92 | 90 | 91 | 90 | 91 | 92 | 94 | 93 | 92 | 91 |
| pm | 53 | 55 | 56 | 58 | 64 | 67 | 66 | 66 | 70 | 70 | 65 | 56 |
| Rain mm | 8 | 20 | 36 | 58 | 198 | 160 | 160 | 175 | 305 | 206 | 66 | 5 |
| **Beirut** | | | | | | | | | | | | |
| Temp. F | | | | | | | | | | | | |
| Max | 62 | 63 | 66 | 72 | 78 | 83 | 87 | 89 | 86 | 81 | 73 | 65 |
| Min | 51 | 51 | 54 | 58 | 64 | 69 | 73 | 74 | 73 | 69 | 61 | 55 |
| Temp. C | | | | | | | | | | | | |
| Max | 17 | 17 | 19 | 22 | 26 | 28 | 31 | 32 | 30 | 27 | 23 | 18 |
| Min | 11 | 11 | 12 | 14 | 18 | 21 | 23 | 23 | 23 | 21 | 16 | 12 |
| Hmdty. % | | | | | | | | | | | | |
| am | 72 | 72 | 72 | 72 | 69 | 67 | 66 | 65 | 64 | 65 | 67 | 70 |
| pm | 70 | 70 | 69 | 67 | 64 | 61 | 58 | 57 | 57 | 62 | 61 | 69 |
| Rain mm | 19 | 11 | 57 | 94 | 56 | 18 | 30 | 0 | 5 | 51 | 132 | 185 |

| | J | F | M | A | M | J | J | A | S | O | N | D |
|---|---|---|---|---|---|---|---|---|---|---|---|---|
| **Berlin** | | | | | | | | | | | | |
| Temp. F | | | | | | | | | | | | |
| Max | 35 | 37 | 46 | 56 | 66 | 72 | 75 | 74 | 68 | 56 | 45 | 38 |
| Min | 26 | 26 | 31 | 39 | 47 | 53 | 57 | 56 | 50 | 42 | 36 | 29 |
| Temp. C | | | | | | | | | | | | |
| Max | 2 | 3 | 8 | 13 | 19 | 22 | 24 | 23 | 20 | 13 | 7 | 3 |
| Min | -3 | -3 | 0 | 4 | 8 | 12 | 14 | 13 | 10 | 6 | 2 | -1 |
| Hmdty. % | | | | | | | | | | | | |
| am | 89 | 89 | 88 | 84 | 80 | 80 | 84 | 88 | 92 | 93 | 92 | 91 |
| pm | 82 | 78 | 67 | 60 | 57 | 58 | 61 | 61 | 65 | 73 | 83 | 86 |
| Rain mm | 46 | 40 | 33 | 42 | 49 | 65 | 73 | 69 | 48 | 49 | 46 | 43 |
| **Bombay** | | | | | | | | | | | | |
| Temp. F | | | | | | | | | | | | |
| Max | 83 | 83 | 86 | 89 | 91 | 89 | 85 | 85 | 85 | 89 | 89 | 97 |
| Min | 67 | 67 | 72 | 76 | 80 | 79 | 77 | 76 | 76 | 76 | 73 | 79 |
| Temp. C | | | | | | | | | | | | |
| Max | 28 | 28 | 30 | 32 | 33 | 32 | 29 | 29 | 29 | 32 | 32 | 31 |
| Min | 12 | 12 | 17 | 20 | 23 | 21 | 22 | 22 | 22 | 21 | 18 | 13 |
| Hmdty. % | | | | | | | | | | | | |
| am | 70 | 71 | 73 | 75 | 74 | 79 | 83 | 83 | 85 | 81 | 73 | 70 |
| pm | 61 | 62 | 65 | 67 | 68 | 77 | 83 | 81 | 78 | 71 | 64 | 62 |
| Rain mm | 2.5 | 2.5 | 2.5 | 0 | 18 | 485 | 617 | 340 | 264 | 64 | 13 | 2.5 |
| **Brussels** | | | | | | | | | | | | |
| Temp. F | | | | | | | | | | | | |
| Max | 40 | 44 | 51 | 58 | 65 | 72 | 73 | 72 | 69 | 60 | 48 | 42 |
| Min | 30 | 32 | 36 | 41 | 46 | 52 | 54 | 54 | 51 | 45 | 38 | 32 |
| Temp. C | | | | | | | | | | | | |
| Max | 4 | 7 | 10 | 14 | 18 | 22 | 23 | 22 | 21 | 15 | 9 | 6 |
| Min | -1 | 0 | 2 | 5 | 8 | 11 | 12 | 12 | 11 | 7 | 3 | 0 |
| Hmdty. % | | | | | | | | | | | | |
| am | 92 | 92 | 91 | 91 | 90 | 87 | 91 | 93 | 94 | 93 | 93 | 92 |
| pm | 86 | 81 | 74 | 71 | 65 | 65 | 68 | 69 | 69 | 67 | 85 | 86 |
| Rain mm | 66 | 61 | 53 | 60 | 55 | 76 | 95 | 80 | 63 | 83 | 75 | 88 |
| **Buenos Aires** | | | | | | | | | | | | |
| Temp. F | | | | | | | | | | | | |
| Max | 85 | 83 | 79 | 72 | 64 | 57 | 57 | 60 | 64 | 69 | 76 | 82 |
| Min | 63 | 63 | 60 | 53 | 47 | 41 | 42 | 43 | 46 | 50 | 56 | 61 |
| Temp. C | | | | | | | | | | | | |
| Max | 29 | 28 | 26 | 22 | 18 | 14 | 14 | 16 | 18 | 21 | 24 | 28 |
| Min | 17 | 17 | 16 | 12 | 8 | 5 | 6 | 6 | 8 | 10 | 13 | 16 |
| Hmdty. % | | | | | | | | | | | | |
| am | 81 | 83 | 87 | 88 | 90 | 91 | 92 | 90 | 86 | 83 | 79 | 79 |
| pm | 61 | 63 | 69 | 71 | 74 | 78 | 79 | 74 | 68 | 65 | 60 | 62 |
| Rain mm | 79 | 71 | 109 | 89 | 76 | 61 | 56 | 61 | 79 | 86 | 84 | 99 |

| | J | F | M | A | M | J | J | A | S | O | N | D |
|---|---|---|---|---|---|---|---|---|---|---|---|---|
| **Cairo** | | | | | | | | | | | | |
| Temp. F | | | | | | | | | | | | |
| Max | 65 | 69 | 75 | 83 | 91 | 95 | 96 | 95 | 90 | 86 | 78 | 68 |
| Min | 47 | 48 | 52 | 57 | 63 | 68 | 70 | 71 | 68 | 65 | 58 | 50 |
| Temp. C | | | | | | | | | | | | |
| Max | 18 | 21 | 24 | 28 | 33 | 35 | 36 | 35 | 32 | 30 | 26 | 20 |
| Min | 8 | 9 | 11 | 14 | 17 | 20 | 20 | 22 | 20 | 18 | 14 | 10 |
| Hmdty. % | | | | | | | | | | | | |
| am | 69 | 64 | 63 | 55 | 50 | 55 | 65 | 69 | 68 | 67 | 68 | 70 |
| pm | 40 | 33 | 27 | 21 | 18 | 20 | 24 | 28 | 31 | 31 | 38 | 41 |
| Rain mm | 5 | 5 | 5 | 3 | 3 | 0 | 0 | 0 | 0 | 0 | 3 | 5 |
| **Calcutta** | | | | | | | | | | | | |
| Temp. F | | | | | | | | | | | | |
| Max | 80 | 84 | 93 | 97 | 96 | 92 | 89 | 89 | 90 | 89 | 84 | 79 |
| Min | 55 | 59 | 69 | 75 | 77 | 79 | 79 | 78 | 78 | 72 | 64 | 55 |
| Temp. C | | | | | | | | | | | | |
| Max | 27 | 29 | 34 | 36 | 36 | 33 | 32 | 32 | 32 | 32 | 29 | 26 |
| Min | 13 | 15 | 21 | 24 | 25 | 26 | 26 | 26 | 26 | 24 | 18 | 13 |
| Hmdty. % | | | | | | | | | | | | |
| am | 85 | 82 | 79 | 76 | 77 | 82 | 86 | 88 | 86 | 85 | 79 | 80 |
| pm | 52 | 45 | 46 | 56 | 62 | 75 | 80 | 82 | 81 | 72 | 63 | 55 |
| Rain mm | 10 | 31 | 36 | 43 | 140 | 297 | 325 | 328 | 252 | 114 | 20 | 5 |
| **Christchurch** | | | | | | | | | | | | |
| Temp. F | | | | | | | | | | | | |
| Max | 70 | 69 | 66 | 62 | 56 | 51 | 50 | 52 | 57 | 62 | 66 | 69 |
| Min | 53 | 53 | 50 | 45 | 40 | 36 | 35 | 36 | 40 | 44 | 47 | 51 |
| Temp. C | | | | | | | | | | | | |
| Max | 21 | 21 | 19 | 17 | 13 | 11 | 10 | 11 | 14 | 17 | 19 | 21 |
| Min | 12 | 12 | 10 | 7 | 4 | 2 | 2 | 2 | 4 | 7 | 8 | 11 |
| Hmdty. % | | | | | | | | | | | | |
| am | 65 | 71 | 75 | 82 | 85 | 87 | 87 | 81 | 72 | 63 | 64 | 67 |
| pm | 59 | 60 | 69 | 71 | 69 | 72 | 76 | 66 | 69 | 60 | 64 | 60 |
| Rain mm | 56 | 43 | 48 | 48 | 66 | 66 | 69 | 48 | 46 | 60 | 64 | 60 |
| **Colombo** | | | | | | | | | | | | |
| Temp. F | | | | | | | | | | | | |
| Max | 86 | 87 | 88 | 88 | 87 | 85 | 85 | 85 | 85 | 85 | 85 | 85 |
| Min | 72 | 72 | 74 | 76 | 78 | 77 | 77 | 77 | 77 | 75 | 73 | 72 |
| Temp. C | | | | | | | | | | | | |
| Max | 30 | 31 | 31 | 31 | 31 | 29 | 29 | 29 | 29 | 29 | 29 | 29 |
| Min | 22 | 22 | 23 | 24 | 25 | 26 | 25 | 25 | 25 | 24 | 23 | 22 |
| Hmdty. % | | | | | | | | | | | | |
| am | 73 | 71 | 71 | 74 | 78 | 80 | 79 | 78 | 76 | 77 | 77 | 74 |
| pm | 75 | 69 | 67 | 66 | 66 | 70 | 76 | 78 | 77 | 76 | 75 | 76 |
| Rain mm | 89 | 69 | 147 | 231 | 371 | 224 | 135 | 109 | 160 | 348 | 315 | 147 |

|  | J | F | M | A | M | J | J | A | S | O | N | D |
|---|---|---|---|---|---|---|---|---|---|---|---|---|
| **Copenhagen** | | | | | | | | | | | | |
| Temp. F | | | | | | | | | | | | |
| Max | 36 | 36 | 41 | 51 | 61 | 67 | 71 | 70 | 64 | 54 | 45 | 40 |
| Min | 28 | 28 | 31 | 38 | 46 | 52 | 57 | 56 | 51 | 44 | 38 | 34 |
| Temp. C | | | | | | | | | | | | |
| Max | 2 | 2 | 5 | 10 | 16 | 19 | 22 | 21 | 18 | 12 | 7 | 4 |
| Min | -2 | -3 | -1 | 3 | 8 | 11 | 14 | 14 | 11 | 7 | 13 | 1 |
| Hmdty. % | | | | | | | | | | | | |
| am | 88 | 86 | 85 | 79 | 70 | 70 | 74 | 78 | 83 | 86 | 88 | 89 |
| pm | 85 | 83 | 78 | 68 | 59 | 60 | 62 | 64 | 69 | 76 | 83 | 87 |
| Rain mm | 49 | 39 | 32 | 38 | 43 | 46 | 71 | 66 | 62 | 59 | 48 | 49 |
| **Delhi** | | | | | | | | | | | | |
| Temp. F | | | | | | | | | | | | |
| Max | 70 | 75 | 87 | 97 | 105 | 102 | 96 | 93 | 93 | 93 | 84 | 73 |
| Min | 44 | 49 | 58 | 68 | 79 | 83 | 81 | 79 | 75 | 65 | 52 | 46 |
| Temp. C | | | | | | | | | | | | |
| Max | 21 | 24 | 31 | 36 | 41 | 39 | 36 | 34 | 34 | 34 | 29 | 23 |
| Min | 7 | 9 | 14 | 20 | 26 | 28 | 27 | 26 | 24 | 18 | 11 | 8 |
| Hmdty. % | | | | | | | | | | | | |
| am | 72 | 67 | 49 | 35 | 35 | 53 | 75 | 80 | 72 | 56 | 51 | 69 |
| pm | 41 | 35 | 23 | 19 | 20 | 36 | 59 | 65 | 51 | 32 | 31 | 42 |
| Rain mm | 23 | 18 | 13 | 8 | 13 | 74 | 180 | 173 | 117 | 10 | 3 | 10 |
| **Djakarta** | | | | | | | | | | | | |
| Temp. F | | | | | | | | | | | | |
| Max | 84 | 84 | 86 | 87 | 87 | 87 | 87 | 87 | 88 | 87 | 86 | 85 |
| Min | 34 | 74 | 74 | 75 | 75 | 74 | 73 | 73 | 74 | 74 | 74 | 74 |
| Temp. C | | | | | | | | | | | | |
| Max | 29 | 29 | 30 | 31 | 31 | 31 | 31 | 31 | 31 | 31 | 31 | 29 |
| Min | 23 | 23 | 23 | 24 | 24 | 23 | 23 | 23 | 23 | 23 | 23 | 23 |
| Hmdty. % | | | | | | | | | | | | |
| am | 95 | 95 | 94 | 94 | 94 | 93 | 92 | 90 | 90 | 90 | 92 | 92 |
| pm | 75 | 75 | 73 | 71 | 69 | 67 | 64 | 61 | 62 | 64 | 68 | 71 |
| Rain mm | 300 | 300 | 311 | 147 | 114 | 97 | 64 | 43 | 66 | 112 | 142 | 213 |
| **Frankfurt** | | | | | | | | | | | | |
| Temp. F | | | | | | | | | | | | |
| Max | 38 | 41 | 51 | 60 | 69 | 74 | 77 | 76 | 69 | 58 | 47 | 39 |
| Min | 29 | 30 | 35 | 42 | 49 | 55 | 58 | 57 | 52 | 44 | 38 | 32 |
| Temp. C | | | | | | | | | | | | |
| Max | 3 | 5 | 11 | 16 | 20 | 23 | 25 | 24 | 21 | 14 | 8 | 4 |
| Min | -1 | -2 | 2 | 6 | 9 | 13 | 15 | 14 | 11 | 7 | 3 | 0 |
| Hmdty. % | | | | | | | | | | | | |
| am | 86 | 86 | 84 | 79 | 78 | 78 | 81 | 85 | 89 | 91 | 89 | 88 |
| pm | 77 | 70 | 57 | 51 | 55 | 52 | 53 | 54 | 60 | 68 | 77 | 81 |
| Rain mm | 58 | 44 | 38 | 44 | 55 | 73 | 70 | 76 | 57 | 52 | 55 | 54 |

|  | J | F | M | A | M | J | J | A | S | O | N | D |
|---|---|---|---|---|---|---|---|---|---|---|---|---|
| **Haifa** | | | | | | | | | | | | |
| Temp. F | | | | | | | | | | | | |
| Max | 65 | 67 | 71 | 77 | 83 | 85 | 88 | 90 | 88 | 85 | 78 | 68 |
| Min | 49 | 50 | 53 | 58 | 65 | 71 | 75 | 76 | 74 | 68 | 60 | 53 |
| Temp. C | | | | | | | | | | | | |
| Max | 18 | 19 | 22 | 25 | 28 | 29 | 31 | 32 | 31 | 29 | 26 | 20 |
| Min | 9 | 10 | 12 | 14 | 18 | 22 | 24 | 24 | 23 | 20 | 16 | 12 |
| Hmdty. % | | | | | | | | | | | | |
| am | 66 | 65 | 62 | 60 | 62 | 67 | 70 | 70 | 67 | 66 | 61 | 66 |
| pm | 56 | 56 | 56 | 57 | 59 | 66 | 68 | 69 | 66 | 66 | 56 | 56 |
| Rain mm | 175 | 109 | 41 | 25 | 5 | 0 | 0 | 0 | 3 | 25 | 94 | 185 |
| **Hamilton, Bermuda** | | | | | | | | | | | | |
| Temp. F | | | | | | | | | | | | |
| Max | 68 | 68 | 68 | 71 | 76 | 81 | 85 | 86 | 84 | 79 | 74 | 70 |
| Min | 58 | 57 | 57 | 59 | 64 | 69 | 73 | 74 | 72 | 69 | 63 | 60 |
| Temp. C | | | | | | | | | | | | |
| Max | 20 | 20 | 20 | 22 | 24 | 27 | 29 | 30 | 29 | 26 | 23 | 21 |
| Min | 14 | 14 | 14 | 15 | 18 | 21 | 23 | 23 | 22 | 21 | 17 | 16 |
| Hmdty. % | | | | | | | | | | | | |
| am | 78 | 76 | 77 | 78 | 81 | 82 | 81 | 79 | 81 | 79 | 76 | 77 |
| pm | 70 | 69 | 69 | 70 | 75 | 74 | 73 | 69 | 73 | 72 | 70 | 70 |
| Rain mm | 112 | 119 | 122 | 104 | 117 | 112 | 114 | 137 | 132 | 147 | 127 | 119 |
| **Harare** | | | | | | | | | | | | |
| Temp. F | | | | | | | | | | | | |
| Max | 78 | 78 | 78 | 78 | 74 | 70 | 70 | 74 | 79 | 83 | 81 | 79 |
| Min | 60 | 60 | 58 | 55 | 49 | 44 | 44 | 47 | 53 | 58 | 60 | 60 |
| Temp. C | | | | | | | | | | | | |
| Max | 26 | 26 | 26 | 26 | 33 | 21 | 21 | 23 | 26 | 28 | 27 | 26 |
| Min | 16 | 16 | 14 | 13 | 9 | 7 | 7 | 8 | 12 | 14 | 16 | 16 |
| Hmdty. % | | | | | | | | | | | | |
| am | 74 | 77 | 75 | 68 | 60 | 58 | 56 | 50 | 43 | 43 | 56 | 67 |
| pm | 57 | 53 | 52 | 44 | 37 | 36 | 33 | 28 | 26 | 26 | 43 | 57 |
| Rain mm | 196 | 178 | 117 | 28 | 13 | 3 | 0 | 3 | 5 | 28 | 97 | 163 |
| **Hong Kong** | | | | | | | | | | | | |
| Temp. F | | | | | | | | | | | | |
| Max | 64 | 63 | 67 | 75 | 82 | 85 | 87 | 87 | 85 | 81 | 74 | 68 |
| Min | 56 | 55 | 60 | 67 | 74 | 78 | 78 | 78 | 77 | 73 | 65 | 59 |
| Temp. C | | | | | | | | | | | | |
| Max | 18 | 17 | 19 | 24 | 28 | 29 | 31 | 31 | 29 | 27 | 23 | 20 |
| Min | 13 | 13 | 16 | 19 | 23 | 26 | 26 | 26 | 25 | 23 | 18 | 15 |
| Hmdty. % | | | | | | | | | | | | |
| am | 77 | 82 | 84 | 87 | 87 | 86 | 87 | 87 | 83 | 75 | 73 | 74 |
| pm | 66 | 73 | 74 | 77 | 78 | 77 | 77 | 77 | 72 | 63 | 60 | 63 |
| Rain mm | 33 | 46 | 74 | 137 | 292 | 394 | 381 | 367 | 257 | 114 | 43 | 31 |

| | *J* | *F* | *M* | *A* | *M* | *J* | *J* | *A* | *S* | *O* | *N* | *D* |
|---|---|---|---|---|---|---|---|---|---|---|---|---|
| **Istanbul** | | | | | | | | | | | | |
| Temp. F | | | | | | | | | | | | |
| Max | 46 | 47 | 51 | 60 | 69 | 77 | 82 | 82 | 76 | 68 | 59 | 51 |
| Min | 37 | 36 | 38 | 45 | 53 | 60 | 65 | 66 | 61 | 55 | 78 | 41 |
| Temp. C | | | | | | | | | | | | |
| Max | 8 | 9 | 11 | 16 | 21 | 25 | 28 | 28 | 24 | 20 | 15 | 11 |
| Min | 3 | 2 | 3 | 7 | 12 | 16 | 18 | 19 | 16 | 13 | 9 | 5 |
| Hmdty. % | | | | | | | | | | | | |
| am | 82 | 82 | 81 | 81 | 82 | 79 | 79 | 79 | 81 | 83 | 82 | 82 |
| pm | 75 | 72 | 67 | 62 | 61 | 58 | 56 | 55 | 59 | 64 | 71 | 74 |
| Rain mm | 109 | 92 | 72 | 46 | 38 | 34 | 34 | 30 | 58 | 81 | 103 | 119 |
| **Jeddah** | | | | | | | | | | | | |
| Temp. F | | | | | | | | | | | | |
| Max | 84 | 84 | 85 | 91 | 95 | 97 | 99 | 99 | 96 | 95 | 91 | 86 |
| Min | 66 | 65 | 67 | 70 | 74 | 75 | 79 | 80 | 77 | 73 | 71 | 67 |
| Temp. C | | | | | | | | | | | | |
| Max | 29 | 29 | 29 | 33 | 35 | 36 | 37 | 37 | 36 | 35 | 33 | 30 |
| Min | 19 | 18 | 19 | 21 | 23 | 24 | 26 | 27 | 25 | 23 | 22 | 19 |
| Hmdty. % | | | | | | | | | | | | |
| am | 58 | 52 | 52 | 52 | 51 | 56 | 55 | 59 | 65 | 60 | 55 | 55 |
| pm | 45 | 52 | 52 | 56 | 55 | 55 | 50 | 51 | 61 | 61 | 59 | 54 |
| Rain mm | 5 | 0 | 0 | 0 | 0 | 0 | 0 | 0 | 0 | 0 | 25 | 31 |
| **Johannesburg** | | | | | | | | | | | | |
| Temp. F | | | | | | | | | | | | |
| Max | 78 | 77 | 75 | 72 | 66 | 62 | 63 | 68 | 73 | 77 | 77 | 78 |
| Min | 58 | 58 | 55 | 50 | 43 | 49 | 39 | 43 | 48 | 53 | 55 | 57 |
| Temp. C | | | | | | | | | | | | |
| Max | 26 | 25 | 24 | 22 | 19 | 17 | 17 | 20 | 23 | 25 | 25 | 26 |
| Min | 14 | 14 | 13 | 10 | 6 | 4 | 4 | 6 | 9 | 12 | 13 | 14 |
| Hmdty. % | | | | | | | | | | | | |
| am | 75 | 78 | 79 | 74 | 70 | 70 | 69 | 64 | 59 | 64 | 67 | 70 |
| pm | 50 | 53 | 50 | 44 | 36 | 33 | 32 | 29 | 30 | 37 | 45 | 47 |
| Rain mm | 114 | 109 | 89 | 38 | 25 | 8 | 8 | 8 | 23 | 56 | 107 | 125 |
| **Kathmandu** | | | | | | | | | | | | |
| Temp. F | | | | | | | | | | | | |
| Max | 65 | 67 | 77 | 83 | 86 | 85 | 84 | 83 | 83 | 80 | 74 | 67 |
| Min | 35 | 39 | 45 | 53 | 61 | 67 | 68 | 68 | 66 | 56 | 45 | 37 |
| Temp. C | | | | | | | | | | | | |
| Max | 18 | 19 | 25 | 28 | 30 | 29 | 29 | 28 | 28 | 27 | 23 | 19 |
| Min | 2 | 4 | 7 | 12 | 16 | 19 | 20 | 20 | 19 | 13 | 7 | 3 |
| Hmdty. % | | | | | | | | | | | | |
| am | 89 | 90 | 73 | 68 | 72 | 76 | 86 | 87 | 86 | 88 | 90 | 89 |
| pm | 70 | 68 | 53 | 54 | 61 | 72 | 82 | 84 | 83 | 81 | 78 | 73 |
| Rain mm | 15 | 42 | 23 | 58 | 122 | 246 | 373 | 345 | 155 | 38 | 8 | 3 |

|  | *J* | *F* | *M* | *A* | *M* | *J* | *J* | *A* | *S* | *O* | *N* | *D* |
|---|---|---|---|---|---|---|---|---|---|---|---|---|
| **Kuala Lumpur** | | | | | | | | | | | | |
| Temp. F | | | | | | | | | | | | |
| Max | 65 | 67 | 77 | 83 | 86 | 85 | 84 | 83 | 83 | 80 | 74 | 67 |
| Min | 72 | 72 | 73 | 74 | 73 | 72 | 73 | 73 | 73 | 73 | 73 | 72 |
| Temp. C | | | | | | | | | | | | |
| Max | 32 | 33 | 33 | 33 | 33 | 33 | 32 | 32 | 32 | 32 | 32 | 32 |
| Min | 22 | 22 | 23 | 23 | 23 | 22 | 23 | 23 | 23 | 23 | 23 | 22 |
| Hmdty. % | | | | | | | | | | | | |
| am | 97 | 97 | 97 | 97 | 97 | 96 | 95 | 96 | 96 | 96 | 97 | 97 |
| pm | 60 | 60 | 58 | 63 | 66 | 63 | 63 | 62 | 64 | 65 | 66 | 61 |
| Rain mm | 158 | 201 | 259 | 292 | 224 | 130 | 99 | 163 | 218 | 249 | 259 | 191 |
| **Lagos** | | | | | | | | | | | | |
| Temp. F | | | | | | | | | | | | |
| Max | 82 | 89 | 89 | 89 | 87 | 85 | 83 | 82 | 83 | 85 | 88 | 88 |
| Min | 74 | 73 | 78 | 77 | 76 | 74 | 74 | 73 | 74 | 74 | 75 | 75 |
| Temp. C | | | | | | | | | | | | |
| Max | 31 | 32 | 32 | 32 | 31 | 29 | 28 | 28 | 28 | 29 | 31 | 31 |
| Min | 23 | 25 | 26 | 25 | 24 | 23 | 23 | 23 | 23 | 23 | 24 | 24 |
| Hmdty. % | | | | | | | | | | | | |
| am | 84 | 83 | 82 | 81 | 83 | 87 | 87 | 85 | 86 | 86 | 85 | 86 |
| pm | 65 | 69 | 72 | 72 | 76 | 80 | 80 | 76 | 77 | 76 | 72 | 68 |
| Rain mm | 28 | 46 | 102 | 150 | 369 | 460 | 279 | 64 | 140 | 206 | 69 | 25 |
| **Lima** | | | | | | | | | | | | |
| Temp. F | | | | | | | | | | | | |
| Max | 82 | 83 | 83 | 80 | 74 | 68 | 67 | 66 | 68 | 71 | 74 | 78 |
| Min | 66 | 67 | 66 | 63 | 60 | 58 | 57 | 56 | 57 | 58 | 60 | 62 |
| Temp. C | | | | | | | | | | | | |
| Max | 28 | 28 | 28 | 27 | 23 | 20 | 19 | 19 | 20 | 22 | 23 | 26 |
| Min | 19 | 19 | 19 | 17 | 16 | 14 | 14 | 13 | 14 | 14 | 16 | 17 |
| Hmdty. % | | | | | | | | | | | | |
| am | 93 | 92 | 92 | 93 | 95 | 95 | 94 | 95 | 94 | 94 | 93 | 93 |
| pm | 69 | 66 | 64 | 66 | 76 | 80 | 778 | 78 | 76 | 72 | 71 | 70 |
| Rain mm | 3 | 0 | 0 | 0 | 5 | 5 | 8 | 8 | 8 | 3 | 3 | 0 |
| **Lisbon** | | | | | | | | | | | | |
| Temp. F | | | | | | | | | | | | |
| Max | 57 | 59 | 63 | 67 | 71 | 77 | 81 | 82 | 79 | 72 | 63 | 58 |
| Min | 46 | 47 | 50 | 53 | 55 | 60 | 63 | 63 | 62 | 58 | 52 | 47 |
| Temp. C | | | | | | | | | | | | |
| Max | 14 | 15 | 17 | 20 | 21 | 25 | 27 | 28 | 26 | 22 | 17 | 15 |
| Min | 8 | 8 | 10 | 12 | 12 | 15 | 17 | 17 | 17 | 14 | 11 | 8 |
| Hmdty. % | | | | | | | | | | | | |
| am | 85 | 80 | 78 | 69 | 68 | 65 | 62 | 64 | 70 | 75 | 81 | 84 |
| pm | 71 | 64 | 64 | 56 | 57 | 54 | 48 | 49 | 54 | 59 | 68 | 72 |
| Rain mm | 111 | 76 | 109 | 54 | 44 | 16 | 3 | 4 | 33 | 62 | 93 | 103 |

|              | J   | F   | M   | A   | M   | J   | J   | A   | S   | O   | N   | D   |
|--------------|-----|-----|-----|-----|-----|-----|-----|-----|-----|-----|-----|-----|
| **London**   |     |     |     |     |     |     |     |     |     |     |     |     |
| Temp. F      |     |     |     |     |     |     |     |     |     |     |     |     |
| Max          | 43  | 44  | 50  | 56  | 62  | 69  | 71  | 71  | 65  | 58  | 50  | 45  |
| Min          | 36  | 36  | 38  | 42  | 47  | 53  | 56  | 56  | 52  | 46  | 42  | 38  |
| Temp. C      |     |     |     |     |     |     |     |     |     |     |     |     |
| Max          | 6   | 7   | 10  | 13  | 17  | 20  | 22  | 21  | 19  | 14  | 10  | 7   |
| Min          | 2   | 2   | 3   | 6   | 8   | 12  | 14  | 13  | 11  | 8   | 5   | 4   |
| Hmdty. %     |     |     |     |     |     |     |     |     |     |     |     |     |
| am           | 86  | 85  | 81  | 71  | 70  | 70  | 71  | 76  | 80  | 85  | 85  | 87  |
| pm           | 77  | 72  | 64  | 56  | 57  | 58  | 59  | 62  | 65  | 70  | 78  | 81  |
| Rain mm      | 54  | 40  | 37  | 37  | 46  | 45  | 57  | 59  | 49  | 57  | 64  | 48  |
| **Madrid**   |     |     |     |     |     |     |     |     |     |     |     |     |
| Temp. F      |     |     |     |     |     |     |     |     |     |     |     |     |
| Max          | 47  | 52  | 59  | 65  | 70  | 80  | 87  | 85  | 77  | 65  | 55  | 48  |
| Min          | 35  | 36  | 41  | 45  | 50  | 58  | 63  | 63  | 57  | 48  | 42  | 36  |
| Temp. C      |     |     |     |     |     |     |     |     |     |     |     |     |
| Max          | 9   | 11  | 15  | 18  | 21  | 27  | 31  | 30  | 28  | 19  | 13  | 9   |
| Min          | 2   | 2   | 5   | 7   | 10  | 15  | 17  | 17  | 14  | 10  | 5   | 2   |
| Hmdty. %     |     |     |     |     |     |     |     |     |     |     |     |     |
| am           | 86  | 83  | 80  | 74  | 72  | 66  | 68  | 62  | 72  | 81  | 84  | 86  |
| pm           | 71  | 62  | 56  | 49  | 49  | 41  | 33  | 35  | 46  | 58  | 65  | 70  |
| Rain mm      | 39  | 34  | 43  | 48  | 47  | 27  | 11  | 15  | 32  | 53  | 47  | 48  |
| **Manila**   |     |     |     |     |     |     |     |     |     |     |     |     |
| Temp. F      |     |     |     |     |     |     |     |     |     |     |     |     |
| Max          | 86  | 88  | 91  | 93  | 93  | 91  | 88  | 87  | 88  | 88  | 87  | 86  |
| Min          | 69  | 69  | 71  | 73  | 75  | 75  | 75  | 75  | 75  | 74  | 73  | 70  |
| Temp. C      |     |     |     |     |     |     |     |     |     |     |     |     |
| Max          | 30  | 31  | 33  | 34  | 34  | 33  | 31  | 31  | 31  | 31  | 31  | 30  |
| Min          | 21  | 21  | 22  | 23  | 24  | 24  | 24  | 24  | 24  | 23  | 22  | 21  |
| Hmdty. %     |     |     |     |     |     |     |     |     |     |     |     |     |
| am           | 58  | 62  | 64  | 72  | 79  | 83  | 82  | 76  | 68  | 61  | 60  | 59  |
| pm           | 63  | 59  | 55  | 55  | 61  | 68  | 74  | 73  | 73  | 71  | 69  | 67  |
| Rain mm      | 23  | 13  | 18  | 33  | 130 | 254 | 432 | 422 | 356 | 193 | 149 | 66  |
| **Melbourne**|     |     |     |     |     |     |     |     |     |     |     |     |
| Temp. F      |     |     |     |     |     |     |     |     |     |     |     |     |
| Max          | 78  | 78  | 75  | 68  | 62  | 57  | 56  | 59  | 63  | 67  | 71  | 75  |
| Min          | 57  | 57  | 55  | 51  | 47  | 44  | 42  | 43  | 46  | 48  | 51  | 54  |
| Temp. C      |     |     |     |     |     |     |     |     |     |     |     |     |
| Max          | 26  | 26  | 24  | 20  | 17  | 14  | 13  | 15  | 17  | 19  | 22  | 24  |
| Min          | 14  | 14  | 13  | 11  | 8   | 7   | 6   | 6   | 8   | 9   | 11  | 12  |
| Hmdty. %     |     |     |     |     |     |     |     |     |     |     |     |     |
| am           | 58  | 62  | 64  | 72  | 79  | 83  | 82  | 76  | 68  | 61  | 60  | 59  |
| pm           | 48  | 50  | 51  | 56  | 62  | 67  | 65  | 60  | 55  | 52  | 52  | 51  |
| Rain mm      | 48  | 46  | 56  | 58  | 53  | 53  | 48  | 48  | 58  | 66  | 58  | 58  |

|  | J | F | M | A | M | J | J | A | S | O | N | D |
|---|---|---|---|---|---|---|---|---|---|---|---|---|
| **Mexico City** | | | | | | | | | | | | |
| Temp. F | | | | | | | | | | | | |
| Max | 66 | 69 | 75 | 77 | 78 | 76 | 73 | 73 | 74 | 70 | 68 | 66 |
| Min | 42 | 43 | 47 | 51 | 54 | 55 | 53 | 54 | 53 | 50 | 46 | 43 |
| Temp. C | | | | | | | | | | | | |
| Max | 19 | 21 | 24 | 25 | 26 | 24 | 23 | 23 | 23 | 21 | 20 | 19 |
| Min | 6 | 6 | 8 | 11 | 12 | 13 | 12 | 12 | 12 | 10 | 8 | 6 |
| Hmdty. % | | | | | | | | | | | | |
| am | 79 | 72 | 68 | 66 | 69 | 82 | 84 | 85 | 86 | 83 | 82 | 81 |
| pm | 34 | 38 | 26 | 29 | 29 | 48 | 50 | 50 | 54 | 47 | 41 | 37 |
| Rain mm | 13 | 5 | 10 | 20 | 53 | 119 | 170 | 152 | 130 | 51 | 18 | 8 |
| **Miami** | | | | | | | | | | | | |
| Temp. F | | | | | | | | | | | | |
| Max | 74 | 75 | 78 | 80 | 84 | 86 | 88 | 88 | 87 | 83 | 78 | 76 |
| Min | 61 | 61 | 64 | 67 | 71 | 74 | 76 | 76 | 75 | 72 | 66 | 62 |
| Temp. C | | | | | | | | | | | | |
| Max | 23 | 24 | 26 | 27 | 29 | 30 | 31 | 31 | 31 | 28 | 26 | 24 |
| Min | 16 | 16 | 18 | 19 | 22 | 23 | 24 | 24 | 24 | 22 | 19 | 17 |
| Hmdty. % | | | | | | | | | | | | |
| am | 81 | 82 | 77 | 73 | 75 | 75 | 75 | 76 | 79 | 80 | 77 | 82 |
| pm | 66 | 63 | 62 | 64 | 67 | 69 | 68 | 68 | 70 | 69 | 64 | 65 |
| Rain mm | 71 | 53 | 64 | 81 | 173 | 178 | 155 | 160 | 203 | 234 | 71 | 51 |
| **Moscow** | | | | | | | | | | | | |
| Temp. F | | | | | | | | | | | | |
| Max | 15 | 22 | 32 | 50 | 66 | 70 | 73 | 72 | 61 | 48 | 35 | 24 |
| Min | 3 | 8 | 18 | 34 | 46 | 51 | 55 | 53 | 45 | 37 | 26 | 15 |
| Temp. C | | | | | | | | | | | | |
| Max | -9 | -6 | 0 | 10 | 19 | 21 | 23 | 22 | 16 | 9 | 2 | -5 |
| Min | -16 | -14 | -8 | 1 | 8 | 11 | 13 | 12 | 7 | 3 | -3 | -10 |
| Hmdty. % | | | | | | | | | | | | |
| am | 82 | 82 | 82 | 73 | 58 | 62 | 68 | 74 | 78 | 81 | 87 | 85 |
| pm | 77 | 66 | 64 | 54 | 43 | 47 | 54 | 55 | 59 | 67 | 79 | 83 |
| Rain mm | 39 | 38 | 36 | 37 | 53 | 58 | 88 | 71 | 58 | 45 | 47 | 54 |
| **Nairobi** | | | | | | | | | | | | |
| Temp. F | | | | | | | | | | | | |
| Max | 77 | 79 | 77 | 75 | 72 | 70 | 69 | 70 | 75 | 76 | 74 | 74 |
| Min | 54 | 55 | 57 | 58 | 56 | 53 | 51 | 52 | 52 | 55 | 56 | 55 |
| Temp. C | | | | | | | | | | | | |
| Max | 25 | 25 | 26 | 27 | 29 | 31 | 31 | 32 | 31 | 29 | 27 | 26 |
| Min | 12 | 13 | 14 | 14 | 13 | 12 | 11 | 11 | 11 | 13 | 13 | 13 |
| Hmdty. % | | | | | | | | | | | | |
| am | 74 | 74 | 81 | 88 | 88 | 89 | 86 | 86 | 82 | 82 | 86 | 81 |
| pm | 44 | 40 | 45 | 56 | 62 | 60 | 58 | 56 | 45 | 43 | 53 | 53 |
| Rain mm | 38 | 64 | 125 | 211 | 158 | 46 | 15 | 23 | 31 | 53 | 109 | 86 |

|          | *J* | *F* | *M* | *A* | *M* | *J* | *J* | *A* | *S* | *O* | *N* | *D* |
|----------|-----|-----|-----|-----|-----|-----|-----|-----|-----|-----|-----|-----|
| **Nassau** | | | | | | | | | | | | |
| Temp. F | | | | | | | | | | | | |
| Max | 77 | 77 | 79 | 81 | 84 | 87 | 88 | 89 | 88 | 85 | 81 | 79 |
| Min | 65 | 64 | 66 | 69 | 71 | 74 | 75 | 76 | 75 | 73 | 70 | 67 |
| Temp. C | | | | | | | | | | | | |
| Max | 25 | 25 | 26 | 27 | 29 | 31 | 31 | 32 | 31 | 29 | 27 | 26 |
| Min | 18 | 18 | 19 | 21 | 22 | 23 | 24 | 24 | 24 | 23 | 21 | 19 |
| Hmdty. % | | | | | | | | | | | | |
| am | 84 | 82 | 81 | 79 | 79 | 81 | 80 | 82 | 84 | 83 | 83 | 84 |
| pm | 64 | 62 | 64 | 65 | 65 | 68 | 69 | 90 | 73 | 71 | 68 | 66 |
| Rain mm | 36 | 38 | 36 | 64 | 117 | 163 | 147 | 135 | 175 | 165 | 71 | 33 |
| **New York** | | | | | | | | | | | | |
| Temp. F | | | | | | | | | | | | |
| Max | 37 | 38 | 45 | 57 | 68 | 77 | 82 | 80 | 79 | 69 | 51 | 41 |
| Min | 24 | 24 | 30 | 42 | 53 | 60 | 66 | 66 | 60 | 49 | 37 | 29 |
| Temp. C | | | | | | | | | | | | |
| Max | 3 | 3 | 7 | 14 | 20 | 25 | 28 | 27 | 26 | 21 | 11 | 5 |
| Min | -4 | -4 | -1 | 6 | 12 | 16 | 19 | 19 | 16 | 9 | 3 | -2 |
| Hmdty. % | | | | | | | | | | | | |
| am | 72 | 70 | 70 | 68 | 70 | 74 | 77 | 79 | 79 | 76 | 75 | 73 |
| pm | 60 | 58 | 55 | 53 | 54 | 58 | 58 | 60 | 61 | 57 | 60 | 61 |
| Rain mm | 94 | 97 | 91 | 81 | 81 | 84 | 107 | 109 | 86 | 89 | 76 | 91 |
| **Oslo** | | | | | | | | | | | | |
| Temp. F | | | | | | | | | | | | |
| Max | 28 | 30 | 39 | 50 | 61 | 68 | 72 | 70 | 60 | 48 | 38 | 32 |
| Min | 19 | 19 | 25 | 34 | 43 | 50 | 55 | 53 | 46 | 38 | 31 | 25 |
| Temp. C | | | | | | | | | | | | |
| Max | -2 | -1 | 4 | 10 | 16 | 20 | 22 | 21 | 16 | 9 | 3 | 0 |
| Min | -7 | -7 | -4 | 1 | 6 | 10 | 13 | 12 | 8 | 3 | -1 | -4 |
| Hmdty. % | | | | | | | | | | | | |
| am | 86 | 84 | 80 | 75 | 68 | 69 | 74 | 79 | 85 | 88 | 88 | 87 |
| pm | 82 | 74 | 64 | 57 | 52 | 55 | 59 | 61 | 66 | 72 | 83 | 85 |
| Rain mm | 49 | 35 | 26 | 43 | 44 | 70 | 82 | 95 | 81 | 74 | 68 | 63 |
| **Ottawa** | | | | | | | | | | | | |
| Temp. F | | | | | | | | | | | | |
| Max | 21 | 22 | 33 | 51 | 66 | 76 | 81 | 77 | 68 | 54 | 39 | 24 |
| Min | 3 | 3 | 16 | 31 | 44 | 54 | 58 | 55 | 48 | 37 | 26 | 9 |
| Temp. C | | | | | | | | | | | | |
| Max | -6 | -6 | 11 | 11 | 9 | 24 | 27 | 25 | 20 | 12 | 4 | -4 |
| Min | -16 | -16 | -9 | -1 | 7 | 12 | 14 | 13 | 9 | 3 | -3 | -13 |
| Hmdty. % | | | | | | | | | | | | |
| am | 83 | 88 | 84 | 76 | 77 | 80 | 80 | 84 | 90 | 86 | 84 | 83 |
| pm | 76 | 73 | 66 | 58 | 55 | 56 | 53 | 54 | 59 | 63 | 68 | 75 |
| Rain mm | 74 | 56 | 71 | 69 | 64 | 89 | 86 | 66 | 81 | 74 | 76 | 66 |

|  | *J* | *F* | *M* | *A* | *M* | *J* | *J* | *A* | *S* | *O* | *N* | *D* |
|---|---|---|---|---|---|---|---|---|---|---|---|---|
| **Papeete** | | | | | | | | | | | | |
| Temp. F | | | | | | | | | | | | |
| Max | 89 | 89 | 89 | 89 | 87 | 86 | 86 | 86 | 86 | 87 | 88 | 88 |
| Min | 72 | 72 | 72 | 72 | 70 | 69 | 68 | 68 | 69 | 70 | 71 | 72 |
| Temp. C | | | | | | | | | | | | |
| Max | 32 | 32 | 32 | 32 | 31 | 30 | 30 | 30 | 30 | 31 | 31 | 31 |
| Min | 22 | 22 | 22 | 22 | 21 | 21 | 20 | 20 | 21 | 21 | 22 | 22 |
| Hmdty. % | | | | | | | | | | | | |
| am | 82 | 82 | 84 | 85 | 84 | 85 | 83 | 83 | 81 | 79 | 80 | 81 |
| pm | 77 | 77 | 78 | 78 | 78 | 79 | 77 | 78 | 76 | 76 | 77 | 78 |
| Rain mm | 252 | 244 | 429 | 142 | 102 | 86 | 53 | 43 | 53 | 86 | 150 | 249 |
| **Paris** | | | | | | | | | | | | |
| Temp. F | | | | | | | | | | | | |
| Max | 42 | 45 | 55 | 61 | 69 | 75 | 80 | 79 | 73 | 61 | 50 | 43 |
| Min | 30 | 31 | 37 | 42 | 49 | 55 | 59 | 58 | 53 | 45 | 38 | 33 |
| Temp. C | | | | | | | | | | | | |
| Max | 5 | 7 | 13 | 17 | 20 | 24 | 27 | 26 | 23 | 16 | 10 | 6 |
| Min | -1 | 0 | 3 | 6 | 9 | 13 | 15 | 14 | 12 | 7 | 4 | 0 |
| Hmdty. % | | | | | | | | | | | | |
| am | 89 | 87 | 87 | 84 | 83 | 82 | 79 | 85 | 89 | 92 | 91 | 90 |
| pm | 80 | 72 | 60 | 56 | 56 | 55 | 50 | 54 | 60 | 69 | 78 | 80 |
| Rain mm | 52 | 46 | 53 | 56 | 69 | 85 | 56 | 89 | 93 | 77 | 80 | 57 |
| **Port-of-Spain** | | | | | | | | | | | | |
| Temp. F | | | | | | | | | | | | |
| Max | 87 | 88 | 89 | 90 | 90 | 89 | 88 | 88 | 89 | 89 | 89 | 88 |
| Min | 69 | 68 | 68 | 69 | 71 | 71 | 71 | 71 | 71 | 71 | 71 | 69 |
| Temp. C | | | | | | | | | | | | |
| Max | 31 | 31 | 32 | 32 | 32 | 32 | 31 | 31 | 32 | 32 | 32 | 31 |
| Min | 21 | 20 | 20 | 21 | 22 | 22 | 22 | 22 | 22 | 22 | 22 | 21 |
| Hmdty. % | | | | | | | | | | | | |
| am | 89 | 87 | 85 | 83 | 84 | 87 | 88 | 87 | 87 | 87 | 89 | 89 |
| pm | 68 | 65 | 63 | 61 | 63 | 69 | 71 | 73 | 73 | 74 | 76 | 71 |
| Rain mm | 69 | 41 | 46 | 53 | 94 | 193 | 218 | 246 | 193 | 170 | 183 | 125 |
| **Prague** | | | | | | | | | | | | |
| Temp. F | | | | | | | | | | | | |
| Max | 49 | 53 | 64 | 73 | 82 | 88 | 91 | 89 | 84 | 71 | 57 | 50 |
| Min | 7 | 10 | 18 | 29 | 36 | 44 | 49 | 47 | 38 | 29 | 24 | 14 |
| Temp. C | | | | | | | | | | | | |
| Max | 10 | 11 | 18 | 23 | 28 | 31 | 33 | 32 | 29 | 22 | 14 | 10 |
| Min | -13 | -12 | -8 | -2 | 2 | 7 | 9 | 8 | 4 | -2 | -5 | -10 |
| Hmdty. % | | | | | | | | | | | | |
| am | 84 | 83 | 82 | 77 | 75 | 74 | 77 | 81 | 84 | 87 | 87 | 87 |
| pm | 73 | 67 | 55 | 47 | 45 | 46 | 49 | 48 | 51 | 60 | 73 | 78 |
| Rain mm | 18 | 18 | 18 | 27 | 48 | 54 | 68 | 55 | 31 | 33 | 20 | 21 |

| | *J* | *F* | *M* | *A* | *M* | *J* | *J* | *A* | *S* | *O* | *N* | *D* |
|---|---|---|---|---|---|---|---|---|---|---|---|---|
| **Rangoon** | | | | | | | | | | | | |
| Temp. F | | | | | | | | | | | | |
| Max | 89 | 92 | 96 | 97 | 92 | 86 | 85 | 86 | 86 | 88 | 88 | 88 |
| Min | 65 | 67 | 71 | 76 | 77 | 76 | 76 | 76 | 76 | 76 | 73 | 67 |
| Temp. C | | | | | | | | | | | | |
| Max | 32 | 33 | 36 | 36 | 33 | 30 | 29 | 29 | 30 | 31 | 31 | 31 |
| Min | 18 | 19 | 22 | 24 | 25 | 24 | 24 | 24 | 24 | 24 | 23 | 19 |
| Hmdty. % | | | | | | | | | | | | |
| am | 71 | 72 | 74 | 71 | 80 | 87 | 89 | 89 | 87 | 83 | 79 | 75 |
| pm | 52 | 52 | 54 | 64 | 66 | 75 | 88 | 88 | 86 | 77 | 72 | 61 |
| Rain mm | 3 | 5 | 8 | 51 | 307 | 480 | 582 | 528 | 394 | 180 | 69 | 10 |
| **Rio de Janeiro** | | | | | | | | | | | | |
| Temp. F | | | | | | | | | | | | |
| Max | 84 | 85 | 83 | 80 | 77 | 76 | 75 | 76 | 75 | 77 | 79 | 82 |
| Min | 73 | 73 | 72 | 69 | 66 | 64 | 63 | 64 | 65 | 66 | 68 | 71 |
| Temp. C | | | | | | | | | | | | |
| Max | 29 | 29 | 28 | 27 | 25 | 24 | 24 | 24 | 24 | 25 | 26 | 28 |
| Min | 23 | 23 | 22 | 21 | 19 | 18 | 17 | 18 | 18 | 19 | 20 | 22 |
| Hmdty. % | | | | | | | | | | | | |
| am | 82 | 84 | 87 | 87 | 87 | 87 | 86 | 84 | 84 | 83 | 82 | 82 |
| pm | 70 | 71 | 74 | 73 | 70 | 69 | 68 | 66 | 72 | 72 | 72 | 72 |
| Rain mm | 125 | 122 | 130 | 107 | 79 | 53 | 41 | 43 | 66 | 79 | 104 | 137 |
| **Rome** | | | | | | | | | | | | |
| Temp. F | | | | | | | | | | | | |
| Max | 52 | 55 | 59 | 66 | 74 | 82 | 87 | 86 | 79 | 71 | 61 | 55 |
| Min | 40 | 42 | 45 | 50 | 56 | 63 | 67 | 67 | 62 | 55 | 49 | 44 |
| Temp. C | | | | | | | | | | | | |
| Max | 11 | 13 | 15 | 19 | 23 | 28 | 30 | 30 | 26 | 22 | 16 | 13 |
| Min | 5 | 5 | 7 | 10 | 13 | 17 | 20 | 20 | 17 | 13 | 9 | 6 |
| Hmdty. % | | | | | | | | | | | | |
| am | 85 | 86 | 83 | 83 | 77 | 74 | 70 | 73 | 83 | 86 | 87 | 85 |
| pm | 68 | 64 | 56 | 54 | 54 | 48 | 42 | 44 | 50 | 59 | 66 | 70 |
| Rain mm | 71 | 62 | 57 | 51 | 46 | 37 | 15 | 21 | 63 | 99 | 129 | 93 |
| **San Francisco** | | | | | | | | | | | | |
| Temp. F | | | | | | | | | | | | |
| Max | 55 | 59 | 61 | 62 | 63 | 66 | 65 | 65 | 69 | 68 | 63 | 57 |
| Min | 45 | 47 | 48 | 49 | 51 | 52 | 53 | 53 | 55 | 54 | 51 | 47 |
| Temp. C | | | | | | | | | | | | |
| Max | 13 | 15 | 16 | 17 | 17 | 19 | 18 | 18 | 21 | 20 | 17 | 14 |
| Min | 7 | 8 | 9 | 9 | 11 | 11 | 12 | 12 | 13 | 12 | 11 | 8 |
| Hmdty. % | | | | | | | | | | | | |
| am | 85 | 84 | 83 | 83 | 85 | 88 | 91 | 92 | 88 | 85 | 83 | 83 |
| pm | 69 | 66 | 61 | 61 | 62 | 64 | 69 | 70 | 60 | 58 | 60 | 68 |
| Rain mm | 119 | 97 | 79 | 38 | 18 | 3 | 0 | 0 | 8 | 25 | 64 | 112 |

|  | *J* | *F* | *M* | *A* | *M* | *J* | *J* | *A* | *S* | *O* | *N* | *D* |
|---|---|---|---|---|---|---|---|---|---|---|---|---|
| **Singapore** | | | | | | | | | | | | |
| Temp. F | | | | | | | | | | | | |
| Max | 86 | 88 | 88 | 88 | 89 | 88 | 88 | 87 | 87 | 87 | 87 | 87 |
| Min | 73 | 73 | 75 | 75 | 75 | 75 | 75 | 75 | 75 | 74 | 74 | 74 |
| Temp. C | | | | | | | | | | | | |
| Max | 30 | 31 | 31 | 31 | 34 | 31 | 31 | 31 | 31 | 31 | 31 | 31 |
| Min | 23 | 23 | 24 | 24 | 24 | 24 | 24 | 24 | 24 | 23 | 23 | 23 |
| Hmdty. % | | | | | | | | | | | | |
| am | 82 | 77 | 76 | 77 | 79 | 79 | 79 | 78 | 79 | 78 | 79 | 82 |
| pm | 78 | 71 | 70 | 74 | 73 | 73 | 72 | 72 | 72 | 72 | 75 | 78 |
| Rain mm | 252 | 173 | 193 | 188 | 173 | 173 | 170 | 196 | 178 | 208 | 254 | 257 |
| **Stockholm** | | | | | | | | | | | | |
| Temp. F | | | | | | | | | | | | |
| Max | 30 | 30 | 37 | 47 | 58 | 67 | 71 | 68 | 60 | 49 | 40 | 35 |
| Min | 23 | 22 | 26 | 34 | 43 | 51 | 57 | 56 | 49 | 41 | 34 | 29 |
| Temp. C | | | | | | | | | | | | |
| Max | -1 | -1 | 3 | 8 | 14 | 19 | 22 | 20 | 15 | 9 | 5 | 2 |
| Min | 15 | 15 | 14 | 1 | 6 | 11 | 14 | 13 | 9 | 5 | 1 | -2 |
| Hmdty. % | | | | | | | | | | | | |
| am | 85 | 83 | 82 | 76 | 66 | 68 | 74 | 81 | 87 | 88 | 89 | 88 |
| pm | 83 | 77 | 68 | 60 | 53 | 55 | 59 | 64 | 69 | 76 | 85 | 86 |
| Rain mm | 43 | 30 | 25 | 31 | 34 | 45 | 61 | 76 | 60 | 48 | 53 | 48 |
| **Sydney** | | | | | | | | | | | | |
| Temp. F | | | | | | | | | | | | |
| Max | 78 | 78 | 76 | 71 | 66 | 61 | 60 | 63 | 67 | 71 | 74 | 77 |
| Min | 65 | 65 | 66 | 58 | 52 | 48 | 46 | 48 | 51 | 46 | 60 | 63 |
| Temp. C | | | | | | | | | | | | |
| Max | 26 | 26 | 24 | 22 | 19 | 16 | 16 | 17 | 19 | 22 | 23 | 25 |
| Min | 18 | 18 | 17 | 14 | 11 | 9 | 8 | 9 | 11 | 13 | 16 | 17 |
| Hmdty. % | | | | | | | | | | | | |
| am | 68 | 71 | 73 | 76 | 77 | 77 | 76 | 72 | 67 | 65 | 65 | 66 |
| pm | 64 | 65 | 65 | 64 | 63 | 62 | 60 | 56 | 55 | 57 | 60 | 62 |
| Rain mm | 89 | 102 | 127 | 135 | 127 | 117 | 76 | 76 | 74 | 71 | 74 | 74 |
| **Tehran** | | | | | | | | | | | | |
| Temp. F | | | | | | | | | | | | |
| Max | 45 | 50 | 59 | 71 | 82 | 93 | 99 | 97 | 90 | 76 | 63 | 51 |
| Min | 27 | 32 | 39 | 49 | 58 | 66 | 72 | 71 | 64 | 53 | 43 | 33 |
| Temp. C | | | | | | | | | | | | |
| Max | 7 | 10 | 15 | 22 | 28 | 34 | 37 | 36 | 32 | 24 | 17 | 11 |
| Min | -3 | 0 | 4 | 9 | 14 | 19 | 22 | 22 | 18 | 12 | 6 | 1 |
| Hmdty. % | | | | | | | | | | | | |
| am | 77 | 73 | 61 | 54 | 55 | 50 | 51 | 47 | 49 | 53 | 63 | 76 |
| pm | 75 | 59 | 39 | 40 | 47 | 49 | 41 | 46 | 49 | 54 | 66 | 75 |
| Rain mm | 46 | 38 | 46 | 36 | 13 | 3 | 3 | 3 | 3 | 8 | 20 | 31 |

| | *J* | *F* | *M* | *A* | *M* | *J* | *J* | *A* | *S* | *O* | *N* | *D* |
|---|---|---|---|---|---|---|---|---|---|---|---|---|
| **Tokyo** | | | | | | | | | | | | |
| Temp. F | | | | | | | | | | | | |
| Max | 47 | 48 | 54 | 63 | 71 | 76 | 83 | 86 | 79 | 69 | 60 | 52 |
| Min | 29 | 31 | 36 | 36 | 54 | 63 | 70 | 72 | 66 | 55 | 43 | 33 |
| Temp. C | | | | | | | | | | | | |
| Max | 8 | 9 | 12 | 17 | 22 | 24 | 28 | 30 | 26 | 21 | 16 | 11 |
| Min | -2 | -1 | 2 | 8 | 12 | 17 | 21 | 22 | 19 | 13 | 6 | 1 |
| Hmdty. % | | | | | | | | | | | | |
| am | 73 | 71 | 75 | 81 | 85 | 89 | 91 | 92 | 91 | 88 | 83 | 77 |
| pm | 48 | 48 | 53 | 59 | 62 | 68 | 69 | 66 | 68 | 64 | 58 | 51 |
| Rain mm | 48 | 74 | 107 | 135 | 147 | 165 | 142 | 152 | 234 | 208 | 97 | 56 |
| **Vancouver** | | | | | | | | | | | | |
| Temp. F | | | | | | | | | | | | |
| Max | 41 | 44 | 50 | 58 | 64 | 69 | 74 | 73 | 65 | 57 | 48 | 43 |
| Min | 32 | 24 | 37 | 40 | 46 | 52 | 54 | 54 | 49 | 44 | 39 | 35 |
| Temp. C | | | | | | | | | | | | |
| Max | 5 | 7 | 10 | 14 | 18 | 21 | 23 | 23 | 18 | 14 | 9 | 6 |
| Min | 0 | 1 | 3 | 4 | 8 | 11 | 12 | 12 | 9 | 7 | 4 | 2 |
| Hmdty. % | | | | | | | | | | | | |
| am | 93 | 91 | 91 | 89 | 88 | 87 | 89 | 90 | 92 | 92 | 91 | 91 |
| pm | 85 | 78 | 70 | 67 | 63 | 65 | 62 | 62 | 72 | 80 | 84 | 88 |
| Rain mm | 218 | 147 | 127 | 84 | 71 | 64 | 31 | 43 | 91 | 147 | 211 | 224 |
| **Vienna** | | | | | | | | | | | | |
| Temp. F | | | | | | | | | | | | |
| Max | 34 | 38 | 47 | 58 | 67 | 73 | 76 | 75 | 68 | 56 | 45 | 37 |
| Min | 25 | 28 | 30 | 42 | 50 | 56 | 60 | 59 | 53 | 44 | 37 | 30 |
| Temp. C | | | | | | | | | | | | |
| Max | 1 | 3 | 8 | 15 | 19 | 23 | 25 | 24 | 20 | 14 | 7 | 3 |
| Min | -4 | -3 | -1 | 6 | 10 | 14 | 15 | 15 | 11 | 7 | 3 | -1 |
| Hmdty. % | | | | | | | | | | | | |
| am | 81 | 80 | 78 | 72 | 74 | 74 | 74 | 78 | 83 | 86 | 84 | 84 |
| pm | 72 | 66 | 57 | 49 | 52 | 55 | 54 | 54 | 56 | 64 | 74 | 76 |
| Rain mm | 39 | 44 | 44 | 45 | 70 | 67 | 84 | 72 | 42 | 56 | 52 | 45 |
| **Warsaw** | | | | | | | | | | | | |
| Temp. F | | | | | | | | | | | | |
| Max | 32 | 32 | 42 | 53 | 67 | 73 | 75 | 73 | 66 | 55 | 42 | 35 |
| Min | 22 | 21 | 28 | 37 | 48 | 54 | 58 | 56 | 49 | 41 | 33 | 28 |
| Temp. C | | | | | | | | | | | | |
| Max | 0 | 1 | 6 | 13 | 19 | 23 | 24 | 23 | 19 | 14 | 6 | 3 |
| Min | -7 | -6 | 2 | 3 | 8 | 12 | 14 | 13 | 9 | 5 | 1 | -2 |
| Hmdty. % | | | | | | | | | | | | |
| am | 83 | 42 | 83 | 83 | 79 | 82 | 84 | 88 | 90 | 89 | 90 | 86 |
| pm | 74 | 71 | 64 | 59 | 55 | 60 | 63 | 63 | 63 | 67 | 78 | 78 |
| Rain mm | 27 | 24 | 25 | 43 | 57 | 88 | 105 | 93 | 58 | 50 | 43 | 43 |

| | J | F | M | A | M | J | J | A | S | O | N | D |
|---|---|---|---|---|---|---|---|---|---|---|---|---|
| **Zürich** | | | | | | | | | | | | |
| Temp. F | | | | | | | | | | | | |
| Max | 36 | 41 | 51 | 59 | 67 | 73 | 76 | 75 | 69 | 57 | 45 | 37 |
| Min | 26 | 28 | 34 | 40 | 47 | 53 | 56 | 56 | 51 | 43 | 35 | 29 |
| Temp. C | | | | | | | | | | | | |
| Max | 2 | 5 | 10 | 15 | 19 | 23 | 25 | 24 | 20 | 14 | 7 | 3 |
| Min | -3 | -2 | 1 | 4 | 8 | 12 | 14 | 13 | 11 | 6 | 2 | -2 |
| Hmdty. % | | | | | | | | | | | | |
| am | 88 | 88 | 86 | 81 | 80 | 80 | 81 | 85 | 90 | 92 | 90 | 89 |
| pm | 74 | 65 | 55 | 51 | 52 | 52 | 52 | 53 | 57 | 64 | 73 | 76 |
| Rain mm | 74 | 69 | 64 | 76 | 101 | 129 | 136 | 124 | 102 | 77 | 73 | 64 |

These figures are partly from the London Weather Centre, from Wexas and from CNN's Valerie Voss. Compiled and processed by Ronald Kirk.

# A TIME TO GO SWIMMING?

Selected centigrade sea temperatures in major PT-hangouts around the world:

| | J | F | M | A | M | J | J | A | S | O | N | D |
|---|---|---|---|---|---|---|---|---|---|---|---|---|
| Acapulco Mexico | 24 | 24 | 24 | 25 | 26 | 27 | 28 | 28 | 28 | 27 | 26 | 25 |
| Agadir Morocco | 17 | 17 | 18 | 18 | 19 | 19 | 22 | 22 | 22 | 22 | 21 | 18 |
| Algiers Algeria | 15 | 14 | 15 | 15 | 17 | 20 | 23 | 24 | 23 | 21 | 18 | 16 |
| Athens Greece | 14 | 14 | 14 | 15 | 18 | 22 | 24 | 24 | 23 | 21 | 19 | 16 |
| Bangkok Thailand | 26 | 27 | 27 | 28 | 28 | 28 | 28 | 28 | 28 | 27 | 27 | 27 |
| Barcelona Spain | 13 | 12 | 13 | 14 | 16 | 19 | 22 | 24 | 22 | 21 | 16 | 14 |
| Cairo Egypt | 15 | 15 | 18 | 21 | 24 | 26 | 27 | 27 | 27 | 24 | 21 | 17 |
| Copenhagen Denmark | 3 | 2 | 3 | 5 | 9 | 14 | 16 | 16 | 14 | 12 | 8 | 5 |
| Corfu Greece | 14 | 14 | 14 | 16 | 18 | 21 | 23 | 24 | 23 | 21 | 18 | 16 |
| Dubrovnik Yugoslavia | 13 | 13 | 13 | 15 | 17 | 22 | 23 | 24 | 22 | 19 | 16 | 14 |
| Faro Portugal | 15 | 15 | 15 | 16 | 17 | 18 | 19 | 20 | 20 | 19 | 17 | 16 |
| Hong Kong | 18 | 18 | 21 | 24 | 25 | 27 | 28 | 28 | 27 | 26 | 24 | 21 |
| Honolulu Hawaii, USA | 24 | 24 | 24 | 25 | 26 | 26 | 27 | 27 | 27 | 27 | 26 | 25 |
| Istanbul Turkey | 8 | 8 | 8 | 11 | 15 | 20 | 22 | 23 | 21 | 19 | 15 | 11 |

| | J | F | M | A | M | J | J | A | S | O | N | D |
|---|---|---|---|---|---|---|---|---|---|---|---|---|
| Kingston Jamaica | 26 | 26 | 26 | 27 | 27 | 28 | 29 | 29 | 28 | 28 | 27 | 27 |
| Las Palmas Canary Islands | 19 | 18 | 18 | 18 | 19 | 20 | 21 | 22 | 23 | 23 | 21 | 20 |
| Lisbon Portugal | 14 | 14 | 14 | 15 | 16 | 17 | 18 | 19 | 19 | 18 | 17 | 15 |
| Los Angeles USA | 14 | 14 | 15 | 15 | 16 | 18 | 19 | 20 | 19 | 18 | 17 | 15 |
| Malaga Spain | 15 | 14 | 14 | 15 | 17 | 18 | 21 | 22 | 21 | 19 | 17 | 16 |
| Malta | 15 | 14 | 15 | 15 | 18 | 21 | 24 | 25 | 24 | 22 | 19 | 17 |
| Miami USA | 22 | 23 | 24 | 25 | 28 | 30 | 31 | 32 | 30 | 28 | 25 | 23 |
| Mombasa Kenya | 27 | 28 | 28 | 28 | 28 | 27 | 25 | 25 | 27 | 27 | 27 | 27 |
| Naples Italy | 14 | 13 | 14 | 15 | 18 | 21 | 24 | 25 | 23 | 21 | 18 | 16 |
| Nassau Bahamas | 23 | 23 | 23 | 24 | 25 | 27 | 28 | 28 | 28 | 27 | 26 | 24 |
| New Orleans USA | 13 | 14 | 14 | 15 | 18 | 21 | 24 | 25 | 23 | 21 | 18 | 16 |
| Nice France | 13 | 12 | 13 | 14 | 16 | 20 | 22 | 23 | 21 | 19 | 16 | 14 |
| Palma Majorca | 14 | 13 | 14 | 15 | 17 | 21 | 24 | 25 | 24 | 21 | 18 | 15 |
| Rio Janeiro Brazil | 25 | 25 | 26 | 25 | 24 | 23 | 22 | 22 | 22 | 22 | 23 | 24 |
| Rome Italy | 14 | 13 | 13 | 14 | 17 | 21 | 23 | 24 | 23 | 20 | 18 | 15 |
| San Francisco USA | 11 | 11 | 12 | 12 | 13 | 14 | 15 | 15 | 16 | 15 | 13 | 11 |
| Stockholm Sweden | 3 | 1 | 1 | 2 | 5 | 10 | 15 | 15 | 13 | 10 | 7 | 4 |
| Sydney Australia | 23 | 24 | 23 | 20 | 18 | 18 | 16 | 17 | 18 | 19 | 19 | 21 |
| Tahiti French Polynesia | 27 | 27 | 27 | 28 | 28 | 27 | 26 | 26 | 26 | 26 | 27 | 27 |
| Tel Aviv Israel | 16 | 16 | 17 | 18 | 21 | 24 | 25 | 27 | 27 | 24 | 21 | 18 |
| Tenerife Canary Islands | 19 | 18 | 18 | 18 | 19 | 20 | 21 | 22 | 23 | 23 | 21 | 20 |
| Tunis Tunisia | 15 | 14 | 14 | 15 | 17 | 20 | 21 | 22 | 23 | 23 | 21 | 20 |
| Vancouver Canada | 8 | 7 | 8 | 9 | 11 | 13 | 14 | 14 | 13 | 12 | 11 | 10 |
| Venice Italy | 9 | 8 | 10 | 13 | 17 | 21 | 23 | 24 | 21 | 18 | 14 | 11 |
| Wellington New Zealand | 17 | 18 | 18 | 17 | 14 | 14 | 13 | 13 | 12 | 14 | 14 | 17 |

# SELECTED CITY ALTITUDES (IN METERS)

Some of the best weather in the world is in high altitude places in tropical countries. One finds "eternal spring" in high plateau areas like Antigua, Guatemala, Cuernavaca, Mexico and Medillin, Colombia. Baguio City, Philippines also can be mentioned. Unfortunately, the political situation and other factors make these places less than ideal.

Other places for perpetual spring are islands cooled by constant trade winds.The French South Pacific (Tahiti, etc.), Netherlands Antilles (Curacao, etc.), Portuguese Azores, Spanish Canaries, and Hawaii (USA) are all in this category.

There is really nowhere in Europe that has a perfect year-round climate. Crete, Cyprus, and Malta come close. The Greek Islands and the Spanish Islands, Majorca, Minorca and Ibiza are like San Francisco: great in the summer but cool, foggy and not very pleasant during the winter months.

In North America, Florida is far too hot and humid in the summers for my taste, but great in winter. Parts of California may be the closest place to paradise. San Diego and Los Angeles have great year-round climates. But urban ghetto Black and hispanic Los Angeles is going the way of New York City – downhill fast. Possibly the nicest community in the world for year-round living, low crime, political stability and lots of yachtsy folks is Newport Beach-- between Los Angeles and San Diego. If you can write us a few pages about the place you think is the best in the world for sunshine, cosmopolitan culture, and easy living, you'll get a free book if we use your material.

Note: A meter in the metric system is 39 inches or a little over 3 feet.

Communities at sea level tend to be humid and hot if they are anywhere near the equator. High altitude places in Europe or North America tend to be crisp, dry, very cold in the winters and have very short (two month?) but usually pleasant summer seasons.

And here is how to get high – or low – depending upon your taste:

| | | | |
|---|---:|---|---:|
| Amsterdam, Netherlands | 5 | Kingston, Jamaica | 8 |
| Asuncion, Paraguay | 77 | La Paz, Bolivia | 3720 |
| Athens, Greece | 0 | Lima, Peru | 153 |
| Auckland, New Zealand | 0 | Lisbon, Portugal | 87 |
| Bangkok, Thailand | 12 | Madrid, Spain | 55 |
| Beirut, Lebanon | 8 | Manila, Philippines | 8 |
| Bogota, Columbia | 2590 | Mexico City, Mexico | 2240 |
| Bridgetown, Barbados | 0 | Montevideo, Uruguay | 9 |
| Brussels, Belgium | 58 | Moscow, Russia | 191 |
| Buenos Aires, Argentina | 14 | Oslo, Norway | 12 |
| Calcutta, India | 26 | Panama City, Panama | 12 |
| Capetown, South Africa | 8 | Port-au-Prince, Haiti | 8 |
| Caracas, Venezuela | 964 | Port-of-Spain, Trinidad | 8 |
| Casablanca, Morocco | 49 | Quito, Ecuador | 2819 |
| Cayenne, French Guiana | 8 | Rabat, Morocco | 0 |
| Copenhagen, Denmark | 8 | Rangoon, Burma | 17 |
| Curacao, Netherlands Antilles | 0 | Rio de Janeiro, Brazil | 9 |
| Damascus, Syria | 213 | Rome, Italy | 14 |
| Dublin, Ireland | 9 | St George's, Grenada | 0 |
| Frankfurt, Germany | 91 | St John's, Antigua | 0 |
| Geneva, Switzerland | 377 | Santiago, Chile | 550 |
| Glasgow, Scotland | 59 | San Diego, California | 20 |
| Guatemala City, Guatemala | 1478 | Singapore | 8 |
| Havana, Cuba | 9 | Stockholm, Sweden | 11 |
| Helsinki, Finland | 8 | Suva, Fiji | 0 |
| Hong Kong | 8 | Sydney, Australia | 8 |
| Istanbul, Turkey | 9 | Tegucigalpa, Honduras | 975 |
| Jerusalem, Israel | 762 | Tehran, Iran | 1220 |
| Juneau, Alaska | 0 | Tokyo, Japan | 9 |
| Kabul, Afghanistan | 2219 | Vienna, Austria | 168 |
| Karachi, Paskistan | 15 | | |

## Chapter 19

# USEFUL ADDRESSES FOR OUT-OF-THE-ORDINARY EXPERIENCES

This planet is a fun place to be. Especially if you know how to get the most out of it. Quality of life is not just about freedom from government, from spouses and from legal wrangles. It is also about seeking out some of those very special opportunities that only a mere handful of the world's most adventurous citizens know about.

For your "pleasure tripping", we have included a number of little-known, if not secret, addresses.

First off, Encounter Overland (at 267 Old Brompton Road, London SW5 9JA, Tel 071-370 6845) offers worldwide adventure travel with tours lasting as long as 29 weeks.

Exodus Expeditions (9 Weir Road, Balham, London SW12 0LT, Tel 081-673 0779) has a free catalog of varied itineraries for offbeat, adventurous living.

Do you dream of kyaking and rafting tours in the Grand Canyon? For us, that dream is more like a nightmare. But if the wet-wet-wet is your cup of tea, Expeditions Inc (Route 4, Box 755, Flagstaff, Arizona 86001, USA, tel 602-774 8176) will be the people to talk to.

On a kinder, gentler note, Explore Asia Ltd (13 Chapter St, London SW1P 4NY, Tel 071-630 7102) will take you trekking and climbing around Nepal and India. And if even that sounds a bit too rough, how about taking it easy on the back of a camel in Samburu? Spectacular camel safaris are organized by Flamingo Tours Ltd (write for more info and latest pricing: PO Box 44899, Nairobi, Kenya).

Whoever said PTs were ordinary. Why not join Globepost Travel Service's motorcycling tours in north-eastern China. They can be contacted at 324 Kennington Park Road, London SE11 3PD.

Go camping in Africa: Guerba Expeditions, 101 Eden Vale Road, Westbury BA13 3QX, Great Britain, Tel 0373 826611 has your ticket. Similar offers, and more, from:

Hann Overland, 2 Ivy Mill Lane, Godstone, Surrey RH9 8NH, Great Britain, tel 0883 744705.

Journey Latin America (14-16 Devonshire Road, Chiswick, London W4 2HD, Great Britain, tel 081-747 3108) has a large selection of South American tours to suit all pockets. Recommended by the authoritative *South American Handbook*.

How about a spot of International Adventure? For that winter sports holiday ABOVE the Arctic Circle, contact: International Adventure, Melbourn St, Rayston, Herts SG8 7BP, Great Britain, Tel 0763 242867.

PT Peter Salisbury is the UK contact for another sports holiday organization, namely the International Long River Canoeist Club. They offer details of thousands of rivers around the world, from the As in France to the Zambezi in Zambia, from the Alesk in Canada/Alaska to the Zare in Zaire. Members in 26 countries are ready to offer help and advice. Write to Peter at 238 Birmingham Road Redditch, Worcs B97 6EL, Great Britain.

And speaking of the Zambezi: Sheerwater (PO Box 125, Victoria Falls, Zimbabwe) offers canoe trips along that river.

More water activity can be found at the London Underwater Centre (13 Glendower Road, London SW14 8NY, Tel 081-876 0735). Scuba diving holidays worldwide for reasonably experienced divers – not, I have to confess, your author. Yet.

Why anyone would want to walk hundreds of miles on end in this day of the car and the airplane, I cannot understand. But each to his own: The Long Distance Walkers Association (Wayfarers, 9 Tainters Brook, Uckfield, East Sussex TN22 1UQ, Great Britain) may have the explanation. If not, check with the Outward Bound Trust (Chestnut Field, Regent Place, Rugby CV21 2PJ, Great Britain, tel 0788 560423) offering walking holidays in off-beat regions of the UK.

Motor Safari (Pinfold Lane, Buckley, Clwyd CH7 3NS, Great Britain, tel 0244 548849) gives you a choice of jeep mountain safaris, squad biking and amphibious vehicles (!) in Wales and Cyprus.

Some nature lovers' travel clubs in the USA are Pacific Crest Club (PO Box 1907, Santa Ana, CA 92702) and the Continental Divide Trail Society (PO Box 30002, Bethesda, MD 20814). In England: The Ramblers Association, 1-5 Wandsworth Road, London SW8 2XX.

Archaeology Abroad (31-34 Gordon Square, London WC1 0PY, tel 071-387 7050) offers you not only the chance to meets lots of young, cultured women. They also provide information about opportunities for archaeological field work and excavations outside Britain. Archaeologists, students of archaeology and specialists who wish to be considered for archaeological work abroad are enrolled and information is provided on request to organizers of excavations who wish to recruit personnel. Others interested in archaeology and preferably with some experience of excavation, are also eligible.

If you are not deemed eligible, you can always BUY your way in. Amathus (51 Tottenham Court Road, London W1P 0HS, Great Britain, tel 071-636 9873) will happily sell you an archaeological tour to Greece.

Long-haul archaeological tours: Jasmine Tours, 23 High St, Chalfont St Peter, Bucks SL9 9QE, England (tel 0753 889577).

Erskine Expeditions (16 Braid Farm Road, Edinburgh EH10 6LF, Great Britain, Tel 031-447 7218) organizes adventure tours in Arctic regions including dog-sledging, mountaineering and cross-country skiing.

If you consider going on an expedition, any expedition, talk to the Expedition Advisory Centre (Royal Geographic Society, 1 Kensington Gore, London SW7 2AR, Great Britain, tel 071 581 2057). It publishes a useful booklet entitled *Joining an Expedition* and provides an information and training service for those planning expeditions. In addition to organizing a variety of seminars and publications including *The Expedition Planners' Handbook and Directory*, the Advisory Centre maintains a database for expedition planners. Check it out! This includes a register of planned expeditions, lists of expedition consultants and suppliers, information on individual countries and a register of personnel who have offered their services to expeditions.

The Explorers Club (46 East 70th St, New York, NY 10021, USA, tel 212-628 8383) was founded in 1904 and dedicated to the search for new knowledge of the earth and outer space. It serves as a focal point and catalyst in the identification and stimulation of institutional exploration, independent investigators and students.

The club has over 3000 members who continue to contribute actively to the constructive role of the explorer. The classes of membership are Member, Fellow, Student, Corporate, each class being divided into Resident (living within 50 miles of the headquarters) and Non-Resident. The club has financed over 140 expeditions and awarded its flag to over 300 expeditions.

The James B Ford Memorial Library contains over 25,000 items, including maps, charts, archives, and photographs, and is probably the largest private collection in North America wholly devoted to exploration.

Abercrombie and Kent (of Sloane Square House, Holbein Place, London SW1W 8NS, Great Britain, tel 071-730 9600 and of 1420 Kensington Road, Suite 11, Oakbrook, IL 60521, USA, tel 312-954 2944) has one of the most extensive tour company programmes with an emphasis on luxury. Specialist holidays worldwide including angling, honeymoons, ballooning and railway tours.

European wine tours: Arblaster and Clarke, 104 Church Road, Steep, Petersfield GU32 2DD, Great Britain, tel 0730 66883.

Expertly guided art and architecture tours: Architectural Tours, 90-92 Parkway, London NW1 7AN, Great Britain, tel 071-267 6497.

Painting holidays in Europe: Artscape Painting Holidays, Units 40 and 41, Temple Farm Industrial Estate, Southend-on-Sea, Essex SS2 5RZ, Great Britain. Tel 0702 617900.

Music holidays with either of two subsidiaries Travel for the Arts and Travel with the Friends (Friends of Covent Garden): Blair Travel, 117 Regent's Park Road, London NW1 8UR, Great Britain, Tel 071-483 2290.

Drawing and art history holidays in Florence: The British Institute, Palazzo Lanfredini, Lungarno Guicciardini, 9, Florence 50125, Italy. Tel 55-284031.

Group photography outings to Norway, Iceland and France: Camera Carriers, 49 Bare Avenue, Morecambe LA4 6BD, Great Britain (tel 0524 411436).

Golfing holidays in the USA: Destination USA, Clipstone House, Hospital Road, Hounslow TW3 3HT, Great Britain. Tel 081-577 1786.

Golfing and spa holidays in Europe: Erna Low Consultants, 9 Reece Mews, London SW7 3HE, Great Britain. Tel 071-584 2841.

Golfing holidays worldwide: Eurogolf, 156 Hatfield Road, St Albans AL1 4JD, Great Britain, tel 0727 42256

Golfing, cooking and spa holidays: Par-tee Tours, Fairway House, North Road, Chorleywood WC3 5LE, Great Britain, Tel 09278 4558.

Astronomical tours (at not so astronomical prices): Explorers Tours, 5 Queen Anne's Court, Peascod Street, Windsor SL4 1DG, Great Britain, Tel 0753 842184.

Music festival tours worldwide: Festival Tours International, BCM Festival Tours, London WC1N 3XX, Great Britain, Tel 071 431 3086

Worldwide music and art history tours: Prospect Music and Art, 454-458 Chiswick High Road, London W4 5TT, Great Britain, Tel 081 995 2151.

Naturist holidays in Europe and America: Peng Travel, 86 Station Road, Gidea Park, Romford RM2 6DP, Great Britain, tel 04024 71832.

Special interest holidays off the beaten track: The Travel Alternative, 27 Park End St, Oxford OX1 1HU, Great Britain, Tel 0865 791636

World's leading guided battlefield tour company: Holts Battlefield Tours, The Golden Key, 15, Market Street, Sandwich, Kent, CT13 9DA, Great Britain, Tel 0304 612248.

Wide range of tours to European gardens: Garden Tours, Premier Suite, Central Business Exchange, Central Milton Keynes MK9 2EA, Great Britain, Tel 0908 609551.

Variety of special interest and activity holidays in France (painting, cookery, language learning, etc.): LSG Theme Holidays, 201 Main St, Thornton LE6 1AH, Great Britain, Tel 0509 231713.

Cooking holidays and art history tours in Italy, France and some Asian destinations: Tours To Remember, 5-6 Kings Court, Kings Square, York Y01 2LD, Great Britain, tel 0904 659966.

Wine and canal holidays in France and Italy: World Wine Tours, Drayton St Leonard, Oxfordshire OX10 7BH, Great Britain, Tel 0865 891919.

Motor racing holidays to Grand Prix events worldwide. As well as golfing, music and archaeological tours. All at: Page and Moy, 136-140 London Road, Leicester LE2 1EN, Great Britain, Tel 0533 552521.

Luxury villas (furnished) for short-term and medium-term hire, most with pool: Continental Villas, 3 Caxton Walk, London WC2 8PW, Great Britain, Tel 071-497 0444. Located in France, West Indies, Spain, Portugal, Italy, Greece and Cyprus.

Safari Consultants are representatives for Johnny Baxendale Four by Four Safaris, Kenya Tour Allen Safaris and Kenya Cordon Bleu Safaris, Kenya. Address: 83 Gloucester Place, London W1H 3PG, Great Britain. Tel 071-287 1133.

Luxury, traditional tented safaris: World Apart, PO Box 44209, Nairobi, Kenya (tel 228961) and c/o Flamingo Tours of East Africa, tel UK 081-995 3505.

# WHERE WE PREPARE FOR OUR TROTTING

The Travel Bookshop is London's first bookshop specializing in travel literature. It opened in 1980 and claims to provide a "complete package" for the traveller, including regional guides, histories, cookery books, relevant fiction and so on. We have found their selection to be very comprehensive and like to browse through one of their country sections before our travels to get the "feel" of the chosen destination.

They produce a general and some regional catalogs of stock and will produce a computer printout for stock on any one particular destination. They are also well-stocked in the map department.

The Travel Bookshop, 13 Blenheim Crescent, London W11, England. Tel (+44) 229 5260.

A competing store with an almost similar name is The Travellers' Bookshop, also in London. It boasts a wide range of antiquarian travel guides as well as the current crop of guide series. The shop will buy your old travel books from you and invites comments about guides and any other aspects of travel for the shop bulletin board.

By mail order, you can buy some excellent books for the independent traveller. Write for the latest free list. In Europe: Regenbogen-Verlag, Schmidstrasse 3, Postfach 3, CH-8025 Zürich, Switzerland.

And In the Americas: Los Amigos del Libro, Casilla Postal 450, Cochabamba, Bolivia.

Also in the world of mail order, a further two publishers tempt us with their selections. Order free catalogs. Vacation Work Publications, 9 Park End St, Oxford OX1 1HJ, England. Tel (+44) 0865 241 978. Publishers of books for budget travellers and for anyone wanting to work or study abroad; and: Wilderness Press, 2440 Bancroft Way, Berkeley, CA 94704, USA. Tel (+1) 415 843 8080. Natural history, adventure travel guides and maps of North America. All mail order, including from abroad, to be paid in US dollars.

# PERIODICALS FOR THAT EVER-TRAVELLING LIFESTYLE

A fellow PT, known to the world as Mr Monk, puts out what can best be described as a "cult magazine" about his own lifestyle. Summed up in the slogan "quit'n the job and hit'n the road". The magazine, titled *MONK*, is a quarterly published from an RV, using a solar-powered Mac. Mr Monk and his ever-present cat Dolly Lama expose America in what *Rolling Stone* magazine named 1991's "Hot Magazine". *Newsweek* also reads *MONK* and called it "'Kuralt meets Kerouac with Laurel and Hardy thrown in". Americans can call 1-800-GET-MONK and order a sample copy for $2.95 or a subscription (4 issues) for ten bucks. Others, write Spy Shop-O-Matic at P.O. Box 5007, Pittsfield, MA 01203-5007, USA with an added $1.50 for handling.

Here is a list of other publications that caught our eye during our travels:

*Adventure Travel* (bi-annual travel magazine), 1515 Broadway, New York, NY 10036, USA, Tel (+1) 212 719 6000.

*Atlantis* (Norwegian-language magazine dealing in offbeat travel), Atlantis Travellers Club, PB 5908, Hegdehaugen 0308, Oslo 3, Norway.

*Australian Gourmet Traveller* (our kind of mag, a consumer publication for travellers who enjoy their food), Australian Consolidated Press, PO Box 4088, 54 Park St, Sydney, NSW 2000, Australia

*Brit* (monthly newspaper for British expatriates in Florida), 35246 US, 19 N Box 137, Palm Harbor, FL 34684, USA, Tel (+1) 813-785 8279

*Business Traveller* (a monthly magazine aimed at the business traveller and featuring airfare cost-cutting information that will show quickly and clearly how to save your air travel costs), 338-396 Oxford St, London W1N 9HE, England, Tel (+44) 71-629 4688

*Camping and Caravaning* (monthly journal for enthusiasts), Greenfields House, Westwood Way, Coventry CV4 8JH, England, Tel (+44) 203 694995.

*Conde Nast Traveller* (at newsstands: glossy, monthly consumer publication featuring travel news, information etc.), 360 Madison Avenue, New York, NY 10017, USA.

*Consumer Reports Travel Letter* (comprehensive examination of major travel questions, with company-by-company, dollars and cents comparisons of competitive travel services based on own 'original, independent, professional' research. Feature length articles on places, issues, etc.) 301 Junipero Serra Blvd, suite 200, San Francisco, CA 94127, USA.

*Destinations*, 444 Front St West, Toronto ON M5V 2S9, Canada

*Executive Travel* (monthly consumer travel publication aimed at the business traveller. Suggestions tend to be on the pricey, expense-account type side), 242 Vauxhall Bridge Road, London SW1V 1AU, England, Tel (+44) 71-821 1155.

*The Expatriate* (monthly title dealing with such issues as investment, pensions information, selection of job ads, health, tax, etc. Mostly for the British expatriate). 56A Rochester Row, London SW1P 1JU, England, Tel (+44) 71-834 9192.

*Expedition Club Austria, Club Nachrichten,* (this is in German, but if you master that language – and are interested in Austria – this is it. A gem of readers' reports, tips and classified ads for lodging, house swapping, travel gear, etc). Postfach 1457, A-1010 Vienna, Austria

*Explore* (quarterly color magazine devoted to adventure travel worldwide) Suite 400, 301-14 St N.W., Calgary, Alberta, Canada T2N 2A1, Tel (+1) 403-270 8890.

*The Explorers Journal* (official quarterly of The Explorers Club, established 1904. Articles and reviews). 46 East 70th St, New York, NY 10021, USA.

*France* (a quarterly publication for Francophiles), Pine House, The Square, Stow-on-the-Wold, Glos GL54 1AF, England, Tel (+44) 451-31398.

*Freighter Travel* News (news and letters, reports on freighter cruises), Freighter Travel Club of America, 1745 Scotch Ave, SE, PO Box 12693, Salem, OR 79309, USA.

*Globe* (newsletter for the Globetrotters Club. Travel information. Articles on individual experiences, news of 'members on the move', tips + a great mutual-aid column for members). The Globetrotters Club, BCM/Roving, London WC1N 3XX, England

*Good Holiday Magazine* (quarterly title for holidaymakers), 1-2 Dawes Court, 93 High St, Esher, Surrey KT10 9QD, England. Tel (+44) 372 469799

*Going Places* (at UK-newsstands. Quarterly glossy dealing in mainstream travel, with lots of destination reports), Pericles Press Ltd, 38 Buckingham Palace Road, London SW1W 0RE, England. Tel (+44) 71-486 5353

*Great Expeditions* (for people who want to travel and explore, offers trips, a free classified ads service, discounts on books, an information exchange, articles and travel notes), PO Box 64699, Station G, Vancouver, BC V6R 4GT, Canada. Tel (+1) 604 734 3938

*The Great Outdoors* (countryside matters), The Plaza Tower, East Kilbride, Glasgow G74 1LW, Great Britain. Tel: (+44) 3552 46444

*Holiday Which?* (Quarterly publication published by the British Consumers' Association, featuring destinations worldwide and reporting on all travel-related news and issues), 2 Marylebone Road, London NW1 4DX, England, Tel (44) 71-486 5544.

*Homes Abroad* (monthly publication for anyone interested in buying property abroad), 387 City Road, London EC1V 1NA, England. Tel: (+44) 71-837 3909)

*Islands* (glossy color title devoted to the world's islands, large and small), 3886 State St, Santa Barbara, CA 93105, U.S.A., Tel: (+1) 805-682 7177.

*International Travel News* (get a free sample copy of this one! A great news source for anyone who travels much. Contributions mostly from readers, almost all of them PTs or closet-PTs).

*Martin Publications Inc,* 2120 28th St, Sacramento, CA 95818, U.S.A.

*The Lady* (we have found some self-catering accomodation in the classified ads section of this one. Also many foreign postings for young females. Plus: Good spot to PLACE an ad), 39-40 Bedford St, Strand, London WC2E 9ER, England, Tel: (44) 71-379 4717.

*London Calling* (monthly magazine for listeners to the BBC's World Service, listing programme times and frequencies), PO Box 7677, Bush House, Strand, London WC2B 4PH, England.

*Lonely Planet Newsletter* (quarterly newsletter giving updates on all the so-called Lonely Planet guidebooks and lots of useful tips from other independent travellers). Lonely Planet Publications, PO Box 617, Hawthorn, Victoria 3122, Australia

*Military Travel News* (pure, concentrated inside-knowledge in this one. Military Travel News is aimed at the US military members on active duty or retired, and dependants, but ANYONE can easily profit from the wealth of secret information in this newsletter. Mostly current low-cost travel information on the USA, Caribbean, Europe, Far East and elsewhere). Travel News, PO Box 9, Oakton, VA 22124, USA.

*The Mouse Monitor* (our own journal of rodent control. Keep those bureau-rats at bay.), Scope International Ltd, 62 Murray Road, Waterlooville, Hants PO8 9JL, England. Tel: (+44) 705 592255, Fax: (+44) 705 591975

*Nomad* (newsletter aimed at people on the move and written by peripatetic publisher, with many readers' reports), BCM-Nomad, London WC1V 6XX, England

*Official Airlines Guide* (The 'OAG' is a monthly airline timetable in pocket format, aimed at the consumer.), Bridge House, Lyons Crescent, Tonbridge, Kent TN9 1EX, England. Tel: (+44) 732 352 668

*The Outrigger* (far out!), c/o Pacific Islands Society, Dr Clerk, 75 Ballards Road, London NW2 7UE, England.

*Passport* (sorry, this is NOT what you think it is. But still worth a read. A newsletter for the discriminating and culturally minded international travellers. Forthcoming cultural events worldwide, plus hotel and restaurant suggestions), 20 North Wacker Drive, Chicago, IL 60606, USA.

*Resident Abroad* (a monthly publication for British expatriates. Although put out by the Financial Times magazine division, we find this a very watered-down version of what could have been a great forum for PTs. Lots of good ads, though), 108 Clerkenwell Road, London EC1M 5SA, England, Tel: (+44) 71-251 9321.

*Safariposten-Denmark* (an annual expedition publication in Danish. There is also a bi-monthly newsletter of the name Globetrotter Nyhedsbrev and a bi-monthly newsletter in English called The Globetrotters Newsletter). Topas Globetrotterklub, Safari House, Lounsvej 29, DK-9640 Farso, Denmark, Tel: (+45) 98 63 84 00.

More for our Danish-language readers: Request a FREE sample copy of PT-style publication *Finansiel Frihed* from expatriate publisher Pia Penlau of Rue du Barry, F-82240 Puylarroque, France. Fax and phone: (+33) 6331 2257.

*The South American Explorer* (The official journal of the South American Explorers Club. With tips, notes, etc), Casilla 3714, Lima 100, Peru. For subscriptions, contact PO Box 18327, Denver, CO 80218, USA.

*Pacific Islands Monthly,* 76 Clarence St, PO Box 3408, Sydney 2001, Australia

*The Pacific Traveller* (glossy bi-monthly focusing on the Asia-Pacific region, with a mixture of destination reports and information for the business traveller). Sky Trend Development Ltd, Mezzanine Floor, 20-22 Old Bailey St, Central Hong Kong

*Sex Havens* by Dr W.G. Hill. Covers over 20 countries and contains clever, detailed information. Published by Scope International and now available price £60/$100. Definitely nothing else as good as this on the market and the result of much back-breaking research by the author.

*South East Asia Traveller* (Patpong road, here we come! Well, not quite. For that, turn to *Sex Havens*. This magazine is mostly geared towards business). Compass Publishing, 336 Smith St, 04-303 New Bridge Centre, Chinatown, Singapore 0105

*The South Sea Digest,* PO Box 4245, Sydney, NSW 2001, Australia

*Travel News* (a weekly trade newspaper. News on upcoming special offers, packages and promos) Francis House, 11 Francis St, Victoria, London SW1P 1BZ, England. Tel: (+44) 71-828 8989

*Travel Trade Gazette* (oldest weekly newspaper for the UK travel industry. Worth a peek). Morgan Grampion House, Calderwood St, London SE18 6QH, England, Tel: (44) 81-855 7777)

*Traveller* (quarterly publication on travel with many useful addresses, some of which are used with the kind permission of the publishers in this book as well). *Wexas International, 45-49 Brompton Road,* Knightsbridge, London SW3 1DE, England, Tel: (+44) 71-581 4130)

*Travel Smart* (a well-written newsletter for sophisticated travellers who expect honest value for their money. Also discount-cruises, supercharters, hotel, car rentals, etc for subscribers), Travel Smart for Business, Communications House, 40 Beechdale Road, Dobbs Ferry, NY 10522, USA.

*Travel Tips* (first person accounts of freighter and passenger ship travel to all parts of the world. Cruise guide, budget travel news, tips on trips), 163-07 Depot Rd, Flushing, NE 11358, USA.

*Tropical Frontier* (USA Newsletter with news, events and travel data on 'the world's most exotic islands' and definitely not Eagle Pass, Texas), PO Box 1316, Eagle Pass, TX 78853, USA.

*Tropical Island Living* (information and news, which we really figure ought to be published from some tropical island), PO Box 7263, Arlington, VA 22207, USA.

## VISA AGENCIES

These people can tell you if you need a visa or not for a particular destination and then help you get it (usually faster and with less hassle, but for a fee). Use them also to lower your profile and avoid standing in lines at various embassies.

All of these services are in England, except for the two last listed, which are in California, USA.
ALLIANCE VISA AND CONSULAR SERVICES, Room 21, Building 8, Manchester Airport, Manchester M22 5PJ. Tel: (+44) 61-489 3201
PORT REPS, PO Box 290, Slough SL1 7LF, Tel: (+44) 6286-4714
PASSPORT AND VISA SERVICES, PVS, (UK) LTD, 10b Parlaunt Road, Langley, Slough, Berks SL3 8BB, Tel (+44) 753 683160
ROSS CONSULAR SERVICES, 6 The Grove, Slough, Berks SL1 1QP, Tel: (+44) 753 820881
THAMES CONSULAR SERVICES, 363 Chiswick High Road, London W4 4HS, Tel (+44) 81-995 2492
THE VISASERVICE, 2 Northdown Street, London N1 9BG, Tel: (+44) 71-833 2709
THOMAS COOK, 45 Berkeley Street, London W1A 1EB, Tel: (+44) 71-499 4000
INTERCONTINENTAL VISA SERVICE, Los Angeles World Trade Center, 350 South Figueroa St, Los Angeles, CA 90071, USA, Tel: (+1) 213-625 7175
VISAS INTERNATIONAL, 3169 Barbara Ct, Suite F, Los Angeles, CA 90068, Tel (+1) 213-850 1191

## ENGLISH LANGUAGE NEWSPAPERS AT YOUR DESTINATION

Major English-speaking nations have not, in the main, been included in this list as information on leading papers is easy to obtain from telephone books or other sources. Also, we don't have the several hundred pages needed to list all the papers in the USA and/or Great Britain. Info here was compiled from *NewsGuides* (Further reading: NewsGuide International Ltd, Park House, 207-211 The Vale, London W3 7QS, England. Tel: 081-7499 8855). For USA readers, an annual paperback called *Editor & Publisher* (available in the reference department of most public libraries) is a good guide to all the newspapers of the world, including all the newspapers in the world; showing ad-rates, circulation, names of major officers (Editor, Publisher, Ad Manager, etc.). Like the *NewsGuides*, they list street addresses, phones and faxes, and state how often published.

What is the use of such a list to PTs? If you are thinking of visiting a place, you can order a few copies of the local rag to look over want ads for apartments, hotels, furnished rooms and houses for rent. You could be interested in the local prices of cars and car rentals. Sex fiends can place "love" ads seeking companionship "and more". Perhaps you can arrange a welcome for you at the airport when you arrive. A sex-starved local may assure that you will always have pleasant memories of your first night in wherever-it-was. Place your own ad or answer ads that you see in the paper. Visiting foreigners are often more atractive to locals than the home-grown supply of partners. Although we have not given street addresses, phone and fax numbers, generally a letter to the newspaper in any town without an exact address will get there. Local papers are always well known to the post offices. Often consulates of your destination country will have a few local papers on display in their free libraries.

ARGENTINA: *Buenos Aires Herald, The Review of the River Plate* (finance)

ANTIGUA: *Nation's Voice, Worker's Voice, Standard, Outlet*

BAHAMAS: *Nassau Guardian, Nassau Tribune, Freeport News*

BANGLADESH: *Bangladesh Observer, Bangladesh Times, News Nation, Holiday, Bangladesh Today, Tide*

BARBADOS: *The Advocate-News, The Nation, Junior Nation, The Sunday Sun, The Bajan*

BELIZE: *Sunday Times, Reporter, Amandala, The Voice, The Beacon, The Tribune*

BERMUDA: *Royal Gazette, Mid Ocean News, Bermuda Sun* and numerous magazines

BOTSWANA: *Botswana Daily News, Botswana Guardian*

BURMA: *The Working People's Daily, The Guardian Daily*

CAYMAN ISLANDS: *Cayman Compass, Horizon Magazine, Nor' Wester, Tourist Weekly, Looking*

CHINA: *China Daily, China Reconstructs, China Pictorial, Peking Review*

COSTA RICA: *Tico Times*

CZECHOSLOVAKIA: *Czechoslovakia Life, Welcome to Czechoslovakia*

DENMARK: *Copenhagen This Week*

COMMONWEALTH OF DOMINICA: *Dominica Chronical*

FIJI: *Fiji Times, Fiji Sun*

FRANCE: *The News, France-USA Contacts* (ads), *International Herald Tribune, Paris Free Voice*

GAMBIA: *Gambia News Bulletin, The Senegambia Sun*

GUYANA: *Guyana Chronical*

HONG KONG: *South China Morning Post, Hongkong Standard*

HUNGARY: *Daily News, Hungarian Week*

ICELAND: *News from Iceland*

IRAQ: *Baghdad Times*

ISRAEL: *Jerusalem Post*

JAMAICA: *The Daily Gleaner, The Star*

JORDAN: *Jordan Times, Jerusalem Star*

KENYA: *The Standard, Nation, Kenya Times, The Weekly Review*

KOREA, SOUTH: *Korea Herald, Korea Times, Korea News Review*

LIBERIA: *The Observer, The New Liberian, The Scope, The Express, The Mirror, The Bong Crier, Afro Media Magazine*

MADAGASCAR: *Madagascar Tribune*

MALAYSIA: *New Straits Times, New Sunday Times, Malay Mail, Sunday Mail, The Star, The National Echo, Sarawak Tribune, Sarawak Vanguard, Malaysia Focus, Sabah Times, Daily Express, Sarawak Herald*

MALTA: *The Times, Weekend Cronicle*

MEXICO: *The News*
NEPAL: *The Rising Nepal, Media Nepal*
OMAN: *Oman Daily Observer, Times of Oman, Akhbar Oman*
PARAGUAY: *Guarani News*
PERU: *Lima Times*
PORTUGAL: *Anglo-Portuguese News, Algarve News / Portugal Post*
QATAR: *Daily Gulf Times, Weekly Gulf Times*
SAMOA: *Samoa News, News Bulletin, Samoa Journal*
SEYCHELLES: *The Nation*
SINGAPORE: *Straits Times*
SPAIN: *The Entertainer* (Costa del Sol only)
SWAZILAND: *Times of Swaziland, Swazi Observer*
TAHITI: *Tahiti Sun Press*
TANZANIA: *Daily News*
TRINIDAD AND TOBAGO: *Trinidad Guardian*
TURKEY: *Daily News, Middle East Review, Outlook*
TURKS AND CAICOS ISLANDS: *Turks and Caicos Current*
UNITED ARAB EMIRATES: *Gulf News, Khaleej Times, Emirate News, Gulf Mirror, Gulf Commercial Magazine, Recorder*

PART FIVE

# THE PT TOOLBOX

# Chapter 20

# OFFSHORE CORPORATIONS AND TRUSTS: DO YOU REALLY NEED THEM?

To many PTs and would-be PTs, corporations are essential tools in making money, discharging liabilities or owning assets globally; often in deep secrecy.

A corporation (or trust) is what lawyers call *a legal entity*. Whereas a company does not eat, sleep or go to the movies, it may own just about anything you care to mention: bank accounts, stocks, bonds, investments, cars, boats and even aeroplanes. So may a trust (a foundation).

The distinction between a "corporation" and a mere "company" is that the former is, by its very definition, a *separate, legal entity* as opposed to an unincorporated, personally-owned company. A corporation may go bankrupt and leave creditors, including the tax man, holding the short end of the stick. An unincorporated company will be inextricably linked to its owner (or owners). If an unincorporated company defaults on a debt or a payment, creditors may immediately turn to the owner and demand payment from him, which is a pretty good reason why you should never operate any business except from behind the protection of a *corporation*. That way, you are only liable for a loss up to whatever capital you have invested in the business, but no claim can be made against you personally in the event that the corporation folds or closes with a negative net worth. Unless, of course, fraudulent conduct by the owner(s) or manager(s) can be proved. Only rarely are owners or managers held personally liable for losses stemming from fraud or gross misconduct, which you should take to read as – only in cases where *criminal misconduct* (or outright fraud) can be proved. Proving such claims may take years. This is the major reason why dejected creditors usually take their licks and abstain from pursuing the matter further.

Shares in a corporation have to be *owned* by someone – or something. Usually, shares are held either by ordinary shareholders, by one or more other companies, institutions or trusts. But a corporation *cannot own itself*. Someone has to own the shares, which also means that someone may be taxed on the wealth represented by the value of the shares, on the dividends or even on the capital gains realized when the shares are ultimately sold (or the corporation is succesfully liquidated).

Enter trusts – or foundations, as they are sometimes called. As opposed to a company or corporation, *no one can own a trust*. By definition, a trust is not only a separate, legal entity, but also *"owns itself"*. No physical or legal person may "own" even the tiniest, little share of a trust. And that, exactly, is why trusts are so phenomenal in their potential uses.

Let us say, for instance, that you live in a high-tax country with very strict tax laws. Every year, you have to file an income tax return (like the US 1040, for instance). On this hideous piece of paper, you will usually be obliged to make a full disclosure of all bank accounts, shares and other assets that you own – under the threat of severe penalties, including jail, for non-disclosure.

The solution to this is *not* to keep your assets in other countries; most high-tax countries tax their citizens on their *global income* and, accordingly, require that all assets (even non-taxable) be disclosed, *regardless* of where they happen to be. Even if you own, say, a loss-making company in another country, or a non-interest bearing bank account (well, they do exist) somewhere you will be legally obliged to disclose this fact on your income tax return. Some countries, including the US, even demand that citizens disclose the *beneficial* ownership of shares, etc., to guard against such assets being legally kept a secret by having them officially registered as belonging to someone else – like an attorney, for instance.

## A WORD ON BIG GOVERNMENT

Any country may, at any time, pass a law that requires their citizens to make an exact statement of all, worldwide assets not only *owned but also controlled*, whether directly or even *indirectly* (e.g. through a power of attorney). Sorry, but those are the facts. It is legally possible for the government in any country to pass such laws and punish citizens for "breaking them", even if those laws constitute a flagrant violation of the constitution of the country in question. A gross example: the United States Constitution states that church and state be kept *separate* and that no official religion may be established. Fine, right? Now take a look at a piece of US coinage and read the fine print – "In God We Trust". Keep religion and state separate? Doesn't much look like it. The law forcing the US Mint to print these four words on US currency was passed at the behest of a fascist, raving maniac senator by the name of Joe McCarthy back in the Fifties. Heard of him? Then you also know what states and governments are *able* to do in terms of passing blatantly illegal and intolerant laws and enforcing them at the point of a gun. It happens everywhere. Germany and France, for instance, still have the *draft*. They also have laws that make it possible to be a "conscientious objector" (e.g. on the basis of religious faith). So far, so good. But to prevent too many people from finding out about these laws, another set of laws exist that make it a crime for anyone to *write* or otherwise *publicize* the fact that a legal loophole exists for anyone who wishes to avoid the draft. In China, most criminal laws are *secret* and even lawyers have a hard time finding out what they have to go on when trying to build a legal defense for clients.

We tell you this to make it painfully clear to you that even though some of the tactics outlined in the following may presently be legal, they may not be so for long. Governments can pass a clearly immoral law with near-impunity. They frequently do so. What you have to protect yourself with is your wits. Even if you live in a country with "across-the-board", full-disclosure laws that make it "technically" illegal for you to indulge in some heavy use of offshore corporations and trusts, it is very tempting to advise you to silently tell Big Brother to "bugger off!", then go about doing what you have to do in total secrecy. After all, your life belongs to you – and so does the money you earn, criminal and anti-human laws notwithstanding.

*Why not hide* as many of your assets as possible from the authorities and everybody else looking to steal from you or do you harm. The way to do this is, first and foremost, *not to disclose your total assets* to begin with. Once you disclose an asset, of any nature, that information will go on file and may later be dug up to help authorities in seizing or attaching that asset. Never mind why they would want to do this, you should only be concerned with keeping assets (like coins, stamps and foreign bank accounts) *totally secret.*

But in order to do this, you must also realize that some day the fact of your ownership may come to light. This is why you have to guard yourself against being second-guessed by authorities or even a blood-thirsty prosecutor. The way to do this is, in essence, the same way that governments discourage citizens from rioting in the streets against a criminal law, by giving your arrangements a *veneer of legality.*

Which brings us back to the question of trusts (and foundations). Nobody can "own" a trust, period. A trusts owns itself and its assets, dispensing with the latter by virtue of decisions arrived at by what would, in corporate terminology, be called the *management or the board of directors , or trustees of a trust.*

The "management" of a trust can be two-tiered. On the top of a pile is *the protector.* It is up to the protector to make sure that the trust's charter is adhered to and that the rules laid down for the dispensing of the trust's assets are followed. The role of the protector is purely that of a *supervisor with veto power over the trustees and power to fire them in his sole discretion.* The day-to-day affairs of the trust are handled, not by corporate officers or managers, but by so-called *trustees.* The trustees will make all decisions concerning the investments and disbursements of funds made by the trust. If the trust wishes to open a bank account, say, or buy a yacht (in keeping with the trust's charter, of course) then it will be the board of trustees which has to arrive at this decision and sign the relevant papers.

But, as you will already have guessed, the trustees may decide to sign a *power of attorney* to someone else who can then, in effect, do whatever he (or she) wishes on behalf of the trust, at his sole discretion – without having to ask permission.

Now, if you own assets that you either do not wish to disclose or wish to guard against future seizure, confiscation or nationalisation by your home government (which is a sure sign of intelligence), you may give your tactics a "veneer of legality" by conducting your financial affairs through the use of a trust and one or more corporations.

# THE SECRET TRUST: ONSHORE OR OFFSHORE?

The difference between "onshore" and "offshore" trusts and corporations is, roughly speaking, that "onshore" means subject to a big-brother, high-tax jurisdiction that obliges trusts and corporate management to file a host of disclosure forms with the local company register (which also handles trusts). This information essentially then will be public, freely given out to anyone for the asking. In addition, annual statements must be made and any profits are taxable. In countries with wealth taxes, the trust or corporation may be obliged to give a percentage of its capital to the State.

On the other hand, an "offshore" location is a country or jurisdiction with very lax (or non-existing) laws about what sort of information, if any, a corporation or trust has to file with the company register – annual statements, identities of managers, protectors and trustees, etc. In an offshore location, this information will usually be much harder to obtain for external third-parties (such as foreign tax authorities). An "offshore" corporation or trust will be *tax-exempt.* For a small, yearly fee payable *in lieu* of any taxes, an offshore corporation or trust may conduct just about any business, anywhere, without any legal requirement to inform the local tax authorities about this. This is the basic distinction between a legal entity that is registered "offshore" as opposed to "onshore". Recap: offshore corporations or trusts pay little or no taxes and their true ownership and activities can be kept secret.

Is there anything immoral or illegal about incorporating a company or trust in an offshore location? In and of itself – no. Most if not all countries recognize the authority of other countries to make their own laws as far as company registers and taxation is concerned (and car registrations, passport issuance, etc., for that matter). Just as it is quite legal to move to another country in order to save taxes (even though your own country may not quite like the idea and usually will attempt to legislate against it), so it is also quite legal to register a company or form a trust in a jurisdiction that extorts little or no taxes.

An American citizen may freely own any number of tax-free corporations in any number of different countries. There is nothing illegal about that. The "iffy" part is the "legal" requirements that he faces to make a full disclosure of his interest in foreign assets on his tax return. Remember most governments think they **own** *"their" citizens* and may confiscate citizens' assets (or send them off to get killed in a silly war) at will. And then keep in mind that governments can only exist because the victims, the citizenry, grant to governments their *sanction* of monstrous laws by abiding by them, however grudgingly.

But what you should be concerned with is that aforementioned "veneer of legality" that you need to give you at least some protection, in case anyone ever makes a connection between you and a vacation home in Monte Carlo that is not in evidence on your latest tax return.

One way to do this is to form a *trust* which owns the villa, or other assets. This automatically relieves you of any law (and certainly very immoral law) requiring you to disclose all your worldwide assets. **You do not own** the villa, the trust does. And neither you nor anyone else owns the trust, since that would be a contradiction in terms. Of course, the trust has to be in an offshore location with no legal requirements that the trust must declare what assets it owns. A trust in, say, the Isle of Man (in the Irish Sea between Ireland and England) may legally own all the stock of IBM and not be obliged to disclose this to a living soul – not on the Isle of Man, anyway.

On the face of it, transferring your assets and business interests outside of your home country to a trust or foundation may be a cure-all for your tax troubles. You can own anything you wish through the trust, retaining complete control over those assets and not be obliged to disclose it to anyone.

But there are two slight catches. First, that a trust may usually not engage in or conduct an active business unless through the (whole or part) ownership of one or more companies (which, as explained, also should be incorporated offshore).

Second, that you cannot *legally* arrange to disburse funds owned by the trust to yourself. It is true that the local *nominees* ("straw men") who lend their names to the trust for use in the company register in exchange for a modest fee could possibly not care less what you do with the assets belong to the trust. Still, the legal requirement – even on the Isle of Man – remains that the trust cannot legally make payments of any nature to anyone unless by following the rules laid down in the trusts' charter documents. And local laws do not allow the incorporation of a (tax-exempt) trust or foundation with rules that allow it to be blatant as a tax-shelter by making no requirements of fund applicants.

The way to *legally* get around both of these requirements is to create an offshore corporation – or several. Say, for instance, that you have quietly transferred a million US dollars to the trust's Swiss bank account by making a donation. You no longer need to disclose this particular one million bucks on your tax return as it no longer legally belongs to you. But you may still want to get some of it back one day. Then what? What you do is basically TRADE with the trust, i.e. *sell something to the trust*. An arm's length transaction with a foreign trust is quite legal. But if a transaction is not reported, who is going to measure the arms? The trust may wish to acquire ownership of, i.e. a newly-incorporated, Delaware company through which to conduct future business in the United States. Let us say that you need a quick, *legal* US $250,000 from the trust, the bank accounts of which you control with a POA. You now buy a US $199 Delaware corporation from any broker specializing in selling newly incorporated, "fresh" corporations – and then pledge as security for a loan your shares in it) to the trust for a cool US $250,199 in cash.

Truth to tell, you may break one law in some country or other if you do not disclose the fact that you don't expect to ever repay the loans and that you are lending yourself your own money. But generally, there is no income tax due on borrowed money until and unless the loan is formally "fugitive". If you need the cash for a new car – or for your daughter's wedding – then who is entitled to say that you "owe" taxes on money on which you have, presumably, paid 40, 50 or even 60 per cent income tax when you first made it?.

## THE ART OF COMPARTMENTALIZING YOUR LIFE

Apart from legal considerations, there are some practical aspects of retaining privacy. If the laws in your country make it absolutely impossible for you to conceal assets legally, even with the use of offshore corporations and trusts, it is up to you and your own conscience whether to go right ahead and break those laws. It is *your life*. Unless you believe in the absolute, unquestioned moral right of a democratically-elected government to pass laws forcing you to disclose everything, right down to the holes in your socks, forget those laws and go about your business. But be discreet. Do not shoot your mouth off, and take great pains to ensure that no one discovers, by a fluke or otherwise, that you happen to control one or more offshore, legal entities. Do it, but keep any and all documents pertaining to concealed assets, offshore corporations and trusts, in a place where they are unlikely to be found or seized. This means not in your home, but preferably in a safety deposit box in a foreign country.

And compartmentalize! As you will remember from the mail drop chapter, Wayne Budd of Canada offers confidential safekeeping of documents. So do others, such as several companies in London. One is The City Safe Deposit, Winchester House, 100 Old Broad Street, London EC2N 1BE, phone (+44) 71 588 2733, which will rent you a very large box for a yearly fee that may be anywhere from £125 to over £1,000 per year, depending on size. Incidentally, such boxes are also very good for keeping spare passports, credit cards, driver's licenses and even a bit of cash if you have to leave the country immediately and don't wish to tip someone off by charging anything to your credit card. Almost every bank in the world rents safety deposit boxes. A small box in Switzerland costs Swiss fr.70 a year (US $50).

To compartmentalize is to keep information about your offshore trusts, corporations *and* where you keep documents such as bearer shares, and communications with the trust you control *TO YOURSELF. Button your lips.*

No one should know where to find your safety deposit box(es) during your lifetime. That you should not pay for such services by credit card is self-evident. Pay cash. Make sure that *no* paper trail is generated that may lead tax, government or other investigators to your documents – since those documents, in turn, may be used to find your assets and bank accounts etc. It is not inconceivable that the US government, among others, may one day be able to conduct a blanket sweep of all bank accounts in Switzerland, looking for those that bear the names of offshore corporations or trusts known or suspected as belonging to American citizens.

For extra secrecy, consider using a "pen-name" supported by alternate identity documents when you buy an offshore corporation or obtain control over an offshore trust. Use a different pen-name when you obtain the safe deposit box in which you stash the documents. If you have to give your lawyer or bankers an address, use a mail drop somewhere on the other side of the Earth. Give that as your "home address". Then use that mail drop for *nothing else*. That's compartmentalizing!. Take a clue from the late Robert Maxwell, who only succeeded in keeping his business affairs going for so long because he put his various businesses into "individual, water-tight compartments". This avoided suspicion from arising until after his death when he was no longer there himself to handle information safekeeping. The half billion he diverted is still unaccounted for. Like the fortunes of Meyer Lasky, Al Capone and Howard Hughes, the public will never know where it went.

## PROPER STORAGE OF DOCUMENTS

Otherwise sensible people often seem to throw caution to the wind when it comes to dealing with important or sensitive documents. One of our clients actually went to jail mainly because he kept customer lists at his office. Here's what happened. Our hero was in the mail order business. He operated from the same address for over a dozen years. During that period he was the subject of exactly one complaint to a Federal agency. He had over 100,000 clients per year for various small catalog items, mainly cutlery, and he offered a money back guaranty. About 1 per cent of his customers took him up on the warranties. He felt he was an honest businessman, and 99 per cent of his customers were satisfied with his products. The 1 per cent that were unhappy always got their money back, "no questions asked". But one day, as the result of this single, totally unwarranted complaint from a non-customer who had somehow received an unsolicited catalog, a bureaucrat decided that his ads were fraudulent. One product, a knife with a blade that would "last forever", was the bureau-rat's particular target.

Without any warning, government agents swooped in on "Mail-order Mike's" office and confiscated ten years of customer records containing over a million names and addresses all neatly coded. First there was a tax investigation to see that Mike had paid the proper income taxes and state sales taxes. He passed with flying colors! Local newspapers then ran favorable articles about Mike's persecution and the unfair treatment he had received. But this only made the bureau-rats more determined to get him. The government agency then sent out a form letter (at taxpayers' expense) to all past customers asking if they were still happy and satisfied with products they bought from ''Mail Order Mike''. They were informed that if not satisfied they could ask for a refund without returning the merchandise. If they felt defrauded in any way, the bureau-rat wrote that they should register their complaints with the Bureau. As a result of the letter, Mike was deluged with requests (forwarded to him by the government) for refunds. Actually, they were from less than two per cent of all past customers on the lists that had been confiscated from him, but 20,000 refund requests all at the same time involved more money than he could afford to pay out. There were three bona-fide complaints that Mike's Miracle Last Forever $9.99 Knife Blade couldn't cut much after eight years. One of these complainants had used it to open several hundred tin cans! The government encouraged him to bring suit for himself and all other knife buyers over the years. He did bring such a *class action* and won a *treble damage* judgment for eight million dollars that sent Mike into bankruptcy. Had he been able to pay it, most of the award would have gone not to the knife buyers but to the clever shyster lawyer for his attorney's fees.

For not being able to make all the requested refunds immediately, and for the three complaints, Mike found himself facing ''Rico Act'' criminal charges of mail fraud and ''organized crime''. To make a long story short, he received a five year jail term. Mike had never, in his worst nightmares, imagined this kind of woe could befall him. With tears in his eyes, he told us that most of the miracle kitchen knives sold up to ten years ago were still in service – as if being honest and selling an honest product was any defense!

Consider his situation: most of his problems could have been avoided if he had no records on file in his office. If anything over a month old was stored elsewhere, the government would have been able to seize at best, 8,000 current customer names – not a million. **All your outdated files should be periodically destroyed.** Those retained for possible future reference should be microfilmed if your budget will stand it, and the microfilms hidden, not at your home or office. It is exceedingly important that computerized information be regularly dumped from your hard disc. If it is necessary to keep computer files for possible future reference, these should be kept on discs or tapes at a secret place, **not your office nor your home.**

What is a suitable secret place? You could rent a garage in a nearby town, preferably in a different name, and keep old records and other such documents there. Don't tell anyone, especially your wife, girlfriend or employees the location, or even that such a place exists. For reasons discussed elsewhere, never leave any records at all stored with your own lawyer or accountant any more. Some towns have ''public storage'' facilities where you can rent the size of storage space you need, be it a small closet or warehouse that will hold five cars. For the most sensitive papers (like alternate identity documents), deeds to foreign property, Austrian bearer savings account passbooks *(sparbuchs),* rare coins, bearer securities and cash you should seriously consider a safe deposit box (certainly in a different name) in an entirely different country. Records at your home and your office are the logical first stop hunting grounds for your enemies – and they don't always go after ''the other guy'''. When your home or office is raided by latter-day Gestapo you'll be glad that your sensitive papers and valuables are safely and secretly filed elsewhere.

## PROPER DISPOSAL OF DOCUMENTS

One cannot stress how important it could be to dispose of personal or sensitive documents in such a way that they do not come back to haunt you. Most people keep receipts, cancelled checks and personal letters in a shoe box or other insecure place at home (or at the office) . . . When the time comes to dispose of them, they simply dump the documents in any wastebasket. A collection of receipts for a year or so, or a series of personal letters may paint an intimate portrait of one's life that could be used against you. Time and time again private investigators and government agents have mined precious information out of garbage cans to be used against people for blackmail, lawsuits – or even criminal prosecutions. When the time comes to dispose of such documents they should be shredded, burned, or cut up in small pieces. Dispose of them in **various** public or community garbage bins (not your private can) so it is impossible to identify you or put together an entire document from the scraps.

A friend of mine collected copies of *Penthouse Magazine* having articles about the Trilateral Commission in them. These were kept in his desk drawer at work. When he left the company, he also left behind five of these magazines. Later, he learned that when the new employer called his old boss for a reference, this former employer said, "He's OK if you want a guy who spends his working days looking at porno photos in sex magazines." The employer then related that my friend left a "huge trove" of girlie mags "hidden in his desk." As a result of this "exposure" my ultra-conservative friend was fired from his new job before he started! Thus, you see that even seemingly unimportant things left where others can find them may cause unexpected future problems. When you make a move or throw something out, be sure it can never be used against you. Destroy it absolutely! In another instance, an individual we knew simply dumped the unwanted "spring cleaning" debris from his apartment out on the street in plastic bags next to and not inside of the garbage cans as required by local ordinances. Some months later he got a police citation and a large bill for the offense of "dumping." It appears that among his papers and junk were several advertising flyers addressed to him. These were used by police to get his name and trace him to a new address!

If your privacy and freedom is important (and it should be!), we suggest you use a "pen-name" or alias wherever possible. Get into the habit of promptly shredding or destroying any letters, bank statements, correspondence, files or mailing labels on adverts or periodicals that arrive in the mail for you. Keep as few papers as possible. Every year or so, get rid of all un-needed records. When you dispose of any personal papers, shredding or burning is best.

# NEXT STEP: PUTTING THE PLAN INTO ACTION

Where and how to set up an offshore corporation or trust in the first place? A good first step is getting hold of the latest issue of *The Gibraltar Financial Services Handbook*, complete with laws and interesting articles. It also carries ads. Order from Diane Sloma, Time Off, PO Box 555, Gibraltar or telephone (+350) 79385

*The International Herald Tribune* has classified ads every day from a number of companies, most of them in Europe, which provide these services. You may phone up (first mistake), give your real name (second mistake), give the name you desire for your corporation or trust (on the phone – third mistake) and pay the whole thing by your credit card (fourth mistake), then arrange to have the incorporation documents mailed to your home or business address (fifth mistake).

Most of these brokers keep extensive records. They have to, since most of them are in highly bureaucratic places where they have to pay taxes. And at least a couple of them have, on occasion, been known to not only have frightfully good memories but also to be very helpful to investigators, lest their businesses be harassed.

The fact that most lawyers and financial services will open their files to the cops is an unfortunate fact of life but there is not a whole lot you can do about it. You have the option of either being very elusive when dealing with corporate agents or risk making yourself the future target of an investigation (or even blackmail). Sorry, but those are the facts. If you wish to deal "above-the-desk" use mail drops, anonymously obtained cashier's checks (and "pen-names").

There are, of course, brokers who do not advertise and charge higher prices in exchange for increased privacy. These are generally companies that will provide the exact same services as advertising brokers, but with the subtle and potentially crucial difference that they say they will destroy your file the second you have acknowledged receipt of your documents. We have tested a few of them and found them to be kindred spirits, even to the extent that a couple of them will insist on being paid in advance for making a phone call to discuss customer requirements. To a (wo)man, they display a reassuringly anarchistic attitude towards official and private investigators alike and will not hesitate to identify a customer as "a certain Mr Donald Duck, currently on a five-year back-packing trek of Nepal" if hard pressed. Prices are, on average, from 10-40 per cent above those normally charged – but then, privacy usually does take some kind of initial, cash outlay to put in place.

How do you use an offshore corporation to save on taxes? One time-honored tactic is to set up or take over a foreign corporation somewhere, then let this corporation engage in loss-making transactions with your primary business.

If tax authorities ever inquire why you have not made a (taxable) profit during the year in question, your accountant will explain you simply explain to them that, in fact, you did – but you also, highly unfortunately, made a large, well-documented extrordinary loss.

Should you wish to put a drain into your corporate coffers on a more constant basis, why not consider the *World Fax & Telex Handbook* swindles? Every day, thousands of businesses around the world receive "offers" for "free listings" in fax and telex handbooks that are rarely, if ever, published by anyone. With the letter is a request that a coupon be returned if the business is interested. What then happens, usually after a few weeks or months, is that the business receives a fairly large invoice for a listing that was never ordered in the first place! If you don't believe this happens, let us merely tell you that according to Interpol estimates, European businesses stupidly pay in excess of £60 million *per year* when honest-looking invoices arrive.

Some people have made this work for them. They quite simply incorporate their own "scams" and arrange to be "swindled" – by a company clandestinely owned and controlled by themselves. And so the world turns.

# Chapter 21

# THE PERFECT FUGITIVE

We have touched upon "getting lost" in other chapters and in other books, but for those who want to escape (or in the terms of the trade "skip out" on) obligations or problems, including criminal charges in their home country, here are a few more suggestions.

Look at your situation from the point of view of the person(s) seeking you: how much time and money do they have to spend on you? Assuming the worst case for you, an *unlimited budget and unlimited time,* from the point of view of the hunter, there are still only a few ways to find a skip:

The investigator can A) follow up leads and B) monitor past contacts.

## LEADS OR PAPER-TRAILS:

If you have spoken for years about buying a garlic farm in Acapulco, it is likely that someone would publish an ad seeking info about you in the Mexican English papers, perhaps with your photo in it. Someone might visit Acapulco and perhaps other resort towns in Mexico to ask questions in the English speaking hangouts. They might circularize all garlic growers associations in Mexico, and maybe even garlic-related concerns in the Spanish speaking world. But they can't get your photo in every paper worldwide, and they can't contact everyone. They can only expend reasonable sums and make reasonable efforts following the clues that you yourself have left behind.

You want to disappear, yet you always leave behind something that could be followed up. To divert the efforts of the posse give out false leads. Leave a wastebasket full of travel brochures with information on your dummy destination circled. Tell everyone you know that you are going to move to a place you will surely not be going. To have your pursuers waste the maximum amount of time, make your "dummy destination" some big city. Throw in clues about what you expect to be doing there, and hotels where you'll be staying. Whatever place you really intended to go, for starters, go somewhere totally different – a place you have picked the last instant at the airport – a place you have never mentioned to anyone. Obviously don't stay very long in any place that you traveled to directly from the hot spot. Hop on buses, trains and boats. Travel through several countries. *Don't go directly to your ultimate destination.* Wait a year or better, two years. By then your file should have cooled off and any inquiries that were made there will have been forgotten.

To discourage face/photo recognition, it is not necessary to go through anything as fancy as plastic surgery. Appearance can be changed by wearing glasses if you didn't before, and wearing contact lenses if you wore glasses. Facial hair, hair color, hair cuts all can drastically change your appearance. You can gain or lose weight. Dress in a different style. If you always wore a business suit, it's time for jeans and plain flannel. If you were casual, it's the time for a tie. But far more important than your appearance is simply choosing new hangouts in countries not likely to be frequented by your old circle of friends. If you are in a new environment with new contacts, you are unlikely to be recognized and reported to your enemies. If you are up to it, go to a place where you'll have to learn a new language. As the vast majority of fugitives stay in their old neighborhoods, and the balance go to similar places where their own language is spoken, the enemy is less likely to look for you and even less likely to find you in a totally foreign country. No harm in choosing a country that does not extradite to your old haunts and one that has generally poor diplomatic relations with your old country. British fugitives often holed up in Spain or South America, and lived quite openly due to the diplomatic chill that stopped most police co-operation for decades.

**NAME CHANGE, NEW PAPERWORK.** Obviously, you must change your name and get paperwork (passport and other ID) for a new identity without links to your past. As explained in the Passport Report, the best passport is NOT from the country where you'll actually be living. Border controls and passport checks are a common way people are tripped up. You must match your paperwork in terms of accent, age, physical description. In the home country, fugitives are usually caught because of informers or because they are arrested on other charges, usually traffic violations. Abroad, fugitives are taken into custody only if they get into local troubles. Even then, with good papers, their true identity is seldom discovered, even if they were front page news in their home country.

If you have a particular trade or profession, inquiries will be made of licensing authorities and other possible related contacts in the places you are thought likely to be seeking new employment. The same is true of hobbies. Suppose you were an avid collector of Nazi era stamps and never missed certain international stamp shows and conventions where these items were featured. You could be sure that a good investigator would look for you at these meets and perhaps even place an ad in your favorite magazines offering some item you were known to want. An irresistible deal would be the bait to bring you in. In California, the police simply sent a notice to the last known addresses of some 5,000 fugitives to the effect that they had won a pair of tickets to an important football game. Over one-third fell for this ploy and came (as required) in person to pick up their prize. Handcuffs, of course, were awarded.

If an unexpired magazine subscription is redirected, or an old bank account is transferred assume an investigator will find out your forwarding address as a result. Credit cards, auto, plane or boat re-registrations, are all leads with a paper trail to be followed up. Moral of story: cut out the paper trail! No clues left behind should lead to your present whereabouts.

**A Portable and Private Home Base** Your home, the place where you sleep should be very private – an address and telephone number not known to **anyone** from your past, and very few new friends. It should be a rented property (not owned) and furnished with things you can either carry with you or abandon. Don't even think about owning property. It will make you immobile and inflexible. You must be ready, willing and able to disappear without a trace within hours of any warnings or problems.

**Earning a Living** If you do not have substantial funds available at your destination, the biggest problem when you arrive in a new place will be earning a living. Turning a quick dishonest sheckel in anything but "the perfect crime," is the fastest way to become a target of local cops and forfeit your freedom. Foreigners are easily recognized and local cops will very often be able to make you tell whom you really are. So don't go into a life of crime in a foreign country. If you don't know the local rules of the game, it is far more likely you'll be caught abroad than at home.

Armed robbery anywhere is one of the surest ways to get nailed and probably killed. Burglary is considerably less risky but things often go awry during the intrusion and even if you get away with the loot, fences to whom stolen goods are sold will often betray new sellers as part of a deal with local police to service their regulars. White collar crimes like loan-point swindles, drug dealing, prostitution, and illegal gambling are all a step up, but will sooner or later lead to apprehension. Contract murder or violence for hire may seem romantic in the movies, but eventually, something goes wrong (usually a betrayal) and the heat is on again. Thus, the best advice for any fugitive is to live cleaner than a saint; to avoid all bad company, fights and possible confrontations. Don't even get into a minor argument over a parking place or the price of lunch. Earn money in a strictly legal field where you are unlikely to make anyone jealous or mad at you.

**GETTING A JOB WITHOUT PROPER PAPERS** is sometimes tough, but so-called "black economy" jobs have long included domestic service – Chauffeuring, personal services, household repairs and cleaning, restaurant and hotel work, day-labor. Often an employer who likes you will hire a lawyer at his own expense to get your papers in order. At a higher level, there are many "Portable Trades and Occupations" requiring no license, no permits, and they permit one to earn serious money. Scope is in the process of putting out an entire book on this subject. But buying and selling things is one obvious option.

**AVOID THE HUMAN TENDENCY TO SEEK CONSTANT IMPROVEMENT IN YOUR STATUS.** Be glad you are surviving and free. "If it works, don't fix it!" Don't make changes that could expose your past for the sake of a minor improvement in earnings or social status. Every time you get a new job or landlord there is the possibility of an investigation.

## PAST CONTACTS

Most otherwise-careful fugitives are traced or caught because of their contacts with old friends or relatives. Break all old ties and you increase your chances of survival to almost 100 per cent. The fluke chance of fate may still get you (see mistakes, below), but the tried and truest method of any skip tracer is to get information via an old friend or relative. Sometimes a clever investigator can make what appears to be a chance contact with say a parent or child. The investigator shows kindness and interest, and merely waits until the information he wants is blurted out. He may offer to act as a safe go-between for mail, messages or deliveries. Gaining your trust if he can't nab you where you are, he'll manoeuver you to a place where he has jurisdiction to put on the cuffs. Moral, don't trust any new contacts (or old ones either).

The best policy, as mentioned, is to cut all ties. If you can't do that, assume that even your nearest and dearest friends or relatives can't keep a secret (they can't) and that they will at best, unwittingly betray you (they will). Assume that every single phone conversation, fax, letter or other communication to past contacts will fall into enemy hands. Certainly not every letter will be intercepted, and not every phone conversation will be tapped, but you only need to make one mistake and the enemy only has to get lucky once. Thus, if your freedom is at stake, don't get overconfident nor sloppy.

You can communicate with a degree of security from a public phone, to a public phone. But do not identify yourself, give place names, or discuss anything suspicious. All international calls are recorded and can be retrieved by computers seeking certain words. Mail-drop operators are especially susceptible to local police pressures and also to bribery by private investigators. If your mail drop becomes known to the enemy, you should assume that all your letters and correspondence is monitored (opened, copied and read).

Assume that family events such as funerals, weddings, graduations, and especially emergency hospitalizations of your nearest and dearest will cause an investigator to lurk in wait on the chance that you will venture back into his happy hunting grounds. Don't depend on a disguise at such events, they will expect you to be dressed as a person of the opposite sex or something equally clever.

**MISTAKES AT THE NEW LOCATION.** When a fugitive settles into a new location, it is common to make new friends, find a new love and during a tender moment, spill the beans about the past. Obviously, this is a major mistake since jealousy or other powerful emotions may make last night's lover tomorrow's foe. Most acquaintances or romantic interests will accept almost any reasonable story you give them. It is best to fabricate a simple, low profile story that fits your accent and new lifestyle. If you have money and highbrow musical or intellectual interests, you could say you were a former school-teacher who inherited an estate from a rich but distant relative with no other heirs. As a result of this good fortune, you promptly retired to wherever you are. This is a better and more believable story than having won a lottery. It is certainly better than the truth – whatever that is. The more unusual or notorious you were back home, the more important it is to invent an ever-so-uninspiring past cover story. Even if you were something very ordinary, like a restaurant chef or car salesman, it is still better to change your past. A new contact might just happen to know someone in your field in your ex-home town. The biggest problem most people have is EGO. They can't let go of the status they had! They blab about who they were and where they used to live. Sooner or later someone at the new location contacts someone from the past, and then the jig is up. It is best to forget the past; burn all old diplomas, letters of recommendation, newspaper articles, photos with celebrities, and so on. Create a background cover story that is incredibly dull, simple and ordinary. Make up new credentials from unverifiable sources if you must. Then, stick to your new story. A fugitive's worst enemy is usually his own big mouth.

To review:

A)   Assume you have left behind clues and a paper trail to follow. Obfuscate this trail with false leads. Go to places and do things that you never thought of doing and have told no one about. When the heat is off, or at least died down a bit, then start making plans for settling down in your ultimate destination.

B)   Cut all past contacts. If you can't do this, eliminate risks by calling old friends only from public phones in foreign countries where you don't live. No one should know exactly where you live. Anyone who knows your phone number can find out where you live.

C)   Don't tell anyone in your new life about your past. Certainly don't encourage anyone to turn you in by telling them your secrets. Make yourself and your past as gray and uninteresting as possible to avoid becoming the subject of gossip.

# CHAPTER 22

# ITALY: TOP CHOICE PT HANGOUT

Italy is one of the best places for an English speaker to disappear and live the good life. Why do we single out Italy? Are other places just as good?

Italy is particularly good for a PT because it is one of the only countries in Europe where the local tax collectors still don't bother foreigners, even if they live in Italy (as tourists) full time. Further, people in general neither like nor co-operate with police or tax collectors. Aside from a spasm of terrorism by the Red Brigades (and bunch of leftist kids with bombs and machine guns), Italy is free from violence directed at low profile middle class tourist types. The Red Brigade people seem to have graduated and gone to work. There are still purse snatchings and jewelry grabs galore. If you park on a public street with a good stereo in your car, take it with you or it will not be there when you get back.

If you are known to be super-rich however, you or your kids may well be kidnapped by the Mafia, Camorra, or other organized crime gangs operating mostly in the south of Italy (especially Sicily and Naples). But convey the image of an ordinary guy and you'll find peace, both from the underworld and the government (which seems to be too often in their service).

Italy is a beautiful place. Great architecture, classical gardens. It's the only country where a redneck truck driver will cruise along listening to Pavarotti sing a classical aria at full volume while he sings along — knowing every word. He will cry real tears for Madame Butterfly, or some other heroine in an opera cassette tape he has heard a hundred times. Besides a general love of art and culture, the food is fresh, healthy, clean and tasty. It can be full of variety if you order something other than spaghetti. By the way, spaghetti is eaten as a starter, like soup, and never as a main course in Italy.

The workers and businesses are either over-regulated and highly taxed or government owned and in the latter case, completely inefficient and corrupt. As a result, up to 40 per cent of the Gross National Product of Italy is produced ''off the books.'' Most Italians are PTs in their own country and when one meets an interesting new friend, finding out what his occupation is may take longer than you will live. Everyone prosperous seems to be employed in ''this and that'' rather than anything specific.

The women, especially the younger ones, are pretty, and although nominally Catholic, are easy going when it comes to carnal sin. Of course we are talking about the northern half of Italy. In the South where there is a good deal of Arab blood in the shorter, wiry, dark skinned black haired people, they still have blood vendettas and shotgun weddings for tourists who mess with a local virgin, or major problems for those who insult another man's honor or religion (in the South again). Like the southern Spaniards and Greeks, who are all of a similar mind and race, these Italians are very emotional, and will do such things as self-flagellation and mutilation in connection with (Catholic) religious festivals. Now that the Catholics have lightened up on their rules, Italy's fastest-growing religion (in the South again) is Muslim fundamentalism. Some Italians want a strong hand without any doubt about what they are expected to do and believe. The South is also much poorer but if you have any sponsorship and manage to marry into and be accepted by an established family, there is an amazing friendliness and instant solidarity with the hundreds of cousins and kinsmen you will never find elsewhere.

Despite religious fervor and even fanatical behavior, the most unexpected thing to find in the North and South alike is a wonderful tolerance of the "strange and different" habits of foreigners. Foreigners who choose to have strange sexual lifestyles as paedophiles, nudists, homosexuals, lesbians, agnostics; those with multiple spouses or communal arrangements are left alone. In Spain or Switzerland, neighbors would make such a person's life unbearable. In Italy, it's live and let live. Naturally, local partners for otherwise forbidden sex must be taken from the prostitutes or outcast classes – not from the "good" families.

Learn the language and you will have a 300 per cent better time of it. Italy has a number of subsidized schools such as the Dante Allegheri in Rome, and the University Per Siena Stranieri in Perugia or Siena. You will get cheap meals, good teachers, great company, and you'll learn fluent Italian in about six months. Passable Italian is yours in three months. Incidentally, enroling in such a school gives you the advantage of official student status so that you can stay for nine months, instead of three, without being liable for tax and obtain temporary plates for an imported car for an extended period.

Before you go, you can read up on the different areas in an excellent magazine similar *to House and Garden* or the British *Country Life* – but with lots more ads.

## HOUSES FOR SALE AND RENT IN ITALY

*Intemationale Ville & Casaii,* Via Anton Giulio Bragaglia 33, 1000123 Roma, Italie. Att: Miss Giulia Trapani. Phone: Rome 06-378-9332 or 378-9282 Fax: 06-3789944 Credit cards accepted. Annual subscription (12 issues) $80US. This highly recommended magazine is similar to the American Previews Real Estate Magazine. Like Previews, it is full of ads and great aerial photos placed by wealthy Italians who want to sell their homes, apartments, castles, villas and chateaux, all over the world. This monthly glossy magazine is loaded with color photos of property for sale and rent. It also has articles and pictures about various regions of Italy. Here's an abundance of ads on places for sale and rent mainly in Italy, but also in France, Brazil, Paraguay – anywhere wealthy Italians own property. The ads are in English (!) making this an exceedingly useful publication for English speakers who may prefer not to do business with people in the normal Anglo-American orbit. Further, most of the deals have not been exposed to the English speaking market as this magazine is sold almost 100 per cent to Europeans. Italians are notorious tax avoiders and PTs. Thus, Italian real estate buyers and sellers may want to make deals involving straw men, gold bars, secret transfers, and dummy companies. Most advertisers and most wealthy Europeans these days speak English. The circulation manager will probably send you a sample issue by airmail if you offer to send them $20. Italy itself is one of the best countries for PTs to own property as the government does not try to collect income taxes from resident foreigners or vacation home owners who do not have any visible income or businesses in Italy.

# Chapter 23

# ESSENTIAL GADGETS AND PRIVACY PARAPHERNALIA

Maintain a list of the goods and gadgets that you either need for privacy purposes right now or that you envisage perhaps needing later.

Most important is information. You should keep not only this book within reach but actively request information, prices and specifications about the goods and services mentioned that may be applicable to your personal situation.

Here is what you should essentially have handy at all times:

1) An inventory of stationery and envelopes in various sizes, colors and shapes. Collect these from hotels, even if you just happen to stop by to ask for directions. Should you stumble over special stationery on your travels, get some and bring it back with you – you never know when it may come in handy. Scotch Magic Tape is indispensable to seal over envelopes whenever you mail anything anywhere, so stock up on it. Also keep an assortment of ballpoint and felt-tipped pens in different colours for various uses. A collection of official-looking stamps and seals ("Confidential", "This is a Certified Copy") is a nice touch.

2) A portable, battery operated telefax machine with at least one extra roll of paper. Store the fully charged fax with all paraphernalia (transformer, acoustic coupler etc.) in a briefcase or inconspicuous custom-made carrying case, ready to grab. Remember that a fax machine, no matter how small or primitive, will always double as a copier. As long as you have your fax with you, you needn't run around to find a Xerox machine.

3) Cash and, if possible, stamps from various countries of interest to you. Depending on your travel habits, keep a bit of cash from various countries in separate envelopes or cheap, nylon wallets with Velcro fastening. Coins may be kept separate by putting them in used film canisters with a label signifying the currency on the outside. If you have foreign phone cards that are not yet fully used up, keep them with your currency from the same country. An assortment of small bills from several countries is very handy if you suddenly need to have a letter remailed from a hotel, as previously explained.

4) A list, preferably coded, with details of your worldwide contacts: people, hotels, mail drops, bank accounts and credit cards (including emergency numbers you may need in case of credit card theft). If you lose your credit cards, call these numbers yourself, one by one. Do not subscribe to one of the services that will let you call one number and then they will take over, calling all card companies for you. This will leave a record of your entire plastic collection with someone else. A record only one person ought to know of – you.

5) A "dedicated travel bag" containing what you will need for a quick trip: essential toiletries plus a change of shirt and underwear; also ankle pouches and/or money belt for passport, cash, spare identity documents etc.

If you often travel by plane, include the following: eyeshades, earplugs, slippers (or pull-over socks) and an inflatable pillow; also one or two cans of a drink. If you suffer stress-related thirst in the taxi on your way to the airport, you will find that sipping even a very lukewarm can of Coke or a mini-brandy will calm you down considerably.

6) If your profession entails the use of a computer, invest in a portable, battery-powered model (preferably of the notebook variety, with an auto-park hard disk to prevent data loss). Consider also a portable, battery-powered printer. Canon has a line of ultra-slim, little bubble-jet wonders that will print your letters etc. even on an airplane without waking up the passenger next to you. Have spare disks and paper, and don't forget your printer cable. The good thing about a portable computer is that you may carry all your crucial files with you anywhere (preferably encrypted and accessible only by entering a password), eliminating or greatly reducing your need of paper files. Such records won't withstand a major attempt to decode them but will be safe in 99.9999 per cent of border crossings.

7) A mini-dictaphone, preferably with an optional, plug-in microphone with a cord at least two feet in length. One of these little recording marvels will enable you to make perfect tapes of phone calls and even face-to-face conversations for later verification if needed. An optional magnet will erase tapes completely after use – or erase sensitive material by putting the dictaphone in front of a radio, recording broadcast nonsense over both sides. A Olympic Pearlcorder is only $120.00. A particularly good and small microcasette recorder is the Olympus L200.

8) Have a collection of road and street maps for the states/countries and cities you either visit or plan on visiting. If travelling to a city or country for the first time, having laid out (and written down) directions *in advance* is preferable to asking your way at gas stations or the Hertz office. It will save you lots of time, aggravation, mileage and gas. File old maps carefully when you get home – you never know when you may have to make a surprise, return visit.

9) Phone books, both personal listings and Yellow Pages, from as many cities as possible. I do not suggest that you travel with 340 pounds of books, but merely that you studiously collect phone books from e.g. hotels on your travels, then bring them back home with you. They often come in handy.

10) Hotel and airline directories. This enables you to plan your itinerary down to the smallest detail without having to use the phone to check flight times, hotel details etc. Make sure that the directories you have are up to date and you will be able to give out the fax numbers of hotels where you will be staying before you even arrive. Very useful pocket guides to various countries and cities are available from both Michelin (the red ones) and, even better, the Wall Street Journal Guides to Business Travel, published with Fodor. With one of these, you will be able to arrange in advance a rendezvous at the best restaurant in a city you have never even been to.

In addition, get as much information together about subjects of present or future, potential interest to you as at all possible. Do it now! It will cost you but a few stamps and envelopes. Then organize the information you collect for quick and easy reference.

You need not invest in fancy file cabinets. Free cardboard boxes, such as those used for four bottles of booze, with home-made labels, will do nicely. Then arrange the information so you can swiftly remove sensitive stuff and leave innocent information in your home or office for investigators or snoops (or your spouse) to go through. Example, keep only one, indexed box with coded details and essential documents (POAs, for instance) pertaining to your automobile registration(s), offshore trusts and corporations, credit cards and bank accounts – in short, the stuff no one but yourself should know about. Consider keeping this information in a nearby storage facility, even if you need to refer to it frequently. Better yet. keep it only on a computer disk with an uninteresting label like "phonograph record inventory".

Then keep additional information in other boxes, depending on the type of information.

# A TRULY PAPERLESS OFFICE IS ALSO TRULY PORTABLE
You CAN cut down on all the paper that threatens to clutter your desk, let alone your life.

Let us give you a full-blown, prime example of how one may organize information and attain maximum portability. One good friend is a contingency fee lawyer – not an ambulance chaser, by any stretch of the imagination, but a truly cosmopolitan fellow who scurries around the globe, securing fair and honest verdicts for his (mostly corporate) clients in far and foreign places. And, of course, some pretty fat fees for himself.

Apart from his formidable brain (he's a member of the Channel Islands chapter of Mensa, with an IQ approaching 180), his physical equipment consists of the following: a custom-tailored, battery-powered notebook computer, a battery-powered, ultra-slim line bubble-jet printer and a portable (though not battery powered) scanner. A scanner is a device used to digitize a visual image, e.g. a document, and store the information in electronic form – on a hard disk, for instance. Basically, two versions exist, hand-held, not unlike a computer "mouse", that one may pass over the pages of a book or newspaper – and "flat-beds" that much resemble a small photocopier. The advantage of a flat-bed scanner is that it is not only capable of scanning a full-size piece of paper, but the material need only be placed *on top* of the scanner – not passed through it, as in the case of most fax machines. If you were to fax anyone a page from this book, for instance, you have to either rip out the page, make a photocopy before faxing – or use a flatbed scanner.

In any event, his notebook computer is built around a powerful 486-type processor, with an expensive, special co-processor for complex mathematical computations. This, in effect, means that he packs more computing power in his briefcase than you would find in a 5-ton "super-computer" a mere ten years ago. As this book goes to press, the 486 has become obsolete, replaced by even more powerful models.

Also built into the computer is a very large-capacity hard disk and a combined modem/faxcard. The former means that he can store information equivalent to about 600,000 closely typed pages (300 copies of this book) in "raw" form and about 200 times that – 12 million pages – once a special piece of packer software has been used to "compress" the data.

The combined modem/faxcard lets him communicate directly, not only with his secretary but also with any fax machine or computer on the globe, including databases containing vast amounts of legal documents and information. As soon as he has written a letter, he can either fax it at the press of a button – or make a printout to send it by mail. But there's more. Instead of studiously making back-up copies, he will hook up the computer to the phone in his hotel room and dial the dedicated phone number of a computer in his office, uploading the entire contents of all files that have been changed or altered since the last back-up procedure to his "back up" computer. Special software is used to compress the data before transmission, vastly cutting down on phone time and costs.

Every document pertaining to a particular case he is working on will immediately be scanned while on location and stored in his computer. Documents can be reviewed at leisure and then downloaded to his machine on the other side of the globe during the night. This means that he carries nary a piece of paper with him, anywhere. Everything he receives and needs is electronically stored on his hard disk and may be brought to the screen for examination in a split-second whenever he needs it. The man is a *pro*. Whenever he receives a document, he will either read it immediately or scan it into his computer for later study. To reduce bulk and avoid paper messes, he will then either immediately shred the material or mail it to his office where it will be if non-essential) or filed. In the case of legal documents, originals may later be needed as evidence at a trial. But if he suddenly finds that he needs to procure a copy of an important letter, he need merely print out a copy of the already scanned document on his portable bubble-jet printer. The copy will be hard to tell from the original, especially if transmitted by fax.

If you need a computer – and chances are that you either do, or soon will – then get equipment that will do the job. Better to buy too much computing power than just enough. As soon as you get started, you will quickly find yourself yearning for more power, more features, more options. Computing pays: If you computerize your files, you will soon find not only your efficiency tremendously increased, but also your creativity enhanced when your mind is not clouded about details or knowledge that you will have a heck of time trying to dig out from somewhere in the piles on your desk.

Your authors are devoted proponents of portable computing. If you are going to spend a night in a hotel, why not use the time to catch up on work rather than waste it on watching old movies?

What to get: a good quality computer, preferably movable and with the latest and most powerful processor. For ease of use, we like to run the user-friendly Microsoft ''Windows'' operating system. Nothing is simpler to learn. If you process much data, especially graphics, make sure that a mathematical co-processor is easy to install without other, costly alterations having to be made to accommodate it. Get a machine with at least one, 3½'' inch disk drive and an internal hard disk – that's simple enough. What is not so obvious is that since no data storage medium is 100 per cent safe, you should also plan ahead. Make back-up copies of your data on a fairly regular basis. The fastest and easiest way to do this is probably by way of a so-called *tape streamer* which will transfer a mirror-image of all the data in your machine onto a tape roughly the size of a VHS-C (compact) video casette. Cost for this potentially life-and-fortune-saving option is usually less than US $1,000. If possible, get a computer that will allow you to plug an external tape streamer directly into one of the ports of the back, without having to install special cards first – this is especially important for the tiny portable and notebook computers that usually have little or no room for additional, internal cards.

The next thing to do – and we hate to say this – is to *get a* brand new *expensive machine!* The reasoning behind this is that, unless you never move about, a cheap computer may prove next to impossible to have repaired, serviced or even upgraded except where you bought it. To illustrate, once upon a time, we flew into Oslo, Norway for a few weeks of sleuthing. Rented a car and found a hotel, hitting the phone for a few calls. Four hours later, we went out into the parking lot to get our suitcases and the laptop computer. Little did we notice that the temperature was freezing. That's normal in Norway in February. We returned to the suite, plugged in the computer, switched it on and – nothing happened! As it transpired, we had accidentally ruined the power supply unit by switching it on before letting it thaw. The computer was a nice, fairly cheap Taiwanese ''no-name'' model with great options But it lacked what turned out to be fundamental feature: serviceability! When we called a vendor in Stockholm, Sweden, we found that for starters they ''were not allowed'' to sell us a new power supply from a local brand machine to see if it would run our Chinese toy. To make the whole thing even more ''hilarious'', they did not have any spare power supplies in stock, knew nothing about whether our machine was distributed in Europe. As it happened, we wound up buying a cheap Polaroid camera, taking several detailed photographs of the machine and sending them by DHL to a friend in the States. He looked at the photos and compared them with various ads in five computer magazines before stumbling on a photo that bore a striking resemblance to our machine. A phone call to the US distributor turned out to be the solution, and after four unproductive days we were lucky to get a replacement power supply from the US outfit by DHL courier delivery.

The point of this little tale is that, especially with portable equipment, you should get a *brand-name machine* – not a little orphan Annie like the machine that ended up costing us many new white hairs. Get something that is serviceable wherever you go. Just because a machine sells briskly in London, England does it mean that anyone knows it (or has spare parts for it) in Paris, France, or Brisbane, Australia. Get a machine that is internationally known, even if it is much more expensive. IBM dealers are everywhere, but the portable models sold by ''Big Blue'' are not usually state-of-the-art any more. Toshiba is very high quality and sold in most countries, and even offers a ''World Guarantee Card'' when you get one of their models. Nice! Other good, fairly ''global'' names are Sharp (cheap but pretty good) and Compaq, which originally made its name selling portable equipment and only later added desktop models. The only discount brands we would consider are Acer and Dell.

As far as wordprocessing software is concerned, two good programs are called "Word Perfect" and "Word For Windows". You can even get a grammar and spell checker with the latter that calls your attention to differences between American, British, Canadian and Australian spelling. If you are a Brit trying to pose as an American in your letters and faxes, at least this will eliminate the risk of exposing yourself by making mistakes when spelling words like "defense"/"defence", "dispatcher"/"despatcher", "check/cheque", or even "asshole"/"arsehole" (American and British spelling, respectively).

If you *know* that you need a computer but have absolutely no idea whatsoever about what to get, read the evaluations in PC magazines or enlist the services of a friend who is a computer nut or if you have no such pals, get a professional computer consultant who will listen attentively and patiently as you lay out your requirements, then make the choice for you. A bit like an interior designer, spending other people's money, but with the difference that computers and software should be thought of as an *investment* in increased productivity and efficiency (and, ahem, privacy!)

## SELF-DEFENSE AND GUNS

Please take a deep breath and relax completely. Just like nuclear weapons, drugs, abortion, the IRS and porno movies, guns are a fact of life. Most people refuse to think rationally about these subjects, having been brainwashed by politicians peddling hystrical rhetoric.

In most countries, the ownership and uses of firearms are closely regulated. Even in the United States, buying a handgun is not as easy as it used to be before Big Government said "no". As humorist P.J. O'Rourke points out, the constitution of the United States asserts the right of all citizens to own and bear arms. Thus, one can merely wonder how it ever came to pass that US lawmakers got away scot-free prohibiting law-abiding, adult taxpayers from carrying firearms on their persons. These regulations don't stop most slum kids from packing a small arsenal.

Compared to the United States, the criminal use of guns is relatively rare in Europe (and, interestingly, in Canada). You may take a nightly stroll through the streets of Lisbon, Portugal or Vancouver, Canada and feel relatively safe. We would not recommend doing that very same thing in most large American cities these days.

However, interesting things have happened. A few years ago, the state of Florida passed a law that permitted citizens to carry *concealed* guns. The result? Practically overnight, the rate of armed muggings and robberies fell by close to 50 per cent. The reason, local muggers suddenly had good reason to fear that any "100-pound weakling" with glasses and carrying a briefcase might, in fact, be waiting for a thief to walk up to him with a switchblade. This could give weak-o a chance to indulge his secret Clint Eastwood dreams and whip out his concealed Uzi, while whispering "Go ahead, move, make my day".

As for you, personally, we suggest two things: one, that you carefully study local regulations concerning gun ownership and use in your locality. If the law permits you to have a gun, even if only a double barrelled shotgun, we suggest you get one for home defense. This is not as crazy as it sounds, things may turn extremely ugly at short notice (or none whatsoever), meaning that either you will be prepared to shoot – or you will get shot yourself. Many Americans who feel sure that a robber would never invade their home justify their ownership of one or more guns (to themselves as well as to others) with the line: Well, in case there's a war, or an earthquake, or a riot, or something . . . As the 1992 riots in south-central Los Angeles, California, all too clearly showed, it takes very little to set off a mob that may claim your property or your life if you are not prepared to give the rabble a whiff of grapeshot. This was Napolean's method of crowd control.

The *unlawful* ownership or use of any firearm carries severe penalties in most countries, ranging from huge fines to prison sentences. In other words, if you use a gun – even for self-defense – some laws say you cannot own in the first place. You may go to jail for saving your own life. In many instances, the ownership of a gun may turn out to be more of a liability than an asset as far as your freedom is concerned. One client owned a number of collector shotguns, a hobby which just happened to be a "serious" crime in his locality. When he banned his wife from their home for reasons of adultery and sued for divorce, she promptly took a taxi to the police station and told the local officials that her husband had "threatened her life" (he hadn't) and that their home was virtually overflowing with "handguns, submachineguns, ammunition and hand grenades" (which it wasn't). That was enough for the swat team to pay an immediate visit to the estranged husband, search the premises – and cart him off to jail for owning beautiful, hand-crafted artistically-engraved, sporting shotguns that had never been used. While he was busy biting the bars until his lawyer could get him sprung, his wife cleaned out the house and looted their joint bank and check accounts. His museum-quality gun collection was confiscated.

If you are looking for good, off-beat places to store just about anything, including guns, a number of books are available. These include titles like *How To Hide Anything, Secret Hiding Places* and *How To Bury Your Goods* (all from Eden Press, 11623 Slater "E", P.O. Box 8410, Fountain Valley, CA 92728, USA). While you're at it, once you've learned from them what you wanted it may be a brilliant idea to hide those books, too . . .

Scope has selected a range of the 50 most useful books for PTs. These are described and priced in the PT Booklist available from Scope free upon request.

So should you get a gun? If it is not illegal – or only "a little bit so" in your area, we suggest you do buy one. But again, be aware of local regulations. Owning a gun may be legal where you live but carrying it on your person or having it in the glove compartment of your car may not.

If you cannot legally obtain a handgun, check out the alternative, shotguns. Ownership of licenced shotguns generally is legal in the UK. For home defense, they are excellent. They also have an advantage over handguns, you do not need to be a very good shot in order to use one successfully – just point in the general direction of a housebreaker and pull the trigger (you may blast a hole in your wall as well as in your target, though). Shotguns come in two basic versions, double barrelled and pump-action. The former holds only two cartridges (one in each barrel) and is painstakingly slow to load, whereas pump-action shotguns have a capacity of being loaded with up to 12 cartridges at a time. You are probably familiar with the Winchester repeating rifle (pump action) from hundreds of cowboy and indian movies where the actors normally get 50 or 60 rounds off before stopping to reload the standard 12-shot model.

Even if no firearms are legally available in your state or country at all, you should still study the subject just a bit. The glossy, monthly US-magazine *Guns & Ammo* is well-written with much good information on the subject for beginners and advanced alike.

One day you may have to relocate to a less safe (or less governed) area of the world. Then you may find yourself in need of a weapon. Even if you have to have a hunters' license to buy a shotgun and don't wish to go to the trouble of getting one, visit the nearest gun dealer and inquire about local regulations. And then get him to show you a gun of the nature that is either most appealing to you – or the "least illegal" to own without a license. If you want to do a bit more thorough job, consider joining a local gun gathering even if only for a month or two. In most countries, this will enable you to (legally) practice on the club's shooting range, and to store a weapon in your home.

## TEACH YOURSELF DEFENSE

If you are on your way to a volatile, high-crime area (or are often visiting one) where handguns are *de rigeur* among the natives, you should learn how to use one at a gun club or a gun dealer. The absolutely best place to do this is in the US, where gun dealers in many states *are allowed to **rent** guns* of any description whatsoever to customers for use on a shooting range operated within the store itself. If you are not American, this makes for a nice and different vacation experience!

Pay a visit to the jolly people at "The Gun Store" on Tropicana Avenue in Las Vegas, Nevada. They sell naïve bumper stickers ("Don't shoot dope, shoot dope dealers – bring back the firing squad") but are otherwise quite relaxed and also extremely friendly. If you are not from Las Vegas they are not permitted to sell you guns – but they love tourists and will be happy to let you rent a gun and use their shooting range at a very nominal charge. Try out an Uzi submachinegun (aim low and lean in over it when shooting as it will kick upwards when on automatic fire), a .45 Automatic (hold correctly or the slide will slice your wrist to the bone) or a Smith & Wesson .357 Magnum. If you happen to be based somewhere in the Pacific Basin, you may also find gun shops across from the Nikko Hotel in Tumon Bay, Guam, with shooting ranges catering to (mostly Japanese) tourists. Guam is an island in Micronesia (North Pacific), a US territory about three hours flight south-east of Tokyo.

Two practical notes about gun practice: first, roll up your shirtsleeves when shooting as gun powder will get on your hands and wrists – it is sticky and hard to wash out. Number two, and much more seriously: do not carry a gun unless necessary. Police and criminals alike find it painfully easy to spot someone who is wearing a gun. Reason, gun-wearers will, without being aware of it, be doing what one officer terms walking 'The Walk'. In plain English, this means that if a gun is tucked in the waistband, the wearer will inadverdently – and constantly – touch his mid-stomach area both while walking, standing and seated. When walking with a gun in a shoulder holster, the arm opposite the gun – the one which would be used to bring it out – will be swinging *less* back and forth than the other arm.

The best non-government shooting ranges in the world are in Pattaya, Thailand where you can play with bazookas, mortars, cannons and tanks.

## OTHER SELF-DEFENSE DEVICES

Non-guns (starter guns, gas guns) are about as illegal to wear – or own, in some countries – as regular handguns. They look like the real McCoy but only make loud noises or spray teargas. Warning: they may still be deadly if pressed towards temple or forehead of target when firing. Do not play around with explosives.Even blanks can blind.

Stun guns are handheld devices, usually a black plastic box the size of two cigarette packs, with two protruding electrodes that will send anywhere from 35,000 to more than 100,000 volts through the body of an attacker when pressed against him and a little button is pushed. It will work through clothing but will *not* affect you even if attacker is touching or holding you.

These little wonders are standard issue for New York cops and are battery-operated, usually by a 9-volt Duracell battery (replaceable). Illegal in many countries for no good reason. Even though high-voltage, there is little amperage, obviously, with a 9-volt battery.

When electrodes are touching skin or tight-fitting clothing of an attacker and the button is pressed for one to four seconds, the jolt of electricity will upset the central nervous system, momentarily shocking ("stunning") and disorienting an attacker who may also lose his sense of direction and balance for up to five seconds – during which short time it is necessary to either escape or switch to hitting or kicking, preferably in groin or solar plexus area.

A sharp, low crackle is the only sound emitted when using a stun gun, which also comes in both police shield, baton and even flashlight variations – some even with optional alarm to summon help and stroboscopic light to disorient attacker. A specialty model is a briefcase with a hand-held radio transmitter which will allow you to zap anyone stealing and running off with it at up to a 100 feet distance (through electrodes hidden in the handle). Very neat and useful but also, unfortunately, pretty heavy due to both batteries and built-in receiver unit. If you don't mind the weight, it is a nice touch if you often carry valuables that you cannot afford to lose yet are unable to fit into suit or coat pockets.

Stun guns are primarily for intimidation. The best design has a wrist strap connected to a pin switch on the unit, so cannot be turned against the victim. Shomer-Tec, PO Box 2039, Bellingham,

Washington 98227, USA, telephone (206) 733-6214, fax (206) 676-5248, is a reliable source of stun guns

Tear gas (mace) comes in neat, little spray cans and is amazingly effective at very close range. The use of tear gas squirted in the eyes of an attacker will cause him to lose the power of sight for up to 15 minutes and causes pain and a high degree of discomfort. A good idea as long as the user does not manage to spray in his or her own eyes. Generally available in most places in the United States, they are illegal in some European countries (including England, which even prohibits the carrying of *loose pepper* for throwing in the eyes of an attacker!) but freely and legally available in others, e.g. Germany and France. Mace and CS are not the same. They are now being replaced by Oleoresin capsicum (OC), sometimes called pepper gas. Stockists include Shomer-Tec. You cannot normally carry such cans of gas on aircraft.

Or how about a light gun? This device looks like a slightly oversized flashlight with a large light bulb containing a special compound. It works very much like the flashlight (blitz) on a camera, only problem is you only get one try as the bulb must be replaced after each "exposure" and to some extent a toy to startle rather than to blind. Cheap and legal, also in England, costing £100 to £150 and available from the Leading Edge (Heathrow terminal three and various malls), The Sharper Image (US mail order with Swiss branch to service Europe) and CCS, 62 South Audley St, London W1, England – tel (+44) 71 629 0223, or Shomer-Tec (see above).

As for knives, unless you were brought up in an extremely bad neighborhood and know how to use a straight razor for more than shaving (and have the scars to prove it), forget knives. Pulling a knife on someone is considered an even more belligerent move than pulling a gun – the problem is that it is much more difficult to use a knife properly than a revolver or a pistol. If taken away from you by an attacker, expect very traumatic repercussions – and an awful lot of stitches. If undeterred, US-based Cold Steel Company offers an evil-looking little S.O.B. called "The Urban Skinner". With a very short, double edged blade it is designed to be held in a clenched fist with only the blade protruding between middle and forefinger. Think twice, then forget it.

**Others.**If you feel uneasy walking in a deserted parking lot late at night, you may derive some sense of security by holding a bundle of keys in your hand, being prepared to squeeze your fist tight around it and let the longest, thinnest key protrude from between either index and middle finger or between middle and ring finger. If you can get one good jab in the face of an attacker, a benign car key may actually cause some useful damage, giving you a chance to flee.

Unarmed self defense is a sensible thing to study. If you are going to do some exercise anyway (which may be a big "if") and if some sort of self defense class is being taught in your area, go for it ! Knowing just a few, rudimentary basics of judo or (much, much better) karate in one of its many forms (Shotokan, Taekwondo, Kyu-Ku-Shinkai, etc.) will make you feel two feet taller. If you are already working out and doing something about your physical well-being, either switch to or supplement your standard regime with karate practise. You need not go for the black belt. The posture and air of radiant self-assurance that you will get from just a few months of dedicated training will be evident from your body language. This may very well cause potential attackers to give up on the idea of bothering you and selecting a less uninviting victim.

Two notes of caution. Unless karate (most highly recommended) or judo classes are quite simply unavailable in your area, do not fall for those pathetic, unspecified, half-ass "self-defense" classes that generally offer nothing but a false sense of security. Also be aware that if you are threatened by a serious knife-artist or someone with a gun, do not be stupid. As my old karate teacher used to say: "A bullet will outspeed a fist any time, any place."

# Chapter 24

# PT PRIVACY HINTS

*PT – Possibility Thinker* – Barry Reid (c/o Eden Press, Box 8410, Fountain Valley, California 92728) says: "Privacy is more than an idea or desire. It is a quality of life which must be CREATED by the person who seeks to enjoy it". He gives the following privacy hints, listed alphabetically:

ACTUAL ADDRESS: If you have grown children, make it clear to them that they should never divulge your address to third parties. Ideally, parents should train their children never to give any information to strangers, period. Agents and investigators at the door should be told to "get a search warrant or go away!"

AGE: Once you are of legal age in your State, why should you always spout out your birthdate? Or give your correct age on questionnaires? Is it really the proper concern of the person asking it? If you are applying for retirement benefits, then it would seem necessary to "prove" that you are now eligible. But in the meantime, it's really no one's business but yours! Your date of birth is often a key number used in "tracking" you through data files. You will short-circuit lots of cross-referencing if you use a different birthdate. Or, when asked your age on a form, simply write "legal".

ARGUMENTS: Avoid arguments or run-ins with neighbors or co-workers. An old, unresolved grudge might be just the spark that sends an investigator to your new location. "Getting even" is a passion few people can resist. Ninety-five per cent of all people in jail were put there by ex-girlfriends, spouses, co-workers, partners, etc., five per cent by "clever police work". Be bland, run away from trouble. Let the other guy have the parking space or be ahead of you in line at the grocery check-out. It isn't worth the risk to assert your "rights".

ARRESTS: Records of arrests and convictions have been a vexing problem for hundreds of thousands of people. While an arrest record without an accompanying record of conviction is virtually meaningless, untold numbers of citizens have suffered all their lives, even if only mentally, because they were at one time arrested. We will not make light of arrest records, but for practical purposes, individuals who were arrested but never convicted should take the attitude that they were never arrested at all. So what? The police often make mistakes, don't they? Officially we still believe people are innocent until proven guilty. Practice that attitude, and concern over a mere arrest should vanish. A mere arrest, without a conviction, is (or at least should be) of no legal significance. Also see convictions.

AUTOMOBILE: Your privacy profile is related directly to the profile of the automobile you own. Avoid expensive luxury cars as well as the splashy, racy types. Drive an ordinary, middle-of-the-road four door sedan in a common color. Look dull. What's a common, boring color? Look around you and notice the cars that you'd never paid any attention to. Red cars are noticed more often by police. Your car should not be more than average for your neighborhood. DON'T use personalized license plates. DON'T have cute bumper stickers or slogans splattered all over the back of your car. Be anonymous. If you need to buy another car, arrange to pay cash to a private seller and delay registration as long as possible. Use a fictitous or company name for alternate title. Your bill of sale will be one proof of your identity.

AUTO REGISTRATIONS: It is often possible to trace a person's whereabouts through auto registrations. These are public records in many countries. If you move, and take your car with you, don't notify the motor vehicle people of your new address. Before fees must be paid again, either sell the car outright or arrange a dummy sale to an anonymous corporation name, a transaction that can often be done by mail. A two-stage dummy sale would be much safer still, especially if one of the transactions took place in another country (or, in the USA, in another state). Registering the car in the name of a business or even an offshore trust with a local maildrop address is a good possibility. The registration of other personal property, such as boats, trailers and airplanes can be handled similarly.

BACKGROUND STORY: Adopt the attitude that personal information such as your school background, national origin, interests, politics, family income, etc are NO ONE'S business but your own. And stick to it! Snooping will thereby become so difficult that suspicion will be cast more on the snooper than on you.

When faced with an overly-inquisitive person, have prepared a set of standard answers which you can deliver without discomfort or concern. Make them suitably vague, yet believable. If a questioner becomes truly obnoxious, give him some out-and-out lies, which, when "reported" in the right places, will make him look like the ass he really is. When asked how much money I have or earn, my standard answer is "Not enough". Name of spouse? "Honey". Phone? "Unlisted".

BANK ACCOUNTS: Every year or every two or three years, consider closing out all your bank accounts and starting with new banks. It does not matter if the new banks are just around the corner or in a different country. But we do recommend never having anything but a nominal pin money account in your home town. Serious money should be kept abroad in countries with bank secrecy. The accounts should be held in pen-names with your second identity created by documents like a banking passport. Hometown banks in your neighborhood are the first places an investigator looks to get leads and a paper trail can follow until he knows everything there is to know about you. What matters is that you BREAK the paper trail that government investigators and others can follow. To break a paper trail, you must withdraw funds in cash, and deposit in cash. If a lot of money is involved, it may be more convenient to purchase bearer securities or gold, common everywhere but in the USA.

CASH SAFETY: Maintain a stash of cash in a secure place in your home for emergencies or bargains that might come along. Many people now have safes in their homes, which is fine. If you plan to keep a lot of valuable items at home, consider having an ordinary safe in an "obvious" place such as your bedroom closet. Use this "decoy" safe for some old stock certificates, copies of deeds, and odds and ends of junk jewelry, coins and a bit of cash. But have another, VERY secure concealed safe in another part of the house or garage that is not nearly as obvious. Use this safe for your really valuable items. If you can handle the job you should install the safe yourself, in total secrecy. Pay cash for the safe and arrange your own delivery. Safe companies DO keep records, and installers remember where they installed, despite what they might tell you to the contrary.

CHECKING ACCOUNTS: Checking accounts should not be used for making sensitive purchases, such as guns, gold, subscriptions, donations, book orders, offshore companies, memberships or luxury items. If you want to maintain a checking account, use it only for day-to-day ordinary purposes, such as groceries and small purchases. Then use an OFFSHORE checking account in a safe tax haven with strict bank secrecy for major purchases. Never use asset transfers from your mother lode account in your home country. Preferably any serious accounts should be in a company name, trust or alias not linked to you. The signature should be different from your domestic one.

CHECK CASHING: For maximum privacy close all your checking and savings accounts, conducting your financial affairs with cash and money orders only. When you need to cash checks take them to the bank on which they were drawn. The bank will have to honor its own checks so long as you have acceptable ID. If the bank is out of the area, mail the check with instructions to convert it to a money order, a series of money orders or a cashier's check, less their charges. You could also "recycle" personal checks by endorsing them over to third parties (provided they are not "crossed" as is common practice in many European countries). If you don't mind the fees, there are a growing number of firms, known as "currency exchanges", that make a business of cashing checks, mostly in the United States. In Europe, this same object can sometimes be achieved more cheaply with a friendly mail drop or mail forwarding secretarial service. They will arrange for an account to be opened for you and checks arriving by mail to be deposited there. Use several mail drops for additional privacy. Get little or no mail at your home. Compartmentalize your activities. If you have several businesses or sources of income, don't mix them up or let your staff know anything about your other activities. In the USA, avoid cashing checks at the same bars. Bars that cash checks are the favorite stomping grounds of FBI agents and all the other snoops, for the simple reason that bars also attract the kinds of people they are looking for. Whenever there is a bank robbery, for example, the first place the FBI checks are all the bars in the vicinity. Bartenders are also known to have great memories . . .

CONVICTIONS: Records of convictions for both misdeameanors and felonies are kept on file with the police for the rest of your life (in most countries). We are only too anxious to point out, however, that once a person has served his time for a felony conviction, he should be restored to full civil rights, without qualification. Anything less than this is tantamount to a "life sentence" of second-class treatment and diminution of opportunities for ALL such convictions. Unfortunately, this is exactly the situation we have. In the USA, so-called "civil disability" laws prevent ex-felons from participating in many professions, even lowly ones like barber, landscaper, taxi driver and mortician. There is one professional area open to virtually all ex-cons, however: unless they have been convicted of treason or other "high crimes", they can still run for Congress, according to the US Constitution. It shouldn't be surprising that many ex-felons who are not Congressmen or Senators have chosen to take on new identities in order to escape the tyranny of non-judicial "life sentences".

CORDLESS TELEPHONES: In most countries, police do not need warrants to record (and presumably use as evidence) conversations heard over cordless telephones, since these phones are actually using the airwaves for transmitting the conversations, rather than wires, which are covered under the federal wiretap laws. Thus, be aware that cordless phones are much less secure. If you must speak on the phone, use a public phone to call a public phone and always vary the phone.

CORPORATIONS: Avoid incorporating your business locally. Corporations are "sitting ducks" for any and all government agencies, and are subject to all kinds of reporting requirements. In all countries, except tax havens, corporations have no rights to privacy – none. Corporations are even REQUIRED to keep records, at least in all the OECD member states. Use an offshore trust or an offshore company. Or, with straw men (nominee directors and shareholders) to front you. Use "collapsible" corporations that hold no real assets and can fold at moment's notice if required. [Author's note: We can refer you to people to set up offshore corporations and trusts. Send £200 minimum consultancy fee to Scope and outline your problems and goals].

CREDIT: Credit bureaux and department stores have credit files on you if you used them to buy on credit in the past. Investigators of all kinds have no trouble at all in obtaining these records. You would be much further ahead privacy-wise, and financially, if you simply quit using credit all together. In Europe, some banks will dispense with the requirement for information if you have a good-sized account with them. $25,000 is the amount required in Switzerland. In France, it is closer to $5,000.

CREDIT CARDS: If you want to continue using charge and credit cards, use them only for ordinary purchases, never for transactions which would reveal your special interests, your complete travel patterns or your lifestyle. Have as many you can switch between, leaving some idle for many months at a time. Also, have some, or better, all of your cards based offshore in tax havens with bank secrecy. As the transaction records are kept in a central place, do not assume your records are secure from a good investigator. But it helps blur things if your credit cards are in alternate identities or company names.

Always ask clerks for all the carbons from the invoice which is imprinted with your card's data at the time of purchase. Fast-moving thieves have gathered carbons from stores' trash bins and made untold millions in charges by telephone. Everything they needed to know about you and your card's account is right there in front of them – on the carbon. For these same reasons YOU shouldn't give out your credit card data over the telephone, either. A "credit survey" is a popular scam to get your card number and pin code and use it in an unauthorized matter.

CREDIT RECORDS: Request your credit records from any and all local credit bureaux in order to check for inaccuracies. Look especially for names of persons or businesses which have *requested* your credit file. If you do not know those individuals, and have never done business with them, there's a good chance they were "used" by an investigator for other than legitimate credit-granting purposes. If you find such items and/or inaccuracies, challenge them in writing, and the credit bureau will be obligated to re-verify them. If they cannot be re-verified, which happens more often than not, the reference MUST be removed from your records. But unless you challenge negative or inaccurate items in the record of your credit profile, they will remain. So-called "credit cleaners" have used this method with amazing success since they know many factors will prevent the credit bureau from being able to re-verify within the legal time limit. Most credit bureaux take the line of least resistance and agree to delete damaging data . . .

In America, the IRS and other government agencies have recently signed agreements with major credit reporting agencies to secure taxpayers' credit records if needed for audits, investigations, etc. According to the US Supreme Court, we have "no reasonable expectation of privacy" when our records are maintained by third parties – at least not in the USA.

DATA FILES: The practices of data-gathering and data-bank cross-referencing are very real threats to everyone's privacy. Once personal information is electronically stored it can take on a life of its own, going far beyond the control of the person who provided it originally, often to his detriment. All of this data, however, is keyed to the person's name, his Social Security number, and often his birthdate for access and use by data processors. If the name(s) and the number(s) don't match up, then the person "isn't there" and as far as the computer knows, doesn't exist. But don't feel entirely secure just because your account is in an alternate identity. Sometimes the alternate identity will be discovered because your best friend turns you in, or because your mail is monitored. Local tax authorities or creditors can seize any account or property within their jurisdiction. The only totally secure account we know of is the Austrian bearer savings account where no one, not even the bank, knows the identity of the holder. The best rule for asset protection is to keep your ass and your assets out of your home country.

DIVORCE: If a divorce situation requires you to gain some quick privacy, consider sharing an apartment or home with a complete stranger. Check the daily newspapers for classified ads under headings like "Rooms to Share", "Rentals to Share" or "Apartments to Share". All records relating to occupancy will already be in someone else's name, and you will be able to make arrangements with the current occupant only, not the landlord and all the utility companies. This room-mate arrangement is well-suited for someone wanting to put lots of "distance" from an ex-spouse, even if it is only a few miles away. A great way to "get lost" fast . . . usually in just one day.

EMPLOYMENT: Never tell neighbors where or for whom you work. Give them misleading information on this subject. If you are paid by check, DON'T deposit the paycheck in any account with your name on it. The best idea is to go to the bank on which it is drawn and cash it there. If you make a regular practice of this, avoid becoming familiar with any tellers or other bank personnel. Vary the times and days for visiting the bank, and go to different branches when possible. You can also use one of the commercial check-cashing services if one is available in your area. Their small charge is a fair price for privacy.

Negative employment records have been covered by using the name of another employer to cover the period during which the negative record came about. The "employer" has sometimes been a company name at a mail drop, which the employee uses to forward very satisfactory reports of his own past employment. Gaps in the work record, due to lay-off, firing or worse, have been covered in the same way. Clever users of this method have researched names of suitable companies which have since gone out of business, knowing that a personnel investigator will have to rely on the applicant's apparent honesty.

For local job references, a good trick is to ask, or pay, a mail drop secretary to give pertinent information about you right over the telephone. Provide the telephone number on the application.

ENVELOPES: Never mail postcards, always put them in an envelope. When sending cash in the mail, be sure someone can't see the banknotes by holding the envelope up to a light or spraying it with oil. First wrap in carbon paper or "school lunch" style aluminium foil.

Also learn from the Swiss banks. Many of them never use a postal meter as this always bears a number. Government employees are always allowed to look at the OUTSIDE of an envelope and even copy it, but in most countries, it is much more difficult to gain access to what is inside. Not only is it a more cumbersome task, laws and even national constitutions bar law enforcement officials from doing so. But foreign -origin mail always can be opened for "postal inspection". The legal reason is to prevent the entry of drugs or pornography. But we really know that most governments simply like to have control over their citizens and the drug suspicion just provides an excuse.

Furthermore, never put a return address on the envelope. If you feel you have to, do NOT put your name or even initial. The address itself is enough. Always use a mail drop address or a PO Box as a return address, *never* your real home address.

FINGERPRINTING: Avoid being fingerprinted. You never know when this information could be used against you. We suggest that you don't apply for jobs or licenses that require fingerprinting. We know of some very clever individuals, however, who have applied for bonding to obtain certain jobs who have used ordinary, commonly-available materials, notably the preparation "newskin" available at many pharmacies, to create entirely new sets of fingerprints which they then used for fingerprinting. Government would love to have everyone fingerprinted, of course. We feel that individual freedom from surveillance and stored records is worth going to some pains to avoid.

HOME DELIVERIES: Don't have milk or other items delivered to you on a regular schedule. The fewer people seen calling at your residence, the safer. Neighbors will often notice home deliveries. Your suppliers can prove to be fertile leads for snoops.

LANDLORDS: Never become overly friendly with a landlord. Hold up your end of any rental agreements, and he will undoubtedly be pleased to leave you completely alone. Landlords are VERY important sources of information for snoops, so consider every conversation with them the same as if you were talking with the FBI or the tax office. The big difference is that not being "under oath", you are perfectly free to lie, mislead, and deceive with impunity. If your landlord asks too many questions, he deserves some false lead answers. Remember, however, that if you burn him for the rent when you leave, you will gain not only an unpaid creditor, but also an enemy who will bend over twice to help skip tracers. The more you have to hide, the more privacy you want; the more honest you have to be. Leaving a trail of unpaid bills and unhappy creditors is a guaranteed way to have some investigator put together all the clues and fit you with a set of steel cuffs.

"LEGAL" ADDRESS: Set up a "legal" address somewhere else. We prefer in a TOTALLY DIFFERENT COUNTRY to the one we actually live in. A tax haven like Sark, Channel Islands (see Scope's *Channel Island Report*) that does not care about you is best. But as regular readers of *Mouse Monitor* know, even a once-reliable mail drop on a place like Sark can be penetrated by government agents. So trust no one completely and compartmentalize your activities and financial interests. TRY TO FIND A MAIL DROP THAT IS NOT OVERLY POPULAR OR WELL-PUBLICIZED. Scope's new book listing 1,200 mail drops worldwide will be good source of information. See also the Scope PT booklist. A commercial service is generally more dependable than a friend who handles things as an unpaid favor.

But perhaps you have a *reliable friend*. Second best is to have your legal address with a kindred spirit, such as in a trustworthy friend's closet, containing some misleading personal effects (books on subjects you have no interest in, and clothes a few sizes away from your own). Your friend, if ever questioned, could then point to something as proof that you WERE there, but that he hasn't heard much since you left for Afghanistan . . .

Use this "legal" address for all your ID you plan on using regularly, such as driver's license or new passports. Provide it also for your employer's records, if needed. In countries where the address is also displayed on the license, police like to ask extra questions of drivers whose licenses display only a post office box number. A street address lends stability and believability to your profile. The street address of your private mail drop and forwarding service could also serve as your "legal" address. Generally, in traffic violation situations, non-local people are treated better than locals. So try to have a non-local or even foreign driver's license for the places where you are frequently behind the wheel.

LEGAL NAME CHANGE: It is our right under the common law to change our names whenever and as often as we like, so long as our intent is not to defraud. Women who marry and adopt their husband's surname have always done this without realizing there never was any legal obligation to do so. The husband, if he wishes, can adopt the wife's surname, or both can take entirely new names. If you want to change your name legally, you can either request the change through a regular court procedure (every state has its official court procedures) or you can simply adopt any new name and begin using it openly. This is called the "use method" of changing names and it is legal in every English-speaking country we know of. You can have your driver's license reissued with the new name, and have all your other identification and official documents changed to the new name, too. You won't be able to have your birth certificate reissued, but that document isn't normally used for ID purposes anyway. A name change can give you lots of additional privacy.

Sometimes an official at the passport office or driving license bureau will insist on "proof" of the name change. Rather than arguing that proof is not necessary, give the bureau-rat the papers he wants, and he will give you the papers you want. Barry Reid has written a book called *Paper Trip* with a name change form included. It can be obtained from the author in California or Scope International.

LETTERS: Consider using a typewriter or computer/printer for all your correspondence. Use cheap white paper (no watermarks) that you purchase by the ream at a supermarket. Never sign anything, or use an illegible ultra-simple scrawl for a signature. On the new electronic models, a type-font like Courier or Helvetica is as common as dirt. The striking pressure will be the same for all letters and it is virtually impossible to prove (aside from fingerprints) that you are the source of any particular correspondence. For correspondence which you might regard as more sensitive, take the extra step of making a photocopy and sending it as the "original". Don't leave fingerprints on it or the envelope which also must be typed, preferably on a paste-on label. Then destroy the actual original. If you are ultra-paranoid, you might also use a foreign maildrop to remail your correspondence. Expat World in Singapore will do this for $1 per item, plus another $1 to cover postage. Remailing to a second country is starting to be a very common practice with Swiss bankers. Obviously, never include your actual home address in any correspondence.

LIVING HABITS: Don't be obvious in your living habits. If your spouse insists upon screaming and yelling at you, get a new spouse. Turn lights off at a decent hour, keep stereo music from annoying neighbors, don't place empty beer kegs on the front porch, and don't have pets that stray or annoy. Don't do major engine overhauls in the driveway, either. Don't annoy your neighbors and it is more likely they won't annoy you. A PT of our acquaintance spent 16 years in Switzerland before he was allowed to apply for citizenship and a passport. At the hearing, a neighbor showed up and testified that this chap frequently went shopping in his car, leaving the garage door open behind him for hours at a time. Inside the garage was the normal mess, which the neighbor testified was a disgrace that shouldn't have been exhibited in such a manner. Citizenship was denied for this complaint alone ! Look around. When in Rome, do as the Romans do.

LIVING TRUST: If you have considerable property and want to enjoy both the benefits of privacy and the elimination of probate hassles for your heirs, have your attorney set up a Leichtenstein Private Foundation. This works like the so-called "living trust". But be sure that it is always set up abroad. In effect, you are disposing of your property during your lifetime, but retaining use of it while you live. The tax man and your creditors get the short end of the stick when you depart this earth if you handle things right. Offshore trusts in tax havens are very good value for money, especially if kept secret. The cost is around $5,000 to set up and $5,000 per year to run. Obviously, if your assets or offshore business operations don't produce a pre-tax income of at least $25,000, there is no point in even thinking about such fancy legal entities. But to protect your assets from ex-wives and bogus lawsuits, not to mention confiscations and taxes, these things are to be considered along with secret accounts of various types. The trusts and foundations are particularly useful when you have heirs who are incompetent to take charge of and manage a substantial "offshore" inheritance without professional guidance.[Contact Scope to set up such vehicles].

MAILING LISTS: You can request that your name be taken off a mail order company's list. In America, you can also contact the Direct Mail Marketing Association (New York City) or Mail Preference Service (London) to have your name taken off most mailing lists. Increasingly, the IRS and other investigative agencies are renting and using use these highly refined mailing lists – legally! – to locate known buyers and readers whose actual or presumed lifestyle may be higher than the one presented for tax purposes.

MAIL ORDER: Always order merchandise by mail under your fictitious name. Pay with a money order, without putting your real name on it. Your receipt is proof enough, should it ever be needed. This practise will assure that your real name will not become part of some "hot list" of known mail buyers. Have all such mail go to your mail drop. Change mail drops every year or two.

MAIL TRACING: If a letter doesn't come back to a tracer/investigator because you kept it or chucked it, he may well try again with something more enticing, or even pay a personal visit. Tracing by mail is the cheapest route for snoopers, so be on the lookout for any mail you are not expecting or seems the slightest bit suspicious. An enticing free offer will often be the opening gambit in any effort to determine your whereabouts. *Watch your mail!* Send someone else to pick up registered or certified mail.

MEDICAL: Whenever you need the services of a physician, dentist, hospital, etc. consider going to a different country or come across as a non-local person in your own country. Then you can easily use an alias and an address other than where you actually live. PAY IN CASH. If you have to, recite – don't display – your "driver's license number" and Social Security number, making sure you slip up with one or two of the digits. Other data, which could be requested (such as employer, birthdate etc) could also be partially misleading. We've never heard of anyone being busted for giving this kind of information who also paid his bill. Fraud is fraud, but identity is YOUR business. Medical records are very definitely NOT confidential. How else would life and health insurance companies be able to decide so imperiously who "deserves" their coverage and at what rates? In many countries, the culprit here is the Medical Information Bureau (or a similar organization) which acts as a clearing-house for insurers or the state. Their records are filed by Social Security number. Medical records are essentially public records and as you may some day be in a lawsuit where your records will be used against you, it is best if only you know where the records are and under what name they are kept. So far you have no legal "duty" to tell the truth on any medical treatment or hospital forms.

MEMBERSHIPS: Cut your ties to all organizations, clubs, unions, lodges or other groups to which you belong. Don't make it obvious, however; just don't renew your memberships. Simply become a "lost" member. If any of your past associates ever ask, have a vague answer like you just don't have the time anymore, or that you are now into bingo . . .

MILITARY: If you had the misfortune of receiving a less-than-honorable discharge from the armed forces (thousands do so annually), all is not lost. First there are ways the discharge can be appealed and upgraded, and you could honestly inform those who need to know that your appeal is "in progress". Second, if it suits the circumstances, references to unfavorable military experience could be "covered" by claiming past employment or attendance at a foreign school during the periods in question. Clever users of school references have used the names of foreign universities in non-English speaking countries (i.e. the Ecole Polytechnique in Paris, France or something similar. A personnel director would rather accept your word that you attended, say, Heidelberg University than to have to draft a letter in German . . .). References to past employers can be based on companies now out of business, or on a letterhead company whose address is that of a mail forwarding service several thousand miles away.

MILITARY DRAFT: If conscription is a threat to your survival in your country, try to avoid it. One method is by moving abroad, or staying in your own country as a "foreign visitor". Try it. It is easier than you think, although you may at some point have to create a totally different identity complete with a foreign driver's license and a foreign passport.

MONEY ORDERS: Keep your name off money orders as the Payer. Use your fictitious name, the name of a prominent Socialist-oriented politician or just leave the line blank.

For almost all purposes, money orders can be considered untraceable since the issuing institutions file paid orders BY THEIR NUMBERS ONLY and not by any other criteria which might tend to reveal you or habits. People and businesses to whom you might remit money orders virtually never record this number, either. They are usually happy to be paid by money order and will consider it the same as cash. When investigators cannot spread out a paper record of all your financial transactions, as with your cancelled checks, you have taken an important step in reducing your financial profile. All tax evasion cases require a paper trail. Without a relatively-complete record of your income and outgoings, there is no case.

NEWSPAPERS: Don't subscribe to any local newspapers delivered by carriers. Buy what you need at a news rack. These cute kids have sometimes been "helpful" sources of information about customers' lifestyles.

OWNING REAL ESTATE: For privacy and mobility, it is always better to rent. But if you must own, keep your real estate investments so cheap or well mortgaged that you could walk away from a deal without feeling you have lost anything significant. If you must own, then hold title under either a co-operative relative's name or a fictitious one (individual or business) created especially for the purpose. Names of imaginary businesses (partnerships or corporations) work well here, as it is perfectly understandable and justifiable for a business (or a trust) to own real property. But be aware that in places like France or Spain, property without an individual owner is assessed for a much bigger annual real estate tax than those where the "true owner" is disclosed on public records. Also in the USA, foreign ownership behind a corporate name must be disclosed or there is a penalty. Real estate makes an owner a sitting duck for shyster lawyers and bureau-rats. It is generally not a thing for a PT. But as you know from our *Think Like A Tycoon*, if you are ready to settle in somewhere for a relatively long time (like five to ten years), it can be a hell of a way to make a lot of money.

PASSPORTS: When travelling abroad avoid using your passport for anything but the official business of entering and leaving. Passports are constant targets of theft.

For maximum privacy, consider getting a second (foreign) passport which your native country knows nothing about. This can be had legally in many countries where national, government sponsored programs make "instant citizens" out of foreign investors in return for a generous donation to the treasury coffers. Read *The Passport Report* and consult Scope for further information on how to acquire a second passport.

Barry Reid once rented a car in Costa Rica. The fine print made him 100 per cent responsible for any loss or damage to the car. There was no insurance available against what eventually happened. He got stuck in the middle of a river (they don't have many bridges in Costa Rica) and as the car started to float downstream with Reid in it, he bailed out. He made it back to San Jose, reported the incident to Avis and felt they should have warned him of the situation where he only narrowly escaped being eaten alive by piranha fish, crocodiles and water snakes. But instead of sympathy, he was told he couldn't leave the country until he had paid $28,000 for the beat-up old Ford that in the USA wouldn't have been worth $1,000. Border officials were always notified in such cases, which were common, and the poor suckers whose cars conked out in the jungle often were held prisoner until they settled up for the new car value. Fortunately, Reid had taken out the car using a driving license, passport and credit card where the name was different than on his spare alternate identity passport. He had this shipped to his hotel by Federal Express. He decided to cash in his return ticket (in the ''wrong'' name) once he was safely back in London and to buy a new ticket in the new name locally and use a different passport on leaving.

PERSONAL PROPERTY: If you ever need to move large amounts of personal property discreetly, and can't handle the job yourself, hire some ''no name'' movers from a city or two away, and have them put your goodies in public storage where only you control access. Weeks or months later, have another mover transfer the property to your new address. Plan this latter move for a time when there is the least chance of surveillance of the facility. Do it all at one time, and avoid intervening visits to ''check up'' on your stored items. If possible give misleading information about yourself and your plans to the storage agent. Pay in cash.

PETS: Pets can be a drag if you need to move in a hurry, so consider your situation carefully if you simply must have a kitty or a puppy dog. Most urban areas require the registering of certain kinds of animals, especially dogs. Avoid registering them as long as possible and lie a little bit when or if a canvassing inspector comes calling. The best pet is a fish you can eat in the event of being obliged to move.

POLICE: Try to avoid all contact with law enforcement people. They are like sponges whenever they deal with the public. They take in endless quantities of information whether you are the victim or the perpetrator. When they are approached by other investigators they enjoy spilling out all they know. To avoid trouble, always avoid cops. Don't try to ride subways for free and don't get parking tickets. Stay clean and invisible. If a fight breaks out in the bar where you are having a drink, try to exit even before the first punch is thrown. If someone insults you on the street (or anywhere else), smile sweetly and move out smartly.

POLITICS: Avoid membership or participation in political groups or other civic organizations. As a rule, these groups are filled with nosey individuals more willing than not to stab someone in the back if it suits their selfish purposes. Political groupies and ''club members'' in general can become your worst enemies just because you don't support the individual or proposition they feel strongly about.

POST OFFICE BOX: Use a post office box for receiving all your mail. You may have to give an address for obtaining the box, but once the box is yours, you can move as often as you want, and the post office will not care.

PRIVATE MAIL BOX: Even better than regular post office boxes are commercially-available, private mail boxes or maildrops. One of their good features is that you can use the street address of the firm as your own. Codes can be used, like ''Apartment G-7'', and you can usually telephone to see if any mail is waiting for you. Most private services will also take phone messages and forward your mail, even under different names and in cover envelopes. With two or more services your mail could be routed in and out of the country, or from one coast to the other, each mailing under yet a different code name.

Sometimes called ''mail drops'' or ''mail forwarding services'', these firms provide the privacy needed by people who simply don't want their mail seen or handled by spouses, employees, nosey neighbors or just plain thieves. Most of these independent operators also provide related services for the convenience of the privacy-seeker.

PROBATE: If you have recently become the beneficiary of a will or have an interest in an estate, notify the executor that further transactions are to be directed through your attorney (see ''Selling real estate''). Your address can then be kept from public records. Since many probate matters can drag on for years, your address or mail drop will have to be known to the executor. It shouldn't bother him that you wish a little privacy. If the estate in question is of great value to you, you would naturally want an attorney to look out for your interest, so this is the perfect excuse. Attorneys should be USED as an additional buffer where appropriate. This is especially true for IRS tax returns. You can, and should, have as the only address they can reach you at the address of your accountant or lawyer. If your lawyer doesn't go along, then use a foreign mail drop and a foreign lawyer – if you file at all. Remember, a good PT is totally invisible to all governments and his real name is never to be found on any record or computer.

PUBLIC RECORDS: Keep your name out of public records, such as business licenses, permits, tax accounts. Operate under a company name or use another person as a front. It's very easy to file ''Fictitious Name Statements'', usually with no ID at all. In the USA, newspapers that carry ''Legal Notices'' will provide all the paperwork and filing with the county recorder. The fee is usually $40 to $50, no questions asked.

Once you start a corporation, you can usually operate bank accounts forever, even if you fail to keep up annual payments on the corporation. The company can operate forever without paying anything, and there is usually no criminal penalty for non-filing as there is for individauls. It is legal. If your corporation is *de facto* not *de jure*, the only penalty is that you probably can't file a lawsuit in the corporation's name.

REGISTERED MAIL: By using either a private or a post office box, the only mail which will arrive at your residence will be the ''Occupant'' variety. Once you establish this pattern, make it a rule NEVER to sign for certified or registered mail. Tell the carrier that you are not the person named on the receipt, or that you believe so-and-so moved months ago, but you don't remember where . . . If he asks who YOU are, he's out of line. He will return the letter marked ''Unable to Deliver at this Address'', etc. Any suspicious or unfamiliar mail with your private address should simply be marked ''Unknown'', ''Deceased'', ''Return to Sender'' and deposited in a public mail box for return.

RENTING: Rent your apartment or house under a fictitious name. Pay rent and utilities with money orders or cash. Also consider the Hong Kong chop account, where you ''sign'' your checks with a little Chinese stamp! Of course, if you pay apartment rent in Kansas City with your Chinese chop account, this probably will defeat your main purpose of keeping a low profile. In a place like Singapore, where half the people have Hong Kong roots and similar accounts, the chop account would be just fine. Cash never has your name on it and money orders do not require your correct name. Or use any name for that matter. A few receipts in any fictitious name can be good enough to ''identify'' you should you ever be stopped without regular ID.

RESIDENCE: Take your name off your doorbell or mailbox and remove any name signs from your house. Keep the address of where you actually live a well-guarded secret. Never carry your actual address on you or in your car. Let only those who are trustworthy and need to know have your actual address. Remember, it is ex-lovers and close business associates who are the ones likely to cause you trouble – not casual acquaintances. A good PT changes addresses every six months.

SCHOOLS: If you do not want your children to attend public school, here are some alternatives:
1,    Find a suitable private school;.
2,    For our freedom fanatics, tell neighbors that you are tutoring the children at home;
3,    Tell the inquisitive truant officer you are a transient visitor from a country that has repealed compulsory attendance laws (many such countries actually exist);
4,    Move every three months or so to prevent rumors from spreading too far;
5,    Keep the children undercover during school hours and out of trouble at all times.

SELLING REAL ESTATE: When you want to sell your real estate, arrange to have an attorney handle the transaction by giving good instructions and the proper power of attorney. Attorneys can generally be counted on to follow their client's instructions, and are usually quite careful about divulging information to third parties (snoops). Short of a court order, your instructions will remain "privileged". He should have several good suggestions for disbursing the funds following the sale, such as a trust account, conversion to all cash, or some kind of offshore tax haven deposit (preferably "routed" through one or two transit countries). Don't be afraid to pay well for these services. If an investigator or other snoop were attempting to invade your privacy, they might ultimately put pressure on him. Since most attorneys enjoy a good battle of wits, protect yourself by keeping him on your side. Wealthy people have always used smart attorneys to cover their moves, and so can you.

SENSITIVE PURCHASES: Make all sensitive purchases with cash, money orders or cashier's checks. Keep receipts of the transactions if taxes or ownership are a consideration, they will be proof enough. Why make the job easy for snoops by channelling all your financial transactions into a neat, easily obtainable file at the bank? There are NO laws requiring you to maintain a personal checking account, period. If you have a checking account, it is best to have it abroad and use it only when absolutely necessary. Banks in many tax havens and elsewhere now have multi-currency accounts where you can switch currencies at any time and write checks in any currency. One such bank is the Jyske Bank of Copenhagen, Denmark.

SKIPPING: Some unscrupulous individuals have been known to skip out on creditors (not pay) by leaving forwarding addresses out of the country, an act which is often enough to make a creditor call off the hounds. Others have letters mailed FROM a foreign country stating that they do not intend to return, so "don't bother trying to collect", etc. Another old trick that sometimes works is writing "Deceased" on the envelope and dropping it in a public mailbox for return to the creditor. Any of these methods could also be used to end relationships other than credit. Obviously, if any serious money is involved, a collection agent will come calling personally at your last known address looking for clues. Likewise, if a spouse or ex-spouse knows you a fan of the Hill series of books, she may be able to figure out where you have gone. So if you have a serious reason to skip, it is best to take off for a place you have never even considered.

SOCIAL SECURITY NUMBERS: Begin creating more privacy for yourself by simply not giving out your Social Security Number (SSN) to ANYONE who is not entitled by law to have it. If you are applying for disability benefits, that's one matter but if you're applying for a homeowner's insurance, why should you? Just because someone asks you for your number is no reason for you to give it to them. Some people make a practice of giving out a fake number on such occasions, knowing that the recipient will NOT be able to verify it, and that the computer file to which it is ultimately sent might not know the difference either. In situations which demand your SSN ask to be shown the laws that require it. Increasingly the SSN is the reference file number used to link your records from one data file to another. You make the job of investigators and snoops all the easier by always giving out the same and/or correct number. Less co-operation leads to greater privacy.

SUBSCRIPTIONS: If you move, do not send in Change-of-Address forms to publishers of magazines or other periodicals, and certainly don't leave them at the local post office. Start over with new subscriptions at your new address (box number!!), under your fictitious name. Pay by money order, don't put your name on it.

TAXES: Sales taxes (called VAT, Value Added, EVA or TVA in Europe) can often be avoided by buying from friends, at swap meets, through classified ads, bartering or by mail from a different country (or in the USA, from out of state, sometimes). Also, in the USA, the states of Texas and Nevada do not have state income taxes. Enterprising individuals establish "residences" in these states to avoid paying taxes in other states. In Europe, the same can be said about Sark, Andorra and Monaco for instance.

As a general rule of thumb, the fewer records you generate and provide, the greater your privacy. Some employers gladly pay cash to avoid payroll paperwork. Their employees gain more money and extra privacy.

It is legally possible for many employees to become independent contractors for their present employers. The change would result in reduced paperwork, less money in taxes, and more privacy for both sides.

TELEPHONE: Your telephone number should be unlisted. If you can apply for service under a fictitious name, all the better. Your fictitious name can be recorded the same as businesses do for the "company names". You will be perfectly "legal", even though the telephone company billings will come to you under a name other than the one most people know you by. When you first apply or register for a phone, if you have an out-of-town visitor who is willing to show his passport and register on your behalf that is fine and you can return the favor in his home town. Or you can use a "Camouflage Passport" as ID. See *The Passport Report* on obtaining alternate identity.

TELEPHONE TRACING: If an investigator is trying to locate you by telephone he may invite you to call him person-to-person, collect. DON'T DO IT. Ignore the request no matter what the excuse is. He might tempt you with some pie-in-the-sky ruse, but what he's really after is your *location*. If you don't give yourself away in the conversation, he will simply call the operator back for the time and charges, and while she's at it, the location of the telephone originating the call. She will be only too happy to oblige. If the security of your location/residence is important, never make collect calls from a phone that is related to you in any way. If you make a "sensitive" phone call, do it from a pay phone or a co-operative person's phone, paying charges upon completion of the call.

TRAVEL: Clever travellers whose outstanding tax liens might hold them up at a national airport drive to a neighboring country and fly from there. Also, travellers to tax havens or offshore banking centers routinely take off from a country other than their own. Their return is routed the same way.

VISITORS: Be very careful about who comes to see you at your residence. Avoid unusual activities at your home that might spark the interest of neighbors. If what you do or the people with whom you must deal are "interesting", it might be best to arrange to meet them someplace else. In the underworld they say, "Keep your nest clean". Think ten times before inviting anyone to "come on up to my place". Once your home address or telephone number is known to a potential enemy your safety and privacy is lost – until you move. Best to keep where you sleep a secret from everyone except the one you sleep with.

# Chapter 25

# A FINAL WARNING

The only barriers that will protect you against your fellow man are those that you put in place by yourself. The world should be a fun place. But it is also a dangerous place unless you use common sense and take care not to invite trouble.

People of intelligence and people of means have always been harassed by lesser mortals. Today is no different. If the economic climate worsens, you will find it increasingly difficult to hold on to what is rightfully yours. You will find that living the life YOU want to live is, in some places, becoming illegal.

Prepare yourself for what the future may bring. If you fail to plan ahead and fail to put the relevant safeguards in place then it is all but certain that you will have regrets later. Do not wait until someone with a court order, a badge or a gun knocks on your door – it will be too late. When you suddenly find yourself in an extremely stressful situation presenting a clear and present danger to your money, your life or your freedom it is hard to think straight. It may be hard to depart the jurisdiction.

Thus, you should immediately start now to actively seek out information about tactics that may become appropriate in your own, personal situation. Take at least the first steps. If you suddenly find yourself in bankruptcy, divorce proceedings, under criminal investigation or similar, there will not be enough *time* for you to get the "missing pieces" and put them together. If you are married, don't tell your spouse everything. Get a mail drop and at least one bank account (preferably offshore) that she does not know about. Tomorrow you may find out that she is working with the enemy and that you need a quick, clean separation with your assets intact. Your spouse may suspect (or find out) that *you* are playing with girls your daughter's age or something else she disapproves of. She starts going through your files, monitoring your mail, bugging your phone etc. To get in a situation when someone in your own house starts monitoring you presents the worst jeopardy – not only are you unprepared for whatever someone else may think of doing to you, but if already under surveillance your adversary knows all your plans and secrets.

Be swift, quick and first and foremost – discreet. Then get cracking.

It is easy to take precautions. Exercise that good, old "due diligence" – that one stares with disbelief when yet another "tax evader" (= someone who asserts his right to keep the fruits of his own labor) or an "insider trader" (= someone guilty of committing the crime of doing his homework better than the rest of class) goes to jail for committing the "crime" of living his only life for himself – not for anyone else.

The well-to-do and capitalists of all stripes are very often smeared. But as reader Eugene Notkin says:

## WASN'T SCROOGE AN ECONOMIC HERO?

"No man is any worse off because another acquires wealth by trade, or the exercise of a profession; on the contrary, he cannot have acquired his wealth except by benefiting others to the extent of what they consider to be its value." said Thomas Huxley.

The Russian peasant, reports Hedrick Smith in his book *The New Russia*, will accept a low standard of living so long as his neighbors are no better off. This obsessive jealousy is the cornerstone of Russia's economic troubles. It is a mentality for failure. The Communists used this to build their empire. Unfortunately, the attitudes in some of the ex-Communist countries may not change for many years to come.

Americans, on the other hand, enjoy a lifestyle that Russians dream of and only the Communist elite can enjoy. But that relatively good life is at risk, not so much because of the socialist-minded politicians who control Washington, the leftist-liberal media and academia, but rather because the non-rich in America now, like the Russians, are thirsting for the blood of the rich. It's a hate that will rain down on the head of anyone with talent, creativity or wealth.

In Japan, artisans of great talent are deemed national treasures. America's greatest are wealthy entrepreneurs, people like H Ross Perot, an IBM salesman who created so much wealth out of nothing. Governments tend to create nothing out of something. Many tycoons are easy heroes to admire. But for the sake of my argument, let's use a fictional rich guy everyone can hate: C.M. Scrooge. "C", his adversaries say, is for cheap and "M" is for mean. Scrooge is a very wealthy American. His wealth passed the $100 million mark years ago. Beside his uncanny ability to make money, he is selfish, mean, niggardly and essentially friendless. Nobody will cry at his funeral.

He drives his employees to produce the most, yet he pays them minimally. Those who do business with him are pushed nearly to the breaking point. Even when business is prodigious, his employees get no Christmas bonus. If he has a charitable bone in his body, no one has yet seen it. Enough said about his faults.

What is most important for us to understand is that bad old C.M. Scrooge is truly a hero, perhaps not voluntarily but a hero nonetheless. It is his promotion of his own selfish interests which makes him so. He cannot help but make America a better place in which to live.

He employs people who might otherwise be on welfare, these people spend their earnings with the butcher, the baker and the candlestick maker. And on and on with a multiplier effect.

Scrooge grudgingly pays substantial taxes which help support a multitude of worthless government employees and other non-productive parasites who also use the butcher, the baker, etc.

He must be enriching the people with whom he does business, otherwise they would not buy or sell from him. His pay may be low, but some of the more talented workers will learn his secrets and become little scrooges.

He himself has his own butcher, baker and candlestick maker to pay. And as we said lots of unavoidable income taxes. Yet still, there are millions of dollars in discretionary income left over. *Whatever* he does with those millions, America will be a better place to live in whether he invests that money or spends it on luxuries.

And last but not least, Scrooge is not immortal. He will die one day. Then, *most* of what he owns will go to the government. His estate taxes, like his income taxes, will have a multiplier effect and every American who shares in the redistribution of his wealth will be somewhat better off.

All the Scrooges and H Ross Perots as well as all the other entrepreneurs are real heroes, vital to our way of life. They are why we live so much better than those under Communism. *Governments cannot replace* the free market's *functioning with anything nearly so efficient.*

Those who throw the Milkens and Helmsleys in jail would do well to ignore the leftist sink-the-rich propaganda and thank their lucky stars for these rich guys who make life in America what it is. It isn't OK to hate them or envy their wealth unless you want to kill the American Dream. Rather, be thankful for the multi-millionaires among us. They are more likely to be contributing to your wellbeing than detracting from it. Instead of saying "Someone should take it away from them", ask "How can I get where they are?"

# THE TEN PRIVACY TENETS

I)   Do not let anyone know where you actually live (= sleep). Preferably, you should actively mislead people about where you live.

II)  Do not let anybody get to know your personal details. Keep your name out of all government computers. Do not receive any packages or sensitive mail in your home.

III) Take care when using the telephone. Use codes in faxes and letters.

IV)  Do not have your vehicle registered in your own name. Consider having a spare set of wheels with license plates, insurance papers and so on in a pen name in a foreign country.

V)   Do not keep serious assets in either your home country, your official domicile nor in your actual country of habitation.

VI)  Do have a place besides your home (self storage, garage or similar) where you keep sensitive documents, an extra set of credit cards, spare cash and – if possible – spare identity papers.

VII) Do have at least one anonymous, offshore corporation that holds title to some assets, especially bank accounts. Offshore corporations should, in turn, be owned by a trust.

VIII) Do take pains to let foreign lawyers and bankers ''get to know you'' under an assumed name. These people may later be useful if you need professional references for your alternate identity. Or use a banking passport.

IX)  Do have a minimum of two maildrops. One near the country where you live and one in another far away country. Test maildrops periodically for efficiency and honesty.

X)   Do strive to persistently compartmentalize both your business and private affairs so that one slip-up does not set a ''domino effect'' in motion. Do not use a maildrop for your bank accounts and financial affairs. Have your bank hold all mail at its office.

Do not have any sensitive information or purchases forwarded from a maildrop to your home or business address – have it mailed either to a hotel in a different city or to a helpful, understanding friend. Hotels are better, by far. Yes, it is a tad more time-consuming – but why on Earth risk shooting yourself in the foot.

The only barriers that will protect you against your fellow man are those you put there yourself.

# Scope International Approved Consultancy Service...

# Your ultimate plan to achieve profit and protection

# INTERLINK CONSULTANCY SERVICES

## CONSULTANCY REQUEST FORM

In previous years, Bill Hill offered a consultancy service to his Report readers. He has now retired from active consulting but the demand continues to grow. Scope has decided not to become directly involved in consulting but we are able to recommend an excellent firm who can offer you clever, legal advice.

As a buyer of Scope's Special Reports, you are exclusively entitled to make use of our recommended professional consultancy service, Interlink. Obviously, we suggest you read our Reports first - where you will usually find the answers to your questions at a very low price - but, if you require specialist advice from professionals who have years of practical experience you need look no further than Interlink.

Scope recommends this firm because we have known the consultants who work with Interlink for many years. We are happy, therefore to refer you to them free of charge as we know that they are engaged in actually putting into effect the advice which they offer.

*Areas of Interlink's expertise include:* **1.** Second passports and travel documents. **2.** Sheltering your assets from prying eyes. **3.** Offshore structures and offshore banking. **4.** Discreet, confidential tax advice. **5.** Currencies / banking. **6.** Imaginative corporate advice. **7.** Diplomatic appointments. **8.** Aircraft and boat registration. **9.** Relocating yourself, your family and your business quickly and efficiently.

If any of the above areas interest you, please contact Interlink on the following fax number: **(Belgium) 32 2225 0573**.

The charge for an initial meeting at which you can discuss your requirements and which can take anything up to half a day, is £750 (US $1200).

This will cover any subsequent advice that you may require in order to achieve your goals. Your meeting will take place in one of several European capitals, within a carefully chosen location, at a time that suits both you and your consultant best.

A written consultation may also be obtained, but we suggest that a personal meeting may be more constructive for you, as questions often arise after receiving your initial answers. Written consultancies are £500/$750.

These are success fees and will only be retained if Interlink are able to provide viable solutions to your requests.

Please note that no consultancies will be given without receipt of the required fee, but if you wish to phone Scope to discuss your requirements, in outline only, in the first instance please call **44 1705 (UK 01705) 631751**.

**Name** _____

**Address** _____

_____

**Telephone** _____ **Fax** _____

**Post to INTERLINK SA**, St Georges House, 31A St Georges Street, Leyton, London, E10 5RH, UK

**1.** I would like a written/phone/fax consultancy and I enclose £500/US $750 (check, money order, traveler's check, or cash sent by registered post). Send a cashiers check/money order/cash if your questions are urgent – personal/corporate checks take up to two weeks to clear.

**2.** I would like a personal consultation and I enclose £750/US $1260 (check, money order traveler's check, or cash sent by registered post). Send a cashiers check/money order/cash if your questions are urgent – personal/corporate checks take up to two weeks to clear.

❏ I have enclosed details of my present situation and goals.

❏ I have enclosed the questions that I would like you to answer.

**NB No questions will be answered without a fee**

*Interlink SA will consider your requirements and send your letter to the ideal consultant or discuss the alternatives with you first.*

## PAYMENTS SHOULD BE MADE TO

# INTERLINK SA

# Other Special Reports Published by Scope International Ltd...

# PT 2 - THE PRACTICE
## FREEDOM AND PRIVACY TACTICS FOR THE NINETIES - AND BEYOND
## by Dr WG Hill

Now is the time to take proper precautions, says WG Hill, father of PT and the world's leading expert on personal tax havens, in this startling book. Contrary to the popular image projected by mainstream media and most governments, your taxes are shooting up and your personal freedom is being taken away, bit by bit. Anyone with a visible pocket will become a victim. The most dangerous place on earth is wherever you are. But in this hands-on guide to low profile and privacy, PT-style, WG Hill shows you how to regain your lost freedom. In more than 200 fact-filled pages, he teaches you the little-known tactics and techniques of living tax-free. For the first time ever in print, he gives away all his privacy secrets and shares with you unique insights on how to escape what he terms "the scam called government". This explosive volume deals with matters that no other books ever dared in a practical, hands-on manner. You will learn all the world's unknown ins and outs of getting, and keeping, a life free from problems, frustrations, harassment, extortion, lawsuits and the implications and ramifications of all of these - the works.

# DO YOU HAVE THE ESSENTIAL KNOWLEDGE FOR A FREE LIFE?

*Answer these simple questions to determine if you have the information and tools necessary for a rich life in complete freedom:*

- Do you know the world's six best ways to transfer cash across borders? Do you know how to triple your interest earnings and gain when currencies change?
- Do you have a collection of untraceable credit cards? Do you have foreign credit cards in a selection of names other than your own?
- Do you know the how-to of no-name bank accounts, where ID is not needed?
- Can you name the ten best low-profile mail tips? Do you have a dead drop?
- Do you own and operate at least one PT-PC in a foreign jurisdiction?
- Will you be able to keep your money safe despite the coming world tax-squad, the new OECD treaties and the international laws already in place? Do you know all the dangers of the nineties and beyond? Are you willing to run the risk of asset stripping and long jail sentences for a "crime" you did not even commit. A so-called crime invented by money-grabbing world governments?

If you answered " no" to one or more of these questions, please do not waste any time in getting *PT2*, the all-new tome for tax exiles and perpetual travelers. In five lengthy parts, WG Hill thoroughly covers ALL privacy and low profile questions. Even those you never dared ask. From such simple things as securing your cars or using all the unknown loopholes of air travel, Hill firmly moves on to invisible ink nineties style, crossing borders sans passports and what he calls the Ten Privacy Tenets. This book gives you the inside facts of essential low profile gadgets and some privacy paraphernalia that would probably be illegal if your government knew that they existed!

Contents also include... True, tried and tested: WG Hill's own telephone tactics, now with a PT shortlist for phone secrecy. .. All about mobile phones, Super Phones, add-on gadgets for your phones. . . How best to transmit faxes... The art of compartmentalizing your life... Never-before-told mail drop secrets... Secure communications... Also: The secret trust, onshore or offshore? And so much more. Stop Press. This volume now comes complete with a bonus - WG Hill s complete guide to banking worldwide, including some secret, super-safe havens for smart money only. Plus a complete course in bearer shares and bonds.

In his introduction, Dr WG Hill writes: This book is dedicated to showing people of intelligence how to stay FREE in every sense of the word While you may consider yourself free, chances are that you are not. The bad news is that even if you are currently living a fairly normal and happy life, events may conspire to turn against you and wind up stealing your money, your freedom - and ultimately, your life. Today, you are a sitting duck - unless you take precautions now. The good news, on the other hand, is that there are plenty of things that you may do yourself to thwart whatever dangers are likely to pop up - in advance, and with just a modicum of effort and expense. Are you ready for true, undiluted, unrestrained freedom in all personal and financial matters?

Do you believe that "an ounce of preparation is worth about a ton of cure"? If so, *PT2 - The Practice* is for you. If you are not content just "letting things happen" then it makes perfect sense to make sure that they don't - or, if they still do, that this will not be to your extreme disadvantage.

## ISBN 0 906619 40 8

*PT2* is available from Scope International Ltd, Forestside House, Forestside, Rowlands Castle, Hampshire PO9 6EE, UK.     Price - £60 UK Sterling (or equivalent) by credit card, cash, check or banker's draft. Price includes postage and packing and please allow 6-8 weeks for surface delivery outside UK. For quicker air mail service add £18 or equivalent (allow 3-4 weeks for delivery). Ordering details and order form are supplied on the last two pages of this Report.

Right now, in this sequel to *PT*, WG Hill gives you the low down, no-nonsense, straight facts about how to set up those seemingly elusive safeguards that may shield you in times of trouble. If you put the information in this book to practical use, you will find that you too can keep your money, your freedom and your life. And forever be home free, PT.

**REMEMBER:** Our no-nonsense money-back guarantee applies to all our publications.

# THE PASSPORT REPORT
## HOW TO LEGALLY OBTAIN A SECOND FOREIGN PASSPORT
## by Dr WG Hill

Why entrust your life and your freedom to any one government? Politicians regard you as an expendable national resource, but you do not "belong" to any one country if you hold several passports and nationalities.

A second passport ensures mobility. Millions of individuals would be alive today if they'd had second passports before the holocaust in Germany, and repression in Argentina, Cambodia, and many other countries.

Many countries now "sell" passports. The wording of their laws describe entrepreneurs, financial benefactors, treaty traders, and special investors in government loan paper as being welcome new citizens. But the bottom line is the same: put up from $10,000 to $100,000 and you can obtain an almost instant passport. Other countries offer instant citizenship if your ancestors were nationals, or if you are of a certain race or religion. Thailand if you are Buddhist, Israel if you are Jewish, Lebanon if you are a displaced Moslem. Almost anyone can qualify for a free passport, and anyone with about $15,000 can have a choice of several more. The Passport Report closely examines the official and unofficial channels in more than seventy countries.

Citizenship can now also be thought of as a business proposition. But what countries offer more advantages? What are the net costs? Taxes, investment opportunities, travel restrictions, financial privacy, social values and retirement are only a few valid considerations closely examined in this Special Report.

A Second passport could save your life, your money and your freedom. The key to this option is your new passport. Specifically, your 'second' passport, one which you can obtain from another country. This valuable document can open opportunities you never thought possible and provide 'back doors' that could literally save your life. The reason governments don't make it easy or publicize such options is that they are concerned with controlling and taxing their own citizens, and could regard popularization of second passport procural as a threat to 'national security'.

Most countries have well established, but little-known, procedures for issuing passports under circumstances which most observers would regard as loopholes. It is knowledge of these exceptions which allows intrepid individuals to obtain multiple foreign passports, and thus choose the countries most suitable for their purposes.

Put another way, it is perfectly legal to obtain several foreign passports so long as one knows the special rules for their issuance. It is of course legal and possible for citizens of most countries to obtain one or more passports without giving up their present citizenship, even though the widespread belief is that certain countries do not permit dual nationality. Yet approximately ten per cent of the populations of countries like South Africa and the United States of America legally hold dual nationality. How dual nationality can be obtained legally is fully explained. In many situations there is no residence requirement, and in a few places there is never even any need to visit.

*The Passport Report* is unquestionably the most detailed and comprehensive guide on this subject. Dozens of contact names and addresses of reliable passport providers and lawyers are given throughout the book.

Here is a brief overview of the contents of *The Passport Report:*
- The first step: psychological preparation.
- Should you hire a lawyer or agency?
- Those who advertise and claim to provide second passports.
- Instant passports and how to get them.
- Non-citizen passports; Diplomatic and service passports; Refugee passports; Provisional passports; Honorary passports.
- How to determine which passport suits you best.
- Over 70 countries examined in detail.
- Eliminating taxes with your second passport.
- Dual nationality: problems and benefits.
- Indirect routes ("back doors").
- Actual case histories detailing exactly how individuals went about securing second passports. Most informative.
- Documents usable in lieu of passports.

*This Report will open your eyes to many ideas and options you've never thought of before. More significantly, it will allow you to appraise realistically the risks of not having a second passport and not having assets properly placed to enable you to escape, survive and prosper. War, revolutions, political changes, personal economic reverses are all possible, if not inevitable at some time or another. Are you prepared?*

*The Passport Report* provides referrals to reliable lawyers, passport providers and specialists for assistance, and consultancies are available to all purchasers. You will find *The Passport Report* to be an invaluable guide.

With over 400 pages packed with unique and vital information, *The Passport Report* is the most detailed and useful book of its kind. Remember our extra-special guarantee applies if it does not deliver more usable and accurate information than any other Report on the same subject, at any price.

*The Passport Report* is available from Scope International Ltd. Price £60.00. See last two pages in this Report for ordering details.

### ISBN 0 906619 19 X

**Guarantee.** If you can find a better Report on the subject, we will not only refund your money but pay for the better Report as well.

# BANKING IN SILENCE
## by Dr WG Hill

*Why You Need To Create Your Own Bank Secrecy Immediately*
THE COMPLETE MANUAL ON HOW TO PROTECT YOUR MONEY

Do you know the US government within two years will be able to gain immediate access to any of your accounts? With their new multi-million dollar systems which are soon to be implemented they will be able to tap in and find out all your banking movements. This system will rapidly spread throughout the entire world.

YOU AND YOUR MONEY ARE IN DANGER. Fifty-six thousand investigations on individuals have taken place in the past three years resulting in thousands of innocent victims being jailed. People who are just trying to protect their own hard-earned money. The systems of the US government are becoming so advanced that in a few years this number will be increased ten fold. Unless you learn about what's going on and protect yourself from it you could be one of those victims.

The rules have changed. The power the US government is gaining is staggering. We are moving into a very different world. Your privacy has been blasted. You must learn the new ways and create your own bank secrecy NOW. Your money is not safe and your usual methods to safeguard it are probably illegal now. You could be jailed.

BEWARE OF THE NEW SYSTEM. The US has already implemented systems to monitor suspicious financial activities. But there is a new system coming to end any shred of banking privacy. The Mother of all databases. The AI/MPP system. It stands for *Artificial Intelligence, Massive Parallel Processing*. It will be able to perform *real-time monitoring of the entire US banking landscape*. It will be able to identify financial movements the minute they are carried out.

*The 388 million American bank accounts will be open for detailed scrutiny at the touch of a button.*

Big Brother will peer into your account any time he pleases. Before long this privacy violation will hit Europe and the rest of the world.

Nowhere is safe any more. No method is safe. *Banking in Silence* is not just a few ideas slapped together to maybe help you obtain a secret bank account. It is a strategic plan to avoid the bureaucrats. Knowledge is power and they are becoming invincible. You have to fight back. This Report is your weapon.

**HERE ARE SOME OF THE VALUABLE THINGS YOU WILL LEARN IN BANKING IN SILENCE:**

**• How politicians launder money**
   Learn the routes the corrupt politicians take to wash their dirty profits.
**• A How To guide to beat the bureaucrats**
   How to cut the paper trail. How to set up a fake paper trail. The warning signals to look out for if you are about to be stung.
**• The beauty of back-to-back loans**
   By borrowing against your own funds on deposit somewhere else, you can get your money back into the country without having to pay tax on it.
**• Where the smart money goes**
   The smart money stays away from the usual tax havens and goes where no tax man would dream of raising his red flag alarm. Countries that on their face value are high tax countries, but have certain deals and concessions that make them very appealing. Find out the secrets of France, Greece, Ireland, The Netherlands, and the Dutch Antilles.

*DISCOVER:*
   • Where you can open up a bank account without having to show ID.
   • How to transfer cash for free and without leaving a paper trail.
   • The advantages of secured credit cards and how to obtain them.
   • How to form your own anonymous company, free, without even incorporating.
   • A country where money laundering is a national habit.
   • The secrets of the Austrian Sparbuch.
*and much, much more . . .*

The information in this useful volume will provide you with the safety you need. This is the most important Report for PTs. It is packed with current up-to-date information. If you are scared, you have a right to be.

Even the banks are scared. Did you know that last year 487 US banks were under investigation for money laundering activities? The US government has gone too far. The power they have over so many countries is disconcerting. When will it stop? It's not going to. Privacy is being outlawed and now only outlaws will have privacy. We implore you to seize your copy of *Banking in Silence* TODAY and act on the wisdom of Dr Hill's infinite, practical advice. Please order on the form at the end of this Report.

**ISBN 0 906619 47 5**

# COMPUTER PRIVACY REPORT
## by Dr WG Hill

We are living in an Information Age. Technology is advancing at a dizzying rate. Don't be alarmed. In his most controversial Report yet, Dr WG Hill shows how you can make sure your private affairs stay private.

Computers are now a necessity for conducting business efficiently and effectively. They are becoming commonplace in the household too. But with the coming of computers, private business has ceased to be private. Through your checks and credit cards the government can now trace your physical whereabouts. It can keep better account of your financial transactions than you do... and all without having to secure a court-ordered warrant! In more and more countries counter measures, such as data encryption methods, are being outlawed.

*The Computer Privacy Report* will give you the latest Privacy Tools and PT techniques used by a handful of the world's leading business moguls. Dr Hill shares his electronic secrets for the first time.

Without the necessary safetyware to protect you, you could wake up one day soon to find yourself defenceless against a fully-computerized, totalitarian government. It will be able to read all your faxes and business letters BEFORE the intended recipient does. And this government will actually have the power to stop transmission if its Central Computer stumbles on key words and phrases deemed to be "suspicious". With supersystems watching your every move there is nowhere to hide. Every cent you make will be taxed and double-taxed to pay for spiralling layers of bureaucracy. What secrets have you got on your hard disk? What would happen if your computer fell into the wrong hands?

Complete privacy is still possible. With computers, your office need have no address, no staff, not even so much as a single desk. It exists in another dimension. Yet you can make real millions from it. You can be open 24 hours a day, 365 days a year. Customers and clients can reach you from all over the world by dialling a local access phone number. They pay you with untraceable electronic cash or with credit cards cleared by secretive banks. Your 'office' clears big money every day but doesn't have to pay taxes. And all legally! Why? Because your office is located in cyberspace. Here, in the world of bits and bytes, neither government nor taxes exist. Dr Hill shows how all of this is possible. Now you too can leave bureaucrats behind for ever!

Roam the globe electronically! This Report will tell you everything you need to know about the SECURE paperless office. You will learn how to use the ten most advanced privacy-protection tricks to keep this office safe from outsiders, con men, competitors, ex-wives and governments.

Dr Hill's new Report is the essential manual for anyone concerned about the future. As we speed towards the 21st century, data encryption is the key to maintaining privacy. With this knowledge, you will be able to keep your electronic affairs totally private.

*The Computer Privacy Report* is available from Scope International Ltd, Forestside House, Forestside, Rowlands Castle, Hampshire PO9 6EE, UK. Price - £60 (or equivalent) by credit card, cash, check or banker's draft.
Price includes postage and packing. Please allow 6-8 weeks for surface delivery outside the UK.
For quicker air mail service add £18 or equivalent (allow 3-4 weeks for delivery).
Ordering details and order form are supplied on the last two pages of this Report.

**ISBN 0 906619 50 5**

# THINK LIKE A TYCOON
## HOW TO MAKE A MILLION OR MORE IN THREE YEARS OR LESS!
## THE TIMELESS CLASSIC BEST SELLER
# by Dr WG Hill

Do you sincerely want to be rich without knocking yourself out? Do you want respect? Do you need love?

Discover the incredible secret that will bring you the happiness only money can buy.

You CAN become a millionaire in three years or less while, at the same time, having three times more fun out of life. Of course you are sceptical. So read on.

My name is WG Hill. I did not make my millions (like some authors) by writing books about things I have not done myself personally. Starting from scratch, without money, special skills, contacts or luck I founded eight totally unrelated part-time FUN businesses. I saw each of them earn me over a million pounds each in three years or less.

While I was making all this money, I managed to go to an average of five parties a week, plus two or three concerts, plays or movies. SEX! My love life didn't suffer either - as I had more "companionship" in a year than most men have in a lifetime. What was the sex-appeal secret of a grumpy, overweight, middle-aged bald guy with crooked teeth and thick glasses? I was doing things that appeared exciting and glamorous to women. I was the action and they came to me! There is no aphrodisiac that comes anywhere close to the appeal of MONEY and POWER!

When thousands of people depend upon you economically, some will fawn and dote upon your every word. Some try to gain your good will with gifts, sexual favors, bribes and offers you can't refuse. When you can refuse, you know that you have arrived. When you can go to the best restaurants in town with your friends and order anything you fancy without considering the price, when you can travel the world free as a bird, you know that you have ARRIVED! If you can live anywhere in the world, have any partners and friends you want, tell off or ignore government bureaucracy, union officials, politicians and former bosses, then you know that you have found FREEDOM !

*With money, everything else will fall into place. Try it!*

Would you trade your present life for what I have just described? Then read on. Years ago I was broke, physically in bad shape and seriously in debt. Then I found concealed in a window box a dusty tattered old book. It had been hidden in the summer cottage of my close friend's father. He was a very rich and powerful man. Later on I discovered that he owed his good fortune to his own discovery of this book many years earlier. Reading the timeless volume I discovered an amazing formula that every single super-rich person seems to have used to gain wealth. It was so incredibly easy to understand that I started to apply it within twenty-four hours. In six months I was a millionaire. I never had to work again.

In Chapter One I learned how to avoid mistakes that keep 94 per cent of the population just plodding along in a miserable rut - dissatisfied with everything. In Chapter Two I discovered how to "Think Like a Tycoon" - how to set and achieve goals. Chapter Three taught me how to achieve these goals quickly - not by moving up some corporate ladder for 30 years. I saw how to make things happen fast plus how to strike it very big in two or three years (at the most). Chapter Four taught me how to use credit and borrow unlimited funds (usually interest free) from bankers and investors. Another important chapter told me why all the "investments" I thought of as sound were really only for suckers.

Although the book I read was written two hundred years earlier, it was like Aladdin's magic lamp for me and changed my life dramatically. After two hours of reading I never earned less than a million a year for the next 30 years. Other millionaires went up and down like a yo-yo, but I just kept having more and more fun by getting richer and richer.

Now, after many adventures, at the age of 49, I have retired (in great comfort I might add) to write my memoirs. Before doing so I wanted to pass on to other ambitious lads the age-old secrets that made me a millionaire at the age of 24.

I took the original timeless secrets of wealth, transformed them into modern English and added my own experiences and a bit of humor. Then I tested out the formula on my best friend, a poverty stricken but talented jazz musician. Let's call my buddy "Warren Trumpet". For years my friend had been insisting that he sincerely wanted to be very rich. I gave him the manuscript of my book. In six months he was a millionaire. In two years more he had gross annual earnings of over FOUR MILLION DOLLARS. As a jazz musician, even with a hit record, *The Girl From Ipanema*, he had never earned more than twenty thousand a year. Warren never had much of an IQ. A highschool dropout, he used to read and write like a ten year old. But that didn't stop him from using my unpublished manuscript to become one of the richest men in the world.

*If he can do it, you can do it.*

Truth is, I'd like to give away these secrets. If everyone used them, the world would be a richer, more productive and happy place. But I learned from the SPCA (Society for Prevention of Cruelty to Animals) that if you give away a puppy dog, that dog is more likely to be mistreated and kicked around than if you SELL that same dog for $100.

I want to give you respect, value and seriously apply this incredible, exciting formula. I will not give it to you for free. On the back page is the order form you must complete and send to Scope International now, if you want to get a copy of my sumptuously bound, gold blocked, limited edition of *Think Like A Tycoon*. How to Make a Million or More in Three Years or Less. (Personal registered copy, not for resale).

**ISBN 0 906619 30 0**

# THE WEALTH REPORT
## CAPITAL PRESERVATION THROUGH GLOBAL INVESTING
## by Adam Starchild

Investing globally is one of the most successful ways to accomplish capital preservation and growth. In *The Wealth Report*, Adam Starchild reveals how you can create an ultimate global portfolio of investments to hedge against inflation, taxes, confiscations, market fluctuations, currency devaluations, economic and political turmoil...

Starchild reveals the little-known investment secrets that he has been giving to his clients for the past few decades. He concentrates not only on preserving your wealth effectively, but also on building it safely and securely. His recommendations are not high-flying investment tips, but rather solid, conservative recommendations that over time will help build a healthy nestegg for you.

*You will learn how to build a secret stash of cash that*
- You can use at any time.
- Is tax-free and seizure proof.
- Pays competitive dividends and interest.
- Has no government reporting requirements.
  *(even for Americans!).*

In fact if you had put $10,000 each year into this investment for the last twenty years you would have $590,697 today! William Bonner, President of Agora Publications (one of the largest financial publishers in the world) called it *"The Ultimate No-Risk Investment"*. And Doug Casey, the editor of *Crisis Investing* newsletter, said *"Do this immediately, even if you do nothing else . . ."*

*You will also discover:*
- How and why you should manage your portfolio from a Swiss base.
- Swiss bank and portfolio management contacts that can get you started on a global path to wealth.
- How and why you should invest in offshore mutual funds (Starchild includes a highly respected offshore fund manager that can provide you with a wide range of funds at lower than usual costs).
- Why gold is considered by many smart investors as "the ultimate asset".
- How to invest in a rare and precious metal even more expensive than gold and with great investor potential!
- The various methods of investing in gold, silver and platinum (including accumulation programs - which you can start with as little as $100 and make periodic purchases thereafter on a regular basis).
- How and where to best form an offshore trust in order to provide tax and creditor protection for your investments.
- How to invest tax-free in the US.

Everything you need to get yourself started on a global path to a secure fortune is in *The Wealth Report*. Starchild's techniques have been used by many of the world's wealthiest people for decades, including presidents, kings, Arab sheikhs . . . And now for the first time they are available to you. They have been tested and proven over time. You will not find a more safe and sure path to financial security than that mapped out for you in this unique work!

### ISBN 0 906619 56 4

*The Wealth Report* is available from Scope International Ltd, Forestside House, Forestside, Rowlands Castle, Hampshire PO9 6EE, UK. Price - £60 UK Sterling (or equivalent) by credit card, cash, check or banker's draft.
Price includes postage and packing, and please allow 6-8 weeks for surface delivery outside UK.
For quicker air mail service add £18 or equivalent (allow 3-4 weeks for delivery).
Ordering details and order form are supplied on the last two pages of this Report.

**REMEMBER:** Our no-nonsense money-back guarantee applies to all our publications.

# THE TAX-FREE CAR REPORT
## DISCOVER HOW TO OWN A LUXURY CAR TAX FREE, USE IT FOR A YEAR OR SO AND THEN SELL IT FOR A PROFIT. AND NOT JUST ONCE BUT AGAIN AND AGAIN!
## by Dr W G Hill

All the information to get you on the road can be found in *The Tax-Free Car Report*. This is your chance to own the car of your dreams tax free. People are doing it everyday. However, these amazing deals are not publicized. This information is not available to the general public.

**You will discover:** • where cars can be bought tax-free at the lowest factory-list prices in the world.
• the longest lasting tax-free license plates. • the nine golden rules of international car ownership.
• little-known secrets about tax-free plates. • the premier source for right-hand drive vehicles.
• everything you need to know about permanent registration.

The last few years have seen many countries trying to corner this lucrative market. It was once a European phenomenon, but now the potential buyer has the global market at his feet. The United States in particular are offering amazing deals on quality luxury cars. There are also excellent deals to be made in the Middle East and the South Pacific. The author, Dr Hill, discusses 14 countries in detail. Over 110 dealers names, addresses and telephone numbers are listed to help you on your way. Dr Hill discusses the entire process of buying tax free.

*The Tax-Free Car Report* **will show you:** • how to approach the dealers • what happens after purchase
• everything you should double check at point of sale • the necessary insurance arrangements
• where the car should be registered, *and* • how to re-sell the car at a later date.

During the past twenty years the author, Dr WG Hill, has personally owned a Rolls, Ferrari, and several Mercedes all tax-free. Let him show you how to save up to 50 per cent off the retail price. Learn everything you need to know to enjoy trouble-free, permanently tax-free international motoring. Those who take Dr Hill's advice are guaranteed to succeed.

**Tax-Free Plates** • where you can obtain the longest lasting tax-free plates
• ways to get new tourist plates in other countries within Europe without having to import the car into your home country
• when to buy so you can maximize the life out of your plates.

**Driving Licenses:** If you have to drive a car, you need a license. WG Hill has found that many people run into problems where these documents are concerned An entire section in *The Tax-Free Car Report* discusses options and alternatives available:
• Licenses from the UK • International driving permits and licenses • US drivers licenses • Isle of Man licenses
• The fast lane to a license

If you haven't got one for whatever reason, or you need another option then you need the situation dealt with quickly and with as little fuss and expense as possible. The company Hill recommends seem to have a formula designed for every conceivable eventuality.

**Permanent Tax-Free Registration:** The problem with tax-free cars has been that the drivers of such vehicles are not really sure what their legal position is. There is a whole section devoted to this subject. Hill explains that it is essential that you know your rights and fully understand the legal position of your actions.

In the past many have failed when purchasing their first tax-free car. Why? The area of permanent registration tends to be their stumbling block. Some have ended up driving a car on expired temporary tax-free plates which they can't renew.

*The Tax-Free Car Report* outlines common problems that first timers fall into and advises how to prepare for the future. The author's experiences ensure you will not find yourself under the scrutiny of policemen, bureaucrats and taxmen.

In *The Tax-Free Car Report*, Dr Hill discusses the necessary registration requirements country by country. He tells you what problems may be encountered, what to do, where to go and how to get around it.

*Also outlined:* • the documents required • how to apply • what criteria you need to qualify the costs
• how long each option is valid for, • what renewal options are available.

*Little-known permanent registration alternatives revealed:*
• the South Pacific option • the United States - State of New York • the South American option.

*Under the International Law Agreement, a car officially and legally registered in any country of the world can drive and stay in any other country for up to 180 days without the need for importation and payment of any taxes or fines.*

*Recommendation* – Dr Hill also recommends several companies who handle all the paperwork and communication regarding permanent registration.

### ISBN 0 906619 56 4

The Tax-Free Car Report is available from Scope International Ltd, Forestside House, Forestside, Rowlands Castle, Hampshire PO9 6EE, UK. Price - £60 UK Sterling (or equivalent) by credit card, cash, check or banker's draft.
Price includes postage and packing, and please allow 6-8 weeks for surface delivery outside UK.
For quicker air mail service add £18 or equivalent (allow 3-4 weeks for delivery).
Ordering details and order form are supplied on the last two pages of this Report.
**REMEMBER:** Our no-nonsense money-back guarantee applies to all our publications.

# THE CHANNEL ISLAND REPORT
## HOW TO ESTABLISH AND MAINTAIN A TAX HAVEN DOMICILE ON A CHANNEL ISLAND (UK) FOR £50 PER MONTH
## by Scope International

A businessman, weary of government red tape, lawsuits and domestic problems, arranged to sell his business and investments for a sizeable sum. If he could keep the proceeds he would enjoy financial security with a very comfortable income. But if he had to pay all the required taxes his economic base would be cut in half.

Being both ethical and cautious, he rejected the appeals of tax shelter promoters and schemes that sounded fraudulent. "If only there was a way to keep my hard-earned money working for me instead of seeing it taken away." So he endeavored to determine whether establishing a tax haven domicile was a good idea for him, and how much time one actually had to spend at such a residence.

### 1. IS MOVING TO A TAX HAVEN LEGAL?

Generally, yes. Almost all countries permit the free movement of their citizens. In peacetime, most nations also permit assets to be transferred abroad. But more importantly we discovered this basic principle of international law: *A government has jurisdiction (power to control) only over those people and property within its frontiers.* Once someone removes himself and the family jewels from a particular country, for all practical purposes that jurisdiction ends. (Exceptions are deportation and extradition for serious crimes).

### 2. DOES IT MAKE ECONOMIC SENSE?

For this particular client, yes indeed! We concluded that anyone who enjoyed traveling a few months a year and who was not absolutely tied down to a nine-to-five job in a high-tax country should at least consider tax havens. A mere change of legal address could typically double the income of retirees. In most cases the tax savings alone could finance all travel and living expenses. Greater financial freedom and flexibility are also factors to consider.

### 3. HOW MUCH TIME MUST ONE SPEND AT A TAX HAVEN?

You don't have to live there. Domicile is normally a question of personal intention, not physical presence. Thus, a person who calls a certain place "home" can travel elsewhere for years, but his domicile will stay the same. True, some tax havens, notably Monaco, have fairly strict rules to the effect that to retain a resident's card one must actually be physically present six months a year. But many other tax havens don't issue residence cards or even keep track of their citizens. A domicile with this sort of informal approach is to be preferred. Residence is proved by such things as a mailing address, telephone listing, apartment lease, or house deed, etc. This particular tax haven is 100 per cent English-speaking, and has far tougher bank secrecy laws than Switzerland.

The government is perhaps the least intrusive of any nation on earth, and is a protectorate of a major power. It is politically stable, located within commuting distance of Paris and London. It is totally free of violent crimes and fraud. Communications are excellent. This Report contains all the information you will need to know about establishing your own tax haven domicile in this unique location.

### ISBN 0 906619 38 6

*The Channel Island Report* is available from Scope International Ltd, Forestside House, Forestside, Rowlands Castle, Hampshire PO9 6EE, UK. Price - £60 UK Sterling (or equivalent) by credit card, cash, check or banker's draft.
Price includes postage and packing, and please allow 6-8 weeks for surface delivery outside UK.
For quicker air mail service add £18 or equivalent (allow 3-4 weeks for delivery).
Ordering details and order form are supplied on the last two pages of this Report.

**REMEMBER:** Consultations with our Channel Island specialist are available to all purchasers and our no-nonsense money-back guarantee applies to all our publications.

*Two Reports in one volume - Double value for money!*

# THE ANDORRA AND SECRET ENCLAVES REPORT
## UNDISCOVERED FISCAL PARADISES OF THE PYRENEES

# THE GIBRALTAR REPORT
## IDEAL BASE FOR YOUR OFFSHORE COMPANY?
# by Dr WG Hill

Dr WG Hill, the world's leading expert on personal tax havens has found another place where real estate values should double in a very short period. It is the ultimate personal tax haven of Andorra, a medieval principality secluded from the rest of the world, yet a short drive from sparkling beaches, mountain lakes and the Mediterranean. The nearest big city is that bustling European economic powerhouse, Barcelona. Andorra is a hidden haven for the few in the know. Property is still affordable. Living costs are low. Natural beauty, powder snow in winter, miles of ski and hiking trails plus the lowest prices in Europe on a huge selection of goods makes this Mini-Switzerland the top personal tax haven in Europe. It's an important place for what it doesn't have: Andorra has never had an economic depression, nor AIDS, nor random violence, nor police intimidation. No nuclear plants are in the vicinity. Andorra has no leftist political parties. It has hardly any government at all. Of the 60,000 people that inhabit this alpine tax refuge, the number employed by the state is less than 100, or 0.4% of the population. There are no taxes whatsoever! Labor unions are strictly forbidden. There is no hint of a "socialist mentality" among the natives. The unregulated banking system is among the safest in the world. It is sound, prosperous, computerized, streamlined, discreet and very customer oriented. Some of the wealthiest people in the world prefer Andorra's low-profile banks to those of secretive Switzerland.

In the all new third edition which has been revised and expanded for 1994, Dr WG Hill reveals the secrets of two Spanish enclaves. Os and Llivia are both small, provincial towns, one tucked away in the French Pyrenees and the other hidden in a Spanish valley. These secret enclaves could be your key to tax freedom. For those interested in becoming prior-taxpayers of North European countries (Sweden, Denmark, Germany), these little spots could provide the ideal solution. As most of our readers are aware, these countries mandate that if one of their citizens moves to a tax haven, he must continue paying taxes to his country of origin. By implementing the plan spelled out in this Report, you could achieve the best of both worlds, all the conveniences of a tax haven, but the fiscal address of high-tax country. Best of all, property prices are even less than those in Andorra-proper.

Dr WG Hill shows you where, how and when to buy bargain property in this unknown alpine paradise and its enclaves. Now is the time to get in, he says. The prices in Campione tripled within two years of his Special Report being issued. Will it be the same in Andorra? In Andorra there is no crime. There is free health care for everyone, including old age pensions. All internal mail is free, too! Schools are free for everyone. Most entertainment is free. Dining out in a first class restaurant before a free classical music concert is cheap. Andorra has 250 restaurants, some of Europe's best skiing and the largest number of Mercedes limousines per capita in the world. Its people are affluent. They do not pay any taxes at all. Andorra is cosmopolitan. More than two thirds of all residents are wealthy, self-made foreigners, most of whom moved to Andorra because they were fed up with government red tape and destructive bureaucracy.

*Chapters include:*

Andorra as a Sex Haven, Shopping in Europe's Bargain Basement (where they give you a discount when you buy with credit cards), Why you should not form an Andorran corporation, How to get local passports, and much, much more. Andorra is located on the north-eastern border of Spain, facing southern France.

On the Spanish Costa del Sol, on the south west coast, is Gibraltar. This sovereign British Crown Colony is fast becoming the preferred European tax haven for offshore corporations. "The Rock of Gibraltar" is the ideal place to register your tax haven company, your trust, your car, yacht or airplane. In this Report, Dr WG Hill examines in great detail the financial advantages of Gibraltar. He also considers quality of living, the real estate market, where to get the most interesting car deals in Europe and how to get the best out of life in Gibraltar. This corporate tax haven is prospering after a 25 year border embargo with Spain. In more than twenty in-depth chapters, Dr Hill covers all the secrets of this unique place where you can drive without a driving license. Where setting up a tax haven corporation "offshore" and buying Branston Pickle, British Bangers or HJ Heinz tinned soups is easy. He answers questions like: "Yachts, casinos - Is this another Monaco?", "Gibraltar, the new Hong Kong?", and "Should you get a Gibraltar Passport?" Other chapters include: Confidential Banking in Gibraltar, How to Set Up Your Own Tax Haven Corporation, Owning a Home in Next-Door Spain *plus* Gibraltar Secret: Why the British Army Pays Your Bills when you Live on Gibraltar.

The Andorra Gibraltar Report, is available from Scope International Ltd, Forestside House, Forestside, Rowlands Castle, Hampshire PO9 6EE, UK. Price £60. See last two pages in this Report for ordering details.

**ISBN 0 906619 31 9**

# THE CAMPIONE REPORT
## SWITZERLAND'S SECRET SEMI-TROPICAL TAX HAVEN
## by Dr WG Hill

WG Hill, the world's leading expert on personal tax havens predicts that Campione, a strange accident of history, anomaly of geography and climatic freak, will be one of the most fashionable tax havens of the next decade.

This Report shows anyone how to become a legal resident of this soon-to-be discovered enclave of the super-rich. Campione is a unique semi-autonomous community located entirely within Switzerland. But as a separate country, it is not subject to any Swiss laws, taxes or tax treaties. Strange as it may seem, becoming a resident of Campione gives one all the advantages of being Swiss, but none of the disadvantages. No compulsory lifetime military camps, no heavy Swiss income taxes, none of the disadvantages of being (as Switzerland is) *outside* the European Union.

Campione is a part of the EU with all the benefits of passport free, visa free travel. Its citizens have the right to travel, work, engage in commerce or perform services anywhere in the EU. Best of all, Campione has "in practice" no income taxes. This Special Report shows you how to achieve these tax benefits even without acquiring residency.

Campione is also one of the few places in the EU where there is no VAT (value added tax), which seriously reduces the price of goods and services.

*The Campione Report tells all the secrets. Here are some more highlights:*
Campione enjoys a freak Mediterranean climate found only in the small Italian Swiss Province of Ticino, where Campione is located. Because it is on lovely Lake Lugano and considerably lower in altitude than the rest of mountainous Switzerland, its white sand beach supports a small grove of tropical palm trees. Your sea-view villa in Campione will be gently caressed by balmy yet non-humid tropical breezes. However, although Campione is in a "Banana Belt", nearby ski slopes are clearly visible. Half an hour on the local funicular railway takes you up to the powder runs!

The cost of living is less than half that of Monte Carlo, Paris, London or New York. There is no pollution, industry or crime. The mountain and lake scenery is breathtaking. The sub-Alpine climate and year-round temperature is second to none. A vibrant social and cultural life is a few minutes away in Lugano or Locarno by regular ferry boat. Take the superhighway due south from Campione and in forty-five minutes you can hear the world's best grand opera at La Scala or visit the fabulous shops of downtown Milan. There are more bankers and stockbrokers locally in Lugano and Chiasso than you can count. The area is second only to Zürich in the proliferation of financial services. All Tokyo, London and Wall Street publications are available at many stands on the day of publication. Locally you can eat in several hundred ethnic gourmet restaurants and see first run English language films in a movie palace the likes of which no longer exist in most big cities. Most of the action is in Lugano, ten minutes across the lake by *vaporetto* bus-boat, or over the one mile long causeway by car.

Shopping, dining, night clubbing, golf, horses, tennis clubs, spectator sports, every pleasure known to man is available. Modern hospitals and internationally known clinics attract the wealthiest people of the world to the area for a variety of cures and treatments. As to morality and personal eccentricity, local Italian Swiss are easy-going and more tolerant than their German Swiss brothers fifty miles to the north.

For an inexpensive, stress-free, tax-free life, Dr Hill suggests, "Move to Campione this year. Buy property soon, before it is over-publicized and discovered. *"You could probably make twenty times your money over the next decade in this semi-autonomous town that practically pays you to live there"*. Only a short drive from Italy, France, Austria, Liechtenstein and Germany, Campione is still a sleepy, peaceful and unspoiled tax haven. But it appears to be heading rapidly towards becoming another Monaco. The ground floor is now. The present population of 3000 is just ten per cent of Monaco's. Monte Carlo has 35,000 people on a similar square mile of waterfront. Campione in 1996 is like Monte Carlo in 1949, before it became 'in' and developed into a mini-Manhattan.

This Special Report gives the who, what, where, when and why. Hill feels that Campione is a great place to escape to, while it is still relatively uncongested. In five or ten years as it becomes overcrowded, it will be the place you can escape from. But your little villa would hopefully be a million dollar hotel or apartment site by then. In the meantime, you have a conveniently located European home base, you can pick up an EU passport and you can enjoy life in Campione, one of the most unusual spots on Earth.

The Campione Report is available from Scope International Ltd, Forestside House, Forestside, Rowlands Castle, Hampshire PO9 6EE, UK. Price £60 UK Sterling (or equivalent). See last two pages in this Report for ordering details.

**ISBN 0 906619 22 X**

# THE MONACO REPORT
## HOW TO BECOME A LEGAL RESIDENT OF TAX-FREE MONTE CARLO
### 1st Edition
## by Scope International

Are you looking for a country with attractive tax laws? With high levels of banking and corporate secrecy? A place which offers a fun lifestyle too? Your search could be over.

Why give away your hard-earned money in taxes to thieving governments? Move to Monaco and say goodbye to income tax! Monaco is the most famous tax haven in the world and people have been moving there for years. Now you can discover why.

*The Monaco Report* is the new survey of the country. But it is more than that. It is the only publication which dares to reveal the information that you want to know. Learn about the amazing personal and corporate advantages on offer. Find out how you can make the most of them and achieve the lifestyle you are looking for.

There is no income tax or direct tax in Monaco! And that is not all. There are no wealth and capital gains taxes on individuals either. This Report takes an uncompromising look at personal taxation in Monaco and points out all the possible benefits.

Learn about Law 214 and stop your assets from falling into the wrong hands. Monégasque inheritance laws would normally allow direct descendants to inherit automatically. But why should disrespectful children be given a share of the pie? With a Law 214 trust you can pass on your possessions at your own discretion!

Monaco has so much to offer! Everyone wants to enjoy the lifestyle. But not everyone can secure a residence card. The Monaco Report looks closely at the application procedure and shows how you can improve your chances. Don't let yourself be misled by inferior information. You must have the whole story and this is the only publication where you'll find it.

Monaco is the perfect base for your company. Why? There is no exchange control and  Monégasque companies do not pay withholding tax on dividends or interest. If less than 25 per cent of turnover is derived outside Monaco, the company does not have to pay any business tax at all!

Many international companies have their headquarters in Monaco. It is the stepping stone for commercial and financial relations between Europe, the US and the rest of the world.  With this Report you can navigate your way through Monaco's intricate company law. Learn about the different enterprise options and find out how foreign nationals can administer business at the lowest tax rates.

Are you frustrated with governments who interfere with your affairs? Discover the strict corporate and financial secrecy that exists in Monaco. The authorities require less information about your company than in other countries and very little is held on public record. As for individual security, you will find all the privacy you need in the Principality. EU members are being forced into line but Monégasque banks continue to observe their own high levels of confidentiality.

Monaco is a truly remarkable country. It is the only tax haven which is famous throughout the world as a sparkling resort area. It may be only two square kilometres in area but it has all the services and cultural activities of a large city. It's all there! Glamor, international arts festivals and sports competitions, casinos, high fashion, designer shopping, golden beaches, world-famous restaurants... You'll love Monaco even without its great tax benefits and respect for privacy! And you don't have to be wealthy. With the information in this Report the pleasures of Monaco are there for everyone to enjoy.

*The Monaco Report* is masterfully written and designed to spare you many months of painful research. It includes a comprehensive appendix which serves as a quick-reference fact-file and directory. Here you will find details of all the financial and leisure services you might need including banks, stockbrokers, consultants, lawyers, accountants, hotels, clubs and theaters.

No other book contains this much  information about Monaco. Save yourself thousands of dollars. Secure your copy of this exciting new Report TODAY.

### ISBN 0 906619 51 3

*The Monaco Report* is available from
Scope International Ltd, Forestside House, Forestside, Rowlands Castle, Hampshire PO9 6EE.
Price - £60 sterling (or equivalent) by credit card, cash or banker's draft.
Price includes postage and packing. Please allow 6-8 weeks for surface delivery outside UK.
For quicker airmail service add £18 or equivalent and allow 3-4 weeks for delivery.
Ordering details and order form are supplied on the last two pages of this Report.

**REMEMBER:** Our no-nonsense, money-back guarantee applies to all our publications.

# THE TAX EXILE REPORT
## CITIZENSHIP, SECOND PASSPORTS AND ESCAPING CONFISCATORY TAXES
## by Marshall J Langer

Are you fed up with paying confiscatory taxes? Are you willing to move and to do whatever else may be legally necessary to escape your present tax burden? If so, *The Tax Exile Report* is for you. This Report is intended for the small minority of well-to-do individuals who are no longer willing to tolerate increasingly unfair tax systems and are prepared to vote with their feet.

Marshall Langer's newly revised Report tells you how to overcome the *tax octopus* - eight different criteria used by the United States and other high-tax countries to tax you on your income *and* your capital. To avoid confiscatory taxes you must eliminate each of the eight tax tentacles, one by one. Langer's Report tells you how to do it.

Langer tells you how to change your residence and your domicile, and when and how to acquire another nationality. He explains how to cope with community property rules. His Report also tells you how to change the source of your income and the location of your assets. He helps you to watch your timing and to deal with problems caused by family members who remain behind.

Should you become a perpetual tourist (PT) or should you move to a new homeland? The Report will help you make the right choice.

*The Tax Exile Report* deals with the special problems involved in leaving high-tax countries, including the US, Britain, Canada, Germany and the Nordic countries. Langer concentrates on demystifying the US rules and telling you how they really work. He tells you how to plan around the US anti-expatriation rules and the departure taxes imposed in other countries. His Report devotes 25 chapters to a review of suitable destination countries, describing the benefits and pitfalls of each of them. Surprisingly these include some of the high-tax countries that others are seeking to escape. Langer explains that most high-tax countries play both ends against the middle. They constantly squeeze their captive 'customers' while seeking to attract new investment from abroad.

*The depth of coverage can best be seen by reviewing the partial summary of the table of contents which follows.*

LEAVING OTHER EU COUNTRIES: France Taxes Citizens Who Move to Monaco, Greece Taxes Transfers by Nonresident Citizens, Netherlands Permits Escape to the Antilles

*A completely new part containing 5 new chapters has been added:*
CHOOSING ONE OR MORE NEW HOME COUNTRIES
A TAX EXILE'S WISH LIST: More Than One Home Country. Home Countries for Residency, Domicile, Citizenship and a Passport.
PASSPORTS AND VISAS: Rating Different Passports. Difficult Passports. Passports Without Citizenship. Visas and Visa-Free Travel.
VISITING WESTERN EUROPE: Seven Schengen Countries. Persons Requiring Schengen Visas. Other EU and Western European Countries.
VISITING NORTH AMERICA: Canadian, US and Mexican Visa Requirements.
VISITING ASIA AND THE PACIFIC. Some Key Asian Countries. Australia and New Zealand.

## SUITABLE PLACES FOR RESIDENCE, DOMICILE, CITIZENSHIP AND PASSPORTS.
*Contains complete chapters on each of these countries:*

| | |
|---|---|
| AMERICA (the US) | IRELAND |
| AUSTRALIA | THE ISLE OF MAN |
| THE BAHAMAS | ISRAEL |
| BERMUDA | MALTA |
| BRITAIN (the UK) | MONACO |
| CAMPIONE | THE NETHERLANDS ANTILLES |
| CANADA | NEW ZEALAND |
| CAPE VERDE | PERU |
| CAYMAN ISLANDS | ST. KITTS AND NEVIS |
| THE CHANNEL ISLANDS | SWITZERLAND |
| COSTA RICA | TURKS AND CAICOS ISLANDS |
| CYPRUS | URUGUAY |
| GIBRALTAR | OTHER EU COUNTRIES |

### TABLES COMPARE SUITABLE COUNTRIES IN VARIOUS PARTS OF THE WORLD

## SHOULD *YOU* BECOME A TAX EXILE?
YOUR ULTIMATE ESTATE PLAN
RESOURCE LIST

<u>STOP PRESS</u>. Departure Tax Would Target Wealthy US Tax Exiles. Clinton Budget Also Targets Foreign Trusts.

*Why is Marshall Langer uniquely qualified to write this Report?*
He is a member of the Florida Bar, and practised law in Miami for more than 35 years. He has worked as an international tax adviser in Europe since 1985, living in Switzerland and in England. He was a partner in the law firm of Shutts & Bowen, Miami, and remains of counsel to that firm. He was also an Adjunct Professor of Law at the University of Miami for many years. In 1990, Langer received the Florida Bar Tax Section's award as Outstanding Tax Attorney of the Year.

Dr Langer is a graduate of the Wharton School of Finance and Commerce of the University of Pennsylvania (BS in Economics) and the University of Miami School of Law (JD *summa cum laude*). He has lectured extensively at tax institutes and seminars throughout the US and Europe, as well as in Japan, Hong King, Australia, Canada, and the Caribbean. He has written numerous articles on international taxation and books on tax and other subjects. He is the author of *The Swiss Report*, published by Scope International. He is also the author of a leading book on tax havens and how to use them, entitled: *Practical International Tax Planning* (the third edition was published in 1985 and is updated annually). In addition, Langer is co-author (with Rufus Rhoades of Los Angeles) of a five-volume set of books on taxes and tax treaties called: *Rhoades & Langer, Income Taxation of Foreign Related Transactions* (updated four times a year).

*The Tax Exile Report* by Marshall J Langer. Price £60 (US $100). See last two pages in this Report for ordering details.

Personal consultations with Dr Langer are available to all purchasers of *The Tax Exile Report.*

**ISBN 0 906619 34 3**

# THE SWISS REPORT
## by Marshall J Langer

Some countries pride themselves on being "like Switzerland", but there is only one Switzerland, the most respected small country in the world. The Swiss Report gives you an inside look at the country and the institutions that make it tick.

Switzerland is not exactly a tax haven but it is the world's greatest money haven. Chances are you already keep some of your money in Swiss banks. The Swiss Report takes you inside this country that is deservedly called "the world's safest place for your money".

The Report describes Switzerland's banks, its world-renowned bank secrecy, and attempts by other countries to end that secrecy. It discusses the controls that limit non-residents to buying small amounts of Swiss real estate. It describes the companies typically used by investors and how you can save money by using a limited liability company instead of a corporation.

Langer considers Switzerland to be both a tax planner's dream and his nightmare. Correctly used in the way spelled out in the Report it can be a base for you to earn money at a tax rate of 11 per cent or less, but it is hard to get that money out of Switzerland without paying a 35 per cent federal tax.

The Report tells you how to visit Switzerland, places to visit, where to stay, how to travel around, where to eat. Would you like to stay longer? The Report also tells you how to live and work in Switzerland, or retire there. Sure there are restrictions on obtaining permits to live in Switzerland. If it didn't have them, millions more would try to live and work there. Residence permits are difficult to obtain, but not impossible, and The Swiss Report tells you how to get them. It even discusses how you can spend up to six months each year in Switzerland as a " Permanent Traveler" (PT), legally remaining a tourist instead of a taxpayer.

Dr WG (Bill) Hill regards Marshall Langer as his "tax guru". Langer is a tax lawyer and the author of several books including the standard reference work on tax havens, Practical International Tax Planning, published by New York's Practising Law Institute. After more than thirty years of law practice in Florida, Langer moved to Europe. He lived in Neuchatel, Switzerland for five years and still operates a company from there. Dr Hill has encouraged Marshall Langer to share his know-how about Switzerland with readers of these Reports. Langer's clients have willingly paid him large fees for many of the insights he has learned as a Swiss-based international tax planner and which he now shares with you in *The Swiss Report*.

### The Report answers these questions:
- Is Switzerland freer than the USA or Great Britain?
- Should you apply for a resident's permit or live there unofficially, as a PT?
- Should you move there at all?
- What's the real cost of living?
- Regional variations?
- How do you avoid or reduce Swiss taxes?
- How can you use Swiss bank accounts and the Swiss secrecy laws to your advantage?
- How safe and secret really are your financial affairs?
- What are the Swiss really like?
- Will you have to do military service?
- How long before you can apply to be a citizen?
- Where can you get a good meal?
- Swiss punctuality and other peculiarities - how do they affect you?
- Should you buy a home or rent?
- How can you benefit from Swiss tax treaties?
- Can you survive with just English?
- Will Switzerland join the European common market?
- Can a foreigner own a Swiss company?
- How can you negotiate a flat income tax in advance?

These and many other questions are answered in *The Swiss Report*. We highly recommend it.

**ISBN 0 906619 28 9**

*The Swiss Report* is available from Scope International Ltd, Forestside House, Forestside,
Rowlands Castle, Hampshire PO9 6EE, UK. Price £60 UK Sterling (or equivalent) by credit card, cash, check or banker's draft. Price includes postage and packing, and please allow 6-8 weeks for surface delivery outside UK.
For quicker air mail service add £18 or equivalent (allow 3-4 weeks for delivery).
Ordering details and order form are supplied on the last two pages of this Report.

**REMEMBER:** Our no-nonsense money-back guarantee applies to all our publications.

# THE TAX HAVEN REPORT
## by Adam Starchild

The words "tax haven" bring to mind far-off corners of the planet with millionaire populations. This population, of course, spends most of its day drinking daiquiris on the beach, its funds secure in various numbered Swiss bank accounts. Not so, according to Adam Starchild (well, he doesn't refute the daiquiri bit). Tax havens need not be the exclusive refuge of the ultra-rich. People of average means need no longer be captive slaves to the State in today's modern jet-set era. In his newly-revised *The Tax Haven Report*, Adam Starchild reveals these secrets of the ultra-rich so that us lesser mortals can take advantage of the many benefits tax havens have to offer.

As modern governments continue to expand and swallow human rights, deficits and taxes grow. All free-minded individuals must seek a means to protect their assets from this out of control monster. As Starchild explains, it is legally possible to pay absolutely no taxes. Your government may want you to think otherwise. The media may love to tattle about the misery of a particular celebrity tax evader, but a very important point remains unnoticed. While tax evasion is illegal, tax avoidance is not. This distinction is crucial, and thus Starchild explains it at great length.

Starchild goes on to cover this exhausting subject from start to finish in a clear, easy-to-understand style. No legal jargon here. He brings over twenty years of experience to the production of this Report and doesn't hop on the bandwagons for the latest "fad" tax havens. In fact, it is not commonly known, but tax havens are just as interested in finding you as you are in finding them. He explains everything from the basic criteria you should use when assessing a tax haven to how you can put them to work to save you that big chunk of your income whisked off each year by Big Brother.

For entrepreneurs and businessmen, he explains the ins and outs of tax haven corporations and trusts, including how they are formed, how they are controlled, where they can be located, and, most importantly, how they can seriously reduce, if not eliminate, the tax burden of your business.

Starchild explains the basics of known and undiscovered tax havens of the world. He divides them into easily identifiable categories, including:

*No-tax havens:* The Bahamas, Bermuda, The Cayman Islands *Foreign-source-income havens:* Panama, Cyprus, Malta, The Isle of Man, Jersey, Guernsey, Gibraltar, Hong Kong *Double-taxation agreement havens:* The Netherlands, Austria, Luxembourg

This Report also includes detailed chapters on both Liechtenstein and Switzerland.

This is essential reading for anyone interested in reducing his tax burden. With over 170 pages of vital information, we are certain that you can develop a successful plan to reduce your tax burden as a result of reading this Report. We are so certain that we do not even hesitate to offer it with our standard money-back guarantee. Unless you are absolutely satisfied return it within 28 days for a full refund.

Adam Starchild has been a business consultant for nearly two decades. He is the author of over a dozen books, four of which are on tax havens, the earliest having been published in 1978. He has also written hundreds of magazine articles, for journals around the world. His articles have appeared in many periodicals and journals including: *The Christian Science Monitor, Credit & Financial Management, International Business, The New York Times, The San Francisco Examiner, Tax Angles, Tax Haven & Shelter Report, Tax Haven News* and *Tax Planning International*.

His consulting clients have ranged from wealthy individuals to banks, trust companies, investment companies, book publishers, import-export companies and tour operators. Often critical of the hype and inflated prices in some of the more famous tax havens, Starchild gives you the benefit of his many years of hands-on experience in setting up trusts in many countries around the world.

### ISBN 0 906619 39 4

*The Tax Haven Report* is available from Scope International Ltd, Forestside House, Forestside,
Rowlands Castle, Hampshire PO9 6EE, UK. Price £60 UK Sterling (or equivalent) by credit card, cash, check or banker's draft. Price includes postage and packing, and please allow 6-8 weeks for surface delivery outside UK.
For quicker air mail service add £18 or equivalent (allow 3-4 weeks for delivery).
Ordering details and order form are supplied on the last two pages of this Report.

**REMEMBER:** Written consultations with Adam Starchild, are available to all purchasers and our no-nonsense money-back guarantee applies to all our publications.

# THE AUSTRIA & LIECHTENSTEIN REPORT
## by Dr Reinhard Stern

Few people are aware that banks in Austria offer all the same advantages of their Swiss counterparts - plus the only true remaining bank secrecy laws in Europe. Now a new Scope Report introduces Austria, the small country with the reputation as one of the world's most popular tourist destinations.

The first part of the book profiles Austria and gives you background information you should have at your fingertips if you plan to visit the country. Its government, its social system and language, its people and their concerns, and much more. You'll be prepared with information on everything from phone calls to vineyards. The Report then moves to specifics for those interested in staying in the country longer. It will help you decide whether Austria is the second residence or retirement haven you've been looking for and, if so, whether to avoid residence requirements or officially apply for a residence permit.

The second part turns to business and delivers newly-available information, some of it has never been published before, on important aspects of banking, investment and economics in Austria. Dr Stern outlines the numerous advantages of investing there, the accounts available to foreigners, and how the policy of banking super-secrecy can enable you to open accounts or purchase securities, future options and bullion coins anonymously. He discusses the best banks to approach for the services you might need and, perhaps more importantly, warns his readers of the mistakes most frequently made by the unwary when undertaking private business there.

Additionally, he introduces two secret enclaves, undiscovered by the public, where Austria's best banks are to be found. Detailed maps included in this section explain how to get to those out-of-the-way secret enclaves. A special section deals with the Vienna stock market, which was the world's top performer several years ago and is likely to be very attractive in the near future.

Favorable tax laws allow foreigners wishing to reside there low-tax or even zero-tax residence status plus tax-free income. Inside information, virtually unknown to the public, is thoroughly discussed.

What kind of businesses exist in Austria, how are they structured, and what status do they have? Should you consider forming a company here? You'll want to know about the corporate taxes and learn your way in *and out* of the loopholes on the real-estate scene, where restrictions on newcomers can otherwise be a barrier. This Report makes it a whole lot simpler.

Liechtenstein is similar to Switzerland in many ways. However, there are also distinctive differences of which investors should be aware. The sections on Liechtenstein answer vital questions on this principality, including setting up accounts, attractive fund management plans and bank secrecy. It advises on taxes, and how to avoid them by setting up private trusts and anonymous commercial Anstalts. You will have information on everything from purchasing real estate anonymously to secret tax loopholes between Austria and Liechtenstein which can be used by PTs and potential offshore investors alike. Clear, easy-to-understand examples will show you how to establish your heirs and beneficiaries, thereby protecting your assets from potential disaster. The Liechtenstein sections also include a discussion of the most favorable banks to administer your affairs.

***HERE ARE JUST A FEW OF THE QUESTIONS THIS UNIQUE REPORT WILL ANSWER FOR YOU:***

- What are the basic do's and don'ts of investments in Austria?
- Austrian bank secrecy: how safe and how secret is it really?
- How do I go about establishing and maintaining anonymity?
- Where are the best banks?
- Which accounts are available to foreigners?
- How can I establish my heirs and protect my assets?
- Where are the super secrecy bank enclaves and how do I use them?
- Exactly what kind of tax breaks does Austria offer foreigners?
- How can I live and do business in Austria without paying taxes?
- Should I establish a business or a holding company in Austria?
- How can I move cash anonymously and across borders safely and discreetly?
- How high is the cost of living in Austria?
- How can I establish residency?
- Should I consider Austria as a place to retire?
- What should I know before buying real estate?
- I'm a PT - is Austria really for me?

Order TODAY using the priority order form at the back of this Report.

**ISBN 0 906619 44 0**

# THE ISLE OF MAN REPORT
## by Charles Cain

*No capital taxes. No capital gains taxes. No inheritance taxes. No wealth taxes. No gift taxes.*

At the heart of the British Isles lies the Isle of Man. This beautiful island shaped slightly like a lozenge is 33 miles long and 13 miles wide. Its old eroded mountains, deep glens, sandy beaches and cliffs make the perfect setting for a tax haven.

It lies only 16 miles from Scotland and is one hour by air to London. With a small population of 70,000 only half are native Manx people, the remainder are clever foreigners enjoying the tax savings and harmonious living of a Manx life.

Author, consultant and international banker, Charles Cain has for the first time in print written his personal guide to his homeland. Born and bred in the Isle of Man, Charles gives you all you will need to know to establish yourself in one of the world's most prestigious tax havens. After being a Managing Director of a Merchant Bank, Charles now provides a specialist consultancy and fiduciary service in relation to offshore corporate and trust structures from his office in Ramsey Isle of Man.

## TAX BENEFITS
In the Isle of Man there are no capital gains taxes, no inheritance taxes, no wealth taxes and no gift taxes. There are only two forms of direct taxation. A small social security contribution payable by employers and employees and a low 20 per cent income tax on companies and associations. Although there is a 20 per cent tax payable on worldwide profits, there are MANY exceptions. In fact most international financial transactions and business are carried out TAX FREE.

## EU CONNECTION
The Isle of Man is ENTIRELY self–governing. No agency of the UK government exists in the Isle of Man. It is ENTIRELY financially self–reliant. It is NOT a member of the EU but enjoys a special associate status and does not have to harmonize its laws or comply with EU directives. Its VAT system is identical to the UK and therefore is treated as being a part of the EU trading system fiscally.

## THE PERFECT BASE FOR YOUR OFFSHORE COMPANY
Private companies in the Isle of Man are not required to file their Annual Audited Accounts at the Public Registry with their Annual Return. In addition there are no restrictions on the number of members or the transferability of shares. Offshore finance is the most important part of the economy.

In the Report, Charles accurately takes you through the logistics of setting up your own private offshore company. He sets out the legal requirements and goes through step by step from incorporating a company right through to winding it up. Everything is here to get you started on the Isle of Man.

You need not waste time and money with expensive consultants. Nobody knows it better.

## HOW TO BENEFIT FROM TRUSTS ON THE ISLE OF MAN
Charles goes into detail and demystifies the sometimes confusing area of trusts. He explains that if the beneficiaries of a trust are resident outside the Isle of Man and the income arises outside the Isle of Man, then the Income Tax Assessor will 'look through' the trust and won't seek to assess it.

All the secrets are revealed in this up and coming haven for those who want to keep what is rightfully theirs.

## WHY THE ISLE OF MAN?
   **1.** Politically and socially stable. **2.** Excellent health services. **3.** Education services.
   **4.** Attractive tax benefits. **5.** High levels of corporate secrecy. **6.** Thriving offshore business center.

The Isle of Man is steeped in history and culture. Medieval bridges, castles and churches to explore. You can walk down ancient roads once used by Vikings. Arts Festivals featuring international artists. It is also home of the most important road racing event in the world with a circuit of over 36 miles. The world famous Isle of Man TT Motorcycle Races.

Charles takes you on a journey through the towns and villages, museums and restaurants. From ancient sites to the hustle of Athol Street, which is rapidly becoming the street of lawyers, accountants, doctors and other professionals. It is said to be the only street in the Isle of Man which is shady on both sides.

The only jurisdiction in the EU where you can run a full trading operation, fully registered for VAT, but totally exempt from all income and capital taxes. A floating diamond in the British Isles.

**Escape the pressures of bureaucracy. Profit from the amazing advantages of this unique island. Charles Cain gives you the facts. No one is more qualified to write this Report. Seize this wonderful opportunity TODAY.**

See the back page of this book for ordering details.

**ISBN: 0 906619 52 1**

# THE RUSSIA REPORT
## by Michael Kavanagh

You've heard about *Glasnost* and *Peristroika*. Forget them. The new buzzword in Russia is *chudo*, which means ECONOMIC MIRACLE. This is your chance to get a slice of the chudo, by purchasing your copy of *The Russia Report*.

This thought–provoking Report has been prepared by an Anglo–Russian consultancy and trading company who have been trading in Russia and the Baltic States since 1989. The three authors: an Anglo–Irish businessman, an Anglo–Latvian businesswoman, and a Russian *biznizman* from St Petersburg combine to give you a detailed account of Russia. The people, the customs, the way of life. When people talk about doing business in Russia, they often don't appreciate the sheer size of the place. The Russian Federation crosses nine time zones and is almost twice the size of the US.

## MONEY TO BE MADE

*The Russia Report* concentrates on Moscow and St Petersburg because they are the areas most accessible to foreigners and where most money is to be made. Since the breakdown of communism, Russia has virtually become a complete free market. In practice, trade is completely unregulated since laws never seem to be enforced. Anyone concerned with making money should not discount Russia. It is a country of enormous opportunity. This Report shows you what's on offer and how to turn it to your advantage. *Avoid some of the pitfalls foreign entrepreneurs often walk into.* Estate agents say that the three things that sell a property are location, location and location. In Russia, the three things necessary to be successful in business are Russian friends, Russian contacts, and Russian acquaintances. The author not only describes the mechanics of doing business in Russia but makes valid suggestions on how to do it. *The Russia Report* also gives guide lines on how to accept and reciprocate Russians' somewhat anarchic ideas about hospitality. If the vodka takes hold, it is acceptable to fall backwards into the potted palms, but not forwards into the dinner.

## SOUND ADVICE BEFORE YOU LEAVE

How do you go about meeting Russian business partners and cultivating relationships with them? Some help can be found from the British Soviet Chamber of Commerce, the Department of Trade and Industry and the Russian Trade Centre but the author's advice is that of an insiders. The author also recommends private consulting agencies who offer to arrange business meetings with appropriate partners there. In a light–hearted and revealing manner the author explains business etiquette. Pack a suit when conducting business as one will not be taken seriously otherwise.

## OPENING A BUSINESS IN RUSSIA

If you are considering doing serious business in Russia, you need to establish a 100 per cent Foreign Owned Company there. Joint ventures no longer exist as a legal entity with no particular advantage to being a Joint Stock Company or Limited Liability Company. The author outlines the procedures, detailing all the appropriate documents that are required.

Once you have set up your 100 per cent Foreign Owned Company, the author guides you through what to do next. How do you avoid tax complications? The simplest way is to own the company offshore in a respectable jurisdiction like the Isle of Man through another offshore company. Discover how simple the mechanics are in this fascinating Report.

## BANKING IN RUSSIA

The good news is that moving money in and out of Russia is a lot simpler than it used to be. Russian banks recognize three kinds of rouble. Cash, bank and convertible roubles. Each having different values and uses, the author's knowledge proves invaluable.

## HOW TO OPEN YOUR OWN BANK

Revealed in this unique Report is the possibility for a foreign company to lend a Russian company money secured against shares in a bank. As the Russian economy begins to settle, ownership of a functioning bank will be greatly sought after.

## BUSINESS OPPORTUNITIES

This in–depth chapter reviews some of the most attractive business opportunities in Russia, along with some to avoid. Potentially very lucrative the author's suggestions concern exporting goods and services to Russia. *Opportunities to consider:* Clothes - A lot of exporters have come badly unstuck by assuming the Russians have no money, and therefore are only interested in something cheap and cheerful. Wrong! The people who can afford to buy imported clothes can afford to buy the best and will do. Fitted Kitchens - Now that the Russians have dressed themselves up, they are turning their attention to their apartments. Soft furnishings and fabrics - At present there are about two locally produced curtain fabrics in the shops. Russians tend to go for over–the–top designs and colors. Sweets and Confectionery - Russians have a very sweet tooth, love the snob value of anything imported, and there's no one so poor that they can't afford a bar of chocolate. *So–called opportunities to stay away from include:* Electrical goods, Cigarettes, Perishables.

Profiling both Moscow and St Petersburg in depth this Report provides you with an amazing insight. To save you time and hassle the author also provides an appendix with current names and addresses of: Banks, embassies, hotels and travel agents. *The Russia Report* deals with the practicalities for the foreign visitor including: Visas and how to obtain them, how to get there and what to expect in customs, getting around the cities, recommendations of where and where not to eat, affordable private and office accommodation Don't be mislead by glossy tourist brochures or public misconceptions. Russia is a land of opportunity. Told by people who have lived and worked there, this Report is the essential guide for anyone concerned about seizing opportunities.

*Over 200 fact–filled pages of priceless information. Get your foot in the door early. Take your slice of the chudo. See enclosed order form to secure your own personal copy of The Russia Report and take advantage of our special offer as a Report Buyer.*

**ISBN: 0 906619 53 X**

# THE MALTA REPORT
## by Ross Shaw

Long viewed as an idyllic holiday and retirement destination, the Mediterranean island of Malta is now developing into a promising financial centre and tax haven. Discover for yourself the many advantages of living and investing in this beautiful island in *The Malta Report*, published by Scope International.

Ross Shaw is a qualified accountant and a PT. He has lived in Malta and has ferreted out the facts and not simply pumped out propaganda. Now living in the Isle of Man, his work on Malta is written objectively with no 'axe to grind'.

*The Malta Report* covers in depth, many areas of PT interest including:
• Residency & Taxation • Real Estate • Banking • Offshore Companies & Trusts • Expatriate Perks and Incentives
Particular attention is given to the PT philosophy, with added emphasis on relocation, taxation, banking and residency.

*The Malta Report* also covers the playground potential of Malta with an extensive section on Entertainment and Nightlife. Discover the rich and exotic culture which has made Malta an attractive destination for hundreds of years.

**Incentives for Expatriates:** Learn about the many perks and incentives used to encourage people to take up residency. Numerous benefits are on offer to you, the foreign resident or investor. You will discover that Malta imposes no VAT or Customs Duty on the import of your personal effects and no death duty, gift duty or wealth tax on real estate transfers.

**Banking:** Malta is fast opening up as a high-profile international financial centre. The recent upgrade of the Malta International Business Authority (MIBA) to the Malta Financial Services Centre (MFSC) is good news for foreign investors. The re-definition clarifies Malta's financial position and divides the island's financial activities into three distinct areas:
• **The Regulatory Unit**, which supervises insurance, investment and banking
• **The Tax Unit**, which covers all tax affairs including new legislation
• **The Business Development Unit**, which is designed to promote Malta as a financial centre

This clarification re-affirms many privileges and incentives which will enable you to take full advantage of Malta as an offshore banking centre. *The Malta Report* covers this in detail, revealing that there are:
• No restrictions on transfer (in or out) of large sums of foreign currency *and ...*
• How you, as a non-resident, can receive gross interest on your savings
• How you can acquire major credit cards, including Visa and Eurocard, with no security pledge

Malta is now becoming increasingly popular amongst US investors. This is demonstrated by the introduction of direct flights between Malta and New York. This has helped to solidify Malta's place within the global financial community and create a credible and attractive banking haven.

**Malta - Switzerland with Shorts and Shades!** Malta, like Switzerland, considers tax evasion a national sport rather than a crime. The Maltese have absolutely no interest in the foreign activities of investors. Foreign tax evaders and avoiders are therefore treated with sympathy. With low or nil taxes in most financial areas, Malta can be readily considered a PT tax haven.

**Business Opportunities you can't afford to miss ...** *The Malta Report* will show you how the island is now becoming a major centre for business development. With ready made factories available on 16 year leases, fully equipped with office and staff facilities, setting up shop in Malta couldn't be easier or less expensive. Malta has the added advantage of very low labour costs amongst an adaptable and skilled workforce.

The island's position, between Europe and Africa, makes it an important hub for international shipping and airfreight. This, and many other opportunities for business are covered in *The Malta Report*. This invaluable Special Report also shows how, as a result of the Maltese government's desire to attract foreign business, the following incentives are available:
• No restrictions on 100 per cent foreign ownership and control of companies
• Guaranteed repatriation of capital and profits
*What more could you want?*

**Get Your Foot In the Door!** Can you afford to be kept in the dark about the PT paradise of Malta? As interest in this country rapidly grows, so the opportunities are being snapped up by those in the know. You too can be involved in this exciting and lucrative financial centre. Get your foot in the door! **Prepare Thoroughly**. *The Malta Report* by Ross Shaw explains it all and will give you the head-start necessary to put you one step ahead of the rest.

**ISBN 0 906619 55 6**

*The Malta Report* is available from Scope International Ltd, Forestside House, Forestside,
Rowlands Castle, Hampshire PO9 6EE, UK. Price £60 UK Sterling (or equivalent) by credit card, cash, check or banker's
draft. Price includes postage and packing, and please allow 6-8 weeks for surface delivery outside UK.
For quicker air mail service add £18 or equivalent (allow 3-4 weeks for delivery).
Ordering details and order form are supplied on the last two pages of this Report.

# HOW TO ORDER

◆ Each individual leather-bound Report is £60 or equivalent in any currency.
◆ All orders are despatched promptly.
◆ Courier service available. Methods and delivery times are quoted on order form.
◆ For quicker service add £18 for air mail.
◆ Bank details, travelers' checks / drafts / money orders made payable to **SCOPE INTERNATIONAL LTD** or currency may be sent. Or quote credit card number and expiry date. Telephone and fax orders will be accepted on the numbers given below.
◆ If you are not satisfied, return the undamaged Report to us within 28 days of receipt and your money will be refunded to you in full.
◆ Please use the order form on the reverse side of this page.

Post, fax or telephone your order to:-
## Scope International Limited
Forestside House, Rowlands Castle, Hants PO9 6EE, England, UK

# TEL: +44 (0) 1705 631751
# FAX: +44 (0) 1705 631322

## SPECIAL OFFER TO READERS OF THIS REPORT!

**Order any 3 of our Special Reports and you may deduct £60!**
**Order any 6 of our Reports and your total saving becomes £135!!**
**Order 9 of our Reports and you will qualify for a massive £225 saving!!!**

*Simply tick the Special Offer box on the order form on the reverse side of this page , mark your choice of Reports and deduct £60, £135 or £225 from the total cost of your order.*

## *LEARN THE SECRETS OF THE SUPER-RICH!*

**None of Scope International's Reports are subsidized, authorized or encouraged by the organizations, countries or institutions written about. All the author has to sell is good, objective information. Satisfaction is guaranteed. If these Reports do not deliver as advertised, they may be returned** *(uncopied of course)* **for a refund.**

# PRIORITY ORDER FORM

Name: _____

Address: _____

_____

Zip/Postcode: _____

Telephone: _____

TEL: _____

FAX: _____

**Courier service unavailable to PO Box addresses
without contact number. Alternative airmail
delivery charged at same price.**

## SPECIAL OFFER DISCOUNTS

| Tick | No. Reports | You Pay | You SAVE |
|---|---|---|---|
| ❑ | 3 | £120 ($200) | £60 ($100) |
| ❑ | 6 | £225 ($370) | £135 ($230) |
| ❑ | 9 | £315 ($520) | £225 ($380) |
| ❑ | 12 | £405 ($670) | £315 ($530) |
| ❑ | 15 | £525 ($870) | £435 ($730) |

### Scope Special Reports *(Please tick)*

| | | |
|---|---|---|
| ❑ PT2 | £60 (US $100) | ............ |
| ❑ The Passport Report | £60 (US $100) | ............ |
| ❑ Banking in Silence | £60 (US $100) | ............ |
| ❑ The Computer Privacy Report | £60 (US $100) | ............ |
| ❑ Think Like a Tycoon | £60 (US $100) | ............ |
| ❑ The Wealth Report | £60 (US $100) | ............ |
| ❑ The Tax-Free Car Report | £60 (US $100) | ............ |
| ❑ The Channel Island Report | £60 (US $100) | ............ |
| ❑ The Andorra & Gibraltar Report | £60 (US $100) | ............ |
| ❑ The Campione Report | £60 (US $100) | ............ |
| ❑ The Monaco Report | £60 (US $100) | ............ |
| ❑ The Tax Exile Report | £60 (US $100) | ............ |
| ❑ The Swiss Report | £60 (US $100) | ............ |
| ❑ The Tax Haven Report | £60 (US $100) | ............ |
| ❑ The Austria & Leichtenstein Report | £60 (US $100) | ............ |
| ❑ The Isle of Man Report | £60 (US $100) | ............ |
| ❑ The Russia Report | £60 (US $100) | ............ |
| ❑ The Malta Report | £60 (US $100) | ............ |

| | |
|---|---|
| **TOTAL GOODS** | |
| **DISCOUNT CLAIMED** | |
| **ADD £5 / US $8** for delivery within the UK | |
| **ADD £10 / US $18** for Surface delivery | |
| **ADD £18 / US $28** for Airmail delivery | |
| **TOTAL PAYABLE** | |

❑ VISA ❑ MASTERCARD ❑ EUROCARD
❑ DINERS ❑ ACCESS

My Card Number is:

| | | | | | | | | | | | | | | | |
|--|--|--|--|--|--|--|--|--|--|--|--|--|--|--|--|
| | | | | | | | | | | | | | | | |

**IMPORTANT:** Please quote Expiry date: ........../..........
Card billing address
(if different): ........................................................

........................................................................

........................................................................

Signature: ............................................................

❑ CHECK / DRAFT ENCLOSED PAYABLE TO:
**SCOPE INTERNATIONAL LTD**
*All Credit Cards Charged at Sterling Prices*

## Scope International Limited (PT)
Forestside House, Rowlands Castle,
Hampshire, PO9 6EE, England, UK

# TELEPHONE: +44 1705 631751
# FAX: +44 1705 631322

## NO-NONSENSE
## MONEY BACK GUARANTEE

*Your money will be refunded in full if you return the
resaleable Reports within 28 days of receipt.*

**All orders are despatched promptly but please
allow the following maximum delivery times:**
Courier 7 days ◆ Airmail 21 days
Surface 10 weeks ◆ UK 14 days
*Above quoted in working days from date of despatch.*